BEATING THE HARNESS RACES

aaron bernstein

ARCO PUBLISHING COMPANY INC.

219 Park Avenue South, New York, N.Y. 10003

Published by Arco Publishing Company, Inc.
219 Park Avenue South, New York, N.Y. 10003

Library of Congress Catalog Card Number 75-18956
ISBN 0-668-03872-1

Printed in the United States of America

Acknowledgments

The author thanks Printing Specialties, Incorporated, and Colonial Press of Chicago for their permission to reproduce copyrighted past performance records, result charts, and other related information.

The author also wishes to thank Greg Magreta, Research Analyst for Harness Tracks of America, whose help and assistance was very valuable.

A special thanks goes to the United States Trotting Association, an organization devoted to the betterment of Harness Racing.

Contents

Introduction

The name of the game is harness racing and we are the players. The ground rules for the game allow each player to have in his possession a racing program, a pencil, one or more packs of cigarettes (strictly optional) and money (never optional).

Unfortunately, the one thing the ground rules don't call for is knowledge. Every person age twenty-one or over has the legal right to place a wager at a racetrack regardless of whether he knows what he's doing or not.

Harness racing, or any kind of horse racing for that matter, has always been associated with gambling. But is the racetrack just a place where you can go to fulfill your gambling needs, or is horse racing a bonafide sport like baseball, basketball or football?

Although some people look at harness racing as a gambler's paradise, it's first of all a sport in the true sense of the word. And it's probably the only sport where the spectator becomes a little bit more than just a spectator. Because for a few moments he becomes an investor in a horse, almost as if he owned part of the animal himself. That alone makes him more directly involved with the sport than he could ever hope to be with any other.

I use the word investor rather than gambler because there's a great difference between the two. If someone goes to the track with little or no knowledge of racing, then he's a gambler, and chances are he'll also be a loser. But if he goes with the ability to logically handicap each race, he's an investor because there's a good chance he'll walk out of the racetrack with more money than when he entered.

Handicapping harness races with a logical approach is based on five important factors: class, form, pace, post position and the driver. Each example race handicapped in this book shows how to use one of the elements to beat the odds, whether by pure handicapping or a systemized type of handicapping.

At present, there are more than fifty harness tracks across North America, so it's impossible to illustrate races from every track. But harness racing is virtually the same at all locations. The only difference is that there are three different sizes of racetracks used to compete on. Since Chicago is the largest city with all three sizes, the example races will take place in the Windy City. The race-tracks used are:

1. Maywood Park—one-half mile
    Each horse travels twice around the racetrack, negotiating four turns.

2. Sportsman's Park—five-eighths of a mile
    Each horse travels around the racetrack one and one-half times, negotiating three turns.

3. Hawthorne Race Course—one mile
    Each horse travels once around the racetrack, negotiating two turns.

While harness racing itself is an exciting sport, it's the pure fun of winning that adds to the excitement. Yes, I said fun, because there are quite a few people that go to the racetrack without this goal in mind. There are many who simply want to win. And if there's a place *not* to go to if you need money, it's the racetrack. An important rule to keep in mind is, if you can't afford to lose at the races—STAY HOME!

CHAPTER 1

Anyone for Harness Racing?

Harness racing began in America shortly after the Revolutionary War. At the time, New England was the major center of racing. Racetracks as we now know them did not exist. "Match races," as they were then called, were held locally along dirt roads. If an owner had a winning trotter in his barn, he made it a point to let his neighbors know about it.

By the early 1800's, harness racing became the most popular form of horse racing in the United States. Then both trotters and pacers were raced under saddle. It wasn't until 1829 that the first sulky appeared on the racing scene. But it took many years before the Standardbred was capable of running faster than when it was raced with a saddle and a rider.

One of the greatest trotters of the 1800's was the world champion Dexter. He was a son of the famous sire Hambletonian. In 1867 he trotted the mile in 2:17 1/4, taking two and one-half seconds off the world record. Interestingly enough, Dexter was known to trot just as fast when saddled as when raced with a sulky. To this day, there are still some tracks in Europe where they prefer to saddle trotters and pacers rather than use the sulky.

In the Gay Nineties, harness racing witnessed the first horse ever to break the coveted two-minute mile. It was the eight year old pacer Star Pointer, who in 1897 went the mile in 1:59 1/4. Just a few years before Star Pointer's achievement, it was believed to be impossible to break the two-minute mark.

While Star Pointer was the subject of much horsetalk, a new foal was born who was to replace him in the not too distant future as harness racing's next hero. He was the great Dan Patch, and he became the biggest name ever in the history of harness racing.

In 1903 as a seven year old, Dan Patch lowered Star Pointer's record for pacing with a mile in 1:59. Trying not to be overshadowed by the accomplishments of Dan Patch was a trotting mare named Lou Dillion. She broke the world's record for her gait by capturing trotting's first two-minute mile. But Dan Patch wasn't to be outdone. A little later in the year, he turned in a sparkling mile of 1:56 1/4, which just about turned him into a national hero.

In the following years, Dan Patch toured the country to the delight of all racing fans. Spectators would come from miles around just to watch him work out on the track for a few minutes. In October, 1905, Dan Patch once again proved his greatness by breaking his own record. This time the mile was in 1:55 1/4, a record that was to stand for the next 33 years.

The years that followed Dan Patch's retirement were lean ones for harness racing. It wasn't until the early 1940's that the sport found new popularity with the introduction of night racing and the mobile starting gate. What was once considered county fair racing came to the big city to stay.

Since the rebirth of harness racing, there have been major improvements in track conditions as well as the sulky. Records which were once thought immortal have continued to fall. The last one of prominence took place on July 1, 1972, when the fastest race in harness racing's history took place. Both the past performances and result chart of that race have been reproduced.

Sir Dalrae, 1973 Horse of the Year. This champion pacer comes from a long line of trotting horses.

That night, Albatross, a great pacer in his own right, amazed the racing fans at Sportsman's Park with a sensational mile in 1:54 3/5, breaking the record which he set just one year before. Will the record ever be broken again? Probably several times over. But that's one of the things that makes harness racing so exciting.

TROTTERS AND PACERS

There are two different types of harness horses, the trotter and the pacer. The only difference between the two is the gait they use in racing. This is important because trotters and pacers have incorrectly been considered different breeds. They are not. They are both members of the Standardbred family. In fact, some of the better pacers over the last few years have actually been bred from trotting horses.

In the trotter's gait, his right front leg and his left hind leg strike the ground at the same time. When these two legs are moving forward, the other two legs are moving backward. Then, as the trotter's body is finished moving forward, the process is reversed. This is described as a diagonal motion of the legs.

In the pacer's gait, both legs on one side move forward while the two legs on the other side move backward. After one set of legs is finished moving forward, the position is reversed. This is described as a lateral motion of the legs. The pacer's front legs do not bend quite as much as the trotter's.

More than 80% of all harness races run today are of the pacing kind. This is quite a contrast from a century ago when virtually all races were trotting events. However, the change didn't take place overnight. It was gradual, and at one time both trotters and pacers were run in the same race. This practice didn't last long because when all things are equal, the pacer is a bit faster than his trotting counterpart. But it did bring about a growing emphasis on speed; hence, the pacing race became the dominant form of the sport.

CLASSIFICATION OF RACES

There are five classifications of harness horses at most racetracks: conditioned races, claiming races, early and late closing events, stakes races, and races of the best horses at the meeting. They may be called free-for-all, junior free-for-all, invitational, or preferred races. A brief description of the five types follows:

Conditioned Races. The conditions for races are written by the Racing Secretary to provide regular opportunities for the horses competing at the racetrack. After the Racing Secretary surveys the horses available, he'll write the conditions to fit these horses and try to bring together fields of equal ability. Then he offers the conditions to the horsemen in the form of a "condition book." The

SPORTSMAN'S PARK

THE FASTEST RACE IN THE HISTORY OF HARNESS RACING

July 1, 1972

ONE MILE PACE

NINTH RACE

"THE GOVERNOR'S CUP"

Purse $25,000

FREE FOR ALL. 3 Years and Up.

RED 1 + 12-1

Driver—HARRY BURRIGHT, Blue-Gold Tr.—F. Griebel (48-7-2-4—.190)

ED BYRD B h 1964, by Poplar Byrd—Reba Frisco—Frisco Dale
Owner: Floyd M. Griebel, Marengo, Ill.

1972 16 0 1 1 $10,225
1971 32 3 5 8 $68,579 2:01^3 May
Lifetime $174,007 6, 2:01^1 (1)

Date	Trk Cond Temp	Class	Dist	Leader's Time ¼	½	¾	Winner's Time	PP	¼	½	¾	Str	Fin	Ind.Time	Odds	Driver	Order of Finish: First, Second, Third	Comment
6-23	^{9}Spk⅝ ft 50°	hcp15000=	m	:30^2	1:02^1	1:31^4	2:01^2	4	4	4^{3¼}	5^4	6^5	5^2	2:01^4	8.20	(H.Burright)	ChiefGDirect, YoungTurk, ShadyCounsel	(closed in str)
6-17	^{9}Spk⅝ ft 65°	hcp12000+	m	:30^1	1:01^2	1:31^3	2:00^1	1	2	3^{1½}	3^1	2^4	3^{4½}	2:01	9.90	(H.Burright)	SongCycle, ShadyCounsel, EdByrd	(rivals too tough)
6-10	^{8}Spk⅝ ft 54°	inv7000−	m	:28^4	1:01	1:30^2	2:00^3	5	5	5^5	5^{3½}	5^{1½}	4^{½}	2:00^4	12.60	(H.Burright)	JakeJackson, RightHonr, GameGne	(passed tiring horses)
6- 3	^{8}Spk⅝ ft 86°	JFA10000=	m	:31^2	1:04	1:33^4	2:01^4	4	4	4^{3½}	4^{2½}	4^4	5^{5½}	2:02^4	12.60	(H.Burright)	SongCycle, ShadyCounsel, ProperTime	(soundly beaten)
5-27	^{9}May ft 70°	w17000^{7172}	m	:29^3	1:00^3	1:30^4	2:01^1	6	6	6	5^{1½}	5^{4½}	2^{4½}	2:02^1	10.20	(H.Burright)	FantasticDream, EdByrd, Dana'sRoybill	(————)
5-20	^{9}May ft 80°	stk12500	m	:30^1	1:01^3	1:31^1	2:01^4	4	5	5	5^{4½}	5^{3½}	5^{2½}	2:02^2	11.50	(H.Burright)	MaidaMillion, SongCycle, ClearBrook	(————)

BLUE 2 = 5-2

Driver—HERVE FILION, Red-Blue-White Tr.—O. Mumford (0-0-0-0—.000)

NANSEMOND B c 1968, by Tar Heel—Adios Scarlet—Adios
Owners: W. Perry, W. Camp, Jr., Va., Capitol Hill Farms, Inc., Que.

1972 4 1 1 0 $24,423 1:59^3 Brd⅝
1971 19 7 5 2 $163,056 1:57^2 Dela
Lifetime $243,273 3, 1:57^2

Date	Trk Cond Temp	Class	Dist	Leader's Time ¼	½	¾	Winner's Time	PP	¼	½	¾	Str	Fin	Ind.Time	Odds	Driver	Order of Finish: First, Second, Third	Comment
6-23	W.R.⅝ ft	invffa25750	m	:28^1	:58^3	1:28^2	1:56^3	6	5	5	5	5^{3¾}	4^{4¾}	1:57^3	3.50	(H.Filion)	Albatross, ByeByeMax, Kentucky	(————)
6-16	Det^1 ft	4yr-stk	m	:29^3	1:00^1	1:30	1:58^2	4	6	6	6	3^{1½}	2^{½}	1:58^2	5.90	(H.Filion)	Albatross, Nansemond, TarportSkipper	(————)
6-11	Brd⅝ ft	jfa	m	:30	1:01	1:30^3	1:59^3	1	2	1	1	1^{1½}	1^{½}	1:59^3	*1.00	(Y.Filion)	Nansemond, MissConnaAdios, LeroyN	(————)
6- 3	R.R. ft	jfa20000	m	:29^2	1:01^2	1:31^4	2:01	8	8	8°	4°	°5^{2½}	4^{2½}	2:01^3	*1.80	(H.Filion)	PublicAffair, SmokeyRainbw, CarbineHanovr	(————)
5-24	Brd⅝ ft	Qua	m	:30^3	1:03^1	1:33^2	2:02^4	6	3	1	1	1^{1½}	1^{3½}	2:02^4	N.B.	(Y.Filion)	Nansemond, ChiefButler, WeeButtons	(————)
5-17	Brd⅝	Qua	m	:30^2	1:04^3	1:34^2	2:04^1	4	3	3	2°	2^{hd}	2^{½}	2:04^1	N.B.	(H.Filion)	J.M.Harry, Nansemond, JetButler	(————)

WHITE 3 = 4-5

Driver—STANLEY DANCER, Blue-Gold Tr.—S. Dancer (0-0-0-0—.000)

ALBATROSS B c 1968, by Meadow Skipper—Voodoo Hanover—Dancer Hanover
Owner: Amicable Stable, Hanover, Penn.

1972 10 7 2 1 $232,259 1:5F^2 L.B.⅝
1971 28 25 2 1 $558,009 1:54^4 Lex^1
Lifetime $741,549 3, 1:54^4 (1)

Date	Trk Cond Temp	Class	Dist	Leader's Time ¼	½	¾	Winner's Time	PP	¼	½	¾	Str	Fin	Ind.Time	Odds	Driver	Order of Finish: First, Second, Third	Comment
6-23	W.R.⅝ ft	inv ffa25750	m	:28^1	:58^3	1:28^2	1:56^3	3	1°	1	1	1^1	1^3	1:56^3	* .35	(S.Dancer)	Albatross, ByeByeMax, Kentucky	(————)
6-16	Det^1 ft	4-yr stk58295	m	:29^3	1:00^1	1:30	1:58^2	1	1	2	1	1^1	1^{½}	1:58^2	* .30	(S.Dancer)	Albatross, NansemondTarportSkipper	(————)
6- 3	R.R. ft	stk91000	1$\frac{1}{16}$	:29^1	:59^2	1:58^2	2:06	1	4	1	1	1^1	1^{1¼}	2:06	N.B.	(S.Dancer)	Albatross, H.T.Luca, DexterHanover	(————)
5-28	Brd⅝ ft	ffa25000	m	:28^4	:58^1	1:28^2	1:56^3	5	5	3	1	1^3	1^{7½}	1:56^3	* .20	(S.Dancer)	Albatross, IsleOfWight, FreedomNow	(————)
4-29	L.B.⅝ ft	ffa40000	m	:29^3	:58^2	1:27^4	1:56^2	5	1°	1	1	1^1	1^{¾}	1:56^2	* .90	(S.Dancer)	Albatross, ByeByeMax, Kentucky	(————)
4-21	^{5}May sy 45°	inv25000	m	:31^2	1:05^1	1:36^4	2:07^4	2	1	1	1^{1½}	1^{1½}	1^{nk}	2:07^4	* .30	(S.Dancer)	Albatross, HailToAll, CafineKid	(————)

GREEN 4 = 8-1

Driver—JOE MARSH, JR., Gray-Blue-Red Tr.—J. Falkner (126-29-16-24—.362)

SONG CYCLE Br. h 1963, by Walter McKlyo—Medley Hanover—Nibble Hanover
Owner: Vornado Stables, Niles, Ill.

1972 10 2 3 0 $27,375 2:00^1 Spk⅝
1971 24 9 2 6 $94,932 1:59^1 Hol^1
Lifetime $491,063 7, 1:58 (1)

Date	Trk Cond Temp	Class	Dist	Leader's Time ¼	½	¾	Winner's Time	PP	¼	½	¾	Str	Fin	Ind.Time	Odds	Driver	Order of Finish: First, Second, Third	Comment
6-23	W.R.⅝ ft	invffa25750	m	:28^1	:58^3	1:28^2	1:56^3	4	4	4	4	4^{3½}	6^8	1:58^1	51.60	(J.MarshJr)	Albatross. ByeByeMax, Kentucky	(————)
6-17	^{9}Spk⅝ ft 65°	hcp12000−	m	:30^1	1:01^2	1:31^3	2:00^1	6	1	1^{½}	1^{½}	1^4	1^3	2:00^1	* .70	(J.MarshJr.)	SongCycle, ShadyCounsel, EdByrd	(outshined rivals)
6- 9	^{9}Spk⅝ ft 50°	fa15000+	m	:31^4	1:04	1:35	2:03^3	6	6	6^4°	4^{2½}°	2^1	2^{1½}	2:03^4	3.20	(J.MarshJr.)	Kentucky, SongCycle, DaringKnight	(back in top form)
6- 3	^{8}Spk⅝ ft 86°	JFA10000=	m	:31^2	1:04	1:33^4	2:01^4	3	3	3^{2½}	2^1	2^{hd}	1^1	2:01^4	*1.50	(J.MarshJr)	SongCycle, ShadyCounsel, ProperTime	(superstar)
5-20	^{9}May ft 80°	stk12500	m	:30^1	1:01^3	1:31^1	2:01^4	2	3	3	2^{nk}	1^{½}	2^{hd}	2:01^4	*1.20	(J.Marsh,Jr.)	MaidaMillion, SongCycle, ClearBrook	(————)
4- 1	Spk⅝ ft	fa18500	m	:30^1	1:03^2	1:33^3	2:03	4	6	7	6	5^{3½}	6^{2½}	2:03^2	6.20	(A.L.Petty)	Kentucky, CafineKid, HailToAll	(————)

BLACK 5 = 9-2

Driver—BRUCE NICKELLS, White-Purple Tr.—B. Nickells (24-4-3-2—.264)

KENTUCKY Br h 1967, by Tar Heel—Milady Hanover—Adios
Owner: Quaker City Stable, Salem, Ohio

1972 14 9 2 3 $110,750 1:58^4 May
1971 24 11 6 2 $168,621 1:57^4 Det^1
Lifetime $257,933 3, 1:57 (1)

Date	Trk Cond Temp	Class	Dist	Leader's Time ¼	½	¾	Winner's Time	PP	¼	½	¾	Str	Fin	Ind.Time	Odds	Driver	Order of Finish: First, Second, Third	Comment
6-23	W.R.⅝ ft	invffa25750	m	:28^1	:58^3	1:28^2	1:56^3	1	2	2	2	2^1	3^{3½}	1:57^1	4.75	(B.Nickells)	Albatross, ByeByeMax, Kentucky	(————)
6-17	Det^1 ft	inv10000	m	:30	1:01^1	1:31^1	2:00	6	2	1	1	1^{½}	1^1	2:00	* .40	(M.Lvnch)	Kentucky, WindyWay, BrambleHall	(————)
6- 9	^{9}Spk⅝ ft 50°	fa15000=	m	:31^4	1:04	1:35	2:03^3	5	5	4^3°	2^1°	1^1	1^{1½}	2:03^3	* .30	(B.Nickells)	Kentucky, SongCycle, DaringKnight	(lives up to name)
5-19	^{5}May ft 74°	stk6400	m	:29^3	:59^3	1:30	1:58^4	5	6	6°	3^{1½}	2^{hd}	1^{1½}	1:58^4	* .90	(B.Nickells)	Kentucky, ByeByeMax, TarportSkipper	(————)
5-12	^{5}May ft 69°	stk20000	m	:28^4	:58^3	1:28^4	1:58^4	6	5	4°	3^1	1^{nk}	1^{1½}	1:58^4	3.60	(B.Nickells)	Kentucky, TarportSkipper, ByeByeMax	(————)
5- 6	L.B⅝ ft	inv12500	m	:29^2	1:02	1:31^2	2:00^1	4	5	5	4°	4^2	1^{1½}	2:00^1	*1.00	(B.Nickells)	Kentucky, DexterHanover, MissConnaAdios	(————)

Selections—CHARLEY HORSE 3—5—2 **Selections—MISS MAREY 3—5—2 (Best Bet)**

NINTH RACE—1 MILE
PACE. Free For All. "The Governor's Cup". 3 Years and Up. Purse $25,000.

Time—:27^3 :57^3 1:25^4 1:54^3 (world record)

Horse	PP	¼	½	¾	Str	Fin	Time	Odds	Driver
3. Albatross	3	1	1^{1¼}	1^{1½}	1^{2½}	1^{1½}	1:54^3	* .20	(S.Dancer)
5. Kentucky	5	2	2^{1¼}	2^{1½}	2^{2½}	2^{1½}	1:55	5.40	(B.Nickells)
2. Nansemond	2	3	3^{3¼}	3^{3½}	3^{4½}	3^{3¾}	1:55^2	7.90	(HervFilion)
4. Song Cycle	4	5	5^{5½}	5^9	4^{9½}	4^{5½}	1:55^4	12.10	(J.MarshJr.)
1. Ed Byrd	1	4	4^{4½}	4^{8½}	5^{13}	5^{15}	1:57^3	30.40	(H.Burright)

Mutuels — (3) 2.40 2:10 2.10 — (5) 2.20 2:10 — (2) 2.10

THE WORLD CHAMPION ALBATROSS commandeered the lead from the great KENTUCKY who had blasted off from the start, and used ultra speed with urging to pace the FASTEST RACE IN HARNESS RACING HISTORY!

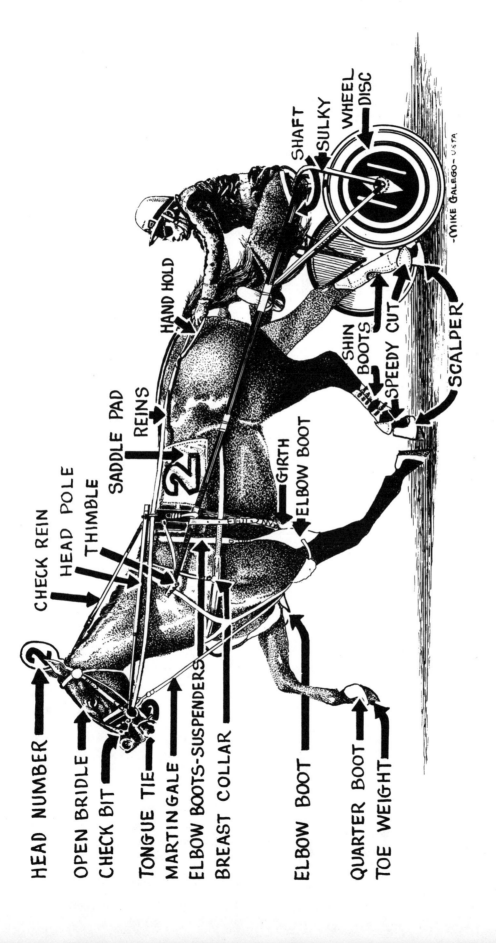

A trotter in motion.

state where the racetrack is located. Stakes races for older horses are usually for state-owned, -bred, or -foaled.

Free-for-all, Junior Free-for-all, Invitational and Preferred Races. These types of races are held for the best horses on the grounds. Every horse at the meeting is eligible for these races, but he must be selected by the Racing Secretary. The top races are the free-for-alls and junior free-for-alls. These horses are the cream of the crop so they race for the highest purse money.

Next in line are the invitational and preferred races. These races are written by the Racing Secretary for horses just short of the free-for-all class. The races may also be separated by the age and sex of the horses.

Some racetracks may use different names for these races, such as "open" or "handicap" races, but they still comprise the best horses on the grounds.

STANDARD ABBREVIATIONS

All racetracks use the same abbreviations for track conditions, finish information, and the horse's color and sex. These are listed below along with an explanation:

Track Conditions
ft—fast
gd—good
sy—sloppy
sl—slow
my—muddy
hy—heavy

Horse's Color
b—bay
blk—black
br—brown
ch—chestnut
gr—gray
ro—roan

Finish Information
ns—nose
hd—head
nk—neck

dis—distanced (lost by more than 25 lengths)
dnf—did not finish
acc—accident

Horse's Sex
c—colt...Male aged four years and under
f—filly...Female aged four years and under
g—gelding...Any desexed male
h—horse...Male aged five years or older
m—mare...Female aged five years or older
r—ridgeling...An incomplete male

BREAKING STRIDE

When a horse makes a "break," he's actually breaking into a gallop. When this happens, the driver must take his horse to the outside of traffic where clearance exists, and try to get him back on his respective gait as soon as possible. While the driver is attempting to do this, he must pull back on his horse so as not to gain any ground while he is galloping. Failure to do so will most assuredly result in immediate disqualification. On occasion, a driver will be able to get his horse on stride quickly enough to come back and win, but more often than not, the horse has too much ground to make up and ends up a badly beaten loser.

If a horse happens to make a break at the finish line and there are one or more horses next to him (within one length) which are in their correct gait, then the expression "lapped on" is used. In this instance, all horses that are lapped on are placed ahead of the breaker.

The most common reason a horse goes off stride is because his driver has asked him to run faster than he's actually capable of going. The horse doesn't know any better so he responds by running the fastest way he knows how—by galloping. Sometimes this can be the result of the inexperience of the driver. A veteran driver usually knows his horse well enough so that he can open him up without causing any problems. At times, though, a horse may simply break stride because he's tired.

From a handicapping standpoint, as far as breaks are concerned, the player is advised to stay away from two things. First, there's the inexperienced driver who can cause his horse to break stride. Second, there's the notorious breaker who is ready and willing to go off stride regardless of who's in the buggy. This type of horse is just not well-mannered and tough to control. There's also the problem of the trotter who has a great tendency to break stride; however, this particular aspect will be discussed separately in the next chapter.

In all, there are three types of breaks that will appear in your program. They will be indicated in the following way:

> x—break
> ix—interference break
> ex—equipment break

Interference and equipment breaks are of little concern to the player, unless they happen to the horse he has bet on to win the race. But as far as handicapping is concerned, these races are simply thrown out because they are not caused by the doings of the driver or the horse.

Related to the interference break is that which occurs when a horse is impeded. It's indicated by the abbreviation *im*. The horse doesn't quite break into a gallop but his momentum is shut off. Most impeded horses lose too much ground and are unable to get back into the race in time. So this type of race would be thrown out also.

Parked Out

The fastest way for any horse to travel around the racetrack is in a position along the rail. When a driver takes his horse to the outside, thus racing alongside a horse that's on the rail, he's what's described as racing "parked out." When a horse is racing in this position, he can travel anywhere from 30 to 50 extra feet around each turn of the track than he would if he were racing along the rail.

The symbol that's used in the program to indicate a parked out horse is a small zero. This appears at either the quarter, half, and/or three-quarter mile pole, as the case may be.

It's usually a very grueling experience for horses to race on the outside for two or more turns. By the time they reach the stretch, they're usually unable to sustain any kind of a meaningful drive because

of traveling the added distance. On the other hand, you'll come across some horses that were able to overcome the adversity of racing parked out for an entire mile. But for most horses, it's just a tiring experience.

When horses race parked, they do so in one of two ways. First there is what's known as racing "without cover." In this instance, the horse races parked out and doesn't have any horses in front of him. This is a very difficult route to travel, especially if it occurs in the early part of the race and the driver isn't able to tuck in or get his horse to the lead. Not only does the horse have to travel the added distance, but he must also break the wind friction, which can take a lot out of the horse.

The second type is when a horse races "with cover." When this is the case, the horse races on the outside but he has one or more horses in front of him breaking the wind friction for him. This is a lot less severe on the horse when compared to racing without cover.

Although it may appear that only the less skilled drivers find themselves parked out, it's actually far from the truth. Many times even the most experienced drivers will shoot their horses out for the lead only to find themselves unable to reach it. The end result is often a parked out mile. Other times it will be late in the race and the driver will want to get his horse within striking distance for the big stretch drive. So he has no other choice but to race on the outside on the final turn. But if he has a lot of horse left and is able to get good cover, you usually can expect him to still come a-running.

From a handicapping standpoint, there will be times when the parked out race is thrown out and times when it plays a very important role. This will be discussed in more detail in a later chapter.

Reading the Past Performances

Up to this point, we've discussed all of the pertinent information plus the abbreviations and symbols that will be found in a horse's past performances. To get a better idea of how the whole ball of wax works, together with how to figure out the horse's speed in his last half, we'll look at a sample past performance.

	Date	Trk Cond Temp	Class	Dist	Leader's Time 1/4	1/2	3/4	Winner's Time	PP	1/4	1/2	3/4	Str	Fin	Ind.Time	Odds	Driver	ORDER OF FINISH First	Second	Third	Comment
	Driver—DWAYNE PLETCHER, White-Black				**Tr.—L. Pletcher**									**(58-10-8-8—.295)**				1973 6 1 0 3	$5,288	2:07 sy Spk⅝	
RED 1	**RIGHT HONOR**	B. h 1964, by Right Time—Sherry's Honor—His Honor																1972 30 6 5 2	$37,562	2:00 Spk⅝	
		Owners: Irma & Lester Pletcher, Shipshewana, Ind.																Lifetime	$235,888	5, 1:59¹ (⅝)	
5-1 =	4- 7	4Spk⅝A ft 56°	w100007273+1		:30⁴	1:01³	1:32	2:02¹	3	4	4⁵	6⁵¼°	66	3²¼	2:02³	7-2	(DwPletcher)	TheGrumbler,	Ghandi,	RightHonor	(closed late)
	3-31	5Spk⅝A sy 44°	nw17008−1		:31	1:04	1:36¹	2:07	4	6	6⁶½	6³¼	5³	1½	2:07	5-2	(DwPletcher)	RightHonor,	TomsChoice,	DocsJerry	(powerful in str.)
	3-19	7Spk⅝ ft 33°	w100007273=1		:31²	1:01²	1:32¹	2:02	7	7	7¹²	7⁶	7⁶½	7⁸	2:03³	*7-5	(DwPletcher)	PerleyHanover,	Ghandi,	EliLang	(followed)
	3- 9	8Spk⅝ gd 40°	w100007273=1		:31	1:04⁴	1:35⁴	2:06²	4	4	5⁵	6³¾°	6³¼	3¾	2:06³	*8 5	(DwPletcher)	MiGrandeAmigo,	CopperCup,	RightHonor	(below par)
	3- 3	8Spk⅝ ft 50°	nw21008−1		:30³	1:02³	1:32³	2:03	7	7	7¹²	7⁹	77	4²½	2:03³	*7-5	(D.Pletcher)	BayStarBoy,	DodgeAcresCleo,	RaceCall	(good last ⅛)
	2-24	10Spk⅝ ft 35°	inv6500=1		:30²	1:01³	1:33	2:02⁴	6	6	6⁷½	66	6⁵½	3¹½	2:03¹	3-1	(DwPletcher)	BannerRanger,	YankeeBaron,	RightHonor	(good close)

We'll start off by reading the top line of the past performance for the pacer Right Honor. Moving across from left to right, it indicates his most recent race was on April 7 in the fourth race at Sportsman's Park, a 5/8ths of a mile track. The track condition was fast and the temperature was 56 degrees at racetime.

Right Honor's last race was conditioned for "Winners of over $10,000 in 1972 and 1973," which was a class hike over his previous race. The distance was one mile and the leader or leaders in the race reached the first quarter in 30 4/5 seconds, the half mile in 1:01 3/5 seconds, the three quarter in 1:32 flat, and the winner's time for the mile was 2:02 1/5 seconds.

Right Honor started from the third post position. He was fourth at the first quarter; fourth at the half mile, 5 lengths behind the leader; sixth at the three quarter mark, 5 1/4 lengths behind the leader while being parked out; sixth, 6 lengths back, at the top of the stretch; and finished the race third, 2 1/4 lengths behind the winner. Right Honor's final time for the mile was 2:02 3/5 seconds.

In that race, Right Honor went off at odds of 7-2. His driver was Dwayne Pletcher. The Grumbler finished first, Ghandi was second, and of course Right Honor finished third. The chartmaker's comment follows the horse's past performance.

The column at the far left indicates that in tonight's race Right Honor is leaving from post position number one. His saddle pad color is red. His morningline odds are 5-1, and below that it denotes that he's staying in the same class tonight.

Moving across from left to right above Right Honor's name, his driver tonight is Dwayne Pletcher who will wear white and black colors. His trainer is L. Pletcher. The driver's percentage at the current meeting is .295.

In 1973, Right Honor had started six times with one win and three thirds. He had earned $5,288 so far and his best winning time for the year was 2:07 at Sportsman's on a sloppy track. In 1972, he started 30 times with six wins, five seconds, and two third place finishes. His earnings were $37,562 and his best winning time for the year was 2:00 minutes flat at Sportsman's Park. His lifetime earnings coming into 1973 were $235,888. His best lifetime mark was 1:59 1/5, as a five year old, on a 5/8ths of a mile track.

To figure out the horse's speed in his last half, let's pick up Right Honor at the half mile pole where he was 5 lengths behind the leader. From that point to the three quarter mark, Right Honor lost ground equaling 1/4 length. But when calculating quarters, 1/4, 1/2, and 3/4's of a length are always rounded off to the nearest full length and one full length is equal to 1/5 of a second. Therefore, Right Honor's third quarter was run in the same time as the leader's which was 30 2/5 seconds.

$$\text{Leader:} \quad 1:01^3 + 30^2 = 1:32$$
$$\text{Right Honor:} \quad 1:02^3 + 30^2 = 1:33$$

The last quarter is calculated the same way. But in this quarter, Right Honor gained 3 lengths from the three quarters to the finish line (5 1/4 to 2 1/4). So his last quarter was run 3/5 of a second faster than the leader's last quarter.

$$\text{Leader:} \quad 1:32 + 30^1 = 2:02^1$$
$$\text{Right Honor:} \quad 1:33 + 29^3 = 2:02^3$$

With a third quarter in 30^2 and the final quarter in 29^3, Right Honor's last half is timed in one minute flat.

$$1:02^3 + 1:00 \ (30^2 + 29^3) = 2:02^3$$

Now that we have the basic information required to read the past performances, all we actually need to know is the understanding of handicapping principles to handicap a race. But unfortunately, the game's not that easy, because there's something just as important as handicapping a race. That's when not to handicap a race—which is what the next chapter is all about.

CHAPTER 2

Eliminating High Risk Races

When you're at the racetrack, there are two things you can do. You can either handicap the race or not handicap the race, and during the course of the racing season, you'll find out that one is just as important as the other. For there are few people, if any, who can go to the racetrack every single night, bet race after race after race, and consistently come out a winner.

That doesn't mean that the player who's determined to make a killing on every single race is a born loser. Nor does it necessarily mean that he doesn't know the first thing about handicapping a race; he may be very skilled at it. But there's a lot more to this game than just that. Whether you wager $2 or $200 a race, the first thing that every player must learn is that patience is just as important as understanding basic handicapping principles.

If you are a serious-minded player and want to win at the racetrack, then you must not only know how to pick winners, but also how to pick losers. This not only will entail choosing the contenders and eliminating the non-contenders in a race, but also will entail eliminating single races.

For some reason, there are people who go to the racetrack who feel if they pass up a race it's as if they were committing an act of treason. It's almost as if they feel it's their patriotic duty to dish out money on races that are so far beyond the comprehension of handicapping that it would make a three year old filly blush. You can always find these people standing in line with one minute to post time, feverishly studying the past performances, trying to pick a winner out of the most terrible field of green two year old trotters you would ever want to lay your eyes on.

A two year old trotting event is probably the classic example of a high risk race. But it's the importance of eliminating *all* high risk races from our attention which we are trying to emphasize, because these races slowly drain a bankroll, which in turn takes away betting power from races in which the player has a fighting chance to win. And it's in *those* races where the logical handicapper chooses a horse which appears to have a marked edge or advantage over his competition. That's what handicapping is really all about.

In all, there are eight situations where the player will find himself handicapping a race under high risk circumstances. Here are brief descriptions of the eight:

TROTTING RACES

When compared to the pacer, the tendency of the trotting horse to break stride is much greater. Because of the diagonal motion of his legs, the trotter is unable to wear the effective type of hopples worn by pacing horses.

Hopples, sometimes spelled hobbles, are worn by virtually all pacers. They are long straps of leather, plastic or nylon and encircle both the front and hind legs of the horse. The straps are connected on the same side of the animal to help keep his legs in unison. However, the trotter is unable to wear this kind of hopple, so you'll rarely come across a trotting race in which no horse in the field breaks stride.

There *is* a special type of hopple occasionally worn by trotters. It runs diagonally under the horse's belly. But the hopple is a far more effective piece of equipment on the pacer because of the lateral motion of his legs.

Because the trotting horse has a great tendency to break stride, the trotting race is the highest risk race the player could possibly wager on. And this is despite whether the race is for high classed animals or not, because trotters entered in free-for-all races are just as capable of breaking stride as the cheapest claimers on the grounds are.

Although you can usually expect trotters to break stride at least three or four times a year, there are a few that don't have this problem at all. So when you come across one that looks well placed, and he shows no breaks in his past performance, it may appear to be a possible exception to the rule of never playing trotting races. But it's not. Even in this situation, the horse is going to be surrounded by potential breakers, which could impede the horse or force him into an interference break.

An example of this very situation is seen on the past performances of the trotter Lincoln's Pay Off.

conditioned for "non-winners of $10,000 in 1972 and 1973," so there was no fear of a class hike. He received the same post position as he had in his last race, and the horse that photoed him out for the win wasn't entered in the field.

The eight horses competing against Lincoln's Pay Off looked like this: Three ran against him in his last race. All three finished far behind, beaten by more than 17 lengths combined. The five remaining horses looked so bad they almost made the other three look good. The five were beaten in their race by more than 70 lengths combined.

Lincoln's Pay Off looked about as well placed as a horse could ever be. Many of the racing fans there that night felt the same way and sent him off as the 7-5 favorite.

FIFTH RACE—ONE MILE TROT—PURSE $4,800
Non-Winners of $10,000 in 1972-73

Time—:31³ 1:02¹ 1:34³ 2:07   Mutuel Pool $87,506

2 Heather Smoke	2	3	3	3³	1⁵	1¹²	2:07	13-1	(DBartlett)
1 Dannys Colt	1	2	2	2²ˣ	5¹⁰	2¹²	2:09²	2-1	(JGraham)
8 Black Label	8	8	8	6¹³	4⁸	3¹²	2:09²	7-1	(JDolbee)
7 Lincolns Pay Off	7	7	6°	4⁸	3⁶	4¹⁷	2:10²	*7-5	(KMaurer)
4 Rosedale Princess	4	1	1	1²	2⁵	5ᵈⁱˢ		34-1	(MCaponetto)
9 Coalmont Jon	9	5	x7	9¹⁷	7²⁰	6ᵈⁱˢ		32-1	(CClickner)
5 RockSprngsRalph	5x	9	9	8¹⁶	6¹⁸	7ᵈⁱˢ		10-1	(APetty)
6 Secret Session	6	6	4°x7	14	8²²	8ᵈⁱˢ		24-1	(KGearhart)
3 Cool Count	3	4	5	5¹²ˣ	9²⁵	9ᵈⁱˢ		9-1	(WRoseboom)

MUTUELS——(2) $29.00 $8.20 $7.40—(1) $5.80 $5.60—(8) $4.20

Brown | **LINCOLN'S PAY OFF**

7

7-2

B g 69 by Speedster—Chancy Hanover—Stars Pride
Owner: John J. Roos, St. Louis, Mo.

1973	9	6	2	0	$6,550	2:03¹ F.P.¹
1972	2	0	1	0	$62	
Lifetime thru 1972					$62	

Driver—KEN MAURER, Green-Gold   Trainer—K. Maurer

4-24	4Haw¹ ft 44°	nw100007²⁷³	1	:32³	1:04¹	1:36¹	2:08	7	1° 1	1¹½	1²½	2ⁿᵏ	2:08	*4-5 (KMaurer)	Rang:Dream, LincolnsPayOff, CoolCount
4-13	F.P.¹ ft	pref2500	1	:30⁴	1:00³	1:31⁴	2:03¹	5	3° 1	1	1²	1²	2:03¹	*4-5 (KMaurer)	LincolnsPayOff, CleverLew, ZekeOaks
4- 6	F.P.¹ ft	pref2400	1	:30	1:01³	1:32	2:03¹	6	6 2°1	1½	11p2	T.dis	*4-5 (KMaurer)	SpeedWash, LincolnsPayOff, ZekeOaks
3-30	F.P.¹ ft	pref2200	1	:32²	1:04¹	1:35¹	2:05³	6	6 6	5°	3¹	1²	2:05³	*9-5 (KMaurer)	LincolnsPayOff, ZekeOaks, SpeedWash
3-23	F.P.¹ ft	w3000	1	:31³	1:02	1:33³	2:04³	2	1 1	1	1¹	1¾	2:04³	*3-2 (KMaurer)	LincolnsPayOff, CleverLew, MysteryPat
3-10	F.P.¹ sy	w3000	1	:34¹	1:06¹	1:39	2:11⁴	1	1 1	1	1¹	1²	2:11⁴	*2-1 (KMaurer)	LincolnsPayOff, CleverLew, RichlandCo.Boy

The Speedster gelding is the epitome of consistency. After virtually running out of competition at Fairmont Park, Lincoln's Pay Off was shipped to Hawthorne where he made an impressive debut on April 24 in a conditioned race for "non-winners of $10,000 in 1972 and 1973." Also complementing the trotter's consistency is the fact that he shows no breaks at all in his past performance.

Lincoln's Pay Off was scheduled to race again one week later on May 1. The event was also

Just by taking one glance at the result chart, it doesn't take very long to figure out the disastrous outcome. During the race, no less than five horses in the field broke stride. Ken Maurer, the driver of Lincoln's Pay Off, had to steer his horse clear of breakers as if he were a football player trying to dodge tacklers. And even though Lincoln's Pay Off didn't go off stride during the race, he was never able to gain his full momentum because of the breakers and finished far out of it, beaten by 17

Delmonica Hanover, Trotter of the Year in 1974.

lengths. So let's remember an important rule. Never play trotting races.

High Class Races

The high class races such as free-for-alls, junior free-for-alls, invitationals, preferreds, opens, and handicap races are always filled with the best horses on the grounds. Very often the player will come across a horse that looks like a solid standout, but in these types of races almost any horse in the field is capable of winning.

None of the six listed high class races should ever be played. Not only are these races reserved for the best horses at the meeting, which brings together fields of similar ability, but you'll very frequently find invaders in the race that have shipped in from other tracks looking for top purses. This only makes high class races more risky than they already are.

We also have to deal with stakes races since they often attract the classier types. The ones that are conditioned for two, three, and four year olds are really nothing more than high class races that exclude older horses. Therefore, these types of races shouldn't be played either.

There is one type of stakes race that is considered for play. These are events conditioned for older horses (four years old and up) that are for state-owned, -bred, or -foaled. In this particular kind of stakes race, the experienced player can often find a superior horse that's able to benefit from a state restricted type of condition.

Young Horses

Our primary concern with young horses is aimed at the two year old. Regardless of what class level the race is scheduled for, two year old events are never played.

The two year old horse is virtually an unproven steed and his dependability is next to none. However, there will be times when you come across a two year old that appears to be maturing much faster than his competitors. But unfortunately, two year olds have something in common with free-for-allers. Whereas a free-for-aller is always capable of winning his race, a two year old is always capable of losing his.

Three year old horses are treated a little differently from two year olds. In the early part of the year, three year old races should not be played. Only by the middle part of the year (around May or June), when they have all had some racing behind them, are their races ever considered for play.

In races conditioned for three year olds only, a colt usually has a slight edge over his filly counterpart when all things are equal. When three year olds race against older horses and all things are equal, the slight edge is given to the older horse.

Non-Winner Races

Non-winner events pertain to the number of races the horse has not won during his lifetime. They start at the base low of the maiden race, or as some racetracks prefer to classify it, "non-winners of one race in lifetime."

The non-winner type of races are usually never classified beyond the "non-winners of four lifetime wins" race. After a horse completes his non-winner races, he'll either go to higher classed conditioned races or is entered in a claiming race for what his owner or trainer thinks his best approximate value is.

It's usually a nightmare when the player attempts to handicap a non-winner race. Maiden races are virtually beyond any handicapping principles. How could you ever possibly rely on a horse that has never won a race in his entire lifetime? Therefore, maiden races should never be played. The best thing you can do when a maiden is scheduled at your racetrack is to use that time to enjoy yourself with a hot dog and a beer.

Races for "non-winners of two lifetime wins" are not much more appealing than maiden races. After all, what has the horse done for you beyond having broken his maiden, and maybe he hasn't even done that. Therefore, these types of races are simply not played either.

Races scheduled for "non-winners of three or four lifetime wins" can be considered for play. But because these races are still somewhat on the risky side, the player should demand that his horse have everything going for him. And what's meant by everything in a non-winner race will be discussed in a later chapter.

CHEAP CLAIMING RACES

On a whole, the player's best betting medium is the claiming race. In this type of race, the handicapper is able to define class relationships between horses much easier than in conditioned races. But this is not to be misunderstood that conditioned races should not be handicapped, because the fact of the matter is the great majority of them are. All we have actually eliminated from conditioned races are a couple of the non-winner events. But the bulk of races the astute player eventually wagers on are claiming races.

The only difficulty you'll run into in handicapping claiming races are ones for bottom claimers.

These are claiming races held for the lowest claiming price a horse can be entered for at your racetrack. This could be a $1,000 claimer at Saratoga or a $3,500 claimer at Sportsman's Park.

The first mark that bottom claimers have against them is that they're the cheapest horses on the grounds. Anytime a bottom claimer makes any noticeable improvement, it's immediately discounted because at this low level class and form are meaningless.

Also weighing heavily against the bottom claimer is that he races less frequently than middle or upper claimers. A bottom claimer can spend two to three weeks on the sidelines waiting for his next race, or more appropriately, recuperating from his last race. By combining all of these poor qualities together, the player would have to do more guessing than actual handicapping.

Ironically, there would be more things going for you if you were to handicap a $2,000 claiming race at Saratoga than a $3,500 claimer at Sportsman's Park. Even though you're working with cheaper claimers at Saratoga, they're not bottom claimers like those at Sportsman's, so they're likely to get to the races more frequently. But when you consider that's the best thing you have going in the race, you really don't have very much. So with this in mind, a minor stipulation is put on claiming races: All claiming races considered for play must be at least $1,500 above the minimum claiming price at your racetrack.

TRACK CONDITIONS

Whenever the condition of the racing strip is listed as anything but fast, it's known as an "off track." Thanks to Mother Nature, the majority of the racing season will be conducted on a fast track. But the majority is not the entirety, so there will still be those evenings when the rains come and the track conditions turn to good, sloppy, slow, muddy, or heavy.

Even when the track conditions are off, most horses still run to their true form. This is simply because the majority of the races are comprised of more non-contenders than actual contenders. If a non-contender has been showing terrible form up until tonight's race, he's likely to show that same terrible form again regardless of what the track conditions are.

Despite the fact that we're still able to eliminate non-contenders on an off track, we really haven't solved anything. They would be eliminated as non-contenders anyway, even if the track was fast. What we're concerned with is the horse we've handicapped to win the race. How will an off track affect his chances? And not only must we know that, but we must also be certain that none of the contenders in the field will race better because the track is off. And if that's not enough, you must also keep in mind that the possibility for a horse to break stride is enhanced because of the slippery conditions.

The best alternative you have to handicapping under these conditions is not to play any races unless they're contested on a fast track. And one of the easiest ways of doing that is not go to the racetrack if it's raining outside. I'll agree this might not sound like the best thing to do, especially if you've already made plans to go to the racetrack with a couple of buddies, but it could very well be the safest thing for your wallet.

There are times, however, when the unexpected may happen. You enter the racetrack on a beautiful clear evening and all of a sudden it's the fourth race and it's raining cats and dogs. You can't possibly sue the local weather forecaster because nobody ever said he was perfect. But what you can do is go home. It's ridiculous to risk any money when there are so many evenings when the track is fast.

If you do decide to stick around on a rainy night, I suggest you be very cautious and only play races if the track is listed as good. At least on a good track, the footing is still somewhat firm and won't bother the horses that much. It's when the track turns to sloppy, slow, muddy, and heavy that races should definitely not be played.

DISTANCES OTHER THAN THE MILE

There are three distinct advantages the player has by handicapping harness races as opposed to thoroughbred races. The first is that the harness

horse runs much closer to his real form than does the thoroughbred. Secondly, you don't have to worry if "Horse A" is carrying six more pounds than "Horse B" since there are no weight assignments. And finally, there's no need to fret about any switch in distances.

Unfortunately this last advantage does not always hold true for all locations. There are a few racetracks that like to throw in an occasional sprint or distance race. But these races are in such a minority that there's no reason to even bother with them. There are far too many races scheduled at the standard mile. And as far as the driver's weight is concerned, it doesn't make any significant difference on a fast track.

WINTER RACING

In Northern racetracks, winter takes its toll on the racehorse as well as the racing fan. By this time of the year, any horse that has an inkling of a future ahead of him has either been shipped to California or Florida for the racing wars, while still others are given a well deserved rest.

What does that exactly leave at major Northern tracks? Not very much. Usually a flock of horses with sub-par ability that have either been campaigning in the neighborhood all year or have been shipped in from some of the minor tracks.

Anything that even resembles form is meaningless at the winter tracks. And if you want to compare final times, forget it. They're not comparable, because as the temperature goes down, the times get slower. When you try to handicap Lucky Louise who won in 2:08 at 30 degrees, to Silly Suzy who got nipped at the wire at 2:10 at 10 degrees, you end up being a meteorologist rather than a handicapper. So up North, the best thing you can do if you have winter racing in town, is to view the whole thing as one big sloppy track. In other words, stay home.

HIGH RISK RACES SUMMARIZED

1.   All trotting events are passed regardless of the class level of the race.
2.   None of the high class races are ever played.

They include: free-for-alls, junior free-for-alls, invitationals, preferreds, opens, and handicaps.

All stakes races are passed with the only exception being ones conditioned for older horses (four years old and up) in which the race is restricted for state-owned, -bred, or -foaled.

3.   Two year old races are never played. Three year old races are passed only in the early part of the year. When three year olds run against older horses early in the year, their chances are dismissed.

4.   Maiden and "non-winner of two lifetime wins" races are never played. Races for "non-winner of three or four lifetime wins" are only played as described in this book.

5.   All claiming races that are for less than $1,500 above the minimum claiming price at your racetrack are passed.

6.   Any race contested on a track listed as anything but fast or good is not played.

7.   All races scheduled at anything other than the standard mile are not played.

8.   Winter racing is not played at any of the icebox tracks.

Handicapping is a game of odds, and the odds are always against you the minute you walk into a racetrack. With taxes and the track's share taken out, there is less money distributed back to the winners of each race than was actually wagered on it. Therefore, what we try to do as handicappers, is to equalize our chances for winning by eliminating all of the high risk races.

To put it into a different perspective, consider your chances for winning if you only wagered on the races listed not for play. I wouldn't hesitate to say that very few people, if any, could survive financially. That's why we, as handicappers, only wager on races that are to our advantage.

In all, there have been only a small percentage of races actually eliminated from play. There are still a ton of conditioned and claiming races to be handicapped. In the next chapter, we'll look at two important factors (class and form) needed to handicap those races. And it's those two factors that produce the contenders in the race.

CHAPTER 3

Choosing the Contenders—Part I

For the player to handicap a race successfully, he must have full knowledge of why or why not each horse has a chance to win the race. By translating why or why not into horsetalk, the whys become the contenders and the why nots the non-contenders.

Our major concern is with the contenders. It's out of that select group that we must locate one horse who deserves to win tonight's race on the basis of his previous race or races. Our only concern with the non-contenders is if one or more of them appears to have a major effect upon our final choice.

If we are going to distinguish the non-contenders from the contenders and then make our final choice, we must use a logical medium. In our words, we must make use of the five basic ingredients of handicapping: class, form, pace, post position, and the driver.

These ingredients, principles, factors, or whatever you prefer to call them, are nothing new to the sport of horse racing. Nor are they anything new to the process of handicapping horse races, whether it be thoroughbred or harness racing. Ever since wagering has been taking place on horse races, it's been these five basic ingredients that have constituted the major proportion of what we call the handicapping process. And if there's any one thing that amazes me about these five ingredients, it's that most people that go to the racetrack have little or no real knowledge of them. In fact, there are quite a number of people that go to the track almost every night and don't even bother to buy a racing program!

If you were to take the single ingredient class and handicap solely on its basis, you would find yourself losing an unusually high number of races. The same is also true for the other four ingredients because it's the total relationship they have with one another that's important. Even form, which is the single most important ingredient, doesn't really mean very much if you don't take into consideration the horse's capable class level. But when you take the combination of class and form, you have an excellent starting point for handicapping a horse, because you have the two most important ingredients that interrelate with one another. And that's why we'll look at these two ingredients first.

CLASS AND FORM

There are two ways we could look at class. The first is from the standpoint of pure class, that combination of qualities the truly class animal possesses. Such as stamina, the physical ability to resist fatigue. He must be game, an inborn quality of courage. He must have endurance, the ability to last under any conditions. He must also have heart, speed, temperament, and be physically sound at all times. And I could go on and on because the truly class animal must possess it all, and he must have it to a greater degree than the horses he will face on the racetrack.

If you want to think of class in these terms, it's all very nice. It's even better if you're looking for a good horse for breeding purposes. But it's not the kind of class we're really interested in in handicapping a race, because it's something which only the best horses have some of, and something the worst horses have none of. Our only interest in class is strictly with the horse's class level in relationship to his current form. And as you will quickly find out, the relationship one has with the other always works both ways.

When we think in terms of the horse's current form, all we're actually doing is making an evaluation of the horse's per-FORM-ance. And in horse racing, performance is simply the ability to win or lose. If a horse is in so-called "good form," then he has shown us the ability to win his races or a determined effort to win his races. If a horse is in "bad form," then it goes without saying—forget him. But good and bad form are really the direct result of class. Because if a horse is in good form, then he's running in his proper class level. Or he can even be running below his proper class level. If a horse is in bad form, then he's running above his proper class level.

Of course, it's impossible for every single horse at a meeting to be running in his proper class level. If they did, it would be an impossible task for us handicappers because all we would have is a series of evenly matched races. But I wouldn't worry too much about this, because it's not the easiest thing in the world for a trainer to properly place his horse week in and week out. And sometimes it's not even a practical thing to do.

In conditioned races under the letter classification system, each horse is classified by the Racing Secretary. So if a trainer has an A-3 pacer in the barn who's gone off form a bit, he can't simply announce to everybody that he's going to race him in B-2 company because that's where he feels his nag can win a race. He has to wait for the Racing Secretary to reclassify his horse. And he could very easily get a B-1 classification where there's still tough going.

At racetracks where the Racing Secretary writes the conditions of the race, a trainer isn't always in a good position to place his horse properly each week. If a horse goes off form, but already has a nice-sized bankroll for the year, he's not going to be eligible for lower classed conditioned races. There are a few type of races where he can drop

his horse down with no regard to his earnings, but it might not be the drastic drop down needed.

In claiming races, a trainer can place his horse wherever he wants. But as I previously said, properly placing a horse is not always a practical thing to do. For instance, let's take a hypothetical $15,000 claimer that has suddenly gone off form. The trainer might have to drop him in for $10,000 to win, or even have a chance to win. But losing a $15,000 claimer for $10,000 via a claim is not the best financial investment a trainer can make. Especially if he knows his horse will be returning to his $15,000 form in a couple of races. So from a trainer's standpoint, a drastic drop down is not always practical.

As you can see, current form is only relevant when the horse's capable class level is taken into consideration. That's why it's impossible for us to handicap solely on the basis of class or current form. If we did, we'd be totally ignorant in evaluating the three class functions of horse racing.

1. When horses are dropped in class.
2. When horses are running within the same class level.
3. When horses are raised in class.

Every single horse that's entered in a race will conform to one of these three class functions. If we're to evaluate a horse in terms of these functions, then we'll have to think like a trainer. In fact, we'll have to act as though we're the trainer of each horse in the race.

Our first decision will be when a horse hasn't raced well at his last class level and therefore should be dropped in class. If the trainer is raising the horse or running him at his last class level, we would eliminate him as a contender. If the trainer does, in fact, drop the horse in class, we'll decide if the drop down is enough to consider him as a contender.

The second decision we'll make is when a horse has raced well at his last class level but should remain there. If it's the trainer's decision to raise his horse in class, again we would eliminate him as a contender. But if the horse is remaining within the same class level or being dropped in class, he would loom as a contender.

Our final decision is when a horse has raced extremely well at his last class level and therefore should be raised in class. If the trainer is not raising his horse in class, he would also loom as a contender. If the trainer does decide to raise his horse in class, we'll determine if the class hike is too much to consider him as a contender.

It's the class-form relationship that's the basis for determining the contenders in each race. Occasionally, a horse will stand out on these two points alone. But more than likely, we'll have to consider the other three ingredients—pace, post position, and the driver. They will be discussed in Chapter 6. But they are not used in determining the contenders but rather in making the final choice from the contenders. So our first order of business will be finding the contenders in conditioned races.

CONTENDERS IN CONDITIONED RACES

When trying to determine if a horse going up in class is a contender, the player enjoys one decisive advantage. He can demand that the horse's last race not only show improvement, but also is an impressive race compared to his recent efforts. In claiming races, we rely very heavily on the class-form relationship to determine this. But in conditioned races, we have to rely a little bit more on the form factor, because class levels of conditioned races can often be deceiving.

Let's say a horse ran in a race for "non-winners of $9,000" last week and this week he's entered against a field for "non-winners of $10,000." Technically speaking, this horse is taking a class hike. But if we technically abide by the rules all the time, we could run into a lot of trouble because the class differences between these two races is very

It's a seven-day-a-week job when you work on the backstretch. (Photo by Kuprion.)

little. In fact, it's very possible that the horses entered in the $9,000 race were classier types. Therefore, each horse must be put in its proper perspective, with the form factor receiving more emphasis than class.

Keep in mind that even though we put more

We'll start off our search for contenders with two horses that are both going up in class in the same race. At first glance, they both appear to be contenders. They're entered in a race conditioned for "non-winners of $16,000 in 1972 and 1973" that took place at Sportsman's Park on July 7.

RED 1 9-2 =	Driver—SONNY GRAHAM, Blue-White **HARRY FITZ**			Tr.—S. Graham					(11-2-4-1—.414)			1973 4 1 1 1 1972 5 3 0 2 Lifetime		$3,190 2:06² gd Spk⅝ $8,687 2:02³ Spk⅝ $8,687 2, 2:02³ (⅝)		
	B c 1970, by Sampson Direct—Irish Lil—Irish Hal Owner: K. D. Owen, Houston, Texas															
	6-28 ⁸Spk⅝ ft 64°	nw140007273+1	:31¹ 1:02² 1:32 2:02³	1	5°	22¼°	11°	11½	2¹	2:02⁴	*4-5 (S.Graham)	SlippinBy, HarryFitz, SherwoodDancer		(wide the mile)
	6-23 ⁵Spk⅝ gd 74°	nw4R—1	:31¹ 1:05³ 1:35³ 2:06²	7	1°	1¹	11½	1²	12¼	2:06²	5-2 (S.Graham)	HarryFitz, DykeM, NativeGem		(easy win)
	6-15 Det¹ ft	3yrstk57105	1 :28⁴ :59 1:29 1:57⁴	1	8	9°	9	10⁸	9¹¹½	2:00	f28-1 (S.Graham)	KeystoneSmartie, ArmbroNesbit, RnBnRtzar		(———)
	6- 9 Lex¹ ft	opn2000	1 :29¹ :59⁴ 1:30² 2:00	4	6	6	5°	4³¼	3⁴	2:00⁴	*2-1 (S.Graham)	PrinceL.bell, FlorhioScotch, HarryFitz		(———)
	8- 9 Haw¹ ft	Qua	1 :31 1:02¹ 1:32³ 2:03	4	1	1	1	1⁷	13½	2:03	NB (J.Moody)	HarryFitz, GaySkipper, SapphireGlow		(———)
	8- 3 Haw¹ ft	Qua	1 :31² 1:01⁴ 1:34 2:04	5	2°	2	2	1⁵	18¼	2:04	NB (S.Graham)	HarryFitz, GuyAdios, Vipsun		(———)
YELLOW 6 6-1 +	Driver—BRUCE NICKELLS, White-Purple **RARE BUTTERFLY**			Tr.—B. Nickells					(68-8-10-4—.219)			1973 14 4 2 2 1972 2 0 0 1 Lifetime		$9,195 2:03³ Haw¹ $146 $11,195 2, 2:11³		
	B m 1968, by Race Time—Butterfly Hanover—Dean Hanover Owner: Hubly Farms, Columbus, Ohio															
	6-20 ⁸Spk⅝ ft 76°	nw80007273—1	:29³ 1:01⁴ 1:31⁴ 2:04	6	2	31¼	31½	2²	11¼	2:04	*4-1 (B.Nickells)	RareButterfly, KeystoneDandy, EmbssyVlo		(well placed)
	5-30 ⁹Spk⅝ ft 59°	FM5000=1	:30⁴ 1:02¹ 1:32 2:02	6	3	55½	53½°	55½	54¾	2:03	12-1 (B.Nickells)	FarvelCounsel, BretsPrincess, Heartlis		(tough trip)
	5-24 ⁶Haw¹ ft 60°	fmnw4R	:30⁴ 1:02² 1:33⁴ 2:03³	3	4	4	4³	3¹	11¼	2:03³	3-1 (B.Nickells)	RareButterfly, GalaNite, Katiller		(rated perfectly)
	5- 8 ⁷Haw¹ ft 60°	fm5500	1 :31⁴ 1:04 1:36³ 2:05³	5	5	8	95½	99½	75¾	2:06⁴	10-1 (B.Nickells)	SandraLil, FemmeFatale, Heartlis		(no chance)
	4-27 ⁵Haw¹ ft45°	FMnw60007273	1 :30² 1:03 1:33⁴ 2:04⁴	1	3	4	44	33	2¾	2:05	7-2 (M.Lynch)	MissDudsun, RareButterfly, MissGertie		(good effort)
	4-16 ⁷Spk⅝A ft 45°	nw80007273—1	:30³ 1:04² 1:33⁴ 2:05³	6	8	8¹³	8¹⁴	78½	63¾	2:06³	4-1 (B.Nickells)	HWExpress, SpyderWright, SoonerRace		(moved late)

emphasis on current form, it doesn't mean the class factor is totally ignored. The only reason we put emphasis on current form is because we don't pay much heed to minor class fluctuations. Those are fluctuations that are within $2,000 of the monetary conditions of the race. So if the horse is going from "non-winners of $10,000" to "non-winners of $12,000" or vice versa, he's considered to be running within the same class level. Anything more than a $2,000 fluctuation is considered to be a definite class hike or drop and will be treated as such.

When we handicap a horse, our primary interest is always with his last race. But before we get into any races, we have to lay down two important ground rules in dealing with horses that were impeded or broke stride in their last race. First, if the horse was impeded, had an interference or equipment break, or broke stride on an off track, his last race is thrown out and he's then handicapped off his previous effort. Secondly, if a horse breaks stride outside of these circumstances, he's automatically eliminated as a non-contender. There are a few other situations where races are thrown out, but they will be dealt with as we go along.

From the number one hole, we have Harry Fitz. Condition wise, this colt is taking a class hike coming off a race for "non-winners of $14,000 in 1972 and 1973." But this is considered a minor class hike, so he's treated as if he's running within the same class level. That means our primary interest is performance with no regard to the class hike. Therefore, for Harry Fitz to become a contender, all he has to do is provide us with a good performance. He certainly qualifies on that count by pacing an entire mile parked out and losing by only one length. Therefore, he would be regarded as a contender.

Also coming off a good effort is the mare, Rare Butterfly. But in her case, the class hike is a definite one. In fact, the class difference between non-winners of $8,000 and non-winners of $16,000 is quite substantial. So not only would Rare Butterfly have to have won her race to be a contender, but it would have to be in a manner that deserves a certain amount of attention, such as a win by a large margin, an unusually large gain of ground in the stretch, or racing well on the outside for two or more turns. So on this basis, she would not be a contender but rather a non-contender.

Aside from eliminating horses by comparing

their chances to the class of the race, there are times when we can also make comparison eliminations between horses. But a comparison elimination should only be used when there's a large class difference between the horses involved.

A comparison elimination could have been made between Harry Fitz and Rare Butterfly. By putting the two horses in their proper perspective, we could easily assume that Harry Fitz's performance would have been a winning one in Rare Butterfly's race, since it took place at a much lower class level. Thus, we would make a comparison elimination of Rare Butterfly. Keep in mind, however, if there was not that large class difference between them, we would have only compared their chances to the class of the race.

Any time a horse makes a definite class hike, his chances for a contending role could be cancelled out. But it's not always the rule, even if the horse is compared to other horses that are not going up in class. This situation is seen in a race conditioned for "non-winners of $8,000 in 1973." The race took place on August 24, at Maywood Park.

improved somewhat in his last race, losing by a smaller margin, he still hasn't reached the point where he indicates that he can handle this class level. We would conclude that Concourse needs a drop in class to improve his chances. He doesn't get one in this race, so he's considered a non-contender.

Leaving from the six post is Folger. It doesn't take very long to eliminate this kind of horse. His last two races at tonight's class level are even less impressive than that of Concourse's. Anytime you come across a horse that reflects the terrible form that Folger's been racing in, he should be quickly eliminated unless there's some sort of gigantic drop in class. Folger doesn't even receive a class drop in this race so he's also labeled a non-contender.

Leaving from the seven post is Joan's Gene. This colt took a drop in class in his last race to "non-winners of $5,000 in 1973." Since he's being raised in class for tonight's race, we demand not only improvement but an impressive race as compared to his previous races. In Joan's Gene's last outing, he showed marked improvement by staying close

RED **1** 5-1	Driver—WILLIAM BECKLEY, Blue-Gold					Tr.—W. Beckley		(35-2-6-7—.219)			1973 17 0 5 1 $7,292							
	CONCOURSE		B c 1969, by Duane Hanover—Takeoff Time—Good Time Owner: David L. Steiner, Lima, Ohio								1972 22 4 4 7 $8,317 2:04 Kenton Lifetime $8,977 3, 2:04							
	8-18 8May ft 77°	nw800⁷³	1 :28³ :59² 1:29¹ 1:59⁴	1 4	7⁶	8⁶	7⁷	57¼	2:01¹	16-1 (W.Beckley)	TheChamp, KeystoneStormy, PocoPilot					(evenly)		
	8-13 5May ft 77°	nw800⁷³	1 :30³ 1:02 1:32⁴ 2:01²	5 2	21¼	23½	2⁹	29½	2:03²	12-1 (W.Beckley)	TheChamp, Concourse, BaronEric					(2nd best)		
	8- 4 3May ft 77°	nw600⁷³	1 :30¹ 1:00⁴ 1:31³ 2:03²	3 1	3²	31¼	31½°	2¹	2:03³	7-1 (W.Beckley)	NobleLand, Concourse, GusMinbar					(boxed in str)		
	7-27 8May sy 79°	nw800⁷³	1 :31¹ 1:05¹ 1:37⁴ 2:09¹	4 4	3²°	43½°	64½	44¼	2:10	7-1 (J.Dolbee)	CafineKid, L.R.Adios, Joan'sGene					(some speed)		
	7-18 8Spk⅝ ft 82°	nw1500⁵⁻²=1	:30⁴ 1:02¹ 1:32⁴ 2:02²	8 9	89½°	9⁸	91⁰	98½	2:04¹	15-1 (W.Beckley)	NobleLand, ArcadiaJake, KeystoneJournal					(evenly)		
	7- 9 8Spk⅝ ft 78°	nw3000⁶−1	:30¹ 1:01⁴ 1:32 2:02	6 2	3²	3³	3²	42¾	2:02³	8-1 (W.Beckley)	MajesticBelleG, WorthyBret, HarkWon					(evenly)		
YELLOW **6** 12-1	Driver—WILLIAM ROSEBOOM, Gold-Purple					Tr.—G. Wentz		(16-0-2-2—.111)			1973 19 0 3 2 $9,748							
	‡**FOLGER**		Ch h 1965, by Top Deck—Lusty Kaye—Lusty Volo Jr. Owner: Virgil Wentz, Rock Springs, Wisc.								1972 29 4 4 7 $18,473 2:03² Was¹ Lifetime $46,943 5, 2:03 (1)							
	8-21 9May ft 66°	‡nw800⁷³	1 :29⁴ :59⁴ 1:30² 2:01	7 7	88°	65½	67½	7¹¹	2:03¹	45-1 (W.Rosebm)	KeystoneJournal, MannartDuer, Minn.BAdios					(no threat)		
	8-13 5May ft 77°	‡nw800⁷³	1 :30³ 1:02 1:32⁴ 2:01²	7 6	68½	67½	6¹³	51⁴	2:04¹	19-1 (W.Rosebm)	TheChamp, Concourse, BaronEric					(too much speed)		
	8- 1 5May ft 67°	‡nw1000⁷³	1 :30³ 1:03¹ 1:33¹ 2:03	6 1	2¹	21¼	3³	4⁸	2:04³	17-1 (W.Rosebm)	NativeExpress, YankeeBaron, Samtree					(away fast)		
	7-21 7Spk⅝ ft 75°	‡nw1750⁶−1	:29³ 1:01¹ 1:31⁴ 2:01³	8 3°	1ʰᵈ	42¼	56½	61¹	2:03⁴	14-1 (L.Rapone)	BigDaddysShdw, Ovrhaul, FlmngosPride					(3-wide leaving)		
	7- 6 7Spk⅝ ft 83°	‡w10000⁷²⁷³=1	:30¹ 1:00⁴ 1:30⁴ 2:00³	8 9	9¹¹	97½	9⁹	94½	2:01³	16-1 (G.Wentz)	YankeeBaron, Overhaul, DanAdios					(dull effort)		
	6-30 6Spk⅝ ft 74°	‡nw2000⁸−1	:29² 1:00³ 1:31¹ 2:01²	7 7	79½	7⁶	5³	22¼	2:01⁴	10-1 (G.Wentz)	FantasticDream, Folger, C.V.Yates					(closed well)		
BROWN **7** 8-1	Driver—MAX LYNCH, Maroon-Blue					Tr.—B. Nickells		(17-1-2-4—.203)			1973 12 4 4 3 $7,197 2:02⁴ Spk⅝							
	JOAN'S GENE		B c 1970, by Gene Abbe—Whirloff Wick—Attorney Owner: Joan Miller, Shaker Heights, Ohio								1972 0 0 0 0 (——) Lifetime (——)							
	8-16 8May ft 74°	nw500⁷³	1 :29⁴ 1:00¹ 1:31⁴ 2:02¹	4 3	21¼	31½	31½°	2½	2:02²	4-1 (M.Lynch)	EdgewoodDevan, JoansGene, OakLndRaidr					(closed well)		
	8- 6 9May ft 75°	nw800⁷³	1 :30⁴ 1:01¹ 1:31² 2:01³	8 8	86½	8⁵	65¼	56½	2:03	8-1 (B.Nickells)	TarrsChief, Dana'sRoybill, NativeGem					(evenly)		
	7-27 8May sy 79°	nw800⁷³	1 :31¹ 1:05¹ 1:37⁴ 2:09¹	5 7	77½	64½°	43½°	3⁴	2:10	7-2 (B.Nickells)	CafineKid, L.R.Adios, Joan'sGene					(fair try)		
	7-17 9Spk⅝ ft 80°	nw3R=1	:30⁴ 1:03³ 1:33⁴ 2:02⁴	6 2	2¹	21½	2¹	12¼	2:02⁴	5-2 (J.Dennis)	JoansGene, FilthyMcNasty, PacingBoy					(good trip)		
	7- 7 3Spk⅝ ft 90°	nw3R=1	:30¹ 1:01 1:31² 2:02	2 4	4⁴	43½	45½	32¼	2:02²	*3-2 (B.Nickells)	BarbaraAlmahurst, TimeMaker, JoansGene					(late close)		
	6-28 7Spk⅝ ft 64°	nw3R+1	:31¹ 1:03 1:32³ 2:03³	5 6	54½	4³	4¹	2ⁿᵏ	2:03³	5-2 (B.Nickells)	LoyalTime, JoansGene, TimeMaker					(bobbled ½)		

From the one post is Concourse. This colt's last two races at tonight's class level are less than desirable. Despite the fact that he finished second on August 13, it's more important to note that he still lost the race by a large margin. Although he

to the leaders and finishing the race well, beaten by only 1/2 length. This showing would be considered an impressive race as compared to his previous races since it is his best effort within the last month. There's also a definite class hike, but it's not a substantial one so it wouldn't eliminate his chances. Therefore, Joan's Gene would qualify as a contender.

The class hike is always capable of producing a strong contender. If the horse is taking a substantial class hike, he should be coming off a strong winning race in order to be a contender. But if the horse is taking a small class hike and he's not coming off a big effort, he best qualifies as a contender when the race is void of class drops and if the horses running at the same class level are far from impressive. This situation is seen in a race conditioned for "winners of over $10,000." The event took place on May 19, at Hawthorne Race Course.

qualify as a contender without the benefit of a class drop. Therefore, he's a non-contender. On the other hand, G. T. Skipper would be a contender since he's already proven himself at this class level by winning his last race.

Although G. T. Skipper is a contender, it doesn't mean that horses running at the same class level must have won their race in order to be contenders. Naturally, a winner would always qualify, but so does a horse that has finished close to a winner. A horse can also qualify as a contender if he has not lost his last race by a large margin, rarely more than five lengths. But he must also show improvement in either his stretch gain or his margin of loss over his previous race. This is why

Blue 3 — **ADIOS ART** — 6-1

B h 68 by Adios Senator—Giny Scot—Grand Tucker
Owner: Oden Ball, Centerburg, Ohio

1973	5	1	1	0	$3.300	2:02^4	Haw^1
1972	25	7	4	2	$32.452	2:00^1	Haw^1
Lifetime thru 1972					$63,128		

Driver—JOE MARSH, JR., Gray-Blue-Red   Trainer—W. Wall

5-12	^{2}Haw^1 ft 52°	w10000	1	:31^1	1:00^1	1:31^3	2:01^1	9	4	1	$1^{1\frac{1}{4}}$	$3^{1\frac{1}{2}}$	$7^{6\frac{3}{4}}$	2:02^3	9-2	(JMarshJr)	G.T.Skipper, TheFooler, NobleSkipper
5- 3	^{6}Haw^1 ft 43°	nw2000^6	1	:31^2	1:01^4	1:32^1	2:02^4	4	5	1	1^2	$1^{2\frac{1}{2}}$	1^1	2:02^4	*1-1	(JMarshJr)	AdiosArt, EdByrd, TimeHonored
4-26	^{8}Haw^1 ft 51°	nw2000^6	1	:32^1	1:02^4	1:34^4	2:04^2	3	3	4°	5^2	1^1	2^{nk}	2:04^2	*2-1	(NWillis)	PocoPilot, AdiosArt, Cleostar
4-16	^{9}Spk⅝ ft 43°	w10000^{7273}	1	:30^3	1:03^2	1:32	2:02^4	1	2	3°	2°	2½	$6^{5\frac{3}{4}}$	2:04	6-1	(RKnox)	BretsPet, FantasticDream, DirectDottie
4-11	^{9}Spk⅝ sy 35°	w10000^{7273}	1	:31	1:02^4	1:34^2	2:06^4	7	8	8	7°	7^5	$6^{1\frac{3}{4}}$	2:07^1	48-1	(RKnox)	Mr.Rebel-dh-PerleyHanover,GameGuy
12- 2	^{8}Was^{1}A ft 52°	w10000^{72}	1	:30^1	1:00	1:32^3	2:02	6	7	7	6	$6^{4\frac{3}{4}}$	$7^{5\frac{1}{4}}$	2:03	14-1	(NWillis)	WithoutWarning,MiGrandaAmigo,PocoPilt

Yellow 6 — **G. T. SKIPPER** — 5-1

B c 69 by Meadow Skipper—Sherry H.—Good Time
Owners: Charles R. and Mildred E. Ralston, Kenton, Ohio

1973	11	2	3	0	$17.975	2:01^1	Haw^1
1972	20	7	4	4	$21.139	2:01^3	Spk⅝
ifetime thru 1972					$21.139		

Driver—WALTER PAISLEY, Green-White   Trainer—E. Clum

5-12	^{2}Haw^1 ft 52°	w10000	1	:31^1	1:00^1	1:31^3	2:01^1	4	1	3	$3^{2\frac{1}{2}}$	1^1	$1^{2\frac{1}{2}}$	2:01^1	3-1	(WPaisley)	G.T.Skipper, TheFooler, NobleSkipper
5- 5	^{9}Haw^1 ft 50°	w10000	1	:29^3	:59^1	1:30	1:59^4	4	2	1°	$1^{1\frac{1}{4}}$	2^2	$6^{7\frac{1}{4}}$	2:01^1	2-1	(JMarshJr)	ShadyCounsel, HeyChris, GameGuy
4-27	^{9}Haw^1 ft 45°	4yr15000	1	:29	:59	1:29^2	1:59^1	5	1	1	1½	$6^{2\frac{1}{2}}$	$8^{5\frac{1}{2}}$	2:00^2	21-1	(WBeckley)	RmlieHnvr,StrIngsHnk,FstClp-dh-ShdyMle
4-21	^{8}Haw^1 sy 58°	fa15000	1	:30^3	1:01^2	1:30^2	2:00^4	3	4	5	7^7	7^6	5^3	2:01^2	15-1	(WBeckley)	SilasTime, KeystonePebble, CecilT.
4-16	^{9}Spk⅝A ft45°	4yrstk52873	1	:30	1:01^1	1:31^2	2:00^3	9	9	x9	9	9^{15}	9^{19}	2:04^2	9-1	(WBeckley)	JayTime, FastClip, SilasTime
4- 7	^{7}Spk⅝A ft 47°	jfa15000	1	:29^3	1:01^2	1:31^1	2:01^3	3	5	5	3°	2½	2^{nk}	2:01^3	19-1	(WBeckley)	BannerRanger, G.T.Skipper, ShiawayLad

Red & Yellow 8 — **TOM'S CHOICE** — 6-1

Br g 63 by Chief Strong—Moomies Queen—Gander
Owner: Harold F. Weber, Pontiac, Ill.

1973	14	3	5	2	$16.162	2:03	Spk⅝
1972	29	5	9	2	$22.846	2:02^3	Was^1
Lifetime thru 1972					$92,604		

Driver—HARRY BURRIGHT, Blue-Gold   Trainer—C. Weber

5- 7	^{5}Haw^1 sy 60°	w7000^{7273}	1	:30	1:00	1:30^2	2:01	5	5	5°	4^3	$2^{2\frac{1}{2}}$	2^2	2:01^2	9-1	(HBurright)	SimonesSkippr,TomsChoice,MiGrndeAmigo
4-28	^{7}Haw^1 ft 43°	w10000	1	:30^4	1:01^3	1:32^2	2:01^4	7	7	6°	$5^{6°}$	$6^{7\frac{1}{4}}$	$8^{6\frac{3}{4}}$	2:03^1	15-1	(HBurright)	HyMinbar, ChiefG.Direct, QuakerByrd
4-21	^{9}Haw^1 sy 58°	w10000	1	:33^3	1:04^3	1:34^2	2:04^3	5	4	4	4^6	$5^{2\frac{1}{4}}$	$2^{\frac{3}{4}}$p1	2:04^4	5-1	(HBurright)	TomsChoice, BayStarBoy, StarboardButler
4- 5	^{10}Spk⅝ 53°	nw1400^8	1	:29^1	1:00^4	1:31^4	2:03	6	6	6	6°	$5^{2\frac{1}{2}}$	$1^{\frac{3}{4}}$	2:03	*6-5	(HBurright)	TomsChoice, DocsJerry, PatrickTime
3-31	^{5}Spk⅝A sy 44°	nw3400^8	1	:31	1:04	1:36^1	2:07	6	7	7	7	6^4	$2^{\frac{1}{2}}$	2:07^1	5-1	(HBurright)	RightHonor, TomsChoice. DocsJerry
3-19	^{7}Spk⅝ ft 33°	w10000^{7273}	1	:31^2	1:01^2	1:32^1	2:02	6	6	6	6°	6^4	5^4	2:02^4	13-1	(HBurright)	PerleyHanover, Ghandi, EllLang

Both Adios Art and G. T. Skipper are running at the same class level as their last race. Adios Art was beaten convincingly in his race and would not

G. T. Skipper was a contender and Adios Art was not. What was also working against Adios Art was the fact that it was G. T. Skipper that beat him last time out. When horses have competed against each other in their last race, you can usually count out the badly beaten loser.

Tom's Choice is also of interest in this race. Previously he raced at this class level quite successfully up until his race on April 28. After turning in a poor effort that day, he was dropped in class for his next race which was conditioned for "winners of $7,000 in 1972 and 1973." He made noticeable improvement and now we must decide if Tom's Choice qualifies to be a contender for "winners of over $10,000."

Actually there's no problem about the decision at all. Tom's Choice is coming off a good race but it's not a powerful race. This would lead us to consider his competition before deciding whether or not he's a contender. And since there's already a horse in the field that has won at tonight's class level (G. T. Skipper), Tom's Choice would not be a contender. But if the race was void of horses that have performed well at a higher class level than Tom's Choice, he would have been a contender.

Up to this point, we've seen horses that have qualified as contenders when going up in class and when running within the same class level. As far as contenders that drop down are concerned, they're treated as if running within the same class level when the monetary conditions of the race are within $2,000. Anything exceeding $2,000 is a definite class drop and is treated as such. So we'll wind up our search for contenders by looking at a race that has all three class functions. It's for "winners of over $8,000 in 1973" and took place at Maywood Park's half miler on September 1.

From the four hole is the Race Time mare Prom Time. Her last race was for $8,000 winners but was restricted for fillies and mares. Technically, this gal is staying at the same class level. But when fillies and mares run in open company, they should show a little bit more than their male counterparts to be on equal terms. Even though Prom Time has raced well against the men at times, she's given no indication in her last two races that she's in a winning mood. Her last race does show some minor improvement, but she still appears to need a class drop in order to contend.

GREEN 4 8-1

Driver—JIM DOLBEE, Green-White-Red Tr.—J. Sullivan (49-11-8-4—.342)

PROM TIME B m 1968, by Race Time—Shadydale Prom—Airliner Owner: Joseph F. Sullivan, Chicago, Ill.

1973	19	3	0	2	$18,302	2:01¹ Haw¹
1972	24	3	5	6	$17,995	2:04² May
Lifetime					$29,665	4, T.T. 1:59¹ (1)

8-29	⁵May ft 83°	§FMw800073	1	:29	:58²	1:28²	1:59	1	3	3³	32°	3³	45¾	2:00¹	6-1 (J.Dolbee)	BeckyHiWin, BretsPet, FarvelCounsel (overmatched)
8-25	¹⁰May ft 78°	§w1000073	1	:30¹	1:00	1:30¹	2:00²	7	8	8⁸	89¼	7⁸	56¾	2:014	38-1 (S.Banks)	TheGrumbler, RoyalGo, JetCoe (no threat)
8-17	⁶May ft 76°	§FM5200	1	:29²	:59¹	1:29⁴	2:00³	4	7	7¹¹	63½	53½	4²	2:01	13-1 (W.Paisley)	HiPeggy, TimeForFrances, BeckyHiWin (closed some)
8-10	⁸May ft 71°	§FMinv6000	1	:30¹	1:00²	1:29²	1:59³	5	1	1¹	3²	4⁵	6⁸	2:01¹	8-1 (W.Paisley)	SandraLil, BeckyHiWin, Bret'sPet (weakened)
8- 1	⁹May ft 67°	§nw1000073	1	:30¹	1:02²	1:32	2:02¹	1	3	11½	12¼	11½	11¼	2:02¹	2-1 (J.Dolbee)	PromTime, TheGrumbler, FantasticDream (easy win)
7-23	⁷Spk⅝ ft 81°	FMinv4200	=1	:30³	1:02¹	1:32³	2:02²	2	3	42½	73¼	6⁴	51½	2:02⁴	12-1 (H.Adams)	BretsPrincess, BrennaScot, HopeImperial (closed some)

BLACK 5 3-1

Driver—JIM CURRAN, Gray-Gold Tr.—R. Farrington (157-29-29-20—.323)

YANKEE BARON B g 1967, by Baron Hanover—Princess J.—Yankee Hanover Owners: Farrington Stables, Inc. and J. Ludy; Richwood, Tipp City, Ohio

1973	24	3	6	5	$25,580	2:00³ Spk⅝
1972	34	9	3	5	$32,903	2:02³ Haw¹
Lifetime					$57,110	4, 2:02¹ (1)

8-22	⁵May ft 69°	§w1000073	1	:30²	1:01³	1:32¹	2:00³	4	5	53°	21°	22½	2³	2:01¹	2-1 (J.Curran)	EliLang, YankeeBaron, DocsJerry (3-wide ¾)
8-17	⁹May ft 76°	§w1000073	1	:28⁴	:58⁴	1:29¹	1:59¹	5	6	8⁷	7⁵	4⁶	32¼	1:59³	4-1 (J.Curran)	AdiosArt, BgDaddysShadow, YankeeBaron (closed some)
8- 6	⁵May ft 81°	nw1000073	1	:30¹	1:01	1:30²	2:004	2	4	4⁴	42½°	32¾	2½	2:00³	*5-2 (J.Curran)	NicksPainter, YankeeBaron, DoctorAndy (good effort)
8- 1	⁵May ft 67°	nw1000073	1	:30³	1:03¹	1:33¹	2:03	2	3	4³	42½	22½	2ⁿˢ	2:03	2-1 (J.Curran)	NativeExpress, YankeeBaron, Samtree (just missed)
7-28	⁹May ft 64°	w1000073	1	:30³	1:02³	1:33	2:02³	8	8	75°	64°	7⁵	75½	2:034	18-1 (J.Curran)	GameGuy, StarboardButler, DoctorAndy (hung out)
7-20	⁵Spk⅝ sy 73°	inv7000	+1	:31	1:03³	1:354	2:06	4	4	4⁶	6⁵	44½	22¼	2:06²	7-1 (J.Curran)	AdidsArt, YankeeBaron, EliLang (good finish)

YELLOW 6 7-2

Driver—JIM FERGUSON, White-Blue Tr.—J. Ferguson (20-7-3-2—.467)

KEYSTONE STORMY Br h 1968, by Lehigh Hanover—Social Hanover—Tar Heel Owners: Double Z Stables, Inc., Middletown, Ohio

1973	17	2	4	0	$8,817	1:59⁴ May
1972	22	4	3	2	$10,288	2:01⁴ V.D¾
Lifetime					$21,457	4, 2:01⁴ (¾)

8-24	⁶May ft 72°	§nw800073	1	:31	1:02³	1:32²	2:014	3	1	1¹	11½	1²	15¼	2:014	*4-5 (J.Ferguson)	KeystoneStormy, TarrsChief, Concourse (tons best)
8-18	⁸May ft 77°	§nw800073	1	:28³	:59²	1:29¹	1:594	6	2°	2¹	2²	22	22¼	2:00¹	3-1 (J.Ferguson)	TheChamp, KeystoneStormy, PocoPilot (2nd best)
8- 9	⁸May ft 80°	§clm13000	1	:29¹	1:00³	1:31	1:594	2	1	2ʰᵈ	11¼	1³	15	1:594	26-1 (J.Ferguson)	KeystoneStormy, ReMark, Mona'sByrd (vastly improved)
8- 3	¹⁰May ft 72°	clm15000	1	:31	1:01	1:31²	2:03²	5	2	2¹	3¹	7⁶	89¼	2:05¹	10-1 (J.Ferguson)	HopeImperial, MeadowClansie, StarCheck (no chance)
7-27	⁶May sy 79°	clm15000	1	:33	1:05³	1:384	2:10	6	7	65½°	3½°	21½	22¼	2:10²	15-1 (J.Ferguson)	Edstime, KeystoneStormy, JimBlackstone (went evenly)
7-17	⁸Spk⅝ ft 80°	clm14000	=1	:30	1:02²	1:32²	2:02	9	6	65½	53°	6⁶	45ᵈʰ	2:03	21-1 (J.Ferguson)	Edstime, KiwiChief, WinningBoy (evenly)

BROWN 7 6-1

Driver—DARYL BUSSE, Gray-Red Tr.—Da. Busse (83-9-8-10—.202)

BIG DADDY'S SHADOW B c 1969, by Shadow Wave—Big Spree—Good Time G. Williams, Kadel & Rursch, Dvnprt, Io., Joy, Tylr Rdg, Ill.

1973	23	4	4	4	$24,495	2:01³ Spk⅝
1972	29	7	4	1	$18,723	2:01² Hol¹
Lifetime					$20,282	3, 2:01² (1)

8-22	⁵May ft 69°	§w1000073	1	:30²	1:01³	1:32¹	2:00³	1	3	42½	63¾°	6¹⁰	4¹¹	2:024	2-1 (Da.Busse)	EliLang, YankeeBaron, DocsJerry (no threat)
8-17	⁹May ft 76°	§w1000073	1	:28⁴	:58⁴	1:29¹	1:59¹	3	5	55½	43½	3⁴	21¼	1:59²	5-1 (Da.Busse)	AdiosArt, BigDaddysShadow, YankeeBaron (nice try)
8-11	¹⁰May ft 77°	§w1000073	1	:28²	:58⁴	1:28	1:57²	8	8	8¹¹°	8¹⁵	7¹⁹	5¹²	1:594	19-1 (S.Banks)	StarboardButler, Jefferson, C.V.Thor (broke 2 minutes)
8- 6	⁵May ft 81°	nw1000073	1	:30¹	1:01	1:30²	2:004	7	7	65°	54½°	54½	4¾	2:01	9-2 (Da.Busse)	NicksPainter, YankeeBaron, DoctorAndy (parked 2 turns)
7-28	¹⁰May ft 64°	inv7500	1	:30	1:01¹	1:304	2:004	4	5	55½	53½	43½	64¼	2:01³	15-1 (Da.Busse)	UncleKenny, GaySkipper, EliLang (evenly)
7-21	⁷Spk⅝ ft 75°	nw17506	=1	:29³	1:01¹	1:314	2:01³	3	7	53½	31¼°	2¹	12¼	2:01³	5-2 (Da.Busse)	BigDaddysShadow, Overhaul, FlamingosPride (easy win)

She doesn't get one in this race, so she's regarded as a non-contender.

Next we come to Yankee Baron. He's taking a minor class drop from "winners of over $10,000 in 1973." So he's treated as if he's running within the same class level, which means he must provide us with a good performance in order to be a contender. Not only does Yankee Baron show a good enough race to be a contender, but he's been in good form for the last month. His last race certainly was no let up because he was parked out at both the half and three-quarter mile poles and still finished the race well. Good form minus a class hike will always equal a contender.

Leaving from the six post is Keystone Stormy. Ever since August 9 when he was put behind the single shaft sulky, he's been a new horse. (The symbol denoting the single shaft precedes the class of the race. It will be discussed in a later chapter.) Keystone Stormy's last race was conditioned for "*non*-winners of $8,000 in 1973," so there is a definite class hike and it's also a substantial one.

The only way Keystone Stormy can become a contender with a substantial class hike is by winning his race in a manner that deserves a certain amount of attention. That kind of race is provided by him since he does boast an overwhelming victory. Therefore, Keystone Stormy would be considered a contender.

Before we get to the next horse, let's quickly clear up a problem that might have been caused by Keystone Stormy. He went from a non-winner to a winner race which constituted a class hike. Even though the monetary conditions were the same, $8,000 in this case, it was still a rise in class. Non-winner races are approximately on a par with winner races when the monetary conditions are doubled. For instance, a race conditioned for "non-winners of $20,000" is approximately equal in class to a race conditioned for "winners of $10,000" and vice versa. If you're not sure the horse you're handicapping is going up or down in class, use this two-for-one ratio as a guide.

Getting back to the race, we have Big Daddy's Shadow from the seven post. He, like Yankee Baron, is also taking a minor drop in class. But he would not be considered a contender because of the poor effort he turned in. You'll also notice that Yankee Baron beat him by 8 lengths while racing under much more difficulty.

As you can see, every horse that has qualified to be a contender in the races we've looked at has shown us nothing less than a decent effort. We always lean towards current form, primarily in the horse's last race. All previous races are used to determine improvement or lack of improvement up to that last race. Class is not as distinct as it is in claiming races because the conditions of the race do not always indicate the true class factor. So we only take notice of definite class fluctuations. Players that handicap with the letter classification system should take notice that a movement from one level to another always constitutes a definite class fluctuation.

When horses go up in class, they must provide us with a deserving performance to become contenders. When they are running within the same class level, they must show us a minimum of a good performance. When they are moving down in class, we give them some leeway on current form proportional to the drop in class. But a horse is never a contender when he shows us nothing, as you will see in the next chapter when we search for contenders in claiming races.

CHAPTER 4

Choosing the Contenders—Part II

When we pick a contender in a claiming race, our choice depends very heavily on how the horse's current form relates not only to the class of horses it faced in its last race, but also to the class of horses it will face in tonight's race.

This is, of course, in general the process we went through to choose contenders in conditioned races. But there was a slight problem caused in conditioned races because the class factor was not always easily identified. To rectify this, we learned a little bit more towards current form by recognizing only definite class fluctuations. This problem is not found in claiming races because the class factor is precise. In fact, it's very precise because we're able to make good use of the claiming prices, which are the class levels used to interpret the horse's current form.

What all of this boils down to is that it's the class-form relationship that will determine the contenders in the race. So once again, we ignore the other three ingredients—pace, post position, and the driver. They are only used when making the final choice from the contenders. This way we avoid two major problems that have plagued many a handicapper. First, there's the mistake of choosing a horse that was dragged along in a fast time because of a quick stepping pacesetter. Second is making an excuse for a horse because he had an outside post position.

The only thing that concerns us when we choose contenders in the race is the class-form relationship. The way it works in claiming races is best described by an example. Let's say we're studying the past performances for a horse that's been running for a $20,000 claiming tag. He has spent his last five races at that class level without winning a race. In fact, he hasn't even been close to the leaders at any point in any one of his races, so he is what we would call being in bad form.

Now let's take a closer look at this horse. It's true that we could label this horse as being in bad form, but that's really only the half of it. There's still the other side of the coin, which is the class side. That's because the bad form was actually caused by the horse running above his proper class level, or if you prefer, his capable winning level. The horse had, like any other horse competing at a racetrack, the ability to win. The only question unanswered is at what level. It may have been $16,000 or $14,000. It may have even been lower than that. But whatever it was, if he was able to run those same five races over again, he would actually be in good form!

As I stated in Chapter 3, it's not always practical for a trainer to drop his horse drastically in claiming price. Most trainers prefer to work their horses up and down the claiming ladder in small steps. So it isn't very likely that you'll find a $20,000 claimer in a $14,000 claiming race his next time out. What the trainer would probably do is to drop him in for about $18,000 hoping that lesser competition will help bring him back to his real $20,000 form. And if the horse wasn't that much off form in the first place, he may even win that $18,000 race. But now we're talking about our job, handicapping. Because if a $20,000 claimer is capable of dropping down to $18,000 and win, it's our job to recognize it.

CONTENDERS IN CLAIMING RACES

The class hike in claiming races is an interesting one. I could easily reproduce several past performance charts that lay down a certain guideline in dealing with contenders in this respect. But instead of doing that, I'd rather you think about this: The large majority of horses that go up in class in claiming races have not won their last race, yet most horses that eventually win their races when going up in class are previous winners. In fact, the ratio is about two to one.

Now that you have thoroughly thought over what I said, let's draw some conclusions. Since most horses that go up in class in claiming races have not won their last race, why should we consider them at a higher class level? We can also benefit from the fact that percentages and ratios bear this out. Although the exact numbers never remain constant, the amount of variance doesn't change very much either. So there is, to say the least, a very exact dividing line separating horses that go up in class in claiming races and eventually win.

Personally, I do not believe it's good judgment to make specific requirements that all contenders should meet outside of the class-form relationship. But I do believe that in this one area of class hikes in claiming races, the player should take advantage of the percentages. And those percentages are going to be much in our favor if we automatically eliminate every horse as a non-contender that's going up in class who hasn't won his last race. True, there are going to be horses that will win regardless of this rule. But their numbers are so few and far between that if we started considering non-winners going up in class, we'd end up losing a lot more races than we'd win.

Now that we have eliminated all the non-contenders, we are still left with the task of choosing the contenders. But now they all have something very much in common. They have ALL won their last race. So how are we going to differentiate one horse that's won, say, a $5,000 claiming race from another horse that's won a $5,000 claiming race, especially if they are both entered in the same race tonight?

The answer is very easy. We'll analyze how each horse handled the pace of the race and then make our decision. And, since we only go through that process for contenders, the easiest thing for us to do is to make every horse that won his last race a contender. But remember, even though a horse is a contender, it doesn't necessarily mean he will become our final choice.

When horses are running at the same class level as their last race, they can qualify to be contenders on two counts. First, if the horse shows an exceedingly good effort in his last race by either winning or finishing close to a winner, it would justify his role as a contender. Secondly, if a horse shows improvement over his previous race in either his stretch gain or his margin of loss, he would also become a contender. Rarely is a horse considered a contender if he was beaten by more than five lengths in his last race.

To get a better understanding of this, we'll look at four horses that are running at the same class level as their last race. They are all entered in the same event, which is for $10,000 claimers. It took place on July 21 at Sportsman's Park.

From the one hole is the free-legged Senator Berry. He's been steadily dropping in class the last month to no avail. His last race shows nothing even remotely reflecting improvement. He took a $2,000 class drop and turned in an even worse performance than in his previous race. He gained no ground and was never close to the leaders at any time. Senator Berry is obviously off form and is quickly eliminated as a contender.

Leaving from the two hole is Billy Clipper. In this pacer's last race, he stayed right behind the leader and took command at the three-quarter mark. He opened up a 3 1/2 length lead in the stretch, but then tired some and crossed the finish line beaten 2 lengths. Although this effort by Billy Clipper doesn't appear to be the greatest, we must take into consideration that he was raised in class for the race. He did win for $7,500, but the class hike to $10,000 isn't a small one. So the fact that he lost by only 2 lengths would actually show

RED **1** 6-1

Driver—JIM CURRAN, Gray-Gold Tr.—R. Farrington (50-6-7-11—.271)
‡SENATOR BERRY Ro g 1967 by Hodgen—Miss Berry—Paul MacPherson
Owner: Farrington Stables & Arnold Cattle Co., Richwood, O., Chgo., Ill.
1973 18 5 1 0 $15,595 2:032 sy Haw1
1972 26 4 4 4 $9,173 2:033 ScD⅝
Lifetime $13,775 5, 2:033 (⅝)

7-16	10Spk⅝ ft 76°	‡clm10000—1	:312	1:033	1:333	2:041	9	9	99½	87¼°	912	98	2:054	9-1	(J.Curran)	BranchDanPrince, BirthdayDelight, Brindntte	(followed)
7- 5	7Spk⅝ ft 71°	‡clm12000=1	:31	1:011	1:314	2:031	8	3°	12¼	33	66	65	2:041	16-1	(J.Curran)	WenevirBert, ByeMe, Knoxella	(used early)
6-27	8Spk⅝ sy 68°	‡clm12500—1	:31	1:044	1:342	2:052	5	7	76¼	76½°	712	87¼	2:064	9-2	(R.Farringtn)	Rozella, WenevirBert, NobleChoice	(no threat)
6-19	7Spk⅝ ft 78°	‡clm14000+1	:29	:592	1:301	2:004	3	6	66	54°	76	910	2:024	9-2	(W.Paisley)	PalMyerFilte, MargaretSue, ArcolaKid	(some speed)
6- 6	7Spk⅝ ft 75°	‡clm13000—1	:311	1:031	1:332	2:023	5	7	75¾°	75¼°x925		924	2:072	*2-1	(J.MarshJr)	Empy, PrinceRccket, Lachamfer	(disappointed)
5-26	10Spk⅝ ft 60°	‡clm14000+1	:314	1:043	1:351	2:043	4	6	53½°	42½°	42½	41¾	2:05	*3-1	(W.Paisley)	Empy, BranchDanPrince, TecklaAdiosB	(parked 2 turns)

BLUE **2** 4-1

Driver—JOE MARSH, JR., Gray-Blue-Red Tr.—J. Marsh, Jr. (231-40-39-30—.310)
BILLY CLIPPER Ch g 1965, by Clipper Ship—Widower Princess—Bay Prince
Owner: Nicholas J. Wall, Cicero, Ill.
1973 12 1 0 2 $4,774 2:033 Spk⅝
1972 38 12 6 5 $37,324 2:00 Haw1
Lifetime $62,111 7, 2:00 (1)

7-11	9Spk⅝ ft 71°	clm10000+1	:311	1:034	1:34	2:044	4	2	21¼	12¼	13½	42	2:051	*6-5	(J.MarshJr)	Mr.Thunderbyrd, ReMark, C.F.Guy	(gave way)
7- 2	10Spk⅝ ft 84°	clm7500—1	:293	1:022	1:323	2:033	1	3	32¼	31¼	11	12	2:033	*5-2	(J.MarshJr)	BillyClipper, Crawdad, BethExpress	(easy win)
6-20	10Spk⅝ ft 76°	clm9000—1	:294	1:02	1:321	2:032	9	9	810°	87¾	810	88¾	2:051	7-1	(J.MarshJr)	TinyForbes, CamdenFrisco, SilverDiller	(needed start)
5-17	8Haw1 ft 53°	clm10000 1	:311	1:02	1:341	2:042	5	7	6	56	55½	53	2:05	4-1	(J.MarshJr)	PlutoHal, DodieDee, TerryJeansRocket	(good race)
5- 8	9Haw1 ft 60°	clm11000 1	:312	1:032	1:342	2:052	2	3	4	41½	32½	53½	2:061	9-2	(J.Marsh,Jr.)	G.T.Winter, FirstLook, LyricEyre	(went evenly)
4- 4	8Spk⅝ gd 35°	clm14000—1	:30	1:024	1:34	2:054	8	8	88	75¾°	96	810	2:074	12-1	(J.MarshJr)	StrongByrd, TinaKnox, KnoxAbout	(showed little)

WHITE **3** 9-2

Driver—LOUIS RAPONE, Blue-Red-Gold Tr.—V. Alesia (56-4-8-6—.187)
EYRE FIRE B g 1962, by Sister's Son— Tactful Rosa—Tactful Guy
Owner: Aldo Stable, Addison, Ill.
1973 23 1 4 1 $10,752 2:083 sy Y.R
1972 37 4 3 5 $20,077 2:031 Spk⅝
Lifetime $94,310 8, 2:02 (1)

7-16	10Spk⅝ ft 76°	clm10000=1	:312	1:033	1:333	2:041	4	6	77	98¼	79	44½	2:051	3-1	(L.Rapone)	BrnchDnPrinc, BrthdyDlght, Brndntte	(passed tiring 1's)
7- 5	10Spk⅝ ft 71°	clm10000+1	:294	1:032	1:332	2:034	7	7	89½	89	76¼	23¼	2:042	7-1	(L.Rapone)	JubileeKnight, EyreFire, DodieDee	(strong last ⅛th)
6-27	7Spk⅝ sy 68°	clm9000—1	:31	1:031	1:333	2:054	3	5	65¼	83¾	74	52¾	2:062	7-1	(H.Cataldo)	MissGertie, Tanner, SpeedyChestnut	(evenly)
6-15	2Spk⅝ ft 79°	clm10000=1	:293	1:003	1:33	2:034	8	5°	62½°	52°	33½x911		2:06	28-1	(H.Cataldo)	TeeniTime, C.R.Purdue, BigMark	(break costly)
6- 4	10Spk⅝ gd 67°	clm10000=1	:311	1:054	1:372	2:07	5	7	88	85½	48	49½	2:09	7-1	(H.Cataldo)	WenevirBert, TerryJeansRocket, C.F.Guy	(went evenly)
5-25	2Haw1 ft 58°	clm10000 1	:32	1:033	1:333	2:05	8	1	1	1hd	75½	72¼	2:052	11-1	(H.Cataldo)	DaddioMac, BillyTime, WenevirBert	(tired)

GREEN **4** 3-1

Driver—GENE VALLANDINGHAM, Red-White-Blue Tr.—R. Rosen (104-12-14-8—.216)
RE MARK Ch g 1967, by Knox Hanover—My Miss Lowe—Desota Hanover
Owner: Ira Berger and K. Clauson, Chicago, Ill.
1973 20 5 1 2 $11,783 2:05 Haw1
1972 19 2 4 2 $2,138 2:122 gd Nor
Lifetime $2,138 2:122 gd

7-11	9Spk⅝ ft 71°	clm10000—1	:311	1:034	1:34	2:044	7	8	99	910	76½	2nk	2:044	9-2	(W.Paisley)	Mr.Thunderbyrd, ReMark, C.F.Guy	(good finish)
7- 3	5Spk⅝ ft 78°	clm12000+1	:303	1:03	1:331	2:023	7	8	810	76½°x9dis	9dis			6-1	(J.MarshJr)	WinterExpress, TinaKnox, MtAiryBill	(brak costly)
6-23	1Spk⅝ gd 74°	clm9000=1	:303	1:042	1:354	2:051	4	5	11	11¼	13½	17¾	2:051	*8-5	(J.MarshJr)	ReMark, SharpStar, ChiefOsceola	(much the best)
6-16	1Spk⅝ sy 68°	clm9000=1	:301	1:024	1:343	2:064	1	7	76½	54½	64¼	36	2:08	*3-2	(W.Paisley)	JubileeKnight, ChiefOsceola, ReMark	(needed room)
6- 6	6Spk⅝ ft 75°	clm9000—1	:294	1:023	1:323	2:023	1	5	56½	55°	64	31¾	2:03	7-2	(W.Paisley)	NearChief, C.R.Purdue, ReMark	(raced well)
5-19	10Haw1 ft 55°	clm10000 1	:304	1:024	1:34	2:043	5	6	x8	x820	9dis	8dis		9-1	(B.Carter)	TeeniTime, NoCredit, SpeedyChestnut	(out of it)

underlying improvement. And if a horse runs a good race within the same class level, and it's one that shows improvement, it would qualify him for the role of contender.

From the three post is Eyre Fire. Although this old-timer did turn in a halfway decent effort his last time out, it's the type of race that can be easily overrated. By making a comparison to his previous race, we see that he closed more ground and finished closer to the winner. So there is no improvement at all, but rather a slight tapering off in form. He would appear to need at least a $1,000 class drop in order to contend. Eyre Fire doesn't get a class drop in this race, so he's also labeled a non-contender.

Leaving from the four post is Re Mark. This gelding showed an exceptional effort in his last race. Good enough to justify his role as contender off that race alone. He trailed the field for three-quarters of the race and then came roaring down the stretch to make up 10 lengths. In his previous race, he appeared to make a speed break unlike the one of May 19. So the drop down to $10,000 company suits him well.

After the four horses were put in their proper perspective, the result was two contenders and two non-contenders. We consider the horse's last race his primary race. If it's an obvious good effort, like that of Re Mark, then the horse simply becomes a contender off that race alone. But if the horse appears to be a borderline case, or if you have any reason to suspect his chances, then by all means consult his previous efforts. This way you can determine improvement or lack of improvement in the horse. If the horse indicates he's getting better, he's a contender. If not, he's a non-contender.

In many races, a very close evaluation of each horse will be needed to decide if the animal is a contender or not. In some races, however, it may require no more than a mere glance to spot who belongs and who doesn't. This situation is seen in a $5,000 claiming race at Maywood Park that took place on August 20.

All four horses, Allen Senator, Color Me Lee, Karen Gray, and Kat Greer, competed in $5,000 claiming races their last time out. (Both Color Me Lee, a four year old, and Karen Gray, a mare,

WHITE **2** 5-1

Driver—JOE MARSH, JR., Gray-Blue-Red — Tr.—L. Drake — (111-27-20-19—.397)

ALLEN SENATOR B g 1967, by Adios Senator—Miss Promover—Ensign Hanover
Owner: Larry Drake, Plymouth, Wisc.

1973 20 1 4 1 $4,991 2:13^{4} gd Aur
1972 39 2 2 7 $4,265 2:09^{4} Sndwh
Lifetime $8,966 4, 2:07^{2}

8- 2 ^{2}May ft 71°	clm5000	1	:32	1:04^{1}	1:35^{2}	2:07^{1}	8	7	53½°	42½°	32	2^{nk}	2:07^{1}	32-1 (W.Paisley)	SweepUp, AllenSenator, EdgewoodWallace	(strong race)
7-23 ^{3}Spk⅝ ft 81°	clm5000=	1	:31^{2}	1:04	1:34	2:04^{3}	7	8	86	87¾	89½x	89½	2:06^{3}	32-1 (A.G.Shaw)	Aquarius, NevadasSonA, J.C.Stormy	(no close)
7- 9 ^{4}Spk⅝ ft 92°	clm5000−	1	:31	1:02^{2}	1:34	2:04^{4}	3	6	69½	65°	36½	49	2:06^{3}	11-1 (A.G.Shaw)	SiouxTime, BartByrd, HarkerFreight	(too much speed)
6-25 ^{5}Spk⅝ ft 83°	clm6000=	1	:30^{3}	1:02^{3}	1:32^{4}	2:03^{3}	6	7	78	85¼	65	69	2:05^{2}	35-1 (C.Abbatiello)	AndysJake, SonnyFarvel, AnniversaryBabe	(no threat)
6-19 ^{5}Spk⅝ ft 78°	clm6000=	1	:30^{2}	1:01^{3}	1:33^{4}	2:04^{1}	9	8	87°	84¾°	87½	711	2:06^{2}	20-1 (A.G.Shaw)	LincolnValntne, MajestcDrm, WllieGrnda	(parkd 2 turns)
6- 7 ^{5}Spk⅝ ft 81°	clm6000−	1	:31	1:04^{1}	1:34^{3}	2:05^{2}	8	9	912	86¾	77¼	45	2:06^{2}	25-1 (A.G.Shaw)	Rik Noc, EllyMarie, FireBomb	(away slow)

BLUE **3** 6-1

Driver—ROBERT MILLER, Burgandy-White — Tr.—H. Poort, Jr. — (1-0-0-0—.000)

COLOR ME LEE B g 1969, by Gary F. Dudley—Fleet's Queen—Fleet Hanover
Owner: Frank A. Rossi, Chicago Heights, Ill.

1973 17 0 3 1 $3,617
1972 12 1 3 2 $3,917 2:08^{3} Was^{1}
Lifetime $3,917 3, 2:08^{3} (1)

7-26 ^{4}May ft 73°	clm6000	1	:30^{2}	1:02^{2}	1:34^{2}	2:06^{1}	3	5	56½	56½	54	44½	2:07^{1}	5-1 (R.Knox)	LdlewhilesVictor, FlamingParker, TimelySpeed	(evenly)
7-17 ^{4}Spk⅝ ft 80°	clm6000=	1	:31^{2}	1:03^{3}	1:34^{3}	2:05	3	5	55	53	53	53¼	2:05^{3}	12-1 (R.Knox)	AdmiralJack, ByrdFarr, AdioGoose	(raced well)
7- 5 ^{3}Spk⅝ ft 75°	clm6000=	1	:30^{3}	1:01^{2}	1:34	2:05	6	9	916	87	816	816	2:08^{1}	6-1 (S.Banks)	BedfrdBrush, FairRowByrd, NthngWhling	(showed little)
6-21 ^{3}Spk⅝ ft 79°	clm6000=	1	:30^{1}	1:03^{4}	1:34^{1}	2:05^{2}	3	6	65°	54½°	65	63¾	2:06^{1}	7-2 (R.Knox)	GrawlnHanovr, KarenGray, JoesDonJuan	(parked 2 turns)
6-11 ^{3}Spk⅝ ft 89°	clm6000−	1	:30^{2}	1:02	1:31^{3}	2:03^{1}	3	5	54	89½	78	35½	2:04^{2}	21-1 (R.Knox)	WindaleGuyTruax, Papa, ColorMeLee	(not good enough)
5-24 ^{5}Haw^{1} ft 60°	nw2R	1	:32^{2}	1:03^{4}	1:35^{4}	2:05^{1}	9	9	9	98½	915	912	2:07^{3}	47-1 (G.Conley)	NativeSue, FlorianaByrd, MiracleDeal	(no chance)

GREEN **4** 8-1

Driver—ROBERT DECKERT, Gold-Blue-White — Tr.—E. Magee — (1-0-0-0—.000)

KAREN GRAY B. m 1965, by Walter McKlyo—Palamarie—Palachuck
Owner: Robert Deckert, Dousman, Wis.

1973 10 0 1 0 $1,440
1972 23 1 2 4 $5,499 2:05^{3} Was^{1}
Lifetime $43,194 4, 2:04^{2} (⅝)

7-26 ^{4}May ft 73°	clm6000	1	:30^{2}	1:02^{2}	1:34^{2}	2:06^{1}	8	8	812	78½°	78	78¼	2:07^{4}	9-1 (R.Deckert)	IdlewhilesVictor, FlamingParker, TimelySpeed	(no close)
7-16 ^{3}Spk⅝ ft 76°	clm6000=	1	:30^{3}	1:03^{4}	1:35	2:05^{2}	6	7	76½°	32½°	33½	34½p4	2:06^{2}	19-1 (R.Deckert)	RooksCreekKathy, Shellio, GayFamous	(parked 2 turns)
7- 4 ^{3}Spk⅝ ft 82°	clm6000=	1	:29^{4}	1:03^{3}	1:34^{3}	2:05^{4}	7	5	54½	52¾	54½	46	2:07	9-1 (R.Deckert)	Chickadee, RomanDancer, SissySassy	(mild bid ¾)
6-21 ^{3}Spk⅝ ft 79°	clm6000=	1	:30^{1}	1:03^{4}	1:34^{1}	2:05^{2}	1	3	32¾	43	42	21	2:05^{3}	24-1 (R.Deckert)	GrawlinHanover, KarenGray, JoesDonJuan	(good trip)
6- 7 ^{4}Spk⅝ ft 81°	clm6000=	1	:29^{2}	1:01^{1}	1:32	2:03^{1}	4	4	45½	66	59½	512	2:05^{3}	49-1 (E.Magee)	AndysJake, WillieGrnda, StlHme-TtieBrke^{dh}	(no threat)
5-24 ^{2}Haw^{1} ft 60°	clm6000	1	:30^{3}	1:02^{1}	1:33^{1}	2:04^{3}	9	9	9	79½°	711	78¾	2:06^{2}	42-1 (R.Deckert)	RitzyRichard, NevedasSonA, HeatherGallon	(no chance)

BLACK **5** 4-1

Driver—JIM CURRAN, Gray-Gold — Tr.—R. Farrington — (95-14-20-8—.292)

KAT GREER B g 1966, by Targhee—Katie Greer—King's Ransom
Owner: Farrington Stables, Inc. & Arnold Cattle Co., Inc., Rchwd, O., Chcgo, Ill.

1973 21 4 2 0 $5,391 2:07^{1} gd Haw^{1}
1972 34 8 8 5 $5,682 2:07^{2} Rock
Lifetime $10,074 6, 2:07^{2}

7-27 ^{1}May ft 79°	clm5000	1	:31^{3}	1:04	1:35^{1}	2:05^{3}	4	4	45¼	45	45½	49	2:07^{2}	4-1 (J.Curran)	BaronBill, BartByrd, Tenochtitlan	(dull effort)
7-18 ^{1}Spk⅝ ft 82°	clm4000=	1	:29^{2}	1:01^{3}	1:32^{1}	2:05^{1}	6	7	66	65°	53½	42¾	2:05^{4}	4-1 (J.Curran)	GeorgieTime, IdlewhilesVictor, MissGift	(raced well)
7- 4 ^{1}Spk⅝ ft 82°	clm4000−	1	:31^{3}	1:04^{1}	1:35^{4}	2:05^{4}	9	3°	11½	1½	1½	25¼	2:06^{4}	11-1 (W.Paisley)	RocksCreekKathy, KatGreer, RosgoKid	(post hurt)
6-13 ^{3}Spk⅝ ft 73°	clm5000=	1	:30^{3}	1:02^{3}	1:33^{4}	2:04^{4}	2	3	32	21°	54	99½	2:06^{4}	15-1 (W.Beckley)	SteppingHal, SilverRoyal, Barwinor	(bid ¾, tired)
6- 4 ^{4}Spk⅝ gd 67°	clm5000=	1	:30^{3}	1:04^{4}	1:37^{1}	2:08^{3}	7	8	810	97	912	88½	2:10^{2}	9-2 (J.MarshJr)	LakewoodQuick, FoxyTime, LandesFortune	(no chance)
5-22 ^{2}Haw^{1} gd 68°	clm5000	1	:31	1:01^{4}	1:33^{2}	2:05^{1}	9	9	9	98	96¾	64¼	2:06	7-1 (W.Paisley)	HarkerFreight, CatCounsel, FoxyTime	(post hurt)

received a 20% allowance in their claiming price.) The improvement in Allen Senator can be seen. He bounced along for two months and showed completely nothing. All of a sudden in his last outing he raced on the outside for two turns and just missed getting up in time to win. His effort is more than enough to qualify him as a contender, even without consulting his previous races.

As for the other three horses, each one has turned in such a poor performance there's no need to consult their previous races either. They're all three non-contenders.

The horse taking a drop in class in a claiming race is always a possible contender. Many times, the class drop produces a strong contender so it's important that you're able to spot the claimer dropping down with a chance to win, as opposed to your typical no-chancer.

The claimer receiving a drop in class is treated a little differently from the horse that's staying at the same class level. Since the horse has competed with higher classed animals in his last race, the emphasis put on current form is eased somewhat. But there's still a very fine line separating the contender from the non-contender. We still demand the horse to have performed well enough in his last effort to make the class drop meaningful. And the best way to learn how to spot this type of fellow is to go through some examples.

We'll look at twelve horses that are dropping down in class. There will be three claiming groups—$5,000, $10,000 and $15,000. Each group will have two contenders and two non-contenders. First the contenders for $5,000:

GREEN **4** 8-1 —

Driver—WALTER PAISLEY, Green-White — Tr.—W. Roseboom — (156-33-24-23—.350)

EDGEWOOD WALLACE B h 1966, by Edgewood Royal—Edgewood Betty—Royal Chief
Owner: Mr. and Mrs. Shelby Baker, Byron, Ill.

1973 21 2 4 2 $7,150 2:07^{1} Spk⅝
1972 24 3 4 4 $10,371 2:05^{2} Spk⅝
Lifetime $22,613 5, 2:05^{2}

6-12 ^{4}Spk⅝ ft 74°	clm6000=	1	:31	1:02^{1}	1:33^{4}	2:05^{1}	5	7	79	75	53½	42½	2:05^{4}	30-1 (J.Willis)	SonnyFarvel, SilverCreekTilly, IroquoisLee	(last ½ gd)
5-30 ^{4}Spk⅝ ft 59°	clm6000+	1	:30^{4}	1:03^{3}	1:35^{1}	2:05^{2}	7	7	79½	84½°	89½	99½	2:07^{2}	6-1 (W.Rosebm)	WillFly, LincolnValentine, BourbonChimes	(no close)
5-18 ^{1}Haw^{1} ft 66°	clm5000 C	1	:30^{1}	1:01	1:32^{3}	2:04^{1}	2	1	1	11½	41½	41¾	2:04^{3}	11-1 (M.Sabatka)	AgnesMeridale, TheWoodpecker, RushStreetBoss	(tired)
5- 5 ^{10}Haw^{1} ft 50°	clm6000	1 1/16	:29^{4}	:59^{4}		1:23^{3}	3	5	4	43	53½	62½	1:24^{1}	13-1 (M.Sabatka)	JerryDuke, ElCaballo, FairmeadeLang	(outpaced)
4-26 ^{2}Haw^{1} ft 51°	clm6000	1	:30^{2}	1:02^{4}	1:35^{1}	2:06^{1}	2	2	2	22½	32	45¼	2:07^{1}	8-1 (M.Sabatka)	SirWarwick. LusciousLady. SissySassy	(early foot)
4-17 ^{6}Haw^{1} ft 56°	clm7000	1	:32	1:05^{4}	1:37^{2}	2:07^{3}	4	1	1	1^{nk}	2¾	53½	2:08^{2}	10-1 (M.Sabatka)	MisterAdios, GrandClara, MelodyWarrior	(tired)

Two young pacers limber up in a morning workout. (Photo by Kuprion.)

WHITE 2 4-1	Driver—STANLEY BANKS, White-Purple			Tr.—K. Vander Schaaf	(163-15-23-24—.219)		1973	12	1	3	0	$5,051	2:05² Spk⅝

PROUD DELIGHT B g 1967, by Ellens Adios—Kud Bee—Scotch War
Owner: Ken Vander Schaaf, Sandwich, Ill.

1972 20 5 6 3 $4,184 2:03² Was¹
Lifetime $6,199 5, 2:03² (1)

8-25	⁴May ft 78°	clm6000	1	:30⁴	1:02⁴ 1:33³ 2:05	4	1	1²½	1²	1²	2½	2:05¹	7-2 (S.Banks)	LoGoAdios, ProudDelight, AaronMeridale (outpaced str)
8-15	⁴May ft 75°	clm7000	1	:31	1:02⁴ 1:33⁴ 2:04⁴	6	1	1¹	1ⁿᵏ	2ⁿᵏ	5²¾	2:05²	2-1 (K.VndrSchf)	SapphireGlow, PeppersAce, WesTee (set early pace)
8- 8	⁸May ft 82°	clm7000	1	:32	1:04³ 1:35¹ 2:06	x3	8	8ᵈⁱ⁹	8ᵈⁱˢ	8ᵈⁱˢ	8ᵈⁱˢ		*9-5 (K.VndrSchf)	BethExpress, MisterAdios, NobleOne (eliminated self)
7-31	⁶May ft 71°	clm7000	1	:29¹	1:00⁴ 1:31⁴ 2:04¹	1	1	1¹½	1ʰᵈ	2½	4¹¼	2:04²	*2-1 (S.Banks)	ChiefsLittleStar, StealHme, NllieWy (set blistering pace)
7-23	¹⁰Spk⅝ ft 81°	clm6000	1	:29²	1:00 1:31¹ 2:02²	1	1	1²½	1¹¾	1³	2²¾	2:03	*3-1 (W.Rosebm)	FlyingFool, ProudDelight, StealHome (too fast pace)
7-16	⁶Spk⅝ ft 76°	clm7000	1	:29²	1:01¹ 1:32⁴ 2:04	9	2	2¹	3¹	2ʰᵈ	5³¼	2:04³	19-1 (S.Banks)	RustyMerrie, NellieWay, AmericanSal (3-wide for lead)

1. Sportsman's Park, June 26: In $6,000 company on May 30, Edgewood Wallace was kept off the pace. He came within striking distance at the three-quarter mark but was unable to close any ground.

In Edgewood Wallace's next race, he was rated in similar fashion. But this time, he was able to chop off 2 1/2 lengths into the winner in the final quarter. Now that Edgewood Wallace is getting the benefit of a $1,000 class drop, he could turn his stretch run into a good stretch kick. Good enough to make him a contender.

2. Maywood Park, September 5: On August 14, against $7,000 claimers, Proud Delight showed good speed for three-quarters of the race. When he was dropped down to $6,000 company, his speed held up much better, only to give way just before reaching the finish line. Now that Proud Delight is being dropped one more notch in claiming price, he's a threat and also a contender in a "possible" effort to make every pole a winning one.

$5,000 Non-Contenders

Orange **9** $5,000 5-1

NEVADA'S SON A

B g 62 by Golden Adios—Nevada's Last—Van Derby
Owners: Farrington Stables, Inc. & Arnold Cattle Co., Inc., Richwood, Ohio, Chicago, Ill.

1973	10	1	0	1	$1,495	2:082	Rock
1972	29	1	4	4	$8,448	2:07	R.R.
Lifetime thru 1972					$36,093		

Driver—WALTER PAISLEY, Green-White **Trainer—R. Farrington**

4-26 2Haw1 ft 51°	clm6000	1	:302	1:024	1:351	2:061	3	4	4	45½	54	55½	2:072	7-2	(RFarrington)	SirWarwick, LusciousLady, SissySassy
4-1610Spk⅝ ft 43°	clm6000	1	:303	1:024	1:343	2:061	8	9	9	8	67½	53¼	2:064	10-1	(JCurran)	BillyTime, CleverRod, FlashysDan
4- 2 Rock sy	clm5000	1	:322	1:054	1:402	2:133	5	5	2°	4°	46½	510¼	2:153	30-1	(JMiritello)	MountainAir, Deena, KaSan
3-27 Rock ft	clm5000	1	:313	1:032	1:361	2:08	3	7	7	7	73½	66	2:091	22-1	(JMiritello)	Deena, BlazeQuick, MayB.Haven
3-17 Rock sy	clm5000	1	:321	1:054	1:381	2:114	8	8	8	6	55½	59½	2:133	15-1	(GMaroun)	MountainHaven, SassBox, ElFaber
3-10 Rock ft	clm6000	1	:312	1:033	1:354	2:063	3	6	3	3°	811	816	2:094	10-1	(GMaroun)	SteadyBullet, VanDelight, SunDanceKid

WHITE **2** 6-1

Driver—PHILIP MILBURN, Blue-Gold **Tr.—M. Priebe, Jr.** **(89-12-17-10—.278)**

BIG DAVID

Br. g 1963, by Tag Me—Mary Guy King—Speed King
Owners: E. & J. Kuk & M. Petros, Oak Park, River Forest, Ill.

1973	26	6	3	5	$14,584	2:052 Spk⅝
1972	15	4	2	3	$7,537	2:044 Was1
Lifetime					$46,519	6, 2:032 (1)

8 24 1May ft 72°	clm6000	1	:301	1:003	1:332	2:05	1	4	46½	44°	56	56¼	2:061	4-1	(J.Dagenais)	WindaleAnnaTruax, CollegeMan, FairyJo	(no excuse)
8-16 4May ft 74°	clm6000	1	:304	1:024	1:34	2:05	3	5	76½	85¼	75¾	73¾	2:054	12-1	(P.Milburn)	IdlwhilesVictor, LncolnVlentine, SeattleCindy	(no threat)
8- 6 4May ft 81°	§clm6000	1	:312	1:032	1:36	2:062	6	x8	86	x816	814	713	2:09	9-2	(P.Milburn)	RooksCrkKathy, PatsysGal, SilverCrkTilly	(made breaks)
7-24 7May ft 81°	clm6000	1	:301	1:031	1:343	2:063	2	2	21°	31½°	53	65¼	2:073	4-1	(P.Milburn)	SonnyFarvel, AdmiralJack, IrishDuane	(parked 2 turns)
7-10 6Spk⅝ ft 76°	clm6000=1		:313	1:033	1:342	2:05	7	8	65°	31½°	35½	25¼	2:06	9-1	(P.Milburn)	Zhivago, BigDavid, LocalLie	(¾ bid, hung)
6-21 4Spk⅝ ft 79°	clm6000—1		:311	1:041	1:353	2:064	5	7	76	52¾°	65	53¼	2:072	9-2	(P.Milburn)	PeppersAce, SenatorHaven, TheIdler	(raced well)

3. Hawthorne Race Course, May 10: On April 26, Nevada's Son A made his Hawthorne Race Course debut. His race is best described as an "even" effort because after securing position, he neither gained nor lost any significant ground.

Since Nevada's Son A was within striking distance throughout the race, it's because he failed to close any ground that makes him a non-contender. His race is good enough to get him by with a $2,000 class drop, but $1,000 just isn't enough to consider him a contender.

4. Maywood Park, September 4: Big David's last race isn't really much different from that of Nevada's Son A's. But what's working even more against Big David is the fact that he's been showing nothing at the $6,000 level for a longer time. The drop to $5,000 company isn't enough to make him a contender, but he would have received serious consideration with $4,000 claimers.

$10,000 Contenders

Red & Yellow **8** $10,000 3-1

C. R. PURDUE

B g 67 by Purdue Hal—Lady Chuck—Parker Byrd
Owner: Ken Vander Schaaf, Sandwich, Ill.

1973	18	7	1	1	$14 839	2:033 sy	Haw1
1972	41	3	7	4	$10.600	2:08	Spk⅝
Lifetime thru 1972					$16,824		

Driver—STANLEY BANKS, White-Purple **Trainer—K. Vander Schaaf**

5- 9 9Haw1 ft 66°	clm14000	1	:31	1:023	1:331	2:032	6	8	8	76	75	55p4	2:042	7-2	(SBanks)	SenatorBerry, CarolChief, Winter
5- 1 9Haw1 sy 62°	clm11000	1	:323	1:051	1:363	2:081	4	4	5	64	66½	1nk	2:081	*9-5	(SBanks)	C.R.Purdue, EyreFire, Knoxella
4-21 5Haw1 sy 58°	clm8000	1	:313	1:02	1:332	2:033	9	2	2	21½	11	15¾	2:033	7-2	(SBanks)	C.R.Purdue, QuickBay, DaveWestern
4-1310Spk⅝ ft 39°	clm7500	1	:304	1:022	1:333	2:044	4	6	6	7°	42	1ns	2:044	5-1	(SBanks)	C.R.Purdue, WesternsJody, GrandAce
4- 4 5Spk⅝ gd 26°	clm6000	1	:31	1:04	1:352	2:072	2	5	5	7	52	11½	2:072	5-1	(SBanks)	C R.Purdue, GrandClara, PlutcHal
3-27 6Spk⅝ ft 38°	Cclm5000	1	:322	1:052	1:363	2:072	5	6	6	5	37	34½	2:082	9-1	(DSheely)	FlubAdubAdoo, Papa, C.R.Purdue

GREEN **4** 3-1

Driver—HARRY BURRIGHT, Blue-Gold **Tr.—M. Lentsch** **(64-6-6-7—.167)**

TEENI TIME

B h 1968, by Race Time—Keens Tarr—Tar Heel
Owner: Matthew Lentsch, South Bend, Ind.

1973	17	2	2	1	$10,452	2:043 Haw1
1972	39	5	5	7	$11,676	2;021 V.D¾
Lifetime					$20,089	4, 2:021 (¾)

5-28 8Spk⅝ sy 52°	clm12000+1		:312	1:052	1:37	2:08	4	3	33	2½°	21½	4¾	2:081	4-1	(H.Burright)	BrilliantSpeed, SummrtmeDirect, FrostyWil	(strong race)
5-1910Haw1 ft 55°	clm10000 C	1	:304	1:024	1:34	2:043	1	2	3	11½	12½	15¼	2:043	*6-5	(J.MarshJr)	TeeniTime, NoCredit, SpeedyChestnut	(much the best)
5-10 7Haw1 ft 62°	clm10000 C	1	:303	1:004	1:312	2:04	9	9	9	88	43½	2hd	2:04	5-1	(H.Burright)	GoldBerry, TeeniTime, ChiefsLittleStar	(strong in stretch)
5- 1 9Haw1 sy 66°	clm11000	1	:323	1:051	1:363	2:081	1	2	3	43	56	41	2:082	9-1	(H.Burright)	C.R.Purdue, EyreFire, Knoxella	(blocked on rail,
4-23 6Haw1 ft 51°	clm10000	1	:313	1:032	1:343	2:05	5	6	6	68	78½	52¾	2:053	7-1	(H.Burright)	PrinceRocket, SilverDiller, OnlyTrouble	(closed some)
4-14 6Spk⅝ ft 49°	clm9000+1		:301	1:022	1:342	2:054	5	2	42¼	42¼°	2½	1hd	2:054	7-1	(H.Burright)	TeenieTime, TyreNavarch, SeattleCindy	(wide hd of str)

5. Hawthorne Race Course, May 19: C. R. Purdue has spent the last six weeks working his way up the claiming ladder in good fashion. In his last race however, he appears to have taken one step too many. But since C.R. Purdue wasn't greatly overpowered, we would consider him a contender at the class level in his previous race. That was an $11,000 win, so he easily qualifies to be a contender in $10,000 company.

6. Sportsman's Park, June 15: Teeni Time is taking a $2,000 drop in class off a race in which he turned in a very game effort. In his previous race, he won big for $10,000, so the drop down is more than enough to consider a contender. Even in $11,000 company, he would appear to be well placed.

7. Sportsman's Park, June 13: Bengal Song typifies the horse on the downgrade. In his last race, he took a $6,000 drop in class and it turned out to be the worst race on his past performances. Although the chartmaker preferred to call it an even effort, it should be noted that Bengal Song is strictly a speed horse. And now that the pacer is without his speed, he's not only considered to be off form, but also a non-contender in $10,000 company.

8. Maywood Park, September 8: On August 25, Dr. Conway gave an indication that he might be coming around to $10,000 form. But as it turned out, it wasn't to be the case. The next week, Dr. Conway went up $1,000 and was completely trounced. If in fact he was coming into form, a $1,000 class hike wouldn't have caused him to be so completely out of the race. Therefore, his drop down back to $10,000 company is discounted and he's labeled a non-contender.

$10,000 Non-Contenders

BLACK & YELLOW **8** 6-1 —

Driver—JOHNNY BLEVINS, White-Blue-Black Tr.—J. Blevins (19-0-4-1—.135)

BENGAL SONG B h 1967, by Lang Hanover—Street Song—Mighty Song
Owner: Richard Schau, Frankfort, Ill.

1973 6 3 0 0 $8,550 2:03^4 Haw^1
1972 24 5 2 1 $15,268 2:03^4 Spk⅝
Lifetime $34,287 4, 2:01^2 (1)

6- 2	^{2}Spk⅝ ft 73°	clm12000—1	:30^3	1:02^3	1:34^2	2:04	7	7	7^{8½}	8^{6¾}	8^{6¼}	6^{6½}	2:05^2	9-2 (J.Blevins)	GinnysGene, Truculent, ItalianBomb	(even effort)
5-25	^{9}Haw^1 ft 58°	clm18000 1	:30^4	1:01^4	1:32^3	2:03^1	1	4	4	2$^{nk\circ}$	2^1	9^5	2:04^1	3-1 (J.Blevins)	RoyalGo-StarGo^{dh}, WendysTed	(tired badly)
5-16	^{9}Haw^1 ft 43°	clm15000 1	:32^1	1:03^1	1:34^1	2:04^1	1	2	1	1^{1½}	1^{2½}	1^{1¼}	2:04^1	*9-5 (J.Blevins)	BengalSong, SpringMeadw, MeadwClansle	(strong mile)
5- 5	^{2}Haw^1 ft 55°	clm13000 1	:31^2	1:03	1:34^2	2:03^4	2	3	1	1^{1½}	1^3	1^1	2:03^4	*2-1 (J.Blevins)	BengalSong, Rozella, SkyHawk	(in peak form)
4-25	^{8}Haw^1 ft 46°	clm11000 1	:31	1:00^4	1:32	2:03^4	1	3	2	2^2	1^{hd}	1^{1¼}	2:03^4	*6-5 (J.Blevins)	BengalSong, JewelThief, PlutoHal	(rail gave edge)
4-16	^{6}Spk⅝Ⓐ ft 45°	clm10000—1	:30^4	1:04^1	1:34^3	2:06^1	2	4	1^{1½}	1½	3^{1¾}	6^{4¾}	2:07^1	*3-2 (J.Blevins)	Crawdad, LoisAmigo, LovinLuLu	(moved early)

RED-YELLOW **8** 8-1

Driver—JOHNNY BLEVINS, White-Blue-Black Tr.—J. Blevins (46-5-4-4—.186)

DR. CONWAY B h 1967, by Don Adios—Volo Dillard—John Dillard
Owner: Terry Brown, Viola, Ill.

1973 20 2 0 3 $8,692 2:05 Spk⅝
1972 33 2 5 4 $14,630 2:01^4 Was^1
Lifetime $47,211 5, 2:01^4 (1)

9- 4	^{8}May gd 73°	§clm11000 1	:30^3	1:03^2	1:34^3	2:05^2	3	4	4^5	5^{5½}	6^{8½}	7^{9¾}	2:07^2	17-1 (J.Blevins)	ArmbroInstep, NobleChoice, SisterDoll	(no threat)
8-25	^{3}May ft 78°	§clm10000 1	:31^3	1:02^3	1:33^1	2:03^4	6	1	1^{1¼}	1^1	2^{hd}	3^{1½}	2:04^1	10-1 (J.Blevins)	BobbyBaron, SengaMarie, Dr.Conwy	(dueled ¾s of mile)
8-17	^{10}May ft 76°	§clm10000 1	:30^2	1:01^4	1:31^4	2:02^2	6	4	4^4	4^4	4^5	3^{4¼}	2:03^1	14-1 (J.Blevins)	DutchKnight, FarmRaker, Dr.Conway	(rallied late)
8- 7	^{10}May ft 81°	clm10000 1	:31^2	1:02^3	1:34^1	2:04^4	2	1	1^1	2^{hd}	4^{2½}	6^{4½}	2:05^4	17-1 (J.Blevins)	SkyHawk, Rozella, DodieDee	(used early)
7-30	^{9}May ft 77°	clm11000 1	:30^3	1:02	1:33^1	2:05	1	3	2^1	5^{2½}	5^4	7^3	2:05^3	15-1 (J.Blevins)	BillyClipper, TinyForbes, Pleasem	(well placed early)
7-20	^{4}Spk⅝ sy 73°	clm10000=1	:32^1	1:06^4	1:38^4	2:10	7	1	1^{1½}	1^{1½}	1½	4^{4½}	2:11	10-1 (J.Blevins)	Rik:Ncc, GinnysGene, BirthdayDelight	(3-wide for lead)

$15,000 Contenders

Red & Yellow **8** $15,000 7-2

KNOX ABOUT
B g 67 by Knox Hanover—Gay Defense—Defense Counsel
Owner: Joseph and Joan Nero and George T. Golemes,
Oak Forest. Oak Park, Ill.

1973 15 5 2 2 $16.747 2:01^1 Haw^1
1972 19 6 4 2 $9.580 2:03^2 H.P.⅝
Lifetime thru 1972 $15,540

Drvier—JOE NERO, Silver-Blue Trainer—J. Nero

5-17	^{9}Haw^1 ft 53°	clm16000 1	:30^1	1:01^1	1:31^3	2:02	6	1°	1	1^2	1^{2½}	3^{1¼}	2:02^1	*1-1 (JNero)	BarkerBlack, GoodTimeLad, KnoxAbout
5- 4	^{6}Haw^1 ft 45°	clm15000 1	:30^1	1:00^2	1:31^2	2:01^1	2	1	1	1^{1½}	1^4	1^{3¾}	2:01^1	5-2 (JNero)	KnoxAbout, LaChamfer, MunciesAdios
4-26	^{9}Haw^1 ft 51°	clm18000 1	:30	:59^3	1:31^2	2:02	7	1	1	1^1	2^2	4^{9½}	2:04	6-1 (NWillis)	FloridaFlash, BigDaddysShadow, Airfare
4-14	^{10}Spk⅝A ft 56°	clm15000 1	:30^3	1:03^4	1:33^2	2:03	9	1	1	1	1^3	1^{1½}	2:03	11-1 (JNero)	KnoxAbout, RuthsChoice, BrilliantSpeed
4- 9	^{8}Spk⅝ gd 33°	clm14000 1	:30^4	1:04^2	1:36	2:08^1	8	5°	1°	1	1^3	1^{3¼}	2:08^1	4-1 (JNero)	KnoxAbout, SummertimeDirct, NobleChoice
4- 4	^{8}Spk⅝ gd 36°	clm14000 1	:30	1:02^4	1:34	2:05^4	4	2	1	1	1^{nk}	3^{4¾}	2:06^4	9-2 (JNero)	StrongByrd, TinaKnox, KnoxAbout

YELLOW **6** 8-1 —	Driver—WILLIAM BECKLEY, Blue-Gold		Tr.—J. Curran			(20-2-1-5—.211)	1973	10	0	1	1	$3,690		
	ANDY'S TOM B g 1967, by Worthy Mon—Andy's Faith—Spahr Owner: B. J. Lind, Chicago, Ill.						1972	28	10	2	2	$27,483	2:01 Haw¹	
										Lifetime		$39,901	5, 2:01 (1)	

6- 4	$8Spk\frac{5}{8}$ gd 67°	clm16000	$-1 :30^1 1:02^3 1:33^2 2:05$	8	1	1^2	14	1^1	$31\frac{3}{4}$	$2:05^2$	14-1 (W.Beckley)	ArrivaByrd, BarkerBlack, Andy'sTom	(hung tough)
5-23	9Haw¹ ft 61°	clm17000	$1 :29^4 1:00^1 1:31^3 2:01^4$	2	4	1	1^1	$32\frac{1}{2}$	$87\frac{3}{4}$	$2:03^2$	16-1 (W.Beckley)	StrongByrd, SkiSlope, TopallAdios	(tired badly)
5-14	9Haw¹ ft 47°	clm19000	$1 :30^2 1:00 1:32^3 2:02^3$	8	8	8	$42\frac{1}{2}$	45	$65\frac{3}{4}$	$2:03^4$	22-1 (W.Paisley)	RightLane, StrohgByrd, KiwiChief	(some speed)
5- 4	9Haw¹ ft 45°	clm20000	$1 :29^4 1:00^1 1:31^3 2:01^2$	3	4	4	5^5	6^6	$86\frac{3}{4}$	$2:02^4$	13 1 (W.Beckley)	PatrickTime, CanTarRebel, aPtPlutocrat	(no chance)
4-27	7Haw¹ ft 45°	clm20000	$1 :29^4 1:02^2 1:34^1 2:04^3$	1	3	3	2^{1o}	2^1	41^{dh}	$2:04^4$	15-1 (W.Beckley)	AlexWejover, CanTarRebel, K·wiChief	(close finish)
4-21	10Haw¹ sy 58°	clm20000	$1 :31 1:02 1:33^1 2:03^1$	2	5	8	7^6	$75\frac{1}{2}$	$85\frac{1}{4}$	$2:04^1$	6-1 (J.Curran)	RightLane. DonRocket, AlexWejover	(even race)

9. Hawthorne Race Course May 22: Knox About is a good example of the drop-down contender. On April 14, he was victorious for $15,000. His next race was for $18,000 where he showed speed for three-quarters but was outclassed when it came time for the stretch battle. The next week, he completed the drop-down cycle by winning again for $15,000.

Now we're up to his primary race where we can see the cycle developing once again. Against $16,000 claimers, it was another speedy endeavor where he just missed winning. That race alone is justification for a contending role, but with his prior accomplishments, he would receive a little extra consideration.

10. Sportsman's Park, June 16: Andy's Tom has been working his way down the claiming ladder for more than a month. His first sign of life occurred on May 23 in a $17,000 claimer where he took the lead after the first quarter and held on to it until the three-quarter mark. When he was dropped in for $16,000, he improved off that performance by taking the lead from the start and holding it for more than three-quarters of the race. Now that he's dropping down one more notch, he's a definite contender to win in $15,000 company.

$15,000 Non-Contenders

Black **5** $15,000 6-1	**PETER BROWN**
	B g 68 by Brown Star—Red Amber—Red Prince
	Owner: M. Finder, J. Baba, Chicago, Morton Grove, Ill.
	1973 10 1 1 2 $6 840 2:08¹ sy Spk\frac{5}{8}
	1972 39 4 8 6 $19.359 2:05⁴ Was¹
	Lifetime thru 1972 $38.304

Driver—PHILIP MILBURN, Blue-Gold		Trainer—J. Baba										
4-17	8Haw¹ ft 56°	clm17500	$1 :30^3 1:01 1:32^1 2:03^2$	6	6	6	6^6	6^4	6^5	$2:04^2$	6-1 (GVallndnghm)	PatPlutocrat, SkiSlope, MountainScout
4-12	Spk\frac{5}{8} ft	clm20000	$1 :30^4 1:03^4 1:34 2:04$	3	6	6	$7°$	$63\frac{1}{4}$	$51\frac{1}{4}$	$2:04^2$	6-1 (WPaisley)	DonRocket, Ajax, C.V.Yates
4- 6	7Spk\frac{5}{8} ft 64°	clm17000	$1 :30^2 1:04^1 1:34 2:04^1$	4	6	$5°$	$2°$	2^{nk}	$42\frac{1}{4}$	$2:04^4$	6-1 (WPaisley)	PrincessJudith, KiwiChief, Lachamfer
3-31	Spk\frac{5}{8}A sy 44°	clm15000	$1 :32^4 1:06 1:37^1 2:08^1$	7	3	3	2	2^2	1^{hd}	$2:08^1$	6-1 (WPaisley)	PeterBrown, Colorama, RichReveller
3-22	9Spk\frac{5}{8} ft 36°	clm20000	$1 :31 1:04 1:33^3 2:04^2$	3x	7	7	6	$76\frac{3}{4}$	$89\frac{1}{2}$	$2:06^2$	7-1 (WPaisley)	C.V.Yates, DonRocket, Jefferson
3-16	8Spk\frac{5}{8} sy 34°	nw24007273	$1 :33^2 1:09^1 1:40^4 2:12$	8	7	7	5	4^2	$43\frac{1}{2}$	$2:12^4$	9-1 (WPaisley)	Ajax, RaceCall, ShadHanover

BROWN **7** 5-1	Driver—JIM CURRAN, Gray-Gold			Tr.—R. Farrington			(103-14-22-10—.287)	1973	26	3	3	3	$13,864	2:07 Rock
	MOONSHOT HANOVER Br h 1967, by Gamecock—Moonlite Hanover—Adios Frrngtn Stables & Arnold Cattle Co., Richwood, O., Chgo. Ill.							1972	29	5	5	2	$21,905	2:03³ Fox\frac{5}{8}
									Lifetime			$94,426	4, 2:01³ (\frac{5}{8})	

8-15	9May ft 75°	§clm17000	$1 :28^3 1:00^2 1:30^3 2:01$	3	4	4^3	$45\frac{1}{2}°$	5^6	$55\frac{1}{2}$	$2:02^2$	7-1 (J.Curran)	VictorysHorn, Pa'Plutocrat, FlagTime	(even effort)
8- 4	11May ft 73°	§clm17000	$1 :31^2 1:02^2 1:31^4 2:01$	3	5	$55\frac{1}{2}$	$56\frac{1}{4}$	59	57	$2:02^2$	7-1 (J.Curran)	NobleSk·pper, PatPlutocrat, TopallAdios	(no threat)
7-31	5May ft 71°	clm16000 C	$1 :31 1:03 1:34 2:04^3$	6	8	$86\frac{1}{2}$	$74\frac{1}{2}$	$43\frac{1}{2}$	$42\frac{1}{4}$	$2:05$	6-1 (J.Graham)	AlexWejover, SteadyBlaze, PalMyerFlite	(no excuse)
7-24	9May ft 81°	clm16000	$1 :30^1 1:00^1 1:31^1 2:02^3$	4	1	$43\frac{1}{2}$	5^2	4^1	$41\frac{1}{4}$	$2:02^4$	*7-5 (J.Graham)	PatPlutocrat, ArrivaByrd, C.V.Yates	(used for lead)
7-12	9Spk\frac{5}{8} ft 88°	clm17000=1	$:29^4 1:03^2 1:33^1 2:02^4$	9	1	$11\frac{1}{2}$	2^{hd}	$1\frac{1}{2}$	$32\frac{1}{2}$	$2:03^2$	12-1 (J.Graham)	BarkerBlack, EasyFaith, MoonshotHanover	(good effort)
7- 4	7Spk\frac{5}{8} ft 82°	clm17500=1	$:29^1 1:01^4 1:30^4 2:01^2$	9	7	$74\frac{1}{2}°$	$55\frac{1}{4}°$	710	$77\frac{1}{2}$	$2:03$	21-1 (J.Graham)	Jefferson, Ajax, SkiSlope	(parkd 2 turns)

11. Hawthorne Race Course, April 26: Peter Brown is making his second major class drop in a row. When he competed against $20,000 claimers on April 12, he turned in a pretty decent race by only getting beaten by less than two lengths. Peter Brown's next race was a disappointment. He made no moves, got beat by a large margin, all with the benefit of a $2,500 drop in class. Since his form seems to be tailing off, we're not inclined to make him a contender for $15,000.

12. Maywood Park, August 21: Moonshot Hanover is telling us in so many words that he's not a contender for $15,000. Follow closely: Going back to Moonshot Hanover's race on July 12 for

$17,000, we see that he raced fairly well that day. Off that race, he would have been an excellent prospect to contend in $15,000 company. Instead, he was dropped in for $16,000 and wasn't quite able to get up in time. After Moonshot Hanover was claimed on July 31, he was sent back up to the $17,000 ranks where he has since then performed poorly. By looking again at that race on July 12, which would have been a $15,000 contending race, you'll see why his last race against the same company is not a contending one.

SUMMARY OF CLASS-FORM CONTENDERS

Understanding the class-form relationship is the key in spotting all horses that figure to be in contention in relation to the class of the race. Although it's mandatory for a claimer going up in class to have won his last race, it's impossible to make specific requirements each contender should meet outside of a good performance. But how do you measure a good performance without keeping in mind the class of the race?

To regulate the contenders by demanding that so-and-so horse must have been within five lengths at the half and finished no worse than fourth is all too often deceiving. But you can weigh the horse's performance against the class of horses it faced in its last race, and then make a logical judgment on how well the horse will perform against tonight's class. Just ask yourself this question: Does the horse fit the conditions of the race? If you have evaluated the horse in terms of class and form that's been discussed, you'll be right much more often than not.

Here is a review of the contenders:

CLAIMERS GOING UP IN CLASS.

All horses that have won their last race are contenders. But even then, the majority will be eliminated when they are rated.

CLAIMERS STAYING AT THE SAME CLASS LEVEL.

Any horse that has raced well in his last race by either winning or finishing close to a winner would be a contender. Close would be considered less than three lengths.

A horse can also qualify as a contender if he wasn't beaten by a large margin, more than five lengths. But he must show improvement in either his stretch gain or his margin of loss over his previous race. If the previous race was at a lower class level, then give leeway on the stretch gain and his loss margin accordingly.

At major tracks, any horse that's running within $500 or less ($250 in the minors) of his last claiming price, is considered to be staying at the same class level.

CLAIMERS GOING DOWN IN CLASS.

If the horse has been steadily dropping in class, or is making his first class drop tonight, he must show good speed for three quarters without tiring badly, or a good stretch drive to finish fairly close to the winner.

If the horse has performed well at tonight's class level in his previous race, then he must show a minimum of an even effort, but still not losing by a large margin.

CONDITIONED HORSES GOING UP IN CLASS.

If a horse is taking a minor class hike (monetary conditions: more than $2,000, but less than $4,000), he must show improvement in either his stretch gain or his margin of loss. The race must also be his best finish (not finish position, but in lengths) within approximately the last three weeks.

If the horse is taking a major class hike (monetary conditions: more than $4,000), his race should be an exceptional win. This is noted by a large gain of ground in the stretch, racing well on the outside for two or more turns, or a win by a large margin.

CONDITIONED HORSES RUNNING WITHIN THE SAME CLASS LEVEL.

For a horse to be considered a contender, he must race as described in CLAIMERS STAYING AT THE SAME CLASS LEVEL. Included in this group are horses running within $2,000 of the monetary conditions of the race.

CONDITIONED HORSES GOING DOWN IN CLASS.

For a horse to be a contender, he must show a good early effort without tiring badly, or a race in which he was not beaten by a large margin. Give leeway if the horse is taking a large class drop.

There will also be horses that are able to drop down while in good form. But make sure you are interpreting the conditions of the race correctly. Refer to the two-for-one ratio discussed earlier.

In the next chapter, we'll look at some horses that are a little more difficult to evaluate. This problem is caused by a third type of contender. We'll also make sure that the race we're about to play is actually a playable race.

CHAPTER 5

Choosing the Contenders—Part III

In the last two chapters, we have concentrated our efforts to distinguish contenders from non-contenders solely on the basis of the class-form relationship. In doing so, we did not have to make an excuse for a horse in regard to the pace or post position factor. Every horse that was determined to be a contender had performed well in relation to his class level regardless if it was a fast or slow pace or he had left from an outside post position.

If you can limit the amount of excuses you have to make for a horse's bad performance, you'll be taking a large step towards separating guesswork from actual handicapping. Naturally, we always excuse a bad race if the horse was impeded, had an interference or equipment break, or broke stride on an off track. But to assume that every horse that's raced poorly from an outside post position needed nothing more than the switch to the inside to turn in an improved effort, is nothing more than pure hogwash. On the other hand, if a horse has raced well from the outside in his last race and tonight he's leaving from an inside post position, we can logically expect an improved effort in most cases. Thus, we separate guesswork from actual handicapping.

Now that I have urged you to stop making excuses for a horse, we'll make a complete about face and discuss "possible" exceptions to this. There are two instances, other than those already discussed, when we can excuse a bad performance by a horse. The first is when a horse's last race took place on an off track. The second is when a horse was parked out in his last race.

Even when considering these two instances, we're not always inclined to immediately throw out the race. The horse must give us some reason in his past performances to do so. If he has already indicated he's going to be a non-contender, there probably won't be any reason to throw his last effort out. But if the horse appears to be a possible contender, then we'll handicap his last ratable race as if it were his primary race. Since we make our final ratings in terms of a fast track, the ratable race must be on the same.

Since a previous race can become a primary race, it can cause a problem. At times, we'll be forced to go back too far in the horse's past performances to get a clear picture of his true form. This could turn a horse into a third type of contender we're going to look at: the unratable contender.

An off track or a parked out race is always capable of turning a horse into an unratable contender. But despite this, the majority of horses will still end up being either contenders or non-contenders. Most of the unratable contenders have been horses that have been on the sidelines or are invading from other tracks.

The unratable contender is always dealt with separately. Although he never becomes a final play, his presence on the racetrack can cause the race to be passed. Because of this, it's very important that you not mistake an unratable contender for a non-contender or even worse than that, a contender. So let us first consider off tracks.

The question of whether or not to throw out a

An exciting moment as three horses fight for the lead. (Photo by Kuprion.)

BLACK **5** 6-1 =

Driver—JIM DOLBEE, Green-White-Red Tr.—W. Wall (102-20-10-15—.300)

SEATTLE CINDY B spayed 1968, by Scottish Pence—Seattle Call—Diplomat Hanover
Owner: Wall Bros., Cicero, Ill.

1973 20 4 4 2 $11,895 2:04^{1} Spk⅝
1972 21 3 6 2 $5,450 2:04^{3} Was^{1}
Lifetime $5,647 4, 2:04^{3} (1)

5-22 ^{8}Haw^{1} gd 68°	clm11000	1	:31^{1}	1:02^{4}	1:34^{2}	2:04	6	7	7	8^{10}	8^{11}	8^{12}	2:06^{2}	6-1 (J.Dolbee)	WesternsJody, NobleChoice, DeltaDirect	(even race)
5-15 ^{9}Haw^{1} ft 56°	clm11000	1	:29^{4}	1:00^{1}	1:32	2:04	6	7	6	6^{8}	4^{3½}	3^{nk}	2:04	6-1 (J.Dolbee)	NobleChoice, ForbesT'me, SeattleCindy	(just missed)
5- 7^{10}Haw^{1} sy 60°	clm10000	1	:30^{4}	1:03^{3}	1:36	2:06	7	7	7	9^{7½}	8^{10}	4^{5¼}	2:07	4-1 (B.Shuter)	ValiantSampson, WesternsJody, NobleScot	(closed late)
4-30^{10}Haw^{1} sy 50°	clm10000	1	:32^{3}	1:04^{2}	1:36	2:07	4	7	7°	6^{5}	2^{½}	2^{¾}	2:07^{1}	9-1 (B.Shuter)	DeltaDirect, SeattleCindy, VarsitySignal	(late bid)
4-19 ^{7}Haw^{1} ft 67°	clm11000	1	:31^{1}	1:01^{4}	1:34	2:04^{1}	8	8	8	8^{7}	x8^{13}	8^{dis}		7-1 (R.Knox)	Rozella, G.T.Winter, HandsomeDate	(no threat)
4-14 ^{6}Spk⅝ ft 49°	clm9000=	1	:30^{1}	1:02^{2}	1:34^{2}	2:05^{4}	9	9	9^{9½}	7^{4½}	6^{2¾}	3^{1¼}	2:06	14-1 (R.Knox)	TeenieTime, EyreNavarch, SeattleCindy	(post hurt)

horse's last race when contested on an off track has been a center of controversy for a long time. There are those who contend that if a horse raced well on an off track in his last effort, he has done so because he liked the conditions. And if a horse raced poorly on an off track his last time out, then he must have disliked the conditions. The result of this thinking would be to throw out every single horse's last race that was contested on an off track, since it is not a true indication of how well the horse will perform on a fast track.

Certainly, there are a number of horses that race well or poorly because they have liked or disliked the conditions. There are notorious "mudrunners" that always race well on an off track. There are also horses that hate the wet conditions so much they practically refuse to run. But it's never wise to immediately throw out the race because an off track, at times, can indicate a horse's true form. This can be best seen on the past performances of Seattle Cindy, who's entered in a $10,000 claimer.

At first observation of Seattle Cindy's last race, the player might be inclined to throw it out since it was contested on a good track. By doing so, we would then handicap her previous race, which took place on May 15. That night, she was flying in $11,000 company, making up eight lengths in the stretch and missing by only a neck. Since she's running for a $10,000 tag tonight, she would be considered a contender.

Now that we have gone through the motions, let's really get down to the brass tacks. Seattle Cindy was, to say the least, completely trounced in her last race. And despite the fact that her last race was negotiated on a good track, there is no reason to believe that she dislikes the wet conditions.

A little closer evaluation of Seattle Cindy's past performances is now needed. Her race on May 7 was on a sloppy track and she was far from completely trounced. If that's not enough, what about the race that took place on April 30? How does a horse that dislikes an off track get beaten by only three parts of a length in the slop?

By using the added information provided in Seattle Cindy's previous races, we would conclude that she neither shows a liking nor a disliking for an off track. Therefore, when she races on a wet surface, it would be an indication of her true form. So despite the fact that Seattle Cindy raced well enough on May 15 to become a contender, the race would play no significance in our handicapping. Her primary race would remain the effort contested on May 22. Since she was a badly beaten loser in $11,000 company, she would be considered a non-contender for $10,000. This formulates our first rule.

1. Any horse whose last race was on an off track and raced poorly, but shows a good race on an off track anywhere in its past performances, is automatically eliminated as a non-contender.

Since it's important to spot horses that are not affected by off tracks, it's just as important to spot the opposite: the horse that isn't able to handle the wet conditions. But this doesn't necessarily mean that the horse figures to contend on a fast track. That depends solely on how well the horse raced in his last ratable race. So let's see how it works both ways.

RED **1** 6-1 –

Driver—JESSIE WILLIS, Maroon-Gray-White Tr.—J. Willis (19-0-2-1—.076)

MAJESTIC DREAM B h 1967, by Majestic Hanover—Sultry Nite—Knight Dream
Owner: William J. McEnery, Evergreen Park, Ill.

1973 11 1 0 1 $2,100 2:07^{2} BmlP
1972 40 7 5 3 $22,963 2:03^{1} Was^{1}
Lifetime $48,228 5, 2:03^{1} (1)

5-28 ^{7}Spk⅝ sy 52°	clm7000—	1	:31^{2}	1:03^{3}	1:34^{4}	2:06^{4}	7	8	8^{11}	8^{9½}	7^{9}	7^{14}	2:09^{3}	9-1 (J.Willis)	ReidsShadow, PaintedMelody, Armbrolvy	(no threat)
5-16^{10}Haw^{1} ft 43°	clm8000	1	:33	1:04^{3}	1:36^{2}	2:06^{4}	7	7°	2	2^{2}	5^{4}	8^{9}	2:08^{3}	18-1 (J.Willis)	Mr.Thunderbyrd, Mose, SengaMarie	(tired badly)
5- 7^{10}Haw^{1} sy 60°	clm10000	1	:30^{4}	1:03^{3}	1:36	2:06	9	9	9	8^{6½}	7^{10}	7^{9¼}	2:07^{4}	20 1 (J.Willis)	ValiantSampson, WesternsJody, NobleScot	(even)
4-28^{10}Haw^{1} ft 43°	clm10000	1$\frac{1}{16}$	:29	:59^{2}		1:22^{3}	1	2	4	6$^{7°}$	5^{4}	6^{5¼}	1:23^{3}	8-1 (J.Willis)	HarkWay, LovinLuLu, SenatorGlib	(soundly beaten)
4-17^{10}Haw^{1} ft 56°	clm10000	1	:32^{2}	1:04	1:35^{4}	2:06^{1}	5	7	7	6^{3}	4^{1½}	3^{1¾}	2:06^{3}	6-1 (J.Willis)	FieldDiamond, SnoVan, MajesticDream	(late bid)
4-10 ^{8}Spk⅝ ft 33°	clm10000=	1	:30^{2}	1:03^{2}	1:33^{2}	2:04^{3}	9	6	6^{7½}	6^{4¾}	5^{4¼}	6^{5}	2:05^{3}	44-1 (J.Willis)	BrilliantSpeed, SnoVan, RuthsChoice	(raced evenly)

By considering the way that Majestic Dream handled an off track in his last race, as well as the race on May 7, we would have enough evidence to surmise that he doesn't exactly cherish the wet conditions. On that basis alone, we would disregard his last race. That leaves us with the race on May 16 as Majestic Dream's primary race. Since he was totally demolished in $8,000 company, he would be considered a non-contender for $6,000, which is what he's entered for tonight.

would not have any precedent to work with.

You may find it useful at times to keep long-term records of how an off track affects certain horses. But since the past performances usually cover the last two months of a horse's racing activities, you'll find that keeping these records is going to be a lot more work than it's really worth. Any race that's taken place more than two months ago is, as far as a horse is concerned, way back in the twilight zone. So what we can do, if there are

BLUE 2 6-1 =	Driver—CARMINE ABBATIELLO, Gold-Red		Tr.—M. Schanks		(0-0-0-0—.000)			1973 11 3 2 0 $7,430 2:024 LA⅝
	FAREX BOY	Br g 1962, by Dartagnan—Baradel—Dillala						1972 29 6 4 4 $17,216 2:023 Hol1
		Owner: Marty Schanks, Des Plaines, Ill.						Lifetime $23,104 10, 2:023 (1)

6-19	9Spk⅝ sy 78°	clm10000=1	:31	1:022	1:334	2:05	4	1	12	11	33	58¾	2:064	5-1 (L.Rapone)	MiMargarita, NoCredit, NobleOne (set early pace)
6-	710Spk⅝ ft 75°	clm10000—1	:294	1:023	1:322	2:031	2	1	11	11¼	12½	21¼	2:032	7-2 (L.Rapone)	Tarline, FarexBoy, J.T.King (weakened at wire)
5-28	8Spk⅝ sy 52°	clm12000—1	:312	1:052	1:37	2:08	7	1	22	31½	76½	810	2:10	6-1 (L.Rapone)	BrilliantSpeed, SummertimeDirect, FrostyWil (used erly)
5-19	2Haw1 ft 55°	clm13000 1	:304	1:01	1:331	2:04	4	4°	1°	22	914	916	2:071	5-1 (M.Schanks)	TecklaAdiosB, RalphAmortzr, LnclnsHghTde (used erly)
5- 9	L.A⅝ ft	clm13000 1	:291	1:021	1:331	2:03	6	1	2	5	31	64p5	2:034	7-1 (RStemermn)	BelleOlympia, ErinFrost, BrennaB. (———)
4-30	L.A⅝ ft	clm13000 1	:293	1:004	1:314	2:022	3	4°	1	3	21	52¼	2:024	4-1 (RStemermn)	BelleOlympia, Deezlebub, JeffersonExpress (———)

Farex Boy, like Majestic Dream, also shows a definite disliking for an off track in his two efforts. So on the same basis, we would disregard his last race. But this time, using the same approach, we come out with a different result.

Farex Boy's primary race is now his effort on June 7. Since he's entered in a $10,000 claiming race tonight, his good effort within the same class level is enough to qualify him for a contending role. So even though we throw out a horse's last race when there's a definite disliking for an off track, it's still up to the horse's last ratable race to determine whether or not he's a contender. This approach is found in our second rule.

2. Any horse whose last race was on an off track and raced poorly, but also shows another poor race on an off track in his past performances, is then handicapped off his last race which took place on a fast track.

When we use rule one, we can spot horses that are not affected by off tracks. Since the rule only deals with horses that have raced poorly, we can automatically eliminate them as non-contenders. By using rule two, we can excuse a horse's bad performance because we have a precedent in his past performances to work with. But if a horse turns in a bad performance, or even if he races well and there are no other races in his past perfor-mances that have taken place on an off track, we

no other races to work with, is to throw the race out and handicap the previous race since it will always have taken place on a fast track. This is described in rule three.

3. Any horse whose last race took place on an off track, and shows no other races on an off track in his past performances, is handicapped off his next to last race.

Rule three serves several purposes. First there's the possibility that the horse raced well only because it was an off track. He is the so-called mudrunner. If this is the case, chances are his previous race will be a dull one. That way, we'll handicap the race that indicates his true form on a fast track. If the horse is actually in good form, then his previous race will indicate that instead, and once again we're covered.

On the other hand, if the horse turned in a bad race, then we're giving him the benefit of the doubt. If his next to last race is good enough to qualify him to be a contender, then we'll treat him as such. If it's just another bad race, then we'll get rid of the horse as a non-contender.

So far, we've dealt with horses that have raced well, horses that have raced poorly, and horses that have shown only one race on an off track. That leaves us with only one more possibility. That's the kind of horse that has performed in middle-of-the-road fashion on two or more occasions. These kinds of horses don't run big races on off tracks, but their form doesn't deteriorate either. They more or less perform in even fashion. So their form is always best evaluated on a fast track. This approach is found in rule four.

4. Any horse that shows two or more races on an off track, which indicate neither a liking nor a disliking for the conditions, is handicapped off his last race which took place on a fast track.

The only time we can hang ourselves by using these four rules is when a horse shows major improvement in his overall form. When dealing with this kind of horse, we'd end up giving him an unfair analysis of his last race on a fast track, because he has improved his form since that race. This kind of horse will be dealt with separately in a later chapter.

The biggest problem that's caused by an off track is when an unratable contender is created. This situation occurs when we have to go back too far in the horse's past performances to get a ratable race. And if the ratable race turns out to be a contending one, we would have an unratable contender.

The past performances of Shiaway Percy reveal why he was considered an unratable contender rather than a contender. He was entered in an $8,000 claiming race (his price is $9,600) which took place on July 3 at Sportsman's Park.

faces tonight. But a race that took place more than seven weeks ago is far too long to consider any horse as a contender. If his race indicated that he was a non-contender, it wouldn't matter if it took place last week, last month, or even last year because non-contenders are never wagered on. But contenders are. And it certainly makes no sense to wager on a horse whose contending race took place almost two months back.

Because of the length of time involved, Shiaway Percy would be labeled an unratable contender and he would not be considered when the contenders are rated. The only function he serves is that he can cause a race to be passed. This will be discussed at the end of the chapter. Rule five describes how horses like Shiaway Percy become unratable contenders.

5. Any horse that has had one or more races thrown out, but qualifies to be a contender off a ratable race that took place more than 30 days ago, is then considered to be an unratable contender.

Horses that have been parked out are also candidates to have their races thrown out. But if a horse has been parked out for only one turn of the track, indicated by one small zero in his past performance line, his race is never thrown out. Although it's true the horse travels an added distance around the racetrack, it's usually done for the benefit of the horse. A driver will often find

BLACK **5** 6-1 =

Driver—STANLEY BANKS, White-Purple **Tr.—K. Vander Schaaf** **(110-14-18-11—.246)**
SHIAWAY PERCY B c 1969, by Uncle Alex—Knight Lassie—Knight Dream
Owner: Ken Vander Schaaf, Sandwich, Ill.

													1973 10 0 0 2	$1,870		
													1972 30 8 2 8	$10,026	$2:08^{2}$ Klmzo	
													Lifetime	$14,933	2, 2:08	
6-19^{10}Spk⅝ sy 78°	clm9600=1	$:32^{2}$	$1:05^{4}$	$1:36^{4}$	$2:06^{4}$	1	3	$4^{2½}$	5^{4}	$4^{3½}$	$3^{3¾}$	$2:07^{3}$	8-1 (S.Banks)	DazzlingDeana, JavelonJeanette, ShiawayPercy		(evenly)
6- 5^{10}Spk⅝ sy 65°	clm9600=1	:32	$1:06^{2}$	$1:37^{3}$	$2:08^{1}$	7	7	$5^{4½}$	$6^{2¾}$	$6^{4¼}$	$5^{1¾}$	$2:08^{3}$	6-1 (S.Banks)	LittlePuff, SengaMarie, IdlewhilesEarl		(closed some)
5-22^{10}Haw¹ gd 68°	clm9600 1	$:31^{2}$	$1:04^{2}$	$1:35^{2}$	$2:05^{3}$	8	9	9	$9^{8¾}$	6^{7}	$6^{4½}$	$2:06^{3}$	6-1 (S.Banks)	BowsBrother, HighJimmy, ChiefRed		(no factor)
5-10^{10}Haw¹ ft 62°	clm12000 1	$:32^{1}$	$1:02^{4}$	$1:34^{1}$	$2:05^{4}$	4	5	6	7^{6}	$6^{1¾}$	3^{nk}	$2:05^{4}$	8-1 (S.Banks)	ChiefRagtime, NoCredit, ShiawayPercy		(just missed)
4-28^{10}Haw¹ ft 43°	clm12000 1$\frac{1}{16}$	:29	$:59^{2}$		$1:22^{3}$	9	8	8	8^{10}	8^{7}	$7^{8¼}$	$1:24^{1}$	15-1 (S.Banks)	HarkWay, LovinLuLu, SenatorGlib		(post hurt)
4-17^{10}Haw¹ ft 56°	clm12000 1	$:32^{2}$	1:04	$1:35^{4}$	$2:06^{1}$	1	3	3	$5^{2½}$	$5^{1½}$	6^{2}	$2:06^{3}$	3-1 (S.Banks)	FieldDiamond, SnoVan, MajesticDream		(even)

Shiaway Percy's last three races have been contested on off tracks. In all three events, he has been neither dominated nor badly beaten. So his status is found in rule four, where we handicap the horse's last race which took place on a fast track. That effort was on May 10 and in it, Shiaway Percy raced extremely well against $10,000 claimers. His effort is more than enough to qualify him for a contending role against the $8,000 claimers he

himself still parked out at the quarter mile pole because he's trying to secure a better position in the race than he would have gotten by going directly to the rail. When it's late in the race, many drivers swing their horses to the outside on the final turn rather than getting stuck behind horses that have little or nothing left. In either case, when a horse has been parked out for only one turn of the track, he has usually finished the race closer to the winner than he would have had the driver decided to spend the entire mile along the rail.

When a horse has raced parked out for two or more turns, then there's a good possibility we can throw his race out. But before we start tossing races out, let us first deal with the horse that has raced well in spite of this, because there's no logical reason whatsoever to cast aside a horse's effort if he has performed well enough in the race to qualify himself for a contending role. Then, when we make our final ratings, we can give these horses extra consideration for racing under adversity. These horses are described in rule six.

6. Any horse that has qualified to be a contender while racing parked out for two or more turns is handicapped off that same race.

Even though there are some horses that race well while parked out for two or more turns, you'll find that the great majority of horses do not hold up well and end up tiring badly. Harness horses are specifically trained to run only the standard mile, so it would serve no purpose, especially when it comes to our bankroll, to consider all of the remaining horses as non-contenders. We'll give the horse the benefit of the doubt and handicap him off his previous race. If the horse is a contender, fine. If not, we can eliminate him. This is described in rule seven.

7. Any horse that has not raced well enough to be a contender while racing parked out for two or more turns is handicapped off his next to last race.

By using rule seven, it's very possible to come up with yet another unratable contender. You may go back to the horse's next to last race only to find out it has to be thrown out because it took place on an off track. Or it may even be another parked out race. If you end up going back more than thirty days ago to find out the horse is a contender, he would come under rule five which would make him an unratable contender.

Whenever a horse has raced on an off track or has been parked out for two or more turns, he is subject to becoming one of the three types of contenders. Whenever a horse has been on the sidelines or is invading from another track, he is subject to becoming only a non-contender or an unratable contender. First, we'll quickly deal with the horse that's been sidelined.

Any time a horse has been away from the races for more than sixteen days, he is no longer considered for a contending role. Yet, the horse isn't totally ignored either. He is still handicapped to determine if he would have qualified as a contender if he had been to the racing wars more recently. If he's a non-contender, he still remains as such. But if he is found to be a contender, then his status is changed to an unratable contender as described in rule eight.

8. Any horse that's been away from the races for more than sixteen days but qualifies as a contender, is then considered to be an unratable contender.

The sixteen-day time limit for this rule may seem a bit contrary because off track and parked out horses are given thirty days in which to qualify as contenders. But taken into consideration is the fact that these horses have not been racing in the interim. If there's any one thing a horse needs to stay in shape, it's competition. Training always helps, but it never replaces a competitive race. So if a horse has been away from the races for more than sixteen days, he'll probably be in need of a race to get back into the grind.

Horses that are shipping in from racetracks outside the local circuit are dealt with the same way as horses that have been sidelined. They too, are handicapped to determine if they qualify as contenders. The only difference is that there's no regard to when their last race took place. If a shipper does qualify as a contender, even if his race took place last week, his status would still be that of an unratable contender.

The biggest problem caused by horses' shipping in is that their class levels are sometimes hard to define. Not only must you take into consideration the class of animals the horse has been racing against, but you must also consider the class of the track itself. Let's say a horse has been steadily beating $8,000 claimers at Freehold Raceway, then is shipped over to the Yonkers oval. Chances are he's not going to be able to do the same in New

York because the class of horses at Yonkers is much better than the class of horses at Freehold. This is also reflected in the purse money they compete for. So if an $8,000 claimer from Freehold is entered for $8,000 at Yonkers, he would actually be taking a class hike.

When trying to determine if a shipper qualifies as a contender, first take into consideration the class of horses at your own racetrack. If the shipper is coming from a racetrack that has classier animals, which is usually reflected by the size of the city the racetrack is located in, he can fit the conditions of the race even if he's entered in a higher class level than he previously raced at, although never to the point of a ridiculously high class hike. If the shipper is coming from a racetrack that has horses of less quality than yours, then he must always be taking a drop in class to fit the conditions of the race.

The final decision is then based solely on the horse's performance. If the horse has raced well enough to become a contender, then his status is changed to that of an unratable contender. If he hasn't raced well, then he's just another non-contender. This is described in rules nine and ten.

9. Any shipper that has raced well enough to become a contender on a par with the conditions of the race, is then considered to be an unratable contender.

10. Any shipper that hasn't raced well on a par with the conditions of the race, is automatically eliminated as a non-contender.

Horses are not considered shippers when competition moves from one racetrack to another within the local circuit unless there's a large difference between the two tracks involved. If a meet moves from a half-mile track to a mile track, it's not advisable to play any races until all local horses have had at least one effort on the track. Usually by three weeks into the meeting, all locals will have tested the racing surface at least once. Any horse who hasn't would be considered a shipper.

When the local competition moves to a racetrack where there's little difference between the two ovals involved, handicapping goes on as usual. This is so long as the two tracks differ by no more than one turn and their speed ratings are no more than one second apart. If there's a larger difference between the two tracks than this, horses are also considered shippers until they have tested the local surface at least once. If you do not know the speed ratings of the racetracks on your local circuit, refer to the speed rating chart at the end of this book.

Now that we have differentiated unratable contenders from contenders and non-contenders, we must decide if their presence on the racetrack is enough reason for us to pass up the race. On the one hand, they are fully qualified contenders because of the class-form relationship we work with. But on the other hand, their current form is somewhat obscure against the local stock.

One unratable contender in a race would not be enough reason to pass up the entire race. There may be some experienced racegoers who would disagree, so let's look at this with a logical winning approach in mind. Let's say a sizable number of races that contained one unratable contender were in actuality won by that unratable contender. On that basis alone, we would have reason enough to pass up those races. But then again, we would have even a better reason just to wager on every single unratable contender that came along.

Wagering on unratable contenders never works. Most races are won by horses that have raced well recently against the local competition. Therefore, instead of passing up a race that has only one unratable contender in it, we'll only pass it up if it has two. This is stated in our final rule.

11. Any race that has two or more unratable contenders in it is not considered for play.

In the next chapter, we'll proceed to rate the contenders. But before doing that, we'll look at the final three ingredients—pace, post position, and the driver.

CHAPTER 6

Rating the Contenders

Now that we have chosen the contenders in the race, it's time to pick out the most likely winner. This is by no means a guarantee that it's impossible for you ever to lose another race. The fact is; most racing fans end up beating themselves at the racetrack. They bet on races that don't deserve a wager and they bet on horses that don't even deserve to be in the race.

The most important thing we have going for us thus far is that we're not going to beat ourselves at the racetrack. We're not going to bet on a race that doesn't deserve a wager because all high risk races have already been eliminated. We're not going to bet on a horse that doesn't deserve to be in the race because we're confining our possible final plays only to contenders. And a contender is simply a horse that fits the conditions of the race.

Now that we know what we have going for us, it's time to get on with the things we have to do. That is, find the one horse who deserves to win tonight's race on the basis of his past performance. The first thing we'll have to consider is pace.

PACE

No horse can be properly handicapped without considering the pace factor. Class and form are the two most important factors because it's their combination that produce the contenders in the race. But it's pace that becomes the most important factor when it's time to make the final choice from the contenders. So the first thing we'll learn about pace is what we don't have to learn.

Item number one: There are no sure fire ways, nor are there any magic formulas, that we can use to predict what the pace of tonight's race will be.

Item number two: Even if there were some way to make an accurate prediction of what the pace of the race will be, we would have no need for it.

We are dealing with two unpredictable animals—man and horse. At the start of each race, some drivers already will have their strategy planned, while others will play it by ear. But who's to say exactly which driver or drivers will shoot their horses out for the lead? Second question. Who's to say if the horse will even respond to what the driver is asking for?

By checking over the past performances, you can usually get some idea of which horses have gate speed and which do not. The average race has two or three horses that will leave the starting gate fast and there's a good chance that one of them is going to be the pacesetter. Occasionally you'll run across an unexpected horse that's gone out for the lead, but for the most part you'll have pretty good success narrowing the field down to two or three possible pacesetters.

Since we know that each race has two or three horses that are likely to set the pace, what do we do now? Actually, I'll take back that question because it's not what we're going to do, but rather what the driver is going to do. When he gets his horse on top, is he going to set a fast or slow pace? An interesting question indeed. Unfortunately the only person who can answer it is the driver himself, and he may not even know it until he gets his horse to the lead.

Let's quickly regroup our facts. We've been able

so far to learn two things about pace. We know there's going to be a pacesetter in every single race. We also know that it's up to the driver just how fast or slow that pace is going to be. I wouldn't exactly classify this as inside information because we really don't know any more about pace than when

racegoer. That way, if you know how to calculate it the hard way, an easier method will cause no problems. It's sort of like learning long division before you know how to do short division. We'll learn a quicker method since time is very important at a racetrack.

	Driver—ROBERT KNOX, Gold-Brown		Tr.—R. Leake	(71-5-15-10—.235)	1973	18	3	4	3	$12,103	2:02 Spr¹

RED & YELLOW 8 9-2 — **PACING PAULINE** — Ch f 1970, by Adios Bomber—Mabel K. Grattan—Dominion Grattan — Owner: Double LLB Stable, South Beloit, Ill. — 1972 10 9 0 1 $11,475 2:04 Spr¹ — Lifetime $11,475 2, 2:04 (1)

8-18	6May ft 77°	FMnw1000007³	1 :30¹ 1:01 1:31² 2:01³	4	7	5⁶	3³°	3³	5²	2:02	9-1 (J.Dennis)	FemmeFatale, Apo;oMeridaje, BrennaScot (raced well)
8-11	Spr¹ ft	3yrstk10070	1 :28² :59 1:30¹ 2:02	5	2° 3	5	31½	1ⁿᵏ	2:02	NB (J.Hankins)	PacingPauline, Max'mize, BarbaraBByrd (———)
8-11	Spr¹ ft	3yrstk5035	1 :28⁴ 1:00² 1:32² 2:02³	9	7 7°	4°	2⁵	2⁶	2:03⁴	NB (J.Hankins)	BarbaraBByrd, PacingPauline, Raquel (———)
8- 4	2May ft 77°	FM4500	1 :30⁴ 1:01² 1:33³ 2:04¹	2	4	6³½	6³¼	4³½	2¹¼	2:04²	9-1 (J.Dennis)	LittleSweetSue, PacngPaulne, PpngTmes (rank 1st turn)
7-29	Camb gd	ffa125	Dash in 2:09¹, Fin. 4								NB (J.Hankins)	CarryOnChief, LittleSweetSue, RobbRanger (———)
7-23	Henry gd	ffa337	Dash in 2:11⁴, Fin. 7								NB (J.Boyer)	LousDude, MrOrion, StormyTide (———)

we started. In fact, when you get down to the real nitty gritty, the quickest way to determine if it's a fast or slow pace is by reading it off the teletimer during the race.

The way in which we regard the pace factor is not by trying to predict how fast or slow the fractions of the race are going to be, but how well the horse handled the pace in the primary race that qualified him as a contender.

The relationship class has with current form is similar to the relationship pace has with the horse's final time. You cannot weigh one factor without taking into consideration the other. The end result of how the horse has handled the pace is going to be reflected in his final time. By combining the two factors we have four possibilities.

$1:01^1$ Fast last half—Slow final time 2:04
$1:01$ Fast last half—Fast final time $2:02^3$
$1:03^2$ Slow last half—Slow final time $2:03^3$
$1:03$ Slow last half—Fast final time $2:02^4$

Without question, the best possible horse to become our final choice would be one that's run the fastest last half in relation to the fastest final time. That way, the pace of the race will always take care of itself. If it happens to be a fast pace, then it's all the better for our type of horse. On the other hand, if it turns out to be a slow pace, then our horse logically figures to be the fastest horse to close off that pace.

Since it's extremely important that a horse's last half is calculated correctly, we'll review how it's done. In Chapter 1, we looked at a long and drawn-out process which should have been mandatory reading if you're an inexperienced

Let us consider Pacing Pauline's last race. At the left, it indicates that the official (or leader's) first half was in 1:01 and the final winning time for the mile was 2:01 3/5. By using nothing more than simple math, we know that the last half of the race was run in exactly 1:00 3/5. (1:01 + 1:00 3/5 = 2:01 3/5).

In Pacing Pauline's last half, she made up 4 lengths (6 to 2). Since 1 length is equal to 1/5 of a second (fractions are always rounded off to the nearest full second), all we do is subtract 4/5 from 1:00 3/5. Therefore, her last half was in 59 4/5 and her final time was 2:02. On the other hand, if Pacing Pauline had lost ground, then those lengths would be added on to the last half.

Some racing programs do not list the number of lengths the horse was behind at the half mile pole. This causes a bit of a problem for the player since he cannot accurately calculate the horse's speed in his last half. This can be rectified however, by taking the difference between the official half mile time and the horse's final time. For instance, the official half mile time in Pacing Pauline's race was 1:01 and her final time was 2:02. Her last half would then come out to be 1:01 (1:01 + 1:01 = 2:02). Obviously, this is nowhere near the real speed she showed, but all is not lost either. Since you'll be calculating every horse in this way, it practically all evens out because every horse's last half will be slower than it actually ran in. However, there is a small margin of error and if your program lists the lengths behind at the half mile pole, you're well advised to use the first method.

Keep in mind that we deal only with pace and

final times with contenders. Non-contenders are no longer considered even if one has the fastest time in the race. Most non-contenders have been beaten by a large margin so their final times are not taken seriously. Ironic as it may sound, a horse is capable of running faster when losing a race than when winning because many times he's "carried" by fast fractions. So remember, we're only interested in speed with contenders, and in doing so, we'll have to consider their post positions.

POST POSITION

In Chapter 2, I stated in part that "the logical handicapper chooses a horse which appears to have a marked edge or advantage over his competition." Included along with the many advantages making up this game of harness racing is post position. When all things are equal, the advantage of post position can be the sole determining factor which separates victory from defeat. That's why handicappers, as well as catch drivers, always are on the lookout for a good horse with an inside post position.

In thoroughbred racing, post position has always been a prime factor. But in harness racing, the post position factor is even more important because each and every horse is required to pull a sulky. Certainly the sulky part of this is no new news. But the effect it has on the horse has often been overlooked.

When the Standardbred is attached to its sulky, the horse is taking up more room on the racetrack (both length and width) than it would if it were saddled like the thoroughbred. So in flat racing, horses are able to stay closer to the competitors in front of them and maintain good position. But good position in a race is even more important in harness racing, and post position is a major determining factor in getting good position in a race. The closer a horse is to the rail, the better are his chances for securing good position.

The difference between an inside and an outside post is also told in the time element involved. Reliable timing devices have figured out that when a horse leaves from the nine post, he has to run almost a full second faster than the horse leaving from the one post. Taken into considera-

tion is the time spent getting to the rail while the horse is moving forward.

By breaking down the time element into horse racing arithmetic, each post position from the two outward to the nine is approximately equal to an added handicap of 1/2 length per post. This is seen on the chart which is based on a norm of 2:05.

Post Position Handicaps
Based on a 2:05 Norm

1.	2:05	6.	2:05$^{2\frac{1}{2}}$
2.	2:05$^{\frac{1}{4}}$	7.	2:05^{3}
3.	2:05^{1}	8.	2:05$^{3\frac{1}{4}}$
4.	2:05$^{1\frac{1}{4}}$	9.	2:05^{4}
5.	2:05^{2}		

Now that we have laid down the facts about post position, we know that if two horses of similar ability were to compete against each other, horse A leaving from the three post and horse B from the six, the definite advantage in post position would go to horse A. Right?

Right...and wrong. In other words, maybe. I can best describe this by going through an example which shows how horse B gets the advantage.

P.P.	Horse	Class	P.P. Last Race	Last Half	Final Time
3	A	$10,000	1	1:02	2:04
6	B	$10,000	8	1:02	2:04

I have made horse A and B as close in ability as possible. Neither horse gets an edge in class and the speed in their last race is equal. Separating these two horses now depends on which animal is getting the advantage in post position.

The advantage in this race would go to horse B. The reason for this is because he received a break in post position of his last race while horse A did not. Both horses raced on equal terms their last time out, horse A from the one post, horse B from the eight. But they do not figure to race on equal terms, since horse A is leaving from a less desirable post than he had in his last race and horse B is getting a break by moving into two post positions.

On the other hand, if horse A was moving in and horse B was moving out, the advantage would have been with horse A.

The way we deal with the post position factor is this: The importance of tonight's post position is not in relation to other horses, but in relation to the post position received in the primary race that qualified the horse as a contender.

Our possible final choice is a horse with a fast final time in relation to a fast last half. We've just combined this with a post position that's hopefully better than what the horse received in his last race. The last factor we'll consider is the driver.

Herve Fillion, harness racing's leading driver with over 5,000 victories.

The Role of the Driver

Regardless of what it says in the Constitution, all drivers are not created equal. To become a top driver takes skill, courage, temperament, and the ability to make quick decisions. Some drivers are better than others and there are no ifs, ands, or buts about it.

When handicapping a race, the driver is the last and also the least important factor that's considered. Far more important are class, form, pace, and post position, because they are the factors used to determine the best horse in the race. If a horse doesn't stand out on at least one of these factors, it probably won't matter how good the man behind the controls is. The role of the driver is one of the most misused handicapping factors. There are many excellent drivers in the business, and racing fans often have their favorite ones. This is all to the good, with only one possible exception. Some racegoers end up betting on drivers rather than horses.

The driver factor is taken into consideration only when there's a better than average driver in the sulky. When the driver factor is used, it is an advantage, never a disadvantage. If two horses of similar ability are entered in the race and one has a leading driver in the bike while the other has an unknown, inexperienced man, the edge would obviously be given to the horse with the leading driver. But by the same token, we wouldn't take anything away from the other horse, because that would be a twofold rating which puts too much emphasis upon the driver factor.

There's nothing to accomplish by decreasing a horse's rating if he has already qualified as a contender on his racing merits. This is especially true if it's the same driver in the sulky as in the horse's last race, even if in your estimation the man is a poor driver. But if the horse has a good driver going tonight, or is switching to a good driver, then the horse deserves an advantage in his rating if the case should warrant it.

A good driver is generally described as a winning driver. Sometimes however, this doesn't always hold true. There are many drivers around who are more than capable but do not win a lot of races because they have yet to make names for themselves. Drivers who have made good reputations for themselves over the years usually end up with horses that have the best chances of winning.

If you frequent the racetrack often, it's a good idea to become aware of the leading men as well as of good drivers that don't happen to boast an impressive record. As a helpful guide, it's best to give horses extra consideration when the driver has been averaging one win or better in every six starts or has a driver's percentage of .275 or better.

Advantage Ratings

Advantage ratings is the first of two rating

systems which will be used to produce the final choice. It deals with exactly what its name implies—advantages, eight in all. The advantages are really nothing more than things the horse has going for him which are based on the five basic ingredients of handicapping.

These ratings will not be applicable for all playable races. Far from it, in fact. The only horse who actually gets rated is the contender who has the fastest final time. This system will produce a final choice in only about 15% of all playable races. All of the remaining races will be rated on the basis of numerical speed ratings. But before we get into that, let's deal with the eight advantages.

1. FASTEST FINAL TIME: The contender who has achieved the fastest final time in his primary race becomes the prime horse and is the only one considered for play. This doesn't necessarily mean the fastest time in the race. A non-contender's final time might be faster, but his time is not significant. If two contenders share the fastest final time, the race is rated on the basis of numerical speed ratings. When a prime horse is found, then proceed to advantages two through eight and see which ones apply to him.

2. FASTEST LAST HALF: The prime horse's last half must be at least 1/5 of a second faster than all other contenders. If it is not faster, or he shares the fastest last half with another contender, this advantage would not apply to him. All last halfs are calculated as stated in this book.

3. EDGE ON CLASS: This only applies if the prime horse raced at a higher class level than all other contenders his last time out. If for some reason the prime horse's class level is obscure against the other contenders, or if you're unable to make a definite class evaluation of one of the contenders, then by all means, do not take this advantage into consideration.

4. BREAK IN POST POSITION: The prime horse is considered to be getting a break in post position only if he is moving in two positions or more over the post position he received in his contending race. If the prime horse is not bettering his post by at least two, then this advantage wouldn't apply to him even if he is leaving from the rail.

5. PARKED OUT RACE: The prime horse receives this advantage only if he was parked out for two or more turns in his contending race.

6. GOOD MOVE IN STRETCH: If the prime horse made up three lengths or more in the last quarter of the race, he receives this advantage. If he was on the lead at the three-quarter mark, then he must have increased his margin by at least three lengths.

7. OFF A WINNING EFFORT: A horse can accomplish nothing better than winning his race. Therefore, if the prime horse is coming off a winning effort, it's also considered an advantage.

8. BETTER THAN AVERAGE DRIVER: For the final advantage to apply, the prime horse must have, in your estimation, a good driver or be switching to a good driver. If you prefer, use the guide mentioned earlier in the chapter.

For a horse to become a final play, he must have, first of all, complied with the first advantage, which is mandatory. From there, the prime horse must comply with at least three of the remaining seven advantages. The only stipulation is that the three advantages cannot be the combination of six, seven, and eight. These three are the least important of the eight, so their combination alone would not be strong enough. Any other combination of three is sufficient, and makes the prime horse the final play.

To get a better understanding of how advantage ratings work, we'll put them to the test in two races. First, an $8,000 claiming race that took place on July 12 at Sportsman's Park.

	Driver—CARL PORCELLI, JR., Blue-Green	Tr.—K. James	(27-4-2-4—.239)	1973 24 2 1 9 $9,344 2:08² BmIP
RED				1972 37 3 12 5 $13,310 2:08² Spk⅝
1	**J. HAZEN ADIOS** B g 1967, by Cape Adios—Beaver Jester—Court Jester			Lifetime $19,266 5, 2:08² (⅝)
6-1 =	Owner: Joseph Livolsi, Chicago, Ill.			

7- 3¹⁰Spk⅝ ft 78°	clm8000=1	:31¹ 1:04¹ 1:35 2:04⁴	1	2	3¹½°	2¹°	2½	2¹	2:05	8-1 (C.PorceliiJr)	SilverDiller, JHazenAdios, AmigosGirl	(good try)
6-22 ²Spk⅝ ft 76°	clm8000=1	:31¹ 1:02⁴ 1:33¹ 2:04⁴	5	8	89½	86	76	43½	2:05³	20-1 (C.PorceliiJr)	HarkWay, NordelRuss, StewartCraig	(closed some)
6-12 ⁵Spk⅝ ft 74°	clm8000—1	:30¹ 1:01³ 1:32⁴ 2:04	8	8	8¹⁴	6⁷	3⁹	3⁴¾	2:05	31-1 (C.PorceliiJr)	RealBlast, HarkWay, J.HazenAdios	(last ½ good)
6- 1¹⁰Spk⅝ ft 73°	clm10000+1	:29³ 1:02⁴ 1:33² 2:03²	3	4	44	44½°	78½	95¾	2:04³	14-1 (W.Rosebm)	PeterJayAdios, Brindanette, CamaroHanover	(evenly)
5-24¹⁰Haw¹ ft 60°	clm8000	1 :30 1:00⁵ 1:31³ 2:02	1	3	3	3³	35	35¾	2:03¹	18-1 (W.Rosebm)	MajorBlack, RealBlast, J.HazenAdios	(went evenly)
5-15 ⁸Haw¹ ft 56°	clm8000	1 :32¹ 1:04² 1:36² 2:06	8	8	7°	8¹¹	88	8¹¹	2:08¹	20-1 (J.Schue)	T.D.Blaze, Hopelmperial, RealBlast	(no threat)

GREEN 4 6-1 =	Driver—DARYL BUSSE, Gray-Red		Tr.—Da. Busse	(119-15-10-14—.212)	1973　8　0　1　1　$2,445

GOODARE
B g 1966, by Times Square—Little Goody—Good Time
Owner: O. Rursch, D. Kadel & G. Williams, Taylor Ridge, Joy, Ill., Davenport, Iowa

1973　8　0　1　1　$2,445
1972　37　7　7　3　$27,614　2:01² Brd⅝
Lifetime　$52,998　4, 2:01¹ (⅝)

6-29	¹Spk⅝ ft 76°	c:m8000=1	:30² 1:02 1:32⁴ 2:03⁴	7	7	78½	74¼	5³	4¾	2:04	22-1 (Da.Busse)	DaddioMac, LusciousLady, MightyLoyal	(closed some)
6-19	¹⁰Spk⅝ sy 78°	clm8000=1	:32² 1:05⁴ 1:36² 2:06⁴	4	8°	73¾°	65°	88	810	2:08⁴	9-2 (Da.Busse)	DazzlngDeana, JavelnJeanette, ShiwayPrcy	(parked mile)
6- 9	¹Spk⅝ ft 78°	clm8500+1	:30¹ 1:00² 1:32² 2:03	6	8	818	75	46½	64¼	2:03⁴	9-1 (Da.Busse)	TinyForbes, Eyreton, LovinLuLu	(slow start)
5- 8	⁶Haw¹ ft 60	clm8000 C	1 :31¹ 1:01³ 1:31⁴ 2:04	6	8	8	815	815	813	2:06³	2-1 (W.Moore)	GinnysGene, MisterAdios, BaronsStorm	(no chance)
4-28	¹Haw¹ ft 43°	clm8500	1 :31¹ 1:02² 1:33⁴ 2:04¹	7	9	7	74¾°	74¼	32¾	2:04⁴	7-2 (W.Moore)	WesternsJody, TerryJeansByrd, Goodare	(raced well)
4- 7	⁶Spk⅝ ft 39°	clm10000=1	:31³ 1:04³ 1:36 2:06²	3	4	4	54½	43	65¾	2:07³	*2-1 (W.Moore)	G.T.Winter, ForbesTime, SilverDiller	(rough trip)

BLACK YELLOW 8 7-2 =	Driver—JIM DOLBEE, Green-White-Red		Tr.—J. Dolbee	(127-21-16-22—.295)	1973　20　5　5　2　$16,961　2:04³ gd Haw¹

SILVER DILLER
Gr. m 1967, by Diller Hanover—Silver Note—Silver King
Owner: David D. Howard, North Vernon, Ind.

1973　20　5　5　2　$16,961　2:04³ gd Haw¹
1972　44　9　8　7　$20,235　2:03¹ Haw¹
Lifetime　$22,490　5, 2:03¹ (1)

7- 3	¹⁰Spk⅝ ft 78°	clm9600=1	:31¹ 1:04¹ 1:35 2:04⁴	2	3	1¹	1¹	1½	1¹	2:04⁴	*6-5 (J.Dolbee)	SilverDiller, JHazenAdios, AmigosGirl	(the best)
6-20	¹⁰Spk⅝ ft 76°	clm10800=1	:29⁴ 1:02 1:32¹ 2:03²	6	6	68	64¾	43½	32½	2:04	7-1 (J.Dolbee)	TinyForbes, CamdenFrisco, SilverDiller	(good try)
6-12	¹⁰Spk⅝ ft 65°	clm10800=1	:30² 1:02 1:33⁴ 2:04	4	3	44	32½	3²	22¼	2:04²	*9-5 (J.Dolbee)	SpeederPick, SilverDiller, LookawaySun	(evenly)
5-29	¹⁰Spk⅝ sy 49°	c:m12000+1	:31⁴ 1:06³ 1:38¹ 2:09⁴	9	1	11¼	1¾	2ⁿᵏ	51½	2:10¹	5-2 (J.Dolbee)	Ferdinand, MiMargarita, SpeederPick	(post hurt)
5-21	⁵Haw¹ ft 65°	c:m10800	1 :30 1:01 1:33² 2:03	6	8	8	85½	43½	22¼	2:03²	5-2 (J.Dolbee)	Brindanette, SilverDiller, MrThunderbyrd	(good stretch)
5-10	⁷Haw¹ ft 62°	clm12000	1 :30³ 1:00⁴ 1:31² 2:04	5	6	4°	32½°	2²	4²	2:04²	*8-5 (J.Dolbee)	GoldBerry, TeeniTime, ChiefsLittleStar	(even trip)

Out of the three contenders, Goodare would become the prime horse since his final time is faster than J. Hazen Adio's or Silver Diller's. The first advantage Goodare meets is the fact that his last half was paced faster than the other two contenders.

J. Hazen Adios	1:00 2/5
Goodare	1:00 1/5
Silver Diller	1:00 3/5

Goodare would not have an edge on class, but he is receiving a break in post position over his previous race. He left from the seven post last time out and moves in three slots tonight to the four hole. He gains a third advantage since he made a good move in the stretch by making up almost four lengths. There's no need to check out any further advantages, because Goodare has already fulfilled the required three. He becomes the final choice and wins by three parts of a length, returning $8.20.

TENTH RACE — 1 MILE
PACE. Claiming price $8,000 — 3 Year Olds and Upward
— Purse $3,700.

Time—:31²	1:03	1:33⁴	2:05¹								Mutuel Pool—$43,883
4. Goodare				4	5	56½	86	64	1¾	2:05¹	3-1 (Da.Busse)
3. Obknoxshus				3	1°	2	21½	2ʰᵈ	2ʰᵈ	2:05²	9-2 (J.Blevins)
8. Silver Diller				8	7	67°	43°	31½	31	2:05²	*2-1 (J.Dolbee)
2. Greenberg O'Brien				2	3°	1²	12½	1ʰᵈ	41½	2:05³	7-1 (G.Kramer)
9. Shiaway Percy				9	9	99½	75½°	53½	52¾	2:05³	17-1 (S.Banks)
7. Crawdad				7	2	34	33	42½	62¼	2:05³	8-1 (J.Willis)
1. J. Hazen Adios				1	4	45½	54	75	73¼	2:05⁴	5-1 (C.PorcelliJr)
6. Danella				6	8	88½°	64½°	87	87¼	2:06³	10-1 (J.Grvngoed)
5. Flat Pass				5	6	78	97	910	98½	2:07	23-1 (W.Short)

Mutuels—(4) 8.20 5.20 4.20—(3) 8.20 5.00—(8) 2.60

Next, we'll consider a $15,000 claimer which consists of four contenders. The race took place at the Maywood twice around on August 25. The 2:01 1/5 turned in by Kiwi Chief is the fastest final time of the four contenders, so he becomes the prime horse. The three horses facing him are all previous winners. Kiwi Chief becomes a final choice by fulfilling the first three advantages. His last half is the fastest of the bunch. (I'll let you calculate this one.) The last time out, he was in for a $15,000 tag, a higher class level than the other three. He's moving in from the six post to the rail, which

RED 1 4-1	Driver—JIM CURRAN, Gray-Gold		Tr.—R. Farrington	(125-17-25-15—.287)	1973　22　2　3　5　$15,713　2:05² Spk⅝

KIWI CHIEF
B g 1963, by Meadow Chief—Kiwi Princess—Van Dieman
Owners: Farrington Sta., Inc.-Arnold Cattle Co., Inc.; R'hw'd, Ohio, Chicago, Ill.

1973　22　2　3　5　$15,713　2:05² Spk⅝
1972　17　0　4　5　$6,394
Lifetime　$24,837　8, 2:03⁴ (1)

8-18	⁷May ft 77°	§clm15000	1 :30³ 1:01 1:31 2:00⁴	6	1°	22	33½	22¾	31½	2:01¹	4-1 (J.Curran)	ReMark, MonasByrd, KiwiChief	(parked early)
8-13	¹⁰May ft 77°	§clm14000	1 :29 1:00 1:31⁴ 2:01³	6	7	76½°	42°	32½x2ⁿᵏ	2:01³	9-1 (J.Curran)	MonasByrd, Kiw'Chief, WinningBoy	(break costly)
8- 4	⁷May ft 73°	§clm14000	1 :30³ 1:02¹ 1:33 2:02⁴	1	3	42¼	53	52¼	41¼	2:03	6-1 (J.Curran)	Mt.AiryBill, WinningBoy, Mona'sByrd	(raced well)
7-27	⁶May sy 79°	clm15000	1 :33 1:05³ 1:38⁴ 2:10	3	6	77½	74½°	77½	76¾	2:11²	7-2 (J.Curran)	Edstime, KeystoneStormy, JimBlackstone	(no chance)
7-17	⁸Spk⅝ ft 80°	clm14000=1	:30 1:02² 1:32² 2:02	4	3	44	74	43½	22¼	2:02²	5-1 (J.Curran)	Edstime, KiwiChief, WinningBoy	(good effort)
7- 4	⁹Spk⅝ ft 82°	clm14000=1	:31 1:03⁴ 1:33² 2:03³	2	3	33½	43½	55	31¼	2:03⁴	2-1 (J.Curran)	HopeImperial, MeadowClansie, KiwiChief	(closed well)

WHITE 2 3-1	Driver—ROBERT KNOX, Gold-Brown		Tr.—R. Knox	(66-5-14-10—.244)	1973　9　4　1　1　$10,143　2:01³ May

‡SPEEDER PICK
Ch h 1963, by Gene Abbe—Josedale Counterwin—Josedale Counterpoint
Owner: Robert Knox, Homewood, Ill.

1973　9　4　1　1　$10,143　2:01³ May
1972　32　4　2　5　$13,721　2:04³ May
Lifetime　$100,499　4, 2:01 (⅝)

8-15	⁸May ft 75°	§‡clm12000	1 :30¹ 1:02¹ 1:33¹ 2:03⁴	5	5	43½°	31°	1¹	1¾	2:03⁴	*1-1 (R.Knox)	SpeederPick, LusciousLdy, RlphAmrtzr	(3-wide for lead)
8- 7	⁸May ft 81°	‡clm14000	1 :29 :59² 1:31² 2:01³	2	3	3½	21½°	2½	11¼	2:01³	3-1 (R.Knox)	SpeederPick, ColMoffitt, Knoxella	(good trip)
7-26	⁸May ft 73°	‡clm9000	1 :29³ 1:01⁴ 1:33 2:05	5	6	74¾	83¾	53	12¼	2:05	9-2 (R.Knox)	SpdrPck, IdlwhlsEarl, ArmbroInstp	(pwrfl 5-wide move)
7-18	¹⁰Spk⅝ ft 82°	‡clm9000=1	:29⁴ 1:01⁴ 1:33² 2:02⁴	2	5	65½	55°	22½	2½	2:03	7-2 (R.Knox)	Amigo'sGirl, SpeederPick, HarkWay	(good close)
7- 7	²Spk⅝ ft 90°	‡clm10000=1	:30¹ 1:03¹ 1:32² 2:02⁴	6	7	75¾°	87	66½	53¾	2:03³	11-1 (R.Knox)	TmelyJoy, TecklaAdiosB, BranchDanPrince	(closed some)
6-29	³Spk⅝ ft 76°	‡clm10000=1	:30 1:01⁴ 1:32³ 2:02³	4	5	55½	53½°	66	44¾	2:03³	4-1 (R.Knox)	ValiantSampson, DodieDee, JubileeKnight	(went evenly)

BLUE 3 5-1

Driver—NELSON WILLIS, Maroon-Gray-White   Tr.—J. Turner   (67-5-5-8—.154)   1973   29   6   3   3 $19,195   2:00² May

VALIANT SAMPSON   B h 1967, by Sampson Direct—Susan Carmel—Adios Paul   1972   36   5   9   5 $6,764   2:05³ Was¹

Owner: John Turner, Downers Grove, Ill.   Lifetime $11,330   5, 2:05³ (1)

8-18	¹¹May ft 77°	§clm12000 C	1	:31	1:00³	1:31²	2:01²	7	2°	1¹	1¹	1²	1¹¼	2:01²	*4-5 (J.Curran)	ValiantSampson, EdgewoodKeene, Winter (the best)

(Race lines:)

- 8-18 ¹¹May ft 77° §clm12000 C 1 :31 1:00³ 1:31² 2:01² 7 2° 1¹ 1¹ 1² 1¹¼ 2:01² *4-5 (J.Curran) — ValiantSampson, EdgewoodKeene, Winter (the best)
- 8-10 ¹⁰May ft 71° §clm11000 1 :30¹ :59⁴ 1:30³ 2:00² 5 2° 1² 1²¼ 1³ 1²¾ 2:00² 4-1 (J.Curran) — ValantSmpsn, EdgwdKeen, DltaDirct (new lifetime mark)
- 7-30 ⁹May ft 77° clm11000 1 :30³ 1:02 1:33¹ 2:05 5 6 6⁵ 7⁴ 8⁵¾ 4¹¾ 2:05² 6-1 (J.Curran) — BillyClipper, TinyForbes, Pleasem (closed some)
- 7-23 ⁸Spk⅝ ft 81° clm11000—1 :29⁴ 1:01¹ 1:32¹ 2:02¹ 3 5 5⁵½ 5³½° 4¹¼ 5¹¼ 2:02² 7-2 (J.Curran) — Tarline, MissGertie, TinyForbes (raced well)
- 7- 7 ¹⁰Spk⅝ ft 90° clm12500+1 :30² 1:01² 1:31⁴ 2:02² 9 9 9⁶¼ 8⁶ 7¹⁰ 6³¾ 2:03¹ 8-1 (J.Curran) — WinningBoy, SharpStar, Slasham (closed some)
- 6-29 ³Spk⅝ ft 76° clm10000 C=1 :30 1:01⁴ 1:32³ 2:02³ 1 2 2¹½ 2¹½ 1³ 1³¼ 2:02³ *5-2 (S.Banks) — ValiantSampson, DodieDee, JubileeKnight (strong effort)

GREEN 4 8-1

Driver—EUGENE WASZAK, White-Blue-Gold   Tr.—E. Waszak   (12-3-1-2—.352)   1973   20   1   2   7 $9,703   2:03¹ May

D's SCOTTY COUNSEL   B g 1968, by Hayes Counsel—Scottys Vision—Scotch Widower   1972   45   5   13   5 $25,256   2:03 Haw¹

Owner: Tony Sabino & Eugene Waszak, Chicago, Ill.   Lifetime $37,725   4, 2:03 (1)

- 8-17 ³May ft 76° §clm13000 1 :30⁴ 1:01² 1:32¹ 2:03¹ 2 1 2ʰᵈ 1¾ 1ⁿᵏ 1ⁿᵏ 2:03¹ 5-1 (E.Waszak) — DsScottyCounsel, RichReveller, ProntoJim (hung tough)
- 8-13 ¹⁰May ft 77° §clm14000 1 :29 1:00 1:31⁴ 2:01³ 7 5° 3³¼° 3²° 5⁹½ 6¹⁴ 2:04² 21-1 (E.Waszak) — MonasByrd, K'w'Chief, WinningBoy (parked mile)
- 8- 7 ⁹May ft 81° clm13000 1 :30 1:01² 1:32 2:03² 4 5 5⁴° 5²½° 5² 3½ 2:03³ 9-1 (E.Waszak) — Tarline, FrontierAnn, DsScottyCounsel (big race)
- 7-31 ⁵May ft 71° clm16000 1 :31 1:03 1:34 2:04³ 7 2° 1ʰᵈ° 8⁵½ 8⁶½ 7⁶½ 2:06 32-1 (E.Waszak) — AlexWejover, SteadyBlaze, PalMyerFlite (tired badly)
- 7-21 ⁴Spk⅝ ft 75° clm14000—1 :30³ 1:01⁴ 1:32¹ 2:01³ 5 2 3²½ 4³¼ 4³ 3⁴ 2:02² 9-1 (E.Waszak) — SharpStar, CashTop, D'sScottyCounsel (evenly)
- 7-16 ⁸Spk⅝ ft 76° clm16000+1 :30 1:00 1:30² 2:00⁴ 9 9 9¹³ 8⁸° 8⁹ 7⁹ 2:02³ 11-1 (E.Waszak) — FloridaFlash, MeadowClansie, Empy (too much speed)

---

rounds out the three. He also has the very capable Jim Curran in the sulky for a fourth advantage, but there's no need to pursue any further ones, since he already has the required three. Although Kiwi Chief wasn't the morningline favorite, he won as expected, returning a modest $6.00 as the people's choice.

Advantage ratings do not take very long to master. After you work with them for an hour or two, you'll probably be picking the final choice out of the race in less than a minute. When advantage ratings do not apply, the final choice is found by numerical speed ratings. We'll deal with these next.

NINTH RACE — 1 MILE
PACE. Claiming price $15,000 — Purse $4,300.

Time—:31   1:01⁴   1:31   2:01⁴   Mutuel Pool—$97,895

1. Kiwi Chief	1	2	2¹½	2⁴½	2²½	1ⁿᵏ	2:01⁴	*2-1 (J.Curran)
3. Valiant Sampson	3	1	1¹½	1⁴½	1²½	2ⁿᵏ	2:01⁴	5-2 (N.Willis)
2. Speeder Pick	2	3	3³	3⁶½	3⁴½	3²	2:02¹	7-2 (R.Knox)
4. D's Scotty Counsel	4	5	5⁵	4⁸½	4⁶½	4³	2:02²	21-1 (E.Waszak)
6. Hope Imperial	6	8	6⁶°	5¹¹	5⁷½	5⁴¼	2:02³	9-2 (J.Dolbee)
7. Cash Top	7	4°	4⁴½°	6¹²	6⁹½	6⁶	2:03	6-1 (Da.Busse)
8. Jim Blackstone	8	7°	8⁹½	7¹⁴	7¹²	7⁹¼	2:03³	60-1 (K.Heeney)
5. Never Say Die A	5	6	7⁷½	8¹⁵	8¹⁶	8¹⁵	2:04⁴	25-1 (W.Paisley)

Mutuels—(1) 6.00 3.40 2.60—(3) 4.20 2.80—(2) 3.00

NUMERICAL SPEED RATINGS

Numerical speed ratings are based upon the first five factors that were found in advantage ratings. The last three factors have been eliminated because they have the least effect upon what these ratings are based on—SPEED.

The idea behind the numerical speed ratings is to locate the horse who ran the fastest last half in relation to the fastest final time. These two factors are the base of the rating, while class, post position, and parked outs are used for adjustments.

The base rating is a combination of the horse's final time and his last half. This is the horse's so-called "pure speed." Each 1/5 of a second over two minutes in the final time is added together with each 1/5 of a second over one minute in the last half. For example:

Final Time - 2:04⁴	24
Last Half - 1:02¹	+11
Base Rating	35

The horse ran 4 4/5 seconds over two minutes. Since each full second is equal to 5/5, all that was needed to do was multiply 4 by 5 and add on the fraction, which comes to 24. No problem, right? The same was done for the last half, which came to 11, and the two were then added together for a base rating of 35.

The class factor is then added or subtracted to the base rating accordingly. Each class fluctuation equals 2 points. Up in class—add 2 points. Same class—no change. Down in class—subtract 2 points.

If the horse is receiving a better post position than he had in his contending race, 1/2 point is subtracted for every post he moves in. If he's moving out, 1/2 point is added on for every post.

If the horse was parked out for two turns in his contending race, then 2 points are subtracted. If three turns, 4 points are subtracted.

Here is how the numerical speed ratings look when put on a chart. The information is taken off the past performance for the pacer Crystal E., who's entered in a $7,000 claiming race.

RED & YELLOW **8** 8-1

Driver—ROBERT KNOX, Gold-Brown Tr.—R. Knox (63-5-11-10—.229)

CRYSTAL E. Blk g 1967, by Crystal Byrd—Crystal Worthy—Worthy Boy
Owner: Priscilla Knox and Robert Rosenbury, Homewood, Ill, Rochester, Ind.

1973	14	2	1	2	\$5,710 2:04^4 Spk⅝
1972	17	1	5	1	\$6,598 2:05^1 May
Lifetime					\$6,598 5, 2:05^1

8-14 ^{7}May ft 70°	clm7000 1	:30^4	1:02^1	1:33^4	2:05^3	3	5	5^4°	3^{2½}°	2½	2½	2:05^4	*2-1 (R.Knox)	SilentTona, CrystalE, BaronsStorm	(3-wide briefly)
8- 4 ^{1}May ft 77°	clm7000 1	:30^3	1:01^1	1:32^4	2:03^2	4	1°	2½	1½	1^{1½}	3^{4¼}	2:04^1	5-1 (R.Knox)	LakewoodQuick, RedsShadow, CrystalE	(tired)
7-27 ^{4}May sy 79°	clm7000 1	:32^4	1:06^1	1:37^1	2:09^1	4	5	3^{6½}°	3^{2½}°	2^4°	3^{3¾}	2:10	3-1 (R.Knox)	BuddyTime, GoranHanover, CrystalE	(tough trip)
7-16 ^{4}Spk⅝ ft 76°	clm6000+1	:31^1	1:03^2	1:34^1	2:04^4	4	2	2^{1½}	2^{1¼}	1½	1^{1¾}	2:04^4	9-1 (R.Knox)	CrystalE, FlyingFool, RushStreetBoss	(in winning form)
7- 3 ^{1}Spk⅝ ft 78°	clm5000=1	:31	1:03^2	1:34^1	2:04^4	3	1°	1^{1½}	1^2	1^{1½}	1¾	2:04^4	24-1 (R.Knox)	CrystalE, CrystalKlata, RushStreetBoss	(wire to wire)
6-18 ^{1}Spk⅝ ft 77°	clm5000=1	:30^3	1:03^3	1:35	2:05^1	6	5	5^5	5^{3½}°	6^{4½}	8^{8½}	2:07	35-1 (R.Knox)	RoyDares, Cindilla, NevadasSonA	(mild bid ¾)

Horse	Final Time	Last Half	Base Rating	Class		P.P.		Park		Adj. Final Rating
Crystal E	29	14	43	-	43	+2½	45½	-2	43½	43½

Crystal E.'s adjusted final rating is 43½. Since these are speed ratings, you can probably already tell that the lower the rating, the faster the horse. Consequently, the contender who has the lowest adjusted speed rating should be at least one full point lower than the next closest contender, rather than 1/2 point. If not, it's best to pass the race.

We'll try the numerical speed ratings out on two races. First, a claiming race for \$17,500 that took place at Sportsman's Park on the Fourth of July.

Ski Slope doesn't require any adjustments, so his base rating of 16 is the same as his adjusted final rating.

Jefferson gets adjustments in the post position and parked out columns. His moving out on post, which adds on 1/2 point. He was parked for two turns so 2 points are then subtracted. His adjusted final rating comes out to 8½.

Gus Minbar's last half was under one minute so it was subtracted from the final time rather than

BLACK **5** 7-2 =

Driver—JIM DENNIS, Green-White Tr.—J. Dennis (102-25-21-7—.382)

SKI SLOPE B g 1966, by Newport Admiral—Starlight Scott—Hoot Mon
Owner: Morris & Victor Zeinfeld, Lincolnwood, Maywood, Ill.

1973	23	2	7	2	\$19,066 2:02^3 Spk⅝
1972	25	4	3	5	\$17,876 2:04 Spk⅝
Lifetime					\$45,990 4, 2:02^1 (1)

6-26 ^{9}Spk⅝ ft 76°	clm17500=1	:29^4	1:02	1:32^2	2:02^3	5	4°	1^{1½}	1^{1½}	1^2	1^{2¾}	2:02^3	2 1 (J.Dennis)	SkiSlope, GusMinbar, AlexWejover	(in good form)
6-20 ^{9}Spk⅝ ft 76°	clm17000=1	:29^1	1:00^3	1:31^1	2:01^4	9	6	8^{5½}°	6^{3¼}°im	8^{9½}	7^{7½}p6	2:03^2	5-1 (J.Dennis)	MoonshotHnvr, HunnertBucks, PrncssJdth	(road trouble)
6-15 ^{5}Spk⅝ ft 79°	clm17000=1	:30	1:00^4	1:31^2	2:01	2	1	2^{1½}	3^{1½}	2^2	2^{nk}	2:01	4-1 (J.Dennis)	Airfare, SkiSlope, TopallAdios	(just missed)
6- 6 ^{8}Spk⅝ ft 75°	clm17000 C--1	:30^2	1:02^1	1:31^4	2:01	3	3	3^3	5^3	6^6	6^{5¼}	2:02	4-1 (G.Conley)	JetCoe, MoonshotHanover, Airfare	(well placed early)
5-30 ^{7}Spk⅝ ft 59°	clm18000+1	:29^4	1:02	1:32^3	2:02^1	4	2	2^1	2^1	4^{2½}	2^{1¼}	2:02^2	6-1 (G.Conley)	TopallAdios, SkiSlope, AlexWejover	(needed room)
5-23 ^{9}Haw^1 ft 61°	clm17000 1	:29^4	1:00^1	1:31^3	2:01^4	1	2	4	6^3	6^5	2^{2¼}	2:02^1	12-1 (G.Conley)	StrongByrd, SkiSlope, TopallAdios	(closed some)

GREEN & WHITE **7** 8-1 =

Driver—GENE VALLANDINGHAM, Red-White-Blue Tr.—R. Young (⟳ 6-9-4—.190)

JEFFERSON Br g 1967, by Race Time—Reggie M.—Direct Brewer
Owner: Richard A. Young, Worth, Ill.

1973	28	3	4	7	\$25,528 2:03^4 Spk⅝
1972	33	6	8	1	\$23,066 2:04^1 Was^1
Lifetime					\$49,270 4, 2:03^2 (1)

6-29 ^{4}Spk⅝ ft 76°	clm18000=1	:29^3	1:00^1	1:30^4	2:01^2	6	4	5^{4½}°	1½°	1^{hd}	5^{1¼}	2:01^3	12-1 (GVllndnghm)	RoyalGo, LincolnsBid, GoodTimeLad	(good effort
6-26 ^{9}Spk⅝ ft 76°	clm17500+1	:29^4	1:02	1:32^2	2:02^3	7	8	8^{8½}	9^7	6^6	7^{4½}	2:03^3	6-1 (B.Shuter)	SkiSlope, GusMinbar, AlexWejover	(slow leaving
6-20 ^{9}Spk⅝ ft 76°	clm16000=1	:29^1	1:00^3	1:31^1	2:01^4	2	4	5^{3¾}	7^4°	4^3	1^{ns}p7	2:01^4	6-1 (B.Shuter)	MoonshotHnvr, HunnertBucks, PrncssJdth	(disqualified
6-15 ^{5}Spk⅝ ft 79°	clm17000−1	:30	1:00^4	1:31^2	2:01	8	8°	5^5°	2^1°	5^4	7^{4½}	2:02	10-1 (B.Shuter)	Airfare, SkiSlope, TopallAdios	(tired badly
6- 6 ^{8}Spk⅝ ft 75°	clm18000=1	:30^2	1:02^1	1:31^4	2:01	7	7	7^{6½}	6^4°	5^5	5^{4¼}	2:01^4	6-1 (B.Shuter)	JetCoe, MoonshotHanover, Airfare	(evenly
5-30 ^{7}Spk⅝ ft 59°	clm18000−1	:29^4	1:02	1:32^3	2:02^1	6	7	7^8	8^7	8^{5½}	5^{1¼}	2:02^2	5 1 (B.Shuter)	TopallAdios, SkiSlope, AlexWejover	(raced well

BLACK & YELLOW **8** 10-1 =

Driver—JOE VOLLARO, Blue-Green- Tr.—J. Vollaro (8-0-1-0—.069)

GUS MINBAR B g 1968, by Greentree Adios—Tilly's Dream—Knight Dream
Vollaro, Pavelka, Seldeen & Shanberg, Inglewood, Van Nuys, Artesia, Long Beach, Cal.

1973	14	1	1	0	\$5,637 2:02^1 L.A⅝
1972	38	6	5	8	\$31,553 1:59^4 Hol^1
Lifetime					\$34,106 4, 1:59^4 (1)

6-26 ^{9}Spk⅝ ft 76°	clm17500=1	:29^4	1:02	1:32^2	2:02^3	1	6	6^{7½}	6^5	5^{5½}	2^{2¾}	2:03^1	32-1 (J.Vollaro)	SkiSlope, GusMinbar, AlexWejover	(closed some
6-15 ^{5}Spk⅝ ft 79°	clm17000−1	:30	1:00^4	1:31^2	2:01	7	9	9^{11}	8^6°	9^{11}	9^{9¾}	2:03	24-1 (J.Dolbee)	Airfare, SkiSlope, TopallAdios	(dull effort
6- 6 ^{8}Spk⅝ ft 75°	clm18000=1	:30^2	1:02^1	1:31^4	2:01	9	9	9^{11}	9^{11}	9^{14}	9^{13}	2:03^3	56-1 (J.Vollaro)	JetCoe, MoonshotHanover, Airfare	(followed
5-30 ^{7}Spk⅝ ft 59°	clm18000=1	:29^4	1:02	1:32^3	2:02^1	2	4	4^4	6^{4½}	7^5	8^3	2:02^4	13-1 (J.Vollaro)	TopallAdios, SkiSlope, AlexWejover	(raced well
5-25 ^{9}Haw^1 ft 58°	clm18000 1	:30^4	1:01^4	1:32^3	2:03^1	5	7	6°	4^{1½}°	7^{3½}	7^{2¾}	2:03^4	9-2 (J.Vollaro)	RoyalGo-StarGo^{dh}, WendysTed	(went evenly
5-18 ^{9}Haw^1 ft 66°	clm21000 1	:31^1	1:01^4	1:31^3	2:01^3	4	6	7	8^{5¼}	7^{5½}	5^{4¼}	2:02^2	20-1 (J.Vollaro)	BgDaddysShadw, PrfectWeapn, RomnLeadr	(went evnly

Horse	Final Time	Last Half	Base Rating	Class		P.P.		Park		Adj. Final Rating
Ski Slope	13	3	16	-	16	-	16	-	16	16
Jefferson	8	2	10	-	10	+½	10½	-2	8½	8½
Gus Minbar	16	-2	14	-	14	+3½	17½	-	17½	17½

added on. His only adjustment thereafter is in the post position column. Since he's going from the rail to the eight post, 3½ points are added. His adjusted final rating is 17½.

The final choice would become Jefferson, since he has far and away the best rating. He beat the 8-5 favorite, Ski Slope, by going wire to wire for an easy victory. He returned $11.60 in the win slot.

SEVENTH RACE — 1 MILE
PACE. Claiming price $17,500 — 3 Year Olds and Upward — Purse $5,200.

Time—:29^1 1:01^4 1:30^4 2:01^2 Mutuel Pool—$96,224

7. Jefferson	7	1°	1 1¼	1 1¾	1 6	1 1½	2:01^2	9-2	(GVllndnghm)
4. Ajax	4	5	6 4½	7 6¾°	5 7¼	2 1¼	2:01^3	6-1	(H.Burright)
5. Ski Slope	5	6	5 3½°	4 3¾	4 7	3 2½	2:02	*8-5	(J.Dennis)
2. Florida Flash	2	3	3 2¼°	2 1¾°	2 6	4 2½	2:02	11-1	(C.Clickner)
1. Noble Skipper	1	4	4 3¼	6 6¼	6 8	5 2¾	2:02	6-1	(W.Paisley)
8. Gus Minbar	8	9	8 5½	9 7¾	8 11	6 6¼	2:02^3	25-1	(J.Vollaro)
9. Moonshot Hanover	9	7	7 4½°	5 5¼°	7 10	7 7½	2:03	21-1	(J.Graham)
3. Alex Wejover	3	2	2 1¼	3 2¼	3 7	8 7½	2:03	10-1	(T.Ratchford)
6. Near Chief	6	8	9 7	8 7¼°	9 13	9 9¾	2:03^2	6-1	(Da.Busse)

Ajax claimed for $17,500 by George LeRoy, trainer—J. Dennis.
Ski Slope claimed for $17,500 by J. Caruso, S Blumberg and L. Airdo, trainer—A. G. Shaw.
Mutuels—(7) 11.60 6.20 3.60—(4) 7.60 4.00—(5) 2.60

Next, we'll take on a $7,000 claimer that was contested at Maywood on August 24. In this race, however, we'll do it a little differently.

GREEN **4** 3-1	Driver—JIM CURRAN, Gray-Gold								Tr.—C. Goins			(122-17-24-14—.287)			1973 21 2 4 2 $7,552 2:03^1 May			
	BOURBON CHIMES	B g 1965, by Ichabod Crain—Geneva Hal—Major Hal													1972 24 4 5 3 $13,652 2:05^2 May			
		Owner: Charles Goins, Lessee, Midlothian, Ill.													Lifetime $40,212 4, 2:01^3 (⅝)			
	8-16 ^{6}May ft 74°	§clm6000	1	:30^2 1:00^2 1:31^2 2:03^3	1	1	1 1	1 2½	1 3	1 5	2:03^3	*3-5	(J.MarshJr)		BourbnChimes, FlashHarry, PaulinesBoy	(much the best)		
	8- 8 ^{2}Mayft 82°	§clm5000	1	:29^1 1:01^1 1:32 2:03^1	3	1	1 2½	1 4	1 4½	1 6¾	2:03^1	2-1	(J.MarshJr)		BourbonChimes, FairRowByrd, Chickadee	(big win)		
	7-25 ^{7}May ft 74°	clm5000	1	:30 1:01^3 1:33^2 2:06	4	5	5 3½	4 1½°	5 4½	4 2	2:06^2	*3-2	(J.Curran)		MightyNalim-QuickGal^{dh}, CombatBoots	(mild bid)		
	7-10 ^{6}Spk⅝ ft 76°	clm6000=1		:31^3 1:03^3 1:34^2 2:05	8	9	8 6½°	5 3°	4 6	4 5¾	2:06^1	20-1	(D.Pletcher)		Zhivago, BigDavid, LocalLie	(¾ bid, hung)		
	6-28 ^{4}Spk⅝ ft 68°	clm6000=1		:30^3 1:02 1:32^4 2:04	7	3°	1½	1 nk	1 nk	7 5¼	2:05	9-1	(D.Pletcher)		MoeWestern, MajesticDream, Armbrolvy	(used early)		
	6-19 ^{5}Spk⅝ ft 78°	clm6000=1		:30^2 1:01^3 1:33^4 2:04^1	7	4°	3 2°	3 1°	7 7	8 11	2:06^2	*5-2	(W.Paisley)		LincolnValentine, MjstcDrm, WillieGrnda	(never saw rail)		
BLACK **5** 5-1	Driver—GENE VALLANDINGHAM, Red-White-Blue								Tr.—J. Wolfe			(74-16-11-6—.326)			1973 18 2 4 2 $9,309 2:04 Spk⅝			
	SAPPHIRE GLOW	Blk m 1964, by Superbole—Gold Glow—Blue Gamble													1972 13 4 0 0 $5,833 2:04^2 Was^1			
		Owner: John Wolfe, Calumet City, Ill.													Lifetime $12,067 8, 2:04^2 (1)			
	8-15 ^{4}May ft 75°	§clm8400	1	:31 1:02^4 1:33^4 2:04^4	1	5	4 3¼	2 nk°	1 nk	1 1¾	2:04^4	*2-1	(GVllndnghm)		SapphireGlow, PeppersAce, WesTee	(good mile)		
	8- 4 ^{1}May ft 77°	clm8400	1	:30^3 1:01^1 1:32^4 2:03^2	6	3°	1½°	2½°	4 3½	6 10	2:05^2	13-1	(GVllndnghm)		LakewoodQuick, ReidsShadow, CrystalE	(parked mile)		
	7-27 ^{2}May ft 79°	clm7200 C	1	:31 1:01^3 1:34 2:06^3	1	3	6 4½	7 4	7 4	7 3	2:07^1	5-2	(J.Curran)		HastiDoc, AnniversaryBabe, MajesticLayne	(blocked)		
	7-18 ^{5}Spk⅝ ft 82°	clm7200=1		:30^1 1:03^1 1:34^3 2:05	4	2	2 1¼	2 nk°	1½	2 2¼	2:05^2	4-1	(J.Curran)		Armbrolvy, SapphireGlow, SeattleCindy	(tired stretch)		
	7- 5 ^{5}Spk⅝ ft 75°	clm7200+1		:29^3 1:00^4 1:33 2:04	1	4	4 3	1½	2 nk	3 1¼	2:04^1	*7-5	(J.Curran)		DameFontane, Pellaire, SapphireGlow	(gd move, hung)		
	6-27 ^{2}Spk⅝ ft 76°	FMclm6000—1		:29^2 1:01 1:33^1 2:04^3	9	7	7 8	7 5°	3 2½	3½	2:04^4	5-1	(J.Curran)		FairyJo, DionnaDiller, SapphireGlow	(good effort)		

Horse	*Final Time*	*Last Half*	*Base Rating*	*Class*	*P.P.*	*Park*	*Adj. Final Rating*
Bourbon Chimes							37½
Sapphire Glow							36

I have provided only the adjusted final ratings for the two horses. It might be a good idea to pick up the nearest pencil and put in the figures yourself to see if you come out with the same final ratings. Be careful though, Sapphire Glow is a mare, so she's entered for $8,400.

The final choice would be Sapphire Glow with a 36, bettering Bourbon Chimes' 37½. (You did pencil in the figures, didn't you?) She wore down Bourbon Chimes in the stretch and drew out to settle the issue. She returned $13.00 to win.

FOURTH RACE — 1 MILE
PACE. Claiming price $7,000 — Purse $3,200.

Time—:30^2 1:00^4 1:32^3 2:04 Mutuel Pool—$54,251

5. Sapphire Glow	5	6	5 8½°	2 1°	1½	1 4½	2:04	5-1	(GVllndnghm)
4. Bourbon Chimes	4	1°	1 5	1 1	2½	2 4½	2:05	*4-5	(J.Curran)
1. Cheslind	1	3	2 5	3 2	4 2½	3 5¾	2:05^1	3-1	(W.Paisley)
2. Ginny's B. Abbe	2	4	3 7°	5 3½	5 4½	4 8¾	2:05^4	29-1	(S.Banks)
6. Wes Tee	6	7	7 12	6 9½	6 9½	5 10	2:06	20-1	(J.Ackerman)
7. Hang Over	7	5°	8 16	7 12	7 12	6 11	2:06^1	46-1	(H.Fabert)
8. Faithful Boy	8	8	6 10°	4 3°	3 2x	7 11	2:06^1	6-1	(J.MarshJr)
3. Jimson	3	2°	4 7½x	8 19	8 22	8 dis		42-1	(L.Banks)

Mutuels—(5) 13.00 3.60 2.80—(4) 2.60 2.20—(1) 2.60

It doesn't take a mathematical genius to do numerical speed ratings. You'll find, with a little practice, that you can add them up in your head and pencil in the final rating next to the horse's name in the program.

Numerical speed ratings are used much more frequently than advantage ratings. But advantage ratings should always take priority over the speed ratings if the race calls for it. Rarely do the two rating systems differ on the final choice, but when they do, you'll find that advantage ratings are correct much more often.

In the next chapter, things won't be so easy. Five races will be handicapped from top to bottom. The non-contenders will be eliminated, the contenders will be chosen, and the final choice will be selected.

CHAPTER 7

Five Playable Races

We have now reached a point where we can put to work the principles set forth in the first six chapters. We will handicap five races, step by step, that are generally representative of races found on an average night's card. Our handicapping endeavors will be aimed at three claiming races and two conditioned events. Since numerical speed ratings are applicable to the great majority of races, they will be used to determine the final choice in four of the five races. Advantage ratings will be used on the other race, but let's not forget that advantage ratings always take priority over numerical speed ratings.

So far, we've studied only partial races when determining if a horse was a contender, non-contender, or an unratable contender. Those horses were specifically chosen because their past performances were able to set a good pattern for future situations. In the last chapter, when we made our final choice, the contenders were already picked out of the race and ready to be rated. So up to now, things have been pretty easy.

The races we'll look at will be neither partial nor easy. The five will be handicapped from top to bottom and nothing whatsoever will be ignored. Horses will be chosen contenders strictly on their racing merits so long as they comply with the class-form relationship. Horses will be eliminated as contenders when they appear to be off form or placed improperly and dealt with accordingly.

The first race we'll work on is a $5,000 claimer that was contested at Sportsman's Park on July 17. The first order of business in each race will be to evaluate each horse.

ONE MILE PACE	FOURTH RACE	Purse $3,000

CLAIMING. Claiming price $5,000 — 3 Year Olds and Upward. Byrd Farr, Color Me Lee, Silver Creek Tilly, Dandy Choice and Julie Way in for $6,000, all others $5,000.

PLEASE ASK FOR HORSE BY PROGRAM NUMBER

	Date	Trk Cond Temp	Class	Dist	1/4	1/2	3/4	Winner's Time	PP	1/4	1/2	3/4	Str	Fin	Ind.Time	Odds	Driver	First	Second	Third		Comment
	Driver—STANLEY BANKS, White-Purple							**Tr.—K. Vander Schaaf**					(157-17-25-17—.233)					1973	14 1 1 1	$3,744 2:07³ Spk⅝		
RED	**BYRD FARR**	B g 1969, by Byrd Whitney—Fancy Pants—Paul MacPherson																1972	8 1 0 1	$2,758 2:10² Spk⅝		
1		Owner: Ken Vander Schaaf, Sandwich, Ill.																Lifetime		$2,938 3, 2:10² (⅝)		
	7- 9	⁴Spk⅝ ft 92°	clm6000=1	:31	1:02²	1:34	2:04⁴		6	3	3⁴½	5⁴½	4⁶½	6¹¹	2:07	8-1	(S.Banks)	SiouxTime, BartByrd, HarkerFreight			(parked briefly)
6-1	6-22	¹Spk⅝ ft 76°	clm6000=1	:31¹	1:03²	1:34³	2:05³		8	1	2¹½	4³½	3³½	4²¾	2:06¹	26-1	(S.Banks)	Papa, SweepUp, MissTrojan			(good effort)
=	6- 8	¹Spk⅝ ft 85°	clm6000=1	:30¹	1:03¹	1:35	2:05³		6	9	8⁵½	5³°	5³½	5⁵½	2:06⁴	9-2	(S.Banks)	IrishDuane, GrawInHnovr, RushStreetBoss			(went evenly)
	5-29	⁴Spk⅝ gd 49°	clm6000=1	:32	1:06²	1:38¹	2:09⁴		4	5	7⁶	5⁴°	4²½	4²¾	2:10²	5-1	(S.Banks)	DunksBoy, Papa, BomberG.			(raced well)
	5-14	²Haw¹ ft 47°	clm7200	1	:31	1:02²	1:33⁴	2:05	4	2	2	2¹	6⁸½	6¹⁵	2:08	8-1	(S.Banks)	SonnyFarvel, MajesticLayne, R.MagicPride		(tired badly)
	4-30	⁴Haw¹ sy 50°	clm8400	1	:31	1:03¹	1:35²	2:06⁴	9	8	8	7⁷¼	7¹¹	7¹⁴	2:09³	29-1	(S.Banks)	RioDean, ClemK, McChancey		(no factor)

61

BLUE **2** 7-2 +

Driver—JIM DENNIS, Green-White Tr.—J. Dennis (144-32-27-10—.350)

1973 5 2 0 0 $2,654 2:05¹ Spk⅝
1972 27 2 1 2 $4,408 2:10² Was¹
Lifetime $26,407 5, 2:02³ (1)

ADIO GOOSE

B g 1965, by Adioway—Shirley Goose—Goose Bay
Owner: Rudolph Gurrola, Elgin, Ill.

7- 5 ¹Spk⅝ ft 75° clm3500=1 :29³ 1:01 1:34¹ 2:05⁴ 4 7 7⁸ 4¹¾° 1³ 1⁴¾ 2:05⁴ *2-1 (J.Dennis) AdioGoose, FrostyAbbe, MissGift (much the best)
6-20 ¹Spk⅝ ft 76° clm3500+1 :30¹ 1:02² 1:33 2:05¹ 2 2 3² 1¹¼ 2½ 1¾ 2:05¹ *5-2 (J.Dennis) AdioGoose, RareEvent, Ballock (well handled)
6-13 Spk⅝ ft 74° Qua 1 :31 1:02⁴ 1:34³ 2:05 8 6 6⁵½ 6⁶¼ 3⁴ 3⁵ 2:06 NB (J.Dennis) HundredPipers, BretsColt, AdioGoose (————)
5- 4 Haw¹ ft Qua 1 :31¹ 1:02³ 1:34⁴ 2:07¹ 3 3 3 3³½ 5⁸½ 6¹⁵ 2:10¹ NB (A.G.Shaw) PalMyerFlite, TalabbeDirect, CharlieRushIn (————)
3-28 Spk⅝ ft Qua 1 :31¹ 1:05 1:36¹ 2:07¹ 8 5 5 5⁸½ 4⁹ 5¹⁴ 2:10 NB (A.G.Shaw) CrystalKing, PellaireByrd, KingWin (————)
1-13 ⁴BmlPA ft 33° clm2500=1 :31¹ 1:06 1:38 2:13² 7 7 7⁷½ 5⁹ 6⁶¾ 6⁵ 2:14² 29-1 (A.G.Shaw) Byemar, LakewoodAmoor, AdamIke (no threat)

WHITE **3** 6-1 =

Driver—HARRY BURRIGHT, Blue-Gold Tr.—H. Poort, Jr. (141-11-15-16—.165)

1973 15 0 3 1 $3,227
1972 12 1 3 2 $3,917 2:08³ Was¹
Lifetime $3,917 3, 2:08³ (1)

COLOR ME LEE

B g 1969, by Gary F. Dudley—Fleet's Queen—Fleet Hanover
Owner: Frank A. Rossi, Chicago Heights, Ill.

7- 5 ³Spk⅝ ft 75° clm6000=1 :30³ 1:01² 1:34 2:05 6 9 9¹⁶ 8⁷ 8¹⁶ 8¹⁶ 2:08¹ 6-1 (S.Banks) BedfrdBrush, FairRowByrd, NthngWhling (showed little)
6-21 ³Spk⅝ ft 79° clm6000=1 :30¹ 1:03⁴ 1:34¹ 2:05² 3 6 6⁵° 5⁴½° 6⁵ 6³¾ 2:06¹ 7-2 (R.Knox) GrawlnHanovr, KarenGray, JoesDonJuan (parked 2 turns)
6-11 ³Spk⅝ ft 89° clm6000—1 :30² 1:02 1:31³ 2:03¹ 3 5 5⁴ 8⁹½ 7⁸ 3⁵½ 2:04² 21-1 (R.Knox) WindaleGuyTruax, Papa, ColorMeLee (not good enough)
5-24 ⁵Haw¹ ft 60° nw2R 1 :32² 1:03⁴ 1:35⁴ 2:05¹ 9 9 9 9⁸½ 9¹⁵ 9¹² 2:07³ 47-1 (G.Conley) NativeSue, FlorianaByrd, MiracleDeal (no chance)
5- 3 ³Haw¹ ft 51° nw2R 1 :30⁴ 1:03¹ 1:35⁴ 2:06² 7 9 8 7²¹ 8ᵈⁱˢ 7ᵈⁱˢ 14-1 (W.Rosebm) GoodLuckGirl, BallardsRodny, MacFarvel (souldn't pace)
4-19 ²Haw¹ ft 67° nw2R 1 :31⁴ 1:04¹ 1:36³ 2:07² 2 8x 8 8²⁰ 8²¹x 8²⁴ 2:12¹ *2-1 (R.Knox) LyricEyre, NellaWind, RockabyWay (followed winner)

GREEN **4** 8-1 —

Driver—WAYNE MOORE, Red-Gold Tr.—W. Moore (47-5-6-4—.184)

1973 22 6 2 1 $11,034 2:06³ gd Spk⅝
1972 32 3 3 9 $8,418 2:04² Nfld
Lifetime $14,963 5, 2:04²

SILVER CREEK TILLY

B m 1967, by Farvel—Tilly Dillon—Congressional
Owner: Four Jacks Racing Stable, Harvey, Ill.

7- 5 ⁵Spk⅝ ft 75° clm7200=1 :29³ 1:00⁴ 1:33 2:04 2 5 5⁴¼ 8⁷ 7⁶¾ 6⁵ 2:05 16-1 (W.Moore) DameFontane, Pellaire, SapphireGlow (evenly)
6-25 ⁵Spk⅝ ft 83° clm7200=1 :30³ 1:02³ 1:32⁴ 2:03³ 7 8 8⁹¼ 6³¾° 8⁸¼ 8¹⁵ 2:06³ 7-1 (B.Gilmour) AndysJake, SonnyFarvel, AnniversaryBabe (3-wide ¾)
6-12 ⁴Spk⅝ ft 74° clm7200=1 :31 1:02¹ 1:33⁴ 2:05¹ 2 6 6⁶ 3²° 2ʰᵈ 2ʰᵈ 2:05¹ 17-1 (W.Moore) SonnyFarvel, SilverCreekTilly, IroquoisLee (just missed)
5-25 ¹Haw¹ ft 58° clm7200 1 :30⁴ 1:01 1:32 2:05 1 3 2° 3²½° 6⁸ 6¹³ 2:07³ 5-1 (H.Burright) GayFamous, KingeryExpress, SonnyFarvel (tired badly)
4-25 ¹⁰Haw¹ ft 46° clm8400 1 :30⁴ 1:02³ 1:34¹ 2:05 1 3 3 3¹ 2¹½x dnf 9-2 (W.Moore) SpeedyQuick, BigDavid, NobleOne (scattered field)
4-16 ⁴Spk⅝ ft 43° clm9600=1 :31¹ 1:04¹ 1:34 2:06 1 3 1¹° 1² 2¹ 4⁵½ 2:07¹ 5-2 (R.Knox) PlutoHal, DaveWestern, J.HazenAdios (outpaced stretch)

BLACK **5** 10-1 =

Driver—ROBERT DECKER, Red-Green Tr.—T. Caygill (23-0-0-4—.058)

1973 12 0 1 1 $1,975
1972 15 1 2 4 $2,276 2:16 Aur
Lifetime $3,575 4, 2:16

ROGER PAINTER

B g 1968, by Painter—Wilmamite—Alemite
Owner: Ed L. Johnson, Fairmount, Ind.

7- 4 ³Spk⅝ ft 82° clm5000=1 :29⁴ 1:03³ 1:34³ 2:05⁴ 6 1 1¹¼ 1½ 3³½ 7⁷ 2:07¹ 18-1 (R.Decker) Chickadee, RomanDancer, SissySassy (3-wide for lead)
6-21 ³Spk⅝ ft 79° clm5000—1 :30¹ 1:03⁴ 1:34¹ 2:05² 5 1 1¹¼ 1¹ 3¹½x3¹¼p4 2:05³ 23-1 (R.Decker) GrawlinHanover, KarenGray, JoesDonJuan (tired break)
6- 8 ²Spk⅝ ft 85° clm6000=1 :30¹ 1:00⁴ 1:31³ 2:03⁴ 5 5 4⁷ 4⁶ 4⁵½ 8¹³ 2:06² 32-1 (R.Decker) FlashHarry, DameFontane, LincolnValentine (tired)
5-29 ⁵Spk⅝ sy 49° clm6000—1 :31 1:04³ 1:37¹ 2:08² 1 3 3²¼ 4²½ 5⁷½ 7⁹ 2:10¹ 12-1 (R.Decker) AndysYankee, AprilArt, FairyJo (weakened)
5-11 ³Haw¹ ft 55° nw3R 1 :30¹ 1:02³ 1:35 2:06² 7 5 5 5³½ 6⁸ 7⁶ 2:07³ 13-1 (R.Decker) AllwinPrince, SpyderWright, DeesSinger (no chance)
4-25 ³Haw¹ ft 50° nw2R 1 :30² 1:02 1:34¹ 2:05² 6 4 1 2² 3⁴½ 3⁵¼ 2:06² 9-2 (R.Decker) EldorasBoy, TommieByrd, RogerPainter (soundly beaten)

YELLOW **6** 6-1 +

Driver—WILLIAM DiBELLA, Red-White Tr.—W. DiBella (3-0-0-0—.000)

1973 8 2 1 0 $1,073 2:07³ E.M.D⅝
1972 4 0 0 0 (——)
Lifetime (——)

DANDY CHOICE

Br g 1969, by Choice H—My Tessie—Calgary Byrd
Owner: Shirley Elaine Hale, Elgin, Ill.

7- 5 ²Spk⅝ ft 75° nw1R=1 :31 1:02 1:32¹ 2:04¹ 5 4 4⁵½ 5¹⁰ 5⁹½ 8¹⁰ 2:06¹ 22-1 (W.DiBella) Cleon, CollegeMan, MajorBill (too much speed)
6-27 ⁴Spk⅝ ft 76° nw1R=1 :31⁴ 1:04¹ 1:35³ 2:07 8 2° 2¹½ 5⁶ 4⁷½ 4⁹¾ 2:09 24-1 (W.DiBella) TwinkleBlue, CleverMo, CharlieRushIn (used early)
6-18 ²Spk⅝ ft 77° 3-4yrnw1R=1 :30² 1:02⁴ 1:33¹ 2:04 4 3 4⁴½ 4⁵¾ 4³½ 4⁹¼ 2:05⁴ 8-1 (W.DiBella) BretsColt, CleverMo, GypsyWave (pulled out hung)
6- 6 E.M.D⅝ ft nw100073 1 :30² 1:01² 1:32⁴ 2:04³ 2 6 6 5° 5³ 4³¾ 2:05² 5-2 (W.DiBella) TimelyLassie, A.G Eddy, IdlewhilesJoe (————)
5-30 E.M.D⅝ ft nw100073 1 :32¹ 1:03⁴ 1:34¹ 2:05² 3 4 4 4 3⁴½ 2⁵ 2:06² 5-2 (W.DiBella) HiLandKnight, DandyChoice, FirePilot (————)
5-25 E.M.D⅝ ft nw1000L 1 :29 1:01⁴ 1:34¹ 2:07³ 2 5 5 5 4⁴ 1¹ 2:07³ 19-1 (W.DiBella) DandyChoice, RoyalMoot, MissPatchenB (————)

GREEN & WHITE **7** 8-1 —

Driver—JAMES MORRISSEY, Green-White-Yellow Tr.—J. Morrissey (19-1-1-3—.135)

1973 15 1 1 3 $4,676 2:11⁴ sy Spk⅝
1972 41 3 5 2 $11,850 2:04¹ Was¹
Lifetime $22,906 7, 2:04¹ (1)

DAZZLING STAR

B g 1965, by Dazzleway—Leola V. Grattan—White Mountain Boy
Owner: J. Morrissey and J. Schilling, Chicago, Ill., St. John, Ind.

7- 5 ⁵Spk⅝ ft 75° clm6000—1 :29³ 1:00⁴ 1:33 2:04 9 6° 7⁵¾ 7⁵½° 8⁷¼ 8⁶½ 2:05² 25-1 (J.Morrissey) DameFontane, Pellaire, SapphireGlow (post hurt)
6-27 ¹⁰Spk⅝ sy 68° clm8000—1 :30² 1:03² 1:34³ 2:06 8 3° 2¹° 5²¾° 8⁸¼ 7⁸ 2:07³ 8-1 (J.Morrissey) BagofGold, LittlePuff, IdlewhilesEarl (hung out)
6-21 Spk⅝ ft 76° Qua 1 :29⁴ 1:02 1:31⁴ 2:04¹ 6 4 4¹⁰ 3⁸½ 3⁶½ 3⁵¾ 2:05² NB (J.Morrissey) BranchRockyGuy, MissPggyFrsco, DzzlngStr (————)
3-16 ⁴Spk⅝ sy 34° clm9000=1 :31¹ 1:04¹ 1:37³ 2:11⁴ 8 2 2³ 1¹¼ 1⁴ 1½ 2:11⁴ 12-1 (J.Morrissey) DazzlingStar, SengaMartin, LaronMarden (big effort)
3- 9 ¹⁰Spk⅝ gd 40° clm9000=1 :31⁴ 1:06³ 1:38⁴ 2:09⁴ 8 2 2¹½ 1ʰᵈ 2¹½ 4² 2:10¹ 10-1 (J.Morrissey) ArmbroHusky, CinderCloud, AljeansDon (parked early)
3- 3 ⁶Spk⅝A ft 53° clm9000—1 :30 1:01³ 1:32⁴ 2:04¹ 3 6 6⁶ 8⁵¼ 8⁶¼ 4³½ 2:05 11-1 (J.Morrissey) SeattleCindy, BluCreed, Mose (away slow)

BLACK & YELLOW **8** 9-2 +

Driver—WALTER PAISLEY, Green-White Tr.—J. Cisna (260-49-45-41—.340)

1973 7 1 0 3 $2,370 2:05 Spk⅝
1972 15 3 3 3 $5,287 2:07² Was¹
Lifetime $5,287 4, 2:07² (1)

ADMIRAL JACK

B g 1968, by Adios Mite—Miss Enchantress—Joe Donlin
Owner: John Cisna, Springfield, Ill.

7- 9 ²Spk⅝ ft 92° clm4000=1 :30³ 1:03³ 1:34¹ 2:05 8 4° 1¹ 3¹½ 2²½ 1ʰᵈ 2:05 15-1 (W.Paisley) AdmiralJack, FannyMorgen, JetwaySue (big trip)
7- 5 Spk⅝ ft 75° Qua 1 :31 1:02³ 1:33⁴ 2:04² 8 7 7⁹½° 8⁷½° 7¹¹ 7¹² 2:06⁴ NB (C.Greene) HighRank, GinnysB.Abbe, CrystalChief (————)
6-14 ¹Spk⅝ ft 74° clm4000=1 :31³ 1:04 1:36 2:06⁴ 7 9 9⁸¼ 9⁵¾ 8⁵¼ 8³¾ 2:07³ 8-1 (J.Cisna) GeeGeeKnox, KirksFlight, CarelessLew (wide leaving)
6- 4 ²Spk⅝ gd 67° clm4000—1 :33² 1:08² 1:40³ 2:11³ 2 4 5⁴ 5⁴ 4⁴½ 3¹¼ 2:11⁴ 9-1 (N.Willis) GeeGeeKnox, WorthyByrd, AdmiralJack (closed some)
4-12 ²Spk⅝ ft 36° clm5000—1 :32³ 1:04 1:35⁴ 2:06³ 1 2 2² 4²¼ 4⁴½ 3⁷¼ 2:08 29-1 (J.Cisna) BethExpress, Talaria, AdmiralJack (good trip)
1-19 ⁷BmlP ft 26° clm6000=1 :31¹ 1:05³ 1:37 2:09² 4 5 5⁵¾ 5⁴ 6⁴ 6⁵ 2:10² 13-1 (N.Willis) CrystalKlata, GrandAce, BigDavid (lacked speed)

GRAY & BLACK **9** 12-1 —

Driver—JERALD GREVENGOED, Gold-Black Tr.—J. Grevengoed (42-2-4-8—.164)

1973 11 0 0 0 (——)
1972 22 3 1 3 $3,939 2:07¹ Spk⅝
Lifetime $4,241 3, 2:07¹ (⅝)

JULIE WAY

B f 1969, by Waylay—Martha Washington—Gene Abbe
Owner: Jerald & Robert Grevengoed, Paw Paw, Ill.

7- 3 ²Spk⅝ ft 78° clm7200—1 :30 1:03 1:33⁴ 2:04¹ 4 5 5⁴½ 7⁴½ 8¹² 8⁸½ 2:06 23-1 (R.Kline) PatrickByrd, FlyingFool, HighJimmy (below par)
6-21 ⁶Spk⅝ ft 71° clm8400—1 :30 1:03 1:34 2:05³ 2 3 3³½ 6⁶¼ 5⁷ 6¹³ 2:08¹ 11-1 (R.Kline) Pompidou, MajesticLayne, BethExpress (below par)
6- 1 ⁹Spk⅝ ft 73° clm12000—1 :29¹ :59⁴ 1:29⁴ 2:01² 2 3 3⁴¼ 3⁶ 8¹⁵ 8¹⁷ 2:04⁴ 22-1 (W.Rosebm) MajorBlack, BillyTime, PalMyerFlite (not good enough)
5-25 ³Haw¹ ft 58° nw3R 1 :31 1:01 1:31¹ 2:01 8 8 8 8⁸½ 8¹⁵ 7¹⁴ 2:03⁴ 54-1 (R.Kline) BigBub, BarbaraAlmahurst, GrandClara (no chance)
5-16 ⁵Haw¹ ft 43° nw3R 1 :31³ 1:02⁴ 1:33² 2:04¹ 4 8 9 8⁸½ 6⁸ 6⁴ 2:05 38-1 (R.Kline) LollipopWave, ReallyBombed, HeatherRuss (no chance)
5- 7 ⁴Haw¹ sy 60° nw3R 1 :31¹ 1:03¹ 1:34² 2:05¹ 8 9 7° 6⁵½ 7⁸ 8⁸¼ 2:06⁴ 56-1 (R.Kline) ChtyChty, MgtyBt'r, BrbraAlmhrst-MssGrtieᵈʰ (nothing)

1. BYRD FARR—Here's a four year old who receives a 20% allowance in his claiming price. Therefore, the $6,000 claiming tag which Byrd Farr has been running for, actually means he's been competing against $5,000 claimers. In his last race, he was prominent for three quarters of the mile. When it came time for the stretch drive, he didn't respond and dropped back from that point on. He crossed the finish line beaten by 11 lengths. Byrd Farr is running against the same class tonight and, on a whole, he's coming off a pretty poor effort. Evaluation—non-contender.

2. ADIO GOOSE—This veteran is coming off back to back wins for $3,500. Since all claimers going up in class who have won their last race are considered to be contenders, there's no problem handicapping Adio Goose. Evaluation—contender.

3. COLOR ME LEE—This young fellow is also receiving a 20% allowance in claiming price. In his last race, the chartmaker was very kind by saying that he "showed little." Actually the four year old showed nothing. He trailed the field from the start by as much as he trailed the field at the end, a total of 16 lengths. Evaluation—non-contender.

4. SILVER CREEK TILLY—Her last race is far from impressive, but the fact that she's dropping $1,000 in class is a tipoff that a little further investigation is needed. In her next to last race, against $6,000 claimers, Silver Creek Tilly lost by 11 lengths in the final quarter. Last time out, the mare closed 2 lengths in the final quarter and improved her loss margin by 10 lengths over her previous race. Her improvement on the track is also complemented by the drop in class tonight. Evaluation—contender.

5. ROGER PAINTER—Here's a frontrunning type who's enjoyed success for three quarters of the race in both his last two efforts. His last time out, he had a 1/2 length lead at the three quarter mark but was eventually passed by six horses in the stretch. He lost his race by 7 lengths, which is not good enough when running against the same class. Evaluation—non-contender.

6. DANDY CHOICE—There's not much to worry about when handicapping this gelding's chances. He went to the starting gate against maidens in his last three races and took quite a beating in all three. He has won a couple of races in the minors, but he's still labeled a maiden because he's yet to win a purse at a major track. Even against this field, Dandy Choice is considered to be taking a class hike. Until he proves his real value against claimers, he's automatically eliminated. Evaluation—non-contender.

7. DAZZLING STAR—There are quite a few problems here. We have to go back four and a half months to get a ratable race. The last two races turned in by Dazzling Star are thrown out because he was parked out for two or more turns. Prior to that, we have a qualifying race which in this situation plays no role. Then we have a three-month layoff, two more off tracks, and before you know it, we're back on March 3. That night he raced well for $9,000, good enough to qualify him as a contender against the $5,000 claimers he faces tonight. But that's cancelled out by the long layoff. Evaluation—unratable contender.

8. ADMIRAL JACK—Here's something you won't see too often. Admiral Jack had the lead at the half, dropped back to third at the three quarter mark, and then came back to win. Since he's also a previous winner within the claiming ranks, he's treated the same as Adio Goose. Evaluation—contender.

9. JULIE WAY—It's another class drop for the filly. She's unsuccessful in eleven starts for the year, and it's very doubtful she'll find her winning ways in this race. The filly pacer has bettered her loss margin in her last two races, but that's due more to the class drops than improving form. Julie Way appears to be headed for another drop in class after this race. Evaluation—non-contender.

Since we've uncovered only one unratable contender, the race is playable. Racewise, we have three contenders—Adio Goose and Admiral Jack, both previous winners, and Silver Creek Tilly, a mare who's benefiting from a drop in class.

The contenders are rated on the basis of numerical speed ratings since the fastest final time is shared by Silver Creek Tilly and Admiral Jack. Here's the chart:

Horse	Final Time	Last Half	Base Rating	Class		P.P.		Park		Adj. Final Rating
Adio Goose	29	16	45	+2	47	-1	46	-	46	46
Silver Creek Tilly	25	17	42	-2	40	+1	41	-	41	41
Admiral Jack	25	7	32	+2	34	-	32	-	32	32

The first thing we need to get is the base rating which, as you know, combines the final time with the last half.

Adio Goose—Final Time   2:05 4/5 =   29
              Last Half   1:03 1/5 = +16
              Base Rating   45

Silver Creek Tilly—Final Time   2:05   =   25
              Last Half   1:03 2/5 = +17
              Base Rating   42

Admiral Jack—Final Time   2:05   =   25
              Last Half   1:01 2/5 = +7
              Base Rating   32

The computation of the base rating is an indication that Admiral Jack could be a standout. His low base rating reveals that he has run the fastest last half in relation to the fastest final time. That's a good sign for any horse, but adjustments could always change that around.

Adio Goose has 2 points added on to his base rating for the class hike. His 47 rating is reduced to 46 since he's moving in two post positions over his last race. He wasn't parked out for two or more turns so his adjusted final rating stays at 46.

Silver Creek Tilly gets 2 points subtracted from her 42 base rating for the drop in class. She's moving out from the two to the four post over her last race which adds on one point for a total of 41. That total is also her adjusted final rating since she encountered no park outs.

Admiral Jack gets only an adjustment in the class column. He's leaving from the same post

position as he had in his last race and was parked out for only one turn of the track. The 2 points added on for the class hike brings his adjusted final rating to 34. His total is 7 points better than the next best rating, so he becomes our final play.

FOURTH RACE — 1 MILE
PACE. Claiming price $5,000 — 3 Year Olds and Upward — Purse $3,000.

Time—:31² 1:03³ 1:34³ 2:05							Mutuel Pool—$95,017		
8. Admiral Jack	8	1°	1½	1½	1¹	1¹¼	2:05	6-1 (W.Palsley)
1. Byrd Farr	1	3	3²½	3¹	3¹½	2¹¼	2:05¹	10-1 (S.Banks)
2. Adio Goose	2	4	4³½	4²°	2¹	3¹½	2:05²	*1-1 (J.Dennis)
4. Silver Creek Tilly	4	6	7⁶½	6⁴	4²½	4²	2:05²	4-1 (W.Moore)
3. Color Me Lee	3	5	5⁵	5³	5³	5³¼	2:05³	12-1 (R.Knox)
7. Dazzling Star	7	8	8⁸½	9⁵½	7⁶	6⁴½	2:06	8-1 (J.Morrissey)
5. Roger Painter	5	2	2¹½	2½°	6⁴	7⁷¾	2:06³	24-1 (J.Dagenais)
6. Dandy Choice	6	7	6⁵½°	7⁴°	8⁸	8⁸¾	2:06⁴	22-1 (W.D Bella)
9. Julie Way	9	9	9⁹°	8⁵°	9⁹	9⁹	2:06⁴	19-1 (J.Grvngoed)

Adio Goose claimed for $5,000 by Gordon Ring and W. Beckley, trainer—W. Beckley

Mutuels—(8) 15.00 7.00 3.00—(1) 9.60 4.80—(2) 2.60

Admiral Jack was sent out for the lead right from the start. He took command at the quarter pole and hit the half mile mark in 1:03 3/5, the exact same time as his last race. He maintained his lead to the wire and won in 2:05, also the same time as his last race. He rewarded his followers with a nice $15.00 payoff.

The even odds favorite, Adio Goose, finished third, 1/2 length in front of Silver Creek Tilly. Both horses were within striking distance coming into the stretch, but neither one could come up with a strong rally. The only real surprise in the race was the much improved effort turned in by Byrd Farr.

The next race we'll work on is a conditioned event for "non-winners of $10,000 in 1973." The race took place at Maywood's half miler on August 22. First we'll locate the contenders in the field of seven.

ONE MILE PACE   NINTH RACE   Purse $4,000

CONDITIONED. Non-winners of $10,000 in 1973 that are Non-winners of a race since July 1st. Also Eligible: 3 & 4 Year Olds that are Non-winners of a race since July 15th.

PLEASE ASK FOR HORSE BY PROGRAM NUMBER

	Date	Trk Cond Temp	Class	Dist	Leader's Time ¼	½	¾	Winner's Time	PP	¼	½	¾	Str	Fin	Ind.Time	Odds	Driver	Order of Finish First	Second	Third	Comment

RED 1 — Driver—WALTER PAISLEY, Green-White   Tr.—J. Cisna   (122-20-23-23—.332)
DANA'S ROYBILL — Ch g 1967, by Painter—Rose's Dusty—Dusty Hanover
Owners: Lang Helt and Hugh L. Fortner, Dana, Ind.
1973 13 1 3 2 $8,702 2:08¹ sy Spk⅝
1972 21 3 0 4 $13,897 2:01¹ Spk⅝
Lifetime $58,869 3, 2:01 (1)
3-1

8-15	5May ft 75°	nw1000073	1	:30¹ 1:00⁴ 1:31³ 2:01³	3 4	52½°	42¼°	4³	33½	2:02²	4-1	(W.Paisley)	CafineKid, MigHanover, DanasRoybil	(parked 2 turns)
8- 6	9May ft 75°	nw800073	1	:30⁴ 1:01¹ 1:31² 2:01³	4 2	21°	11	1 hd	22¼	2:02	*8-5	(W.Paisley)	TarrsChief, Dana'sRoybill, NativeGem	(brushed twice)
7-20	8Spk⅝ sy 68°	w100007273=1	1	:30³ 1:03¹ 1:34⁴ 2:05³	2 2	31¼	31½	24	36	2:06⁴	9-1	(B.Shuter)	StarboardButler, NobleKnightTime, DnasRybl	(no close)
7-14	9Spk⅝ ft 75°	w100007273=1	:30	1:00⁴ 1:31 2:00⁴	1 3	42¾	21°	1½	42½	2:01²	7-1	(W.Paisley)	NicksPainter, RightGood, Overhaul	(str bid, hung)
7- 7	7Spk⅝ ft 90°	w10000=1	:30	1:02 1:31⁴ 2:01¹	5 6	66½	76°	56	5³	2:01⁴	13-1	(W.Paisley)	BlueBreak, RobbRanger, Doc'sJerry	(raced well)
6-30	4Spk⅝ ft 78°	w10000+1	:30	1:01⁴ 1:30³ 2:00¹	7 7	32¼°	1 hd°	78¼	711	2:02²	15-1	(P.Milburn)	AdiosArt, DoctorTom, YankeeBaron	(tired badly)

WHITE 2 — Driver—DAN SHETLER, JR., Purple-Gold-White   Tr.—D. Shetler, Jr.   (15-1-3-4—.267)
STEADY BLAZE — B g 1969, by Steady Beau—Dear Amelia—Targhee
Owners: Derek Norwood & John Murnane, Chicago, Mt. Prospect, Ill.
1973 23 2 4 4 $12,711 2:01³ Spk⅝
1972 17 3 2 2 $7,223 2:05¹ Was¹
Lifetime $7,223 3, 2:05¹ (1)
9-2

8-14	9May ft 70°	§clm19200	1	:30³ 1:00⁴ 1:31² 2:01⁴	6 3°	2 hd°	1½°	1½	21¼	2:02	5-1	(D.ShetlerJr)	L.R.Adios, SteadyBlaze, AndysTom	(big race)
8- 4	11May ft 73°	clm20400	1	:31² 1:02² 1:31⁴ 2:01	6x 8	8²⁵	8²⁴	8²⁵	8²⁴	2:05⁴	6-1	(D.ShetlerJr)	NobleSkipper, PatPlutocrat, TopallAdios	(break costly)
7-31	5May ft 71°	clm19200	1	:31 1:03 1:34 2:04³	8 1	2 hd	1 hd	1 hd	2 nk	2:04³	9-1	(D.ShetlerJr)	AlexWejover, SteadyBlaze, PalMyer, Flite	(just missed)
7-24	5May ft 81°	clm19200	1	:30¹ 1:00¹ 1:31¹ 2:02³	7 6	54°	41½°	3½	51½	2:03	7-2	(D.ShetlerJr)	PatPlutocrat, ArrivaByrd, C.V.Yates	(3-wide ¾)
7-14	4Spk⅝ ft 75°	nw180007273=1	:31² 1:02¹ 1:32⁴ 2:02³	6 4°	1 ns°	2¾°	44	910	2:04³	7-1	(D.ShetlerJr)	HarryFitz, GoodBox, MigHanover	(rough mile)
7- 7	5Spk⅝ ft 90°	nw160007273=1	:29² :59⁴ 1:29⁴ 2:01³	5 2°	21½	1½	1½	11¼	2:01³	5-1	(D.ShetlerJr)	SteadyBlaze, MigHanover, NobleLand	(well handled)

BLUE 3 — Driver—JOE MARSH, JR., Gray-Blue-Red   Tr.—J. Marsh, Jr.   (128-33-21-22—.401)
WORTHY BRET — B c 1970, by Bret Hanover—Worthy Eleda—Worthy Boy
Owner: Golden Ventures Stable, South Holland, Ill.
1973 24 2 4 7 $19,846 2:05¹ sy Haw¹
1972 13 4 1 2 $9,225 2:04² Was¹
Lifetime $9,225 2, 2:04² (1)
5-2

8-15	Spr1 ft	3yrstk12930	1	:28¹ :57 1:28 1:57	4 4	4	4	4⁵	41⁰	1:59	NB	(J.MarshJr)	MelvinsWoe, OtaroHanover, GaySkipper	(————)
8-15	Spr1 ft	3yrstk12930	1	:30¹ :59⁴ 1:29⁴ 1:58¹	6 6	6	6	5³	46	1:59⁴	NB	(J.MarshJr)	MelvinsWoe, OtaroHanover, GaySkipper	(————)
8- 6	5May ft 81°	nw1000073	1	:30¹ 1:01 1:30² 2:00⁴	4 6	77	75	66½	53¼	2:01²	6-1	(R.Knox)	NicksPainter, DoctorAndy, WorthyBret	(closed some)
7-24	5May ft 81°	w100007273	1	:30 1:00³ 1:31⁴ 2:01³	6 6	64°	32°	33	32¾	2:02¹	5-1	(J.MarshJr)	QuakerByrd, ChiefG.Direct, WorthyBret	(3-wide ¾)
7- 9	8Spk⅝ ft 78°	nw30006=1	:30¹ 1:01⁴ 1:32 2:02	9 4°	11	11½	1½	2¾	2:02¹	3-1	(J.MarshJr)	MajesticBelleG, WorthyBret, HarkWon	(used early)
7- 2	9Spk⅝ ft 84°	nw30006=1	:30² 1:02⁴ 1:32¹ 2:01⁴	3 3	3³	3³	32½	41½	2:02¹	*6-5	(J.MarshJr)	Majorca, HarkWon, KeystoneJournal	(evenly)

GREEN 4 — Driver—GARY SCURLOCK, Blue-White   Tr.—D. Guerrettaz   (0-0-0-0—.000)
FANTASTIC DREAM — B c 1969, by Lehigh Hanover—Adorable Dream—Knight Dream
Owner: Gary L. Scurlock, Newton, Ill.
1973 20 1 2 2 $10,810 2:01² Spk⅝
1972 32 12 3 2 $47,144 2:00³ Haw¹
Lifetime $52,610 3, 2:00³ (1)
5-1

8-11	10May ft 77°	w1000073	1	:28² :58⁴ 1:28 1:57²	3 4	45	47½	515	713	2:00	18-1	(N.Willis)	StarboardButler, Jefferson, C.V.Thor	(too much speed)
8- 1	9May ft 67°	nw1000073	1	:30¹ 1:02² 1:32 2:02¹	3 5	54°	43½°	43	33¼	2:02¹	7-1	(D.Guerrettz)	PromTime, TheGrumbler, FantasticDream	(big race)
7-24	5May ft 81°	w100007273	1	:30¹ 1:00³ 1:31⁴ 2:01³	7 7	75½	63½	54½	64½	2:02³	38-1	(D.Guerrettz)	QuakerByrd, ChiefG.Direct, WorthyBret	(evenly)
7-13	9Spk⅝ ft 77°	inv6000=1	:30⁴ 1:04 1:34¹ 2:02⁴	2 3	32¼	41¾°	47	66¼	2:04	12-1	(G.Scurlock)	UncleKenny, G.T.Skipper, ShadHanover	(tired in str)
7- 6	8Spk⅝ ft 83°	inv6500+1	:30¹ 1:01 1:30 1:59⁴	4 6	86	87½	711	713	2:02	17-1	(N.Willis)	ShadyMile, AdiosArt, TheGrumbler	(no chance)
6-30	6Spk⅝ ft 78°	nw20008=1	:29² 1:00³ 1:31¹ 2:01²	1 3	34½	32½	21	12¼	2:01²	*2-1	(J.Graham)	FantasticDream, Folger, C.V.Yates	(strong in stretch)

BLACK 5 — Driver—GLEN KIDWELL, Blue-Gold   Tr.—G. Kidwell   (5-0-0-1—.067)
SINCERA — B m 1967, by Adios Bomber—Franselka—Selka's King
Owners: Chancey Acres and Glen Kidwell; Kenosha, Wis., Marengo, Ill.
1973 24 0 2 4 $9,927
1972 39 5 8 8 $29,627 2:02¹ Spk⅝
Lifetime $79,365 5, 2:02¹ (⅝)
8-1

8-13	5May ft 77°	nw800073	1	:30³ 1:02 1:32⁴ 2:01²	3 5	56½	34°	411	616	2:04³	28-1	(G.Kidwell)	TheChamp, Concourse, BaronEric	(too much speed)
7-28	7May ft 64°	FMnw800073	1	:30¹ 1:00² 1:32 2:03¹	6 8	88	62¼°	53	6⁴	2:04	24-1	(G.Kidwell)	MaryAmigo, Majorca, HiPeggy	(mild bid ¾)
7-16	9Spk⅝ ft 76°	FM4200=1	:32 1:04¹ 1:35 2:04³	9 9	89°	63¾°	64½	93¼	2:05¹	16-1	(G.Kidwell)	MaryAmigo, Front'erAnn, SweetMove	(hung out)
7- 9	9Spk⅝ gd 78°	FM4300=1	:31² 1:03² 1:33² 2:04¹	1 3	3¹	42°	34½	31½	2:04³	7-2	(G.Kidwell)	MaryAmigo, PipingTimes, Sincere	(closed some)
6-30	5Spk⅝ ft 76°	FM5000=1	:30² 1:02 1:31³ 2:02	5 4	44½	55¼	65¼	31½	2:02²	24-1	(G.Kidwell)	FirstCash, MaryAmigo, Sincere	(raced well)
6-15	3Spk⅝ ft 79°	FM6000=1	:30⁴ 1:02² 1:32³ 2:01²	7 9	87¼	75	66	76¾	2:02⁴	17-1	(G.Kidwell)	BeckyHiWin, FirstCash, MajesticBelleG	(dull effort)

YELLOW 6 — Driver—MAX LYNCH, Maroon-Blue   Tr.—B. Nickells   (17-1-2-4—.203)
RARE BUTTERFLY — B m 1968, by Race Time—Butterfly Hanover—Dean Hanover
Owner: Hubly Farms, Columbus, Ohio
1973 18 4 2 2 $9,525 2:03³ Haw¹
1972 2 0 0 1 $146
Lifetime $11,195 2, 2:11³
8-1

8-11	9May ft 77°	FM4500	1	:30¹ 1:01 1:32 2:03	2 5	64	65	64	63¾	2:03⁴	16-1	(B.Nickells)	MajsticBelG, JustlyWicked, PipingTimes	(needed room)
8- 4	2May ft 77°	FM4500	1	:30⁴ 1:01² 1:33³ 2:04¹	4 1°	2¾	2½	22	64¾	2:04	9-1	(M.Lynch)	LittleSweetSue, PacingPauline, PipingTimes	(used early)
7-16	9Spk⅝ ft 76°	FM4200=1	:32 1:04¹ 1:35 2:04³	3 4	45	21½°	32	52¼dh	2:05	9-1	(B.Nickells)	MaryAmigo, FrontierAnn, SweetMove	(raced well)
7- 7	6Spk⅝ ft 90°	nw160007273+1	:29⁴ 1:01 1:30⁴ 2:01¹	6 3°	44°	85¼	86¾	89¾	2:03¹	26-1	(B.Nickells)	BretsTune, HarryFitz, BrennaScot	(parked 2 turns)
6-20	8Spk⅝ ft 76°	nw800073=1	:29³ 1:01⁴ 1:31⁴ 2:04	6 2	31¼	31½	22	11¼	2:04	*4-1	(B.Nickells)	RareButterfly, KeystoneDandy, EmbssyVio	(well placed)
5-30	9Spk⅝ ft 59°	FM5000=1	:30⁴ 1:02¹ 1:32 2:02	3 6	55½	53½°	55½	54¾	2:03	12-1	(B.Nickells)	FarvelCounsel, BretsPrincess, Heartlis	(tough trip)

GRAY 7 — Driver—HANK FABERT, Gold-Brown   Tr.—H. Fabert   (4-1-0-0—.250)
ADIOS MUCHACHO — B g 1969, by Addio Byrd—Frisk Along—Frisco Flyer
Owner: Roger V. Pierson, Princeton, Ill.
1973 26 7 5 5 $9,993 2:02¹ E.M.D⅝
1972 31 5 4 2 $1,202 2:10 gd Sndwh
Lifetime $1,581 3, 2:10
8-1

8-15	5May ft 75°	nw1000073	1	:30¹ 1:00⁴ 1:31³ 2:01³	7 8	86¼	77¼°	79	712	2:04	20-1	(H.Fabert)	CafineKid, MigHanover, DanasRoybil	(3-wide briefly)
8- 4	Lat1 ft	pref1500	1	:29² 1:00³ 1:31⁴ 2:01	4 1	2	32	64¾	2:02	3-1	(H.Fabert)	ScottieS, Ashlawn, Canoe	(————)
7-28	Lat1 ft	inv2000	1	:29³ :59 1:29 1:58³	4 2	2	2	21½	69	2:00²	9-1	(H.Fabert)	NaughtyWillie, MilesToGo, HurryHome	(————)
7- 7	Lat1 ft	inv2000	1	:29² :58³ 1:28¹ 1:58	6 6°	7	7	711½	716	2:01¹	18-1	(H.Fabert)	GalionPam, MilesToGo, HurryHome	(————)
6-30	Lat1 ft	inv2000	1	:29² :58⁴ 1:28 1:58⁴	4 4	4	4	310	212	2:01¹	6-1	(H.Fabert)	LoBuka, AdiosMuchacho, FirstCorners	(————)
6-23	Lat1 ft	inv2000	1	:29 :59 1:29 1:59²	2 2	2	1	2³	216½	2:02³	7-1	(H.Fabert)	MilesToGo, AdiosMuchacho, LoBuka	(————)

1. DANA'S ROYBILL—We have a couple of good efforts in a row for the six year old son of Painter. In his last race, he was parked out for two turns of the track and still turned in a strong effort. If Dana's Roybill had tired in the race, we would have given him the benefit of the doubt and handicapped him off his previous race. But when a horse performs well on the outside, that effort always remains his primary race. As far as class is concerned, Dana's Roybill is well placed. He's running for the same conditions as he raced for in his last start. Evaluation—contender.

2. STEADY BLAZE—Here's another horse that's turned in a game effort. Steady Blaze was on the outside for three turns of the track and gave very grudgingly in the stretch; an extremely powerful race considering he never saw the rail. Steady Blaze's last four races have been among the claiming ranks. Prior to those races, he competed in conditioned events which attracted much classier types than he's facing tonight. But there's no drop in class for this race because he went down in class when he stepped into claimers. His class status for this race is interpreted to be in relatively the same company. But that doesn't take anything away from Steady Blaze since he's coming off a good race. Evaluation—contender.

3. WORTHY BRET—Here's a situation you'll come across quite frequently during the summer months. Horses that have competed in stakes races at state or county fairs and then return to their local pari-mutuel racetrack. If Worthy Bret had turned in a couple bad races against low quality stakes horses, we could get rid of him as a non-contender. But the Bret Hanover offspring doesn't fall into that category. He faced some high caliber "Grand Circuit" types. And considering he was still in the race at the stretch call against that kind of competition, he raced pretty respectably. However, Worthy Bret would not be a contender because his efforts were not on the local circuit. Evaluation—unratable contender.

4. FANTASTIC DREAM—This is a good example of why horses are not picked as contenders simply on the basis of their final times. Fantastic Dream's last race is easily the fastest final time turned in at Maywood Park out of the seven-horse field. But he was never a factor in his race after the first half, which, in turn, totally discounts his fast time. He's taking a class drop tonight, since he's coming off a race for $10,000 winners, but it's not nearly enough to outweigh a 13-length defeat. Evaluation—non-contender.

5. SINCERA—It's been a very tough year for this pacing mare. She's gone 24 straight races without once visiting the winner's circle. Her last race was conditioned for "non-winners of $8,000," but she's not taking a class hike here. The monetary conditions are still within $2,000 of tonight's race, so she's handicapped as if remaining within the same class level. But the class factor is still working against Sincera. She lost her race by 16 lengths and it's going to take quite a reversal in form to change that. Evaluation—non-contender.

6. RARE BUTTERFLY—This is our second look at the mare Rare Butterfly. It's also the second time we see her in a very difficult position. Her last three races have been restricted for fillies and mares with the purse value listed. Now that she's returning to open company, she's going to have to show a little bit extra to race on equal terms with the rest of the field. And you can see by her past performances that she doesn't fulfill that requirement. Evaluation—non-contender.

7. ADIOS MUCHACHO—We only have one race to go on for Adios Muchacho, but he's indicated very precisely what to expect. In tonight's race, Adios Muchacho is running under the same conditions as his last start and that's why he's so easily eliminated. He was a badly beaten loser and was never close to the leaders at any point in the race. It appears that Adios Muchacho will have to drop in class before he receives any consideration. Evaluation—non-contender.

Once again, we've uncovered only one unratable contender in the race, which makes it a playable affair. The field has been limited to two contenders—Dana's Roybill and Steady Blaze, both of who are coming off game efforts.

Steady Blaze has the fastest final time, but he doesn't have enough advantages to go along with it to make the final choice in that respect. The race calls for numerical speed ratings, and here's the chart:

Horse	*Final Time*	*Last Half*	*Base Rating*	*Class*		*P.P.*		*Park*		*Adj. Final Rating*
Dana's Roybill	12	5	17	-	17	-1	16	-2	14	14
Steady Blaze	10	6	16	-	16	-2	14	-4	10	10

The base rating between the two horses is very close. Steady Blaze's final time is 2/5 of a second faster than the final time turned in by Dana's Roybill. But when the last half is added on, things get even closer. Dana's Roybill closed 1/5 of a second faster than Steady Blaze.

Dana's Roybill—	Final Time	2:02 2/5 =	12
	Last Half	1:01 =	+5
	Base Rating		17
Steady Blaze—	Final Time	2:02 =	10
	Last Half	1:01 1/5 =	+6
	Base Rating		16

Even though two horses may have a close base rating, it doesn't necessarily mean their adjusted final ratings will be close. The maximum adjustments are capable of changing the difference between two or more horses' base rating by as much as 16 points. Dana's Roybill and Steady Blaze weren't changed quite that drastically with their adjustments, but it was enough to make a clear choice between the two. That's despite the fact that there wasn't any need for adjustments in the class column.

Dana's Roybill is moving in from the three post to the rail which reduces his point total to 16. He was parked out for two turns of the track which takes 2 more points away. His adjusted final rating stands at 14.

Steady Blaze is getting an even bigger break in post position. He's going from the six to the two which takes off 2 points for a total of 14. Since he was parked out for three turns of the track, 4 points are subtracted rather than 2. That brings his adjusted final rating to 10, which makes him the final choice.

NINTH RACE — 1 MILE

PACE. Conditioned — Non-winners of $10,000 in 1973 that are Non-winners of a race since July 1st — Also Eligible: 3 & 4 Year Olds that are Non-winners of a race since July 15th — Purse $4,000.

Time—:30^1 1:01^1 1:31^3 2:01^1 Mutuel Pool—$78,050

2. Steady Blaze	2	1	1^2	1^1	1^2	1^{nk}	2:01^1	3-1	(D.ShetlerJr)
1. Dana's Roybill	1	2	2^2	2^1	2^2	2^{nk}	2:01^1	*8-5	(W.Paisley)
4. Fantastic Dream	4	6	$4^{5½}$	4^4	3^4	$3^{4½}$	2:02^1	5-1	(G.Scurlock)
3. Worthy Bret	3	4	3^4	3^3	$4^{6½}$	$4^{6½}$	2:02^3	2-1	(J.MarshJr)
6. Rare Butterfly	6	3°	$5^{5½}$°	$5^{6½}$	6^9	$5^{9¾}$	2:03^1	37-1	(M.Lynch)
5. Sincera	5	7	$6^{7½}$	$6^{6½}$	5^9	6^{10}	2:03^1	28-1	(G.Kidwell)
7. Adios Muchacho	7	5°	$7^{9½}$	7^{14}	7^{17}	7^{17}	2:04^3	33-1	(H.Fabert)

Mutuels—(2) 8.00 3.60 3.60—(1) 3.20 2.60—(4) 3.00

The race turned out to be strictly a two-horse affair. Steady Blaze was out for the lead from the outset. Dana's Roybill stayed right behind and pressed the issue throughout, but he was never able to catch the top one. Steady Blaze made every pole a winning one. He paid $8.00 to win.

The next race we'll work on is for claimers running for an $8,000 price tag. The race took place on July 16 at Sportsman's Park. Again, the evaluations come first.

ONE MILE PACE **SEVENTH RACE** **Purse $3,700**

"ILLINOIS RETAIL LIQUOR ASSOCIATION"

CLAIMING. Claiming price $8,000—3 Year Olds & Up. Wes Tee, Lovin Lu Lu, Will Fly, Lunar Hill, Senga Marie and Ram's Princess in for $9,600, all others $8,000.

PLEASE ASK FOR HORSE BY PROGRAM NUMBER

Driver—JACK ACKERMAN, Black-Gold **Tr.—J. Ackerman** **(31-5-1-5—.201)**

RED **1** 10-1 =

WES TEE Br c 1969, by Miracle Freight—Dixie Maid—Yankee Scot
Owner: Lyman F. Montgomery, Sandwich, Ill.

1973	23 4 2 0	$4,451	2:05^1 Spk5/8
1972	18 1 1 3	$1,475	2:07 Lat^1
	Lifetime	$1,475	3, 2:07 (1)

Date Trk Cond Temp	Class	Dist	Leader's Time 1/4	1/2	3/4	Winner's Time	PP	1/4	1/2	3/4	Str	Fin	Ind.Time	Odds	Driver	Order of Finish: First, Second, Third	Comment
7- 6 ^{10}Spk5/8 ft 83°	clm9600=	1	:30^1	1:02	1:33^1	2:05	5	x7	8^{12}	7^7°	$6^{7½}$	6^7	2:06^2	23-1	(J.Ackerman)	E.Barb, BigMark, LunarHill	(break costly)
6-27 ^{10}Spk5/8 sy 68°	clm9600=	1	:30^2	1:03^2	1:34^2	2:06	2	7	$8^{5¾}$	$8^{4¼}$	$9^{8¾}$	$6^{7¼}$	2:07^2	16-1	(J.Ackerman)	BagofGold, LittlePuff, IdlewhilesEarl	(no factor)
6-14 ^{6}Spk5/8 ft 69°	clm9600—	1	:31^2	1:03^2	1:35	2:05	2	4	$4^{5½}$	7^4	7^8	$7^{9¾}$	2:07	12-1	(J.Ackerman)	RockSpringsCag, MunciesAdios, ChiefRagtime	(tired)
6- 1 ^{10}Spk5/8 ft 73°	clm12000=	1	:29^3	1:02^4	1:35^2	2:03^2	9	8	$8^{8¼}$	$8^{7½}$	8^9	$7^{5½}$	2:04^3	19-1	(J.Ackerman)	PeterJayAdios, Brindanette, CamaroHanover	(slow start)
5-22 ^{5}Haw^1 gd 68°	nw4R	1	:32^1	1:04^2	1:35^2	2:05^2	8	1	1	2^1	5^5	$7^{6½}$	2:06^4	21-1	(J.Ackerman)	NardinsBlitz, RocketMan, NoFear	(fast leaving)
5-12 ^{1}Haw^1 ft 52°	clm15600	1	:30^2	1:02	1:33^1	2:04	2	3	4	$5^{3½}$	$5^{4½}$	$6^{4¾}$	2:05	18-1	(J.Ackerman)	TinaKnox, SummertimeDirect, Levitas	(even trip)

BLUE **2** 6-1 =

Driver—WILLIAM ROSEBOOM, Gold-Purple Tr.—V. Wentz (23-0-0-3—.043) 1973 23 0 3 5 $7,378
LOVIN LU LU B m 1967, by Don Adios—Lu Lu Byrd—Poplar Byrd 1972 32 3 8 5 $15,710 2:044 Spk⅝
Owner: Eugene Czyl & Joseph Landowski, Homewood, Harvey, Ill. Lifetime $34,972 4, 2:043
7- 310Spk⅝ ft 78° clm9600=1 :311 1:041 1:35 2:044 8 8 88 74½° 88½ 88¼ 2:062 14-1 (W.Rosebm) SilverDiller, JHazenAdios, AmigosGirl (no threa
6-1910Spk⅝ sy 78° clm9600—1 :322 1:054 1:364 2:064 5 9 84¾ 86½ 913 914 2:093 5-1 (N.Willis) DzzlingDeana, JavelonJanette, ShiawayPercy (weakened
6- 9 1Spk⅝ ft 78° clm10200—1 :301 1:002 1:322 2:03 5 6 68 42½° 25 33¼ 2:033 7-2 (W.Paisley) TinyForbes, Eyreton, LovinLuLu (raced well
5-3110Spk⅝ ft 74° clm10800=1 :291 1:021 1:331 2:033 1 3 32½ 41½° 21½ 43¾ 2:042 7-1 (W.Rosebm) HopeImperial, TommyLobell, BowsBrother (tired some
5-21 5Haw1 ft 65° clm10800 1 :30 1:01 1:332 2:03 7 2 3 63½ 55½ 56½ 2:042 15-1 (W.Rosebm) Brindanette, SilverDiller, MrThunderbyrd (even race
5-10 8Haw1 ft 62° clm12000 1/16 :27 :571 1:222 8 4 3° 33½ 55½ 711 1:243 22-1 (W.Rosebm) ArrivaByrd, RocketMan, H.W.Express (no threat

WHITE **3** 6-1 —

Driver—NELSON WILLIS, Maroon-Gray-White Tr.—N. Willis (95-7-15-12—.204) 1973 23 10 3 2 $7,014 2:042 Lex1
INDIANA CHARMER Blk g 1965, by Mighty Indian—Pamela K—Goose Bay 1972 40 18 2 5 $7,940 2:054 W.R⅝
Owner: Wm. H. Anderson, Sr., Shelbyville, Ind. Lifetime $10,174 7, 2:054 (⅝)
7- 4 6Spk⅝ ft 82° clm9000—1 :30 1:011 1:314 2:031 2 5 42¾ 1½° 42 89½ 2:051 9-1 (N.Willis) AprilArt, RckSprngsCg, TmmyLbll (moved parked, tired
6-23 Lat1 ft ffa1500 1 :30 :594 1:301 2:001 7 4 4 4 44 57¼ 2:013 13-1 (T.Tharp) KellytuckKnight, Deuce, HalosPrincess (————
6-16 Lat1 ft pref1500 1 :311 1:021 1:333 2:031 5 1 3 3 42 34½ 2:04 9-1 (T.Tharp) DrMahrud, HurryHome, IndianaCharmer (————
5-28 Lex1 sl clm4500 1 :33 1:054 1:401 2:132 7 4° 4° 4° 1½ 13¼ 2:132 •4-5 (M.Arnold) IndianaCharmer, PasonTag, QuickTurn (————
5-23 Lex1 sl clm4500 1 :37 1:124 1:49 2:203 6 3 3 3 21 12½ 2:203 •3-5 (M.Arnold) IndianaCharmer, DsUninvitedVlo, VckyAdios (————
5-18 Lex1 ft stk1500 1 :30 1:012 1:323 2:011 1 4 4 2° 52¾ 610 2:031 15-1 (T.Tharp) JarrettownDave, Waterford, MrRhythm (————

GREEN **4** 6-1 —

Driver—GENE VALLANDINGHAM, Red-White-Blue Tr.—G. Vallandingham (88-11-10-6—.211) 1973 24 4 1 4 $5,571 2:024 Spk⅝
WILL FLY B c 1969, by Miracle Freight—Easter Fly—Dragon Fly 1972 24 1 5 2 $3,046 2:074 H.P⅝
Owner: Thecla Japely, Brookfield, Wis. Lifetime $3,046 3, 2:074 (⅝)
7- 4 6Spk⅝ ft 82° clm10800—1 :30 1:011 1:314 2:031 3 2° 11¼ 3¾ 52 77¼ 2:043 5-1 (GVllndnghm) AprilArt, RockSpringsCag, TommyLobell (used earl
6-25 7Spk⅝ ft 83° clm12000—1 :293 1:012 1:312 2:02 7 4° 2hd° 77° 816 818 2:053 7-1 (W.Paisley) Knoxella, TinaKnox, TrryJeansRockt (dueled for lead ½
6-15 4Spk⅝ ft 79° nw90007273=1 :301 1:024 1:342 2:04 9 7 77½ 42° 68½ 610 2:06 5-1 (GVllndnghm) NativeGem, P.B.Mar, ChittyChitty (no chanc
6- 8 3Spk⅝ ft 85° clm8400+1 :30 1:014 1:322 2:024 5 1 11 1hd 12 11¼ 2:024 4-1 (GVllndnghm) WillFly, AprilArt, CircleEddie (strong mil
5-30 4Spk⅝ ft 59° clm7200—1 :304 1:033 1:351 2:052 4 2 22 21 2½ 11¼ 2:052 18-1 (GVllndnghm) WillFly, LincolnValentine, BourbonChimes (perfect tri
5-19 3Haw1 ft 55° nw3R 1 :311 1:024 1:341 2:033 6 7 7 711 925 925 2:083 27-1 (GVllndnghm) NobleSon, EasySkipper, JubileeKnight (too much spee

BLACK **5** 6-1 —

Driver—JOE MARSH, JR., Gray-Blue-Red Tr.—J. Sullivan (205-36-35-25—.313) 1973 18 4 3 3 $16,006 2:034 Spk⅝
FROSTY WIL Ch g 1967, by Greatheart Pick—Kwik Kop—His Chief 1972 38 4 4 6 $15,690 2:052 Spk⅝
Owner: Thomas Sullivan, Chicago, Ill. Lifetime $38,369 4, 2:052 (1)
6-2010Spk⅝ ft 76° clm9000—1 :294 1:02 1:321 2:032 7 7 78¼° 76¾ 77 76 2:043 10-1 (B.Shuter) TinyForbes, CamdenFrisco, SilverDiller (even
6- 810Spk⅝ ft 85° clm11000—1 :302 1:021 1:32 2:022 7 8 88° 86° 74 55¼ 2:032 6-1 (B.Shuter) VarsitySignal, TommyLobell, Slasham (tough tri
5-28 8Spk⅝ sy 52° clm12000+1 :312 1:052 1:37 2:08 3 6 65½ 62¾° 43½ 3¾ 2:081 •7-2 (J.MarshJr) BrillntSpeed, SmmrtimeDirect, FrostyWil (couldn't clos
5-21 6Haw1 ft 58° clm10000 1 :313 1:032 1:34 2:04 5 5 5 75½ 52½ 21¼ 2:041 •2-1 (J.Dolbee) DillerVolo, FrostyWil, WorthyReward (last ½ goo
5-12 1Haw1 ft 52° clm13000 1 :302 1:02 1:331 2:04 8 9 9 87½ 78½ 78¼ 2:053 9-1 (J.Dolbee) TinaKnox, SummertimeDirect, Levitas (even tr
5- 410Haw1 ft 45° clm12500 1 :294 1:01 1:324 2:031 7 8 8 66½ 32½ 24dh 2:04 9-2 (J.Dolbee) SequoiaHanover, MerryRuler-FrostyWildh (closed som

YELLOW **6** 7-2 =

Driver—JAMES MORRISSEY, Green-White-Yellow Tr.—J. Morrissey (19-1-1-3—.135) 1973 9 0 1 3 $2,092 2:063 Spk⅝ Qua
LUNAR HILL B c 1969, by Knight Time—Leta Hill—Tar Heel 1972 18 5 2 0 $10,592 2:034 Y.R
Owner: H. E. Wagley, Chicago, Ill. Lifetime $10,592 3, 2:034
7- 610Spk⅝ ft 83° clm9600—1 :301 1:02 1:331 2:05 6 1 11½ 11½ 12 31½ 2:052 5-1 (J.Morrissey) E'Barb, BigMark, LunarHill (hung toug
6-27 7Spk⅝ sy 68° clm10800+1 :31 1:031 1:333 2:054 2 3 43½ 41½° 41½ 42½ 2:062 7-1 (J.Morrissey) MissGertie, Tanner, SpeedyChestnut (needed sta
6-21 Spk⅝ ft 76° Qua 1 :31 1:04 1:35 2:063 3 4 47 35 24 1ns 2:063 NB (J.Morrissey) LunarHill, WonderByrd, DeMarYoung (————
3-23 2Spk⅝ ft 45° clm8400 C—1 :311 1:03 1:351 2:064 5 6 79 86 64 53¼ 2:072 •8-5 (E.Waszak) MortiesPride, SengaMarie, LuckyPeak (late ra
3-15 7Spk⅝ ft 46° nw25008+1 :292 1:013 1:32 2:024 7 8 812 75¼ 65¼ 64½ 2:034 10-1 (E.Waszak) GameGuy, PreciousCheval, PrincessJudith (tough fo
3-10 2Spk⅝A ft 48° clm8400=1 :294 1:012 1:342 2:053 8 1° 12½ 11¼ 11½ 33¾ 2:062 11-1 (E.Waszak) ZanStar, DameFontane, LunarHill (blistering spee

GREEN & WHITE **7** 12-1 =

Driver—JIM CURRAN, Gray-Gold Tr.—R. Farrington (30-5-3-7—.300) 1973 14 0 2 3 $5,386
FIRST LOOK B g 1966, by Adios Kidd—Gay Look—Southern Brigade 1972 36 4 5 3 $13,472 2:03 Haw1
Owner: Farrington Stables, Inc. & Arnold Cattle Co., Inc., Richwood, O., Chicago, Ill. Lifetime $17,119 6, 2:03 (1)
7- 410Spk⅝ ft 82° clm8000=1 :31 1:032 1:34 2:043 7 8 98¼° 74° 88 88½ 2:062 11-1 (J.Curran) SengaMarie, PortSam, LittlePuff (parked 2 tur
6-2710Spk⅝ sy 68° clm8000 C—1 :302 1:032 1:343 2:06 7 1 31 31½ 77¼ 88¼ 2:073 9-1 (S.Banks) BagofGold, LittlePuff, IdlewhilesEarl (used ea
6-16 1Spk⅝ sy 68° clm9000—1 :301 1:024 1:343 2:064 2 3 32¼ 31½ 32 47¼ 2:081 10-1 (J.Grvngoed) JubileeKnight, ChiefOsceola, ReMark (well placed ea
6- 1 9Spk⅝ ft 73° clm10000—1 :291 :594 1:294 2:012 7 8 813 812 714 712 2:034 19-1 (J.Grvngoed) MajorBlack, BillyTime, PalMyerFlite (not good enou
5-22 8Haw1 gd 68° clm11000 1 :311 1:024 1:342 2:04 9 9 9 911 78 78 2:053 15-1 (J.Grvngoed) WesternsJody, NobleChoice, DeltaDirect (even ra
5- 8 9Haw1 ft 60° clm11000 1 :312 1:032 1:342 2:052 5 6 5° 52½ 43 21 2:053 9-1 (J.Grvngoed) G.T.Winter, FirstLook, LyricEyre (closed go

BLACK & YELLOW **8** 9-2 =

Driver—DARYL BUSSE, Gray-Red Tr.—O. Jaffke (125-16-12-15—.221) 1973 25 4 2 5 $10,790 2:043 Spk⅝
SENGA MARIE B m 1966, by Adios Pick—Greta Han—Ogden Hanover 1972 42 4 9 5 $7,234 2:10 Reg
Owner: Norma G. Jensen Edmonton, Alberta Lifetime $27,224 4, 2:05 (¾)
7- 410Spk⅝ ft 82° clm9600=1 :31 1:032 1:34 2:043 6 7 88 95½ 44½ 11¼ 2:043 28-1 (M.Lynch) SengaMarie, PortSam, LittlePuff (powerful str mo
6-26 8Spk⅝ ft 76° clm9600=1 :292 1:013 1:323 2:032 2 5 74 88 96 77¼ 2:044 9-1 (M.Lynch) RockSpringsCag, ZanStar, TarportPalmer (shuffled ba
6-14 6Spk⅝ ft 69° clm9600=1 :312 1:032 1:35 2:05 6 9 99 53° 42¼ 54½ 2:06 14-1 (W Moore) RckSpringsCag, MunciesAdios, ChiefRgtime (away sl
6- 510Spk⅝ sy 65° clm9600=1 :32 1:062 1:373 2:081 2 5 64¾° 73¼° 52¼ 2nk 2:081 4-1 (W.Paisley) LittlePuff, SengaMarie, IdlewhilesEarl (good last
5-2410Haw1 ft 60° clm9600 1 :30 1:003 1:313 2:02 3 4 4 46½ 48 46p5 2:031 5-1 (J.Searle) MajorBlack, RealBlast, J.HazenAdios (no chan
5-1610Haw1 ft 43° clm9600 1 :33 1:043 1:362 2:064 1 4 5 54½ 43 31¾ 2:071 8-1 (J.Searle) Mr.Thunderbyrd, Mose, SengaMarie (closed sor

GRAY & BLACK **9** 10-1 =

Dirver—STANLEY BANKS, White-Purple Tr.—R. Monckton (153-17-25-15—.235) 1973 9 3 0 1 $5,108 2:031 Spk⅝
RAMS PRINCESS B f 1969, by Rams Counsel—Miss Kalabash—Guy Ambassador 1972 21 0 4 2 $2,415
Owner: Georgia C. Nehlig, Cicero, Ill. Lifetime $5,317 2, 2:084 (1)
7- 410Spk⅝ ft 82° clm9600=1 :31 1:032 1:34 2:043 4 5 55½° 31¼° 22 53 2:051 6-1 (S.Banks) SengaMarie, PortSam, LittlePuff (parked 2 tu
6-26 8Spk⅝ ft 76° clm9600+1 :292 1:013 1:323 2:032 9 9 96½ 910 85 55¼ 2:042 11-1 (J.D.Holford) RockSpringsCag, ZanStar, TarportPalmer (post h
6-11 4Spk⅝ ft 89° clm7200+1 :302 1:02 1:33 2:042 4 5 55 66° 43½ 1¾ 2:042 •2-1 (S.Banks) RamsPrncss, TamsnJove, JavelonJeanette (strong fin
6- 1 1Spk⅝ ft 79° clm6000+1 :292 1:01 1:312 2:031 3 4 45 46° 31 1hd 2:031 6-1 (S.Banks) RamsPrincess, AgnesMeridale, RomanDancer (late r
5-22 1Haw1 gd 68° clm4200 1 :31 1:024 1:354 2:071 9 4° 1 12½ 11 33½ 2:08 6-1 (S.Banks) KingSelka, SmokePuff, RamsPrincess (used ea
5-15 Haw1 ft 55° Qua 1 :312 1:02 1:341 2:04 2 2 3 33 35 312 2:062 NB (S.Banks) ByeByeBill, KeystoneJournal. RamsPrincss (————

1. WES TEE—If Wes Tee had broken stride on an off track, his race would have been automatically thrown out. But since he broke stride on a fast track, he's automatically eliminated from consideration. Evaluation—non-contender.

2. LOVIN LU LU—There's lots of room for improvement for this particular racing mare. In almost every one of her races, she's been able to get within striking distance after three quarters of the mile. But not once, in any of the races on her past performances, has she gained ground from that point on. Evaluation—non-contender.

3. INDIANA CHARMER—For the second time this chapter, we've come across a horse in which we have only one race to work with. And once again, we're able to make an easy elimination off that race. Indiana Charmer made a good move at the three quarter mark to take command. Unfortunately, his success was short lived. By the stretch call, he dropped back 2 lengths and by the time he reached the finish line, he stopped completely. He's getting a $1,000 class drop for tonight's race, but it's not nearly enough to make him a contender. Evaluation—non-contender.

4. WILL FLY—There's not much difference between Will Fly and Indiana Charmer. Both are coming off the same race and they were both badly beaten losers. Will Fly didn't stop quite as much as Indiana Charmer did, but he's still a long way from a contending role with only a $1,000 drop in class. Evaluation—non-contender.

5. FROSTY WIL—It isn't very likely Frosty Wil will make it to the winner's circle. The six year old gelding is working on his third class drop in a row and he still appears to be running above his head. Last time out, Frosty Wil was lowered $2,000 in class and failed to show any improvement in form over his previous race. Just off that effort alone, he hasn't raced well enough to get by even if he was taking another $2,000 class drop. The fact that Frosty Wil is only dropping down one notch for tonight's race is reason enough to ignore his chances. Evaluation—non-contender.

6. LUNAR HILL—After uncovering five non-contenders in succession, we've finally come across a horse that's performed well enough to become a contender. Lunar Hill capitalized on the $1,000 drop in class he received in his last race. He lost by only a length and a half after showing good speed for more than three quarters of the mile. Another class drop would greatly enhance his chances, but he's still in a good position since he's staying within the same class level. Evaluation—contender.

7. FIRST LOOK—We have to go back more than six weeks to get a ratable race. Last time out, First Look was parked out for two turns of the track. But that race is tossed out because he didn't hold up well. Then we have two consecutive off track efforts, but they're disregarded also because his past performances indicate he has trouble on wet surfaces. We finally get a race we can handicap back on June 1, but it's far from an impressive effort. He was never closer than 12 lengths during the entire race. A good performance would have turned First Look into an unratable contender, but he doesn't even qualify for that. Evaluation—non-contender.

8. SENGA MARIE—A good effort within the same class level will always put a horse into a contending role. That's the kind of race provided by Senga Marie, and in pretty good fashion to boot. The seven year old mare was 8 lengths behind at the half mile mark and she was still able to muster up enough speed to cross the finish line first. The class factor is also in her favor since she's entered at the same level. Evaluation—contender.

9. RAMS PRINCESS—This young filly also raced well her last time out. She was on the outside of the track for two turns and held up extremely well. In the race that was eventually won by Senga Marie, she was a definite factor during the entire contest. Rams Princess will have to be reckoned with here, since she's also staying within the same class level. Evaluation—contender.

With no unratable contenders in the race, our first priority turns directly to Senga Marie. She has the fastest final time out of the three contenders and advantage ratings are definitely in her favor. Just look at the difference there is when we calculate each one's last half.

Lunar Hill - 1:03 2/5
Senga Marie -   59 3/5
Rams Princess - 1:00 3/5

That good stretch drive turned in by Senga Marie gives her a second advantage. She made up 5 1/2 lengths in the final quarter and, in doing so, fulfilled a third advantage—winning her race. She meets the required three advantages which makes her our final choice.

SEVENTH RACE — 1 MILE
PACE. Claiming $8,000. 3 Years & Up. Purse $3,700.

Time—:30 1:023 1:334 2:034 Mutuel Pool—$122,709

8. Senga Marie	8	8	97½	74°	41¾	12¼	2:034	4-1	(Da.Busse)
7. First Look	7	7	76¾°	63°	31½	22¼	2:041	12-1	(J.Curran)
4. Will Fly	4	5	53¾°	2nk°	11½	33¾	2:043	7-2	(GVllndnghm)
1. Wes Tee	1	4	43¾	84½	74¼	44¾	2:044	13-1	(J.Ackerman)
5. Frosty Wil	5	6	64¾°	41½°	21½	54¾	2:044	*5-2	(J.MarshJr)
9. Ram's Princess	9	9	87¼	95½	86¼	65¾	2:05	15-1	(S.Banks)
6. Lunar Hill	6	3°	11¼	31¼	64¼	77½	2:052	6-1	(J.Morrissey)
2. Lovin Lu Lu	2	2	31¼	1nk	53¾	813	2:062	11-1	(W.Rosebm)
3. Indiana Charmer	3	1°	21¼	53	912	921	2:08	9-1	(N.Willis)

Mutuels—(8) 10.20 5.20 4.20—(7) 10.40 7.20—(4) 3.60

The race turned out to be almost an instant replay of Senga Marie's last effort. As the field hit the halfway point, she was dead last. Then, at the three quarter pole, she moved into contention by securing good cover on the outside. That was all she really needed. Senga Marie unleashed another fierce stretch drive and won the race going away. She paid $10.20 to win.

For some unexplainable reason, Frosty Wil was sent off as the 5-2 favorite. For those of you who want to test this race on numerical speed ratings, you'll find that Senga Marie was a clear choice.

The next race we'll work on is also a claiming affair. It was contested at Hawthorne Race Course's mile track which has the longest stretch run in the country. The race took place on May 17 and brought together a field of $10,000 claimers. Some of the evaluations are out of the ordinary, which makes this one a good exercise.

8 RACE

ONE MILE PACE — Claiming Price $10,000. — Purse $6,100

PLEASE ASK FOR HORSE BY PROGRAM NUMBER

PROGRAM NUMBER

Red **1** $12,000 7-2

DODIE DEE

Br m 67 by Philip Scot—Helen Ann—Royal Chief
Owner: Magic J. Stable, Michigan City, Ind.

1973	14	0	1	0	$2,793	
1972	33	6	7	2	$19,027	2:033 Spk⅝
Lifetime thru 1972					$25,552	

Driver—JOHNNY BLEVINS, White-Blue-Black **Trainer—J. Blevins**

Date	Trk Cd Tem	Class	Dis	Leader's Time ¼	½	¾	Winner's Time	PP	¼	½	¾	Str	Fin	Ind Time	Odds	Driver	Order of Finish First, Second, Third
5- 9	7Haw1 ft 66°	clm10800	1	:304	1:02	1:341	2:044	3	7	7°	32	21	21¼	2:05	3-1	(JBlevins)	IdlewhilesEarl, DodieDee, TerryJeansByrd
4-28	1Haw1 ft 43°	clm10200	1	:311	1:022	1:334	2:041	4	6	8	86¾	63½	42¾	2:044	15-1	(JBlevins)	WesternsJody, TerryJeansByrd, Goodare
4-18	10Haw1 sy 61°	clm10800	1	:302	1:033	1:372	2:09	2	6	6	53½	1½	53½	2:094	9-1	(JBlevins)	IdlewhilesEarl,RosedalePrince,MissLekram
4-11	6Spk⅝ sy 35°	clm10800	1	:331	1:063	1:38	2:103	4	5	7	7	615	410dh	2:123	24-1	(JBlevins)	BoldGene, Mose, Crawdad
4- 3	7Spk⅝ ft 37°	clm10800	1	:311	1:04	1:34	2:051	6	7	8	9	99¼	98¾	2:07	65-1	(JBlevins)	RuthsChoice, Brindanette, LovinLuLu
3-24	10Spk⅝ ft 48°	clm10800	1	:31	1:04	1:35	2:06	9	9	9	9	915	917	2:092	24-1	(JBlevins)	WorthyReward,PretzelBendr,RosedlePrnce

White **2** $10,000 9-2

PLUTO HAL

B g 67 by Rocket Byrd—Peggy Jean Hal—Purdue Hal
Owner: Peter J. Guido, Chicago, Ill.

1973	16	2	3	4	$8.904	2:06 Spk⅝
1972	39	5	8	7	$16,317	2:053 Was1
Lifetime thru 1972					$24,949	

Driver—WALTER PAISLEY, Green-White **Trainer—L. Lettau**

Date	Trk Cd Tem	Class	Dis	Leader's Time ¼	½	¾	Winner's Time	PP	¼	½	¾	Str	Fin	Ind Time	Odds	Driver	Order of Finish First, Second, Third
5- 3	10Haw1 ft 43°	clm10000	1	:311	1:042	1:36	2:063	3	2	1	12¼	14	2nk	2:063	*3-2	(JMarshJr)	WorthyReward, PlutoHal, Cheslind
4-25	8Haw1 ft 46°	clm11000	1	:31	1:004	1:32	2:034	6	2	3	34½	32	31¼	2:04	10-1	(WPaisley)	BengalSong, JewelThief, PlutoHal
4-16	4Spk⅝ ft 43°	clm8000	1	:311	1:041	1:34	2:06	5	2	3	2	11	1½	2:06	9-2	(WPaisley)	PlutoHal, DaveWestern, J.HazenAdios
4-11	10Spk⅝ sy 35°	clm7000	1	:311	1:06	1:393	2:102	5	2	2	2	12½	18¼	2:102	5-2	(JMarshJr)	PlutoHal, YoungBrooks, JustaBreak
4- 4	5Spk⅝ gd 36°	Cclm6000	1	:31	1:04	1:352	2:072	3	1	3	6	41½	32½	2:08	4-1	(WPaisley)	C.R.Purdue, GrandClara, PlutoHal
3-27	7Spk⅝ ft 38°	clm6000	1	:311	1:034	1:351	2:062	6	6°	6°	6°	86	810	2:082	32-1	(ATitusJr)	ClemK., AllenSenator, Cinarkin

Blue

3

$12,000

5-1

TERRY JEAN'S ROCKET

B g 69 by Rocket Byrd—Hootnanny—Hardy Hanover
Owners: Morris M. & Victor Zeinfeld, Lincolnwood, Maywood, Ill.

1973	8	0	2	2	$2.318		
1972	6	1	0	3	$3.148	2:06^1	L.A.⅝
Lifetime thru 1972					$11,100		

Driver—TOM RATCHFORD, Gold-White **Trainer—J. Dennis**

5- 1	L.A.⅝	ft	nw5500	1	:31^1	1:02^4	1:34	2:05	5	6	6	6	6^3	4^4	2:05^4	4-1	(JDennis)	TotalFreight, ShyVariety, CountParee
4-26	L.A.⅝	ft	nw5000	1	:31^1	1:02	1:33	2:03	3	6	5	4	4^{1½}	3^{2¾}	2:03^3	*8-5	(JDennis)	SingleSmith,FireballJude,TerryJeansRcket
4-19	L.A.⅝	ft	nw5000	1	:30^2	1:02	1:32^3	2:02^1	4	1	2	2	2^1	2^{2½}	2:02^3	9-2	(JDennis)	RacingColor,TerryJeansRockt,SingleSmith
4-13	L.A.⅝	ft	nw5000	1	:29^3	:59^3	1:32^1	2:03^4	1	4	4	1	1^1	4^{4¾}	2:04^4	9-2	(JDennis)	Beretta, GrapeVine, PeterJayAdios
4- 3	L.A.⅝	ft	nw5000	1	:31^2	1:04	1:35	2:04^4	5	2	2	1	1^1	2^{¾}	2:05	*6-5	(JDennis)	ButlerBoy,TerrysJeansRockt,PetrJayAdios
3-22	L.A.⅝	ft	nw6500^{7273}	1	:30	1:02	1:34^1	2:03^4	6	6ix	5	5	5^{4½}	4^{8½}	2:05^2	23-1	(JDennis)	W.P.Adios, DutchHillPrince, SportsArena

Green

4

$10,000

6-1

LITTLE PUFF

B h 68 by Poplar Byrd—Charlotte—Southern Tryax
Owners: Misty Farm & Walter P. Myers, Salem, Ill.

1973	7	2	1	1	$5,602	2:04^1	L.A.⅝
1972	18	2	3	4	$6.991	2:02^4	Haw^1
Lifetime thru 1972					$13,719		

Driver—JERRY GRAHAM, Green-Orange **Trainer—J. Graham**

5- 8	^{9}Haw^1	ft 60°	clm11000	1	:31^2	1:03^2	1:34^2	2:05^2	3	4	6x	9^{16}	8^{15}	8^{18}	2:09	5-2	(JGraham)	G.T.Winter, FirstLook, LyricEyre
4-30	^{7}Haw^1	sy 50°	clm13000	1	:30^4	1:02	1:33	2:03^2	8	2°	2	3^2	4^3	5^{7¾}	2:05	19-1	(JGraham)	SenatorBerry, GoranHanover, C.F.Guy
4-20	^{6}Haw^1	sy 64°	clm12000	1	:34^2	1:05^1	1:37^2	2:06^4	2	2	3	3^{3½}	3^{2½}	2^{3¼}	2:07^2	5-1	(JGraham)	SenatorBerry, LittlePuff, NobleChoice
4- 5	L.A.⅝	ft	clm12000	1	:30^4	1:02	1:32^2	2:02^2	6	7	7	7	8^5	5^{3¾}	2:03	16-1	(JGraham)	RickyCounsel, Koranie, DsScottyCounsel
3-30	L.A.⅝	ft	clm9000	1	:30^2	1:03^2	1:33^4	2:04^1	8	1	1	1	1^{1½}	1^{nk}	2:04^1	9-1	(JGraham)	LittlePuff, G.B.Goldenboy, OnlyTrouble
3-22	L.A.⅝	ft	clm8500	1	:31^1	1:02^4	1:33^2	2:04^2	1	4	4	4	4^2	1^{½}	2:04^2	6-1	(JGraham)	LittlePuff, GameJack, JeffersonExpress

Black

5

$10,000

10-1

NOBLE SCOT

B g 66 by Scottish Pence—Prim Bay—Goose Bay
Owner: Duncan Price, Homewood, Ill.

1973	16	1	1	1	$5.843	2:06^2	Spk⅝
1972	41	3	5	5	$17,135	2:09^1	BmlP
Lifetime thru 1972					$40,519		

Driver—DUNCAN PRICE, Red-White-Blue **Trainer—D. Price**

5- 7	^{10}Haw^1	sy 60°	clm10000	1	:30^4	1:03^3	1:36	2:06	5	6	6	5^{3½}	3^{5½}	3^{3½}	2:06^4	17-1	(DPrice)	ValiantSampson, WesternsJody, NobleScot
4-30	^{10}Haw^1	sy 50°	clm10000	1	:32^3	1:04^2	1:36	2:07	3	6	5°	4^{3½}	5^4	4^{4¼}	2:07^4	21-1	(DPrice)	DeltaDirect, SeattleCindy, VarsitySignal
4-19	^{7}Haw^1	ft 67°	clm11000	1	:31^1	1:01^4	1:34	2:04^1	3	4	4	4^5	7^8	7^{10}	2:06^1	27-1	(DPrice)	Rozella, G.T.Winter, HandsomeDate
4-13	^{3}Spk⅝	ft 39°	clm10000	1	:30^4	1:02^4	1:33^1	2:04^2	5	8	8	8	8^{13}	8^{11}	2:06^3	24-1	(DPrice)	ChiefsLittleStar,HandsmeDate,DeltaDirect
4- 5	^{8}Spk⅝	ft 53°	clm11000	1	:29^4	1:02^2	1:33^2	2:05	6	7	7	8	7^7	5^6	2:06^1	25-1	(DPrice)	Dr.Conway, StewartCraig, FirstLook
3-28	^{8}Spk⅝	sy 50°	clm10000	1	:32^2	1:06^2	1:37^4	2:10^1	6	3°	1	3	3^{3¼}	4^5	2:11^1	9-1	(DPrice)	FrostyWil, FirstLook, Dr.Conway

Yellow

6

$10,000

6-1

BILLY CLIPPER

Ch g 65 by Clipper Ship—Widower Princess—Bay Prince
Owner: Nicholas J. Wall, Richwood, Ohio

1973	8	0	0	2	$2,399		
1972	38	12	6	5	$37,324	2:00	Haw^1
Lifetime thru 1972					$62,111		

Driver—JOE MARSH, JR. Gray-Blue-Red **Trainer—J. Marsh, Jr.**

5- 8	^{9}Haw^1	ft 60°	clm11000	1	:31^2	1:03^2	1:34^2	2:05^2	2	3	4	4^{1½}	3^{2½}	5^{3½}	2:06^1	9-2	(JMarshJr)	G.T.Winter, FirstLook, LyricEyre
4- 4	^{8}Spk⅝	gd 36°	clm14000	1	:30	1:02^4	1:34	2:05^4	8	8	8	7°	9^6	8^{10}	2:07^4	12-1	(JMarshJr)	StrongByrd, TinaKnox, KnoxAbout
3-27	^{8}Spk⅝	ft 38°	clm15000	1	:30^1	1:04^3	1:34^4	2:05^1	2	3	3	1	1^{nk}	7^5	2:06^1	9-2	(JMarshJr)	WardenIllmo, Avanti, CarolChief
3-20	^{8}Spk⅝	ft 35°	clm15000	1	:31^2	1:04^1	1:34^1	2:05^3	4	3	4	7	4^{2¾}	4^3	2:06^1	7-2	(JMarshJr)	SpringMeadow, Avanti, CarolChief
3-13	^{8}Spk⅝	sy 56°	clm14000	1	:32^3	1:05^3	1:38	2:10^2	3	1	1	1	1^{1½}	3^{2½}	2:11	5-2	(JMarshJr)	SpringMeadow.DyamiteWomen,BillyClipper
3- 7	^{7}Spk⅝	ft 52°	clm15000	1	:30^2	1:02^2	1:33^2	2:03^4	3	2	2	2	2^3	4^{4¾}	2:04^4	5-2	(JMarshJr)	RichReveller, SkiSlope, Avanti

Brown

7

$10,000

12-1

ARMBRO HUSKY

Br h 64, by Capetown—Armbro Elite—Tar Heel
Owners: S. Halford & L'Dorado Farms, Crete, So. Holland, Ill.

1973	15	5	3	1	$11.815	2:06^3	Spk⅝
1972	38	6	5	9	$15,989	2:03	Spk⅝
Lifetime thru 1972					$55,514		

Driver—NELSON WILLIS, Maroon-Gray-White **Trainer—S. Halford**

5- 8	^{9}Haw^1	ft 60°	clm11000	1	:31^2	1:03^2	1:34^2	2:05^2	9	9	8°	7^5	x9^{25}	9^{dis}		18-1	(WMoore)	G.T.Winter, FirstLook, LyricEyre
5- 1	^{9}Haw^1	sy 62°	clm11000	1	:32^3	1:05^1	1:36^3	2:08^1	7	6	6x	5^{3½}	4^5	7^2	2:08^3	7-1	(WPaisley)	C.R.Purdue, EyreFire, Knoxella
4-23	^{10}Haw^1	ft 51°	clm13000	1	:32^1	1:04^4	1:35^4	2:05^4	5	6	7	9^8	9^{4½}	7^{5½}	2:07	3-1	(WPaisley)	EdgewoodKeene,BillsDaughtr,StwartCraig
3-27	^{8}Spk⅝	ft 38°	clm15000	1	:30^1	1:04^3	1:34^4	2 05^1	5	7	7	6°	8^3	6^{4¼}	2:06	5-1	(WPaisley)	WardenIllmo, Avanti, CarolChief
3-21	^{8}Spk⅝	ft 35°	clm13000	1	:30^4	1:03	1:33^1	2:04^2	1	3	3	3	2^5	2^{nk}	2:04^2	5-2	(WPaisley)	DeansTreasure, ArmbroHusky, AdiosTwo
3-16	^{6}Spk⅝	sy 34°	clm12500	1	:32^2	1:06^2	1:37^3	2:11	3	6	6	5	4^{4½}	2^{1¼}	2:11^1	4-1	(WPaisley)	StrongByrd, ArmbroHusky, DeansTreasure

Red & Yellow
8
$10,000
15-1

DOCTOR C.

B g 66 by Amortizor—Roberta Giers—R. K. Giers
Owner: William J. McEnery, Evergreen Park, Ill.

1973	6	0	0	0	$235	
1972	25	1	1	2	$7.227	$2:05^3$ Spk$\frac{5}{8}$
Lifetime thru 1972					$47,043	

Driver—JESSIE WILLIS, Maroon-Gray-White   Trainer—J. Willis

3-31 ^{2}Spk$\frac{5}{8}$A ·y 44°	clm9000	1	$:30^3$	$1:03^3$	$1:37^2$	$2:08^4$	9	2	2	5	9^{18}	9^{dis}		43-1	(JWillis)	NearChief, Mose, DutchKnight
3-21 ^{10}Spk$\frac{5}{8}$ ft 35°	clm9000	1	$:30^4$	1:05	$1:36^1$	$2:06^4$	8	9	9	9	9^{11}	9^{14}	$2:09^3$	11-1	(JWillis)	BillCarlith, JerryDuke, DillerVolo
3-15 Spk$\frac{5}{8}$ ft 52°	Qua	1	$:30^4$	$1:04^2$	$1:36^1$	$2:09^2$	6	1	2	3	$3^{1\frac{1}{2}}$	2^{hd}	$2:09^2$	NB	(JWillis)	AmysChick, DoctorC., FirePilot
3-10 ^{10}Spk$\frac{5}{8}$ sy 58°	clm10000	1	$:31^1$	1:05	1:38	$2:09^4$	5	1	1	1	$2^{1\frac{1}{2}}$	7^{14}	$2:12^3$	10-1	(JWillis)	HangOver, Edstime, FrostyWil
3- 6 ^{9}Spk$\frac{5}{8}$ ft 65°	clm12500	1	$:30^3$	$1:02^4$	$1:34^3$	$2:06^3$	3	3	3	4	$5^{3\frac{3}{4}}$	$5^{4\frac{3}{4}}$	$2:07^3$	13-1	(JWillis)	Levitas, MerryRuler, SummertimeDirect
2-28 ^{7}Spk$\frac{5}{8}$ ft 41°	nw2000^6	1	$:30^4$	1:03	1:34	$2:04^4$	2	5	5	8	$7^{5\frac{3}{4}}$	$8^{5\frac{1}{2}}$	2:06	8-1	(JWillis)	Ajax, ShadHanover, MagicTime

Orange
9
$10,000
6-1

VALIANT SAMPSON

B h 67 by Sampson Direct—Susan Carmel—Adios Paul
Owner: Ken Vander Schaaf, Sandwich, Ill.

1973	19	3	2	2	$10.070	2:06 Haw^1
1972	36	5	9	5	$6,764	$2:05^3$ Was^1
Lifetime thru 1972					$11,330	

Driver—STANLEY BANKS, White-Purple   Trainer—K. Vander Schaaf

5- 9 Haw^1 ft 71°	‡Qua	1	$:32^1$	1:03	$1:35^4$	$2:07^2$	3	1	1	1^{2}x	3^2	$1^{2\frac{1}{4}}$	$2:07^2$	NB	(SBanks)	ValiantSampson,KystneJournl,CinderCloud
5- 7 ^{10}Haw^1 sy 60°	clm10000	1	$:30^4$	$1:03^3$	1:36	2:06	2	4	4	$2^{1\frac{1}{4}}$	1^4	$1^{2\frac{1}{4}}$	2:06	9-2	(SBanks)	ValiantSampson, WesternsJody, NobleScot
4-25 ^{8}Haw^1 ft 46°	clm11000	1	:31	$1:00^4$	1:32	$2:03^4$	2	4	4	4^6	4^3	$4^{3\frac{1}{2}}$	$2:04^3$	9-2	(SBanks)	BengalSong, JewelThief, PlutoHal
4-16 ^{6}Spk$\frac{5}{8}$ ft 43°	clm12000	1	:31	$1:02^4$	$1:32^4$	$2:03^4$	7	1	1	1	$1_{\frac{1}{2}}$	$5^{4\frac{1}{4}}$	$2:04^3$	14-1	(SBanks)	FrostyWil, PrinceRocket, FirstLook
4-11 ^{8}Spk$\frac{5}{8}$ sy 35°	clm12000	1	$:31^1$	$1:04^2$	$1:37^1$	$2:09^1$	8	5	5	3	$4^{1\frac{1}{2}}$	4^6	$2:10^2$	38-1	(SBanks)	TinaKnox, FrostyWil, FirstLook
4- 2 ^{7}Spk$\frac{5}{8}$ ft 42°	clm12000	1	$:30^3$	1:04	$1:33^4$	$2:05^4$	8	1	1	1	1^1	6^9	$2:07^3$	48-1	(SBanks)	TecklaAdiosB,NobleChoice,SummrtmDirct

1. DODIE DEE—A pretty good effort was turned in by this mare her last time out. But unfortunately, she has only one half of the class-form relationship working in her favor. The 20% allowance which is given to Dodie Dee for her female status translates her last race into a $9,000 claimer. Since Dodie Dee is going up in class off a race she didn't win, she's automatically eliminated. This is something that can easily be overlooked, so it's important to keep your eyes out for the allowances given in claiming races. Evaluation—non-contender.

2. PLUTO HAL—Here's a six year old gelding that just missed a winning effort his last time out. He grabbed the lead at the half mile mark, worked his way up to a 4-length lead in the stretch, then was caught from behind and lost the race by a head. Pluto Hal was dropped down $1,000 for the race and it appears his present form is best among $10,000 company. Evaluation—contender.

3. TERRY JEAN'S ROCKET—This is the kind of horse that gives handicappers a nightmare. The young gelding is not only shipping in from a track outside the local circuit, but he's also making his first appearance in a claiming race which makes his class status somewhat obscure against the rest of the field. Terry Jean's Rocket has been competing at Los Alamitos, which is about one step above the class of horses found at Hawthorne Race Course. Therefore, he would meet the conditions of tonight's race even if he was taking a small class hike. But the facts actually reveal the opposite—a small class drop. Conditions reading "non-winners of $5,000" generally attract horses worth a few thousand dollars more than tonight's claiming level. However, Terry Jean's Rocket still would be a contender since his races haven't been on the local circuit. Evaluation—unratable contender.

4. LITTLE PUFF—A rather easy evaluation is made for this horse. He's automatically eliminated for breaking stride on a fast track. Evaluation—non-contender.

5. NOBLE SCOT—Scratched.

6. BILLY CLIPPER—After all things have been put in their proper perspective, this veteran performed pretty well in his last race. He was dropped down $3,000 in class and made considerable improvement over his next to last race. Another thing that shouldn't go overlooked is the fact that Billy Clipper was on the sidelines for more than a month going into that race. He's receiving another class drop tonight and he's very capable of improving off his last effort. Evaluation—contender.

7. AMBRO HUSKY—Just another horse,

who's eliminated for breaking stride on a fast track. Evaluation—non-contender.

8. DOCTOR C—There's absolutely nothing working in the way of a contending role for this horse. He hasn't been on the racetrack for more than six weeks. The last couple of races he competed in were about as bad as you'll ever see in a racing program. To top everything off, he's going up in class for tonight's race. Evaluation—non-contender.

9. VALIANT SAMPSON—This is the third horse in the race we can eliminate for breaking stride on a fast track. Valiant Sampson broke stride in a qualifier, which is probably the worst kind of race a horse could make a break in. Evaluation—non-contender.

The race is playable since we've uncovered only one unratable contender. That was Terry Jean's Rocket and on paper he doesn't look too bad. He's well placed as far as class goes and he's shown pretty good form recently on the West Coast. But the fact still remains that he's a shipper, and shippers do not win often enough. He hasn't competed against local horses and he's yet to test the present raceway. Two horses of this type would make the race unplayable, but the presence of one is not enough reason to pass up a potentially winning wager.

The field's been narrowed down to just two contenders—Pluto Hal and Billy Clipper. The fastest final time belongs to Billy Clipper, but he doesn't have the required three advantages to make him a final choice in that respect. The race calls for numerical speed ratings and here's the chart:

time should always be used instead of the official half mile time whenever it's available.

Pluto Hal	—Final Time	2:06 3/5 =	33
	Last Half	1:02 1/5 =	+11
	Base Rating		44

Billy Clipper	—Final Time	2:06 1/5 =	31
	Last Half	1:02 4/5 =	+14
	Base Rating		45

The only adjustment we have to make for Pluto Hal is in the post position column. He's moving in from the three post to the two which takes off 1/2 point away from his base rating. That brings his adjusted final rating to 43 1/2.

Billy Clipper has a 45 base rating which turns out to be the same as his adjusted final rating. He gets 2 points knocked off for the drop in class but then 2 points are added on because he's moving out in post position from the two hole to the six.

The final choice in the race would be Pluto Hal. His adjusted final rating is 1 1/2 points better than Billy Clipper's rating.

EIGHTH RACE—ONE MILE PACE—PURSE $6,100
Claiming Price $12,000-$10,000.
Scratched—NOBLE SCOT

DODIE DEE claimed for $12,000 by L. B. & M. Stables, Tr.—P. Milburn

Time—:31¹   1:02   1:34²   2:04²   Mutuel Pool $103,492

2 Pluto Hal	2	4	3	3³	2½	11½	2:04²	3-1	(WPaisley)
1 Dodie Dee	1	5	4	44½	33½	21½	2:04⁴	*5-2	(JBlevins)
3 TerryJeansRocket	3	6	5	66½	44½	31½	2:04⁴	5-1	(TRatchford)
9 Valiant Sampson	8	1	1	1²	1½	41¾	2:04⁴	9-1	(SBanks)
6 Billy Clipper	5	7	6	56	55½	53	2:05	4-1	(JMarshJr)
8 Doctor C.	7	3	2	2²	66x	61⁴	2:07¹	34-1	(JWillis)
7 Armbro Husky	6	8	7	714x	7dis	7dis		13-1	(NWillis)
4 Little Puff	4	2°x8	8dis	8dis	8dis			5-1	(JGraham)

MUTUELS—(2) $8.00 $3.80 $2.60—(1) $3.80 $3.20—(3) $3.20

Pluto Hal was the benefactor of a perfect trip

Horse	Final Time	Last Half	Base Rating	Class		P.P.		Park		Adj. Final Rating
Pluto Hal	33	11	44	-	44	-½	43½	-	43½	43½
Billy Clipper	31	14	45	-2	43	+2	45	-	45	45

The program we're working with doesn't list the lengths the horse was behind at the half mile pole. So to calculate the last half, we take the difference between the official half mile time and the horse's final time. But it's only calculated this way when the situation calls for it. The horse's actual half mile

from his driver. He stayed close to the leaders and didn't have to make a move for the first three quarters of the race. Then, in the final quarter, he eventually wore down the frontrunning Valiant Sampson and proved to be the best in the race. He returned a modest $8.00 to win.

Coming in second in the race was Dodie Dee. She turned in a good effort which probably would have been a winning one if she was up against $9,000 claimers. Terry Jean's Rocket also raced well and he could very well improve off his effort now that he's had a race on the local surface.

Another thing that's important to point out is the breakers that were entered in the field. All three horses that broke stride in their last race were leaving on the outside of Pluto Hal. That doesn't present a problem. But had the situation been the opposite, or you come across a situation where there's one or more breakers leaving on the inside of the horse you're wagering on, it's very advisable

to be cautious. If the animal is a speed horse and it appears that he'll be clear of the potential breakers from the start, then proceed as usual. But if the horse is likely to find himself behind the potential breakers during the race, then I suggest you play it safe and cut your wager in half.

The last race we'll work on is a conditioned event for "Winners of $10,000 or more in 1972 and 1973." The race took place at Sportsman's Park on July 6. Nine horses were entered in the field and, as you'll see by the evaluations, it's a very interesting race.

ONE MILE PACE   # SEVENTH RACE   **Purse $5,700**

"15th WARD REGULAR REPUBLICAN ORGANIZATION"

CONDITIONED — 3 Year Olds and Upward — Winners of $10,000 or more in 1972-73.

PLEASE ASK FOR HORSE BY PROGRAM NUMBER

	Date	Trk Cond Temp	Class	Dist	1/4	1/2	3/4	Winner's Time	PP	1/4	1/2	3/4	Str	Fin	Ind.Time	Odds	Driver	First	Second	Third	Comment

RED 1 6-1 =
Driver—JACK ACKERMAN, Black-Gold — Tr.—J. Ackerman — (27-3-1-5—.193) — 1973 3 0 0 1 $456 2:06³ Spk⅝ Qua — 1972 34 6 6 2 $30,818 2:00⁴ Spk⅝
ARCADIA JAKE Ch g 1968, by Hayes Counsel—Memory Lane—Brookdale — Owners: Wildman, Roschman et al., Indianapolis, Ind. — Lifetime $88,816 3, 1:59¹ (1)
6-29 5Spk⅝ ft 76° nw25006-1 :30³ 1:02⁴ 1:32³ 2:02² 9 2° 11½ 31½ 42 31¾ 2:02⁴ 9-2 (J.Ackerman) ByeByeRoger, SteadyBlaze, ArcadiaJake (blocked)
6-22 7Spk⅝ ft 76° inv6000-1 :29 1:01 1:30¹ 2:00 9 9 98½° 97½° 97 97½ 2:01³ 35-1 (J.Ackerman) C.V.Thor, BrindaAnnsWinner, JetCoe (overmatched)
6-16 6Spk⅝ sy 68° w100007273-1 :28⁴ 1:00² 1:32 2:05⁴ 4 6 6¹² 67¼ 86¼ 79 2:07³ 14-1 (J.Ackerman) YankeeBaron, AdiosArt, Chaw (needed start)
6-13 Spk⅝ ft 74° Qua 1 :32 1:04 1:36 2:06³ 7 2° 14 12 13 16¾ 2:06³ NB (J.Ackerman) ArcadiaJake, FlamingEyre, MissPeggyFrisco (———)
11-24 6Was¹ ft 38° w100007172 1 :32¹ 1:02² 1:33² 2:03¹ 2 2 12½ 1½ 21½ 74¾ 2:04¹ 9-1 (J.Ackerman) FntsticDrm, LstaSkyRdr, MiGrndeAmgo (weakened in str)
11-18 7Was¹ ft 33° w100007172 1 :31² 1:02⁴ 1:34² 2:03³ 8 8 8¹⁰ 97 96 6¾ 2:04² 15-1 (J.Ackerman) ShadyCounsel, RustyWidower, YankeeBaron (away slow)

BLUE 2 10-1 =
Driver—JIM DOLBEE, Green-White-Red — Tr.—E. Clum — (112-16-15-20—.277) — 1973 18 3 0 0 $10,345 2:00⁴ Haw¹ — 1972 26 6 4 3 $29,961 2:00 Spk⅝
RIGHT GOOD Ch h 1968, by Right Time—Wayfield—King's Counsel — Owner: Sho-Mor Inc., Park Ridge, Ill. — Lifetime $66,724 4, 2:00 (⅝)
6-30 9Spk⅝ ft 74° w10000-1 :29³ 1:02¹ 1:31⁴ 2:01³ 3 6 87¼ 86 75¼ 52¾ 2:02¹ 12-1 (J.Dolbee) GameGuy, Doc'sJerry, RobbRanger (raced well)
6-23 8Spk⅝ gd 66° w100007273-1 :30 1:04 1:34² 2:04¹ 1 3 3³ 63½ 65 64½ 2:05¹ 9-1 (J.Dolbee) ShadyMile, YankeeCreed, ShadHanover (evenly)
6-16 9Spk⅝ sy 65° inv7500-1 :30 1:04² 1:36 2:04⁴ 5 5 55½ 55 6¹² 69½ 2:08⁴ 12-1 (J.Dolbee) Kentucky, QuakerByrd, DoctorAndy (soundly beaten)
6- 9 8Spk⅝ ft 78° inv7000+1 :29⁴ 1:01⁴ 1:31¹ 2:00¹ 5 4 44¼ 43 36½ 44¾ 2:01¹ 12-1 (J.Dolbee) TheGrumbler, QuakerByrd, ShadyCounsel (raced well)
6- 2 7Spk⅝ sy 65° inv7000-1 :30² 1:03² 1:33² 2:03¹ 2 4 45½ 46 6¹¹ 88½ 2:05 7-2 (W.Paisley) ChiefGDirect, GuyDaniel, NobleSon (out of it)
5-26 9Spk⅝ ft 60° hcp15000-1 :30 1:02¹ 1:32² 2:00² 1 3 32¾ 42½ 65½ 67¾ 2:02 9-1 (J.Dolbee) DancerGeorge, GdByeClmbs, SlasTme (soundly beaten)

WHITE 3 6-1 =
Driver—STANLEY BANKS, White-Purple — Tr.—H. Vander Schaaf — (124-15-21-12—.247) — 1973 18 4 4 2 $16,675 2:02 sy Haw¹ — 1972 33 4 6 4 $14,066 1:59² Haw¹
DAN ADIOS B g 1968, by Ellen's Adios—Kud Bee—Scotch War — Owner: John H. Den Herder, Sioux Center, Iowa — Lifetime $15,567 4, 1:59² (1)
6-23 7Spk⅝ gd 66° w100007273-1 :31² 1:06 1:36¹ 2:06² 2x 9 87¼ 85¾° 87¾ 97¾ 2:08 7-2 (S.Banks) CafineKid, TeddyRip, WorthyBret (broke early)
6-14 8Spk⅝ ft 69° w100007273-1 :31² 1:01² 1:31 2:01¹ 9 9 9¹⁷ 9¹⁵ 9¹⁵ 914 2:04 8-1 (J.Grvngoed) ShadHanover, JetCoe, GameGene (trailed)
6- 2 6Spk⅝ sy 65° w100007273-1 :29¹ 1:00¹ 1:30¹ 2:01¹ 9 9 98½° 85 64¼ 2"" 2:01¹ 17-1 (S.Banks) NativeExpress, DanAdios, WorthyBret (pwrful str. rush)
5-25 8Haw¹ ft 58° w100007273-1 :31² 1:01 1:31² 2:00³ 6 6 74½° 88½ 88½ 2:02² 20-1 (J.Grvngoed) Ha'Brunt, G.T.Skipper, EliLang (no chance)
5-12 9Haw¹ ft 52° w10000 1 :29⁴ 1:01 1:31¹ 2:00⁴ 4 6 9 96¾° 62¾ 22 2:01¹ 12-1 (S.Banks) RightGood, DanAdios, SimonesSkipper (last ½ good)
5- 5 9Haw¹ ft 50° w10000 1 :29³ :59¹ 1:30 1:59⁴ 7 9im7 69½ 67½ 56½ 2:01¹ 20-1 (J.Grvngoed) ShadyCounsel, HeyChris, GameGuy (road trouble)

GREEN 4 3-1 =
Driver—MERRITT DOKEY, White-Red-Black — Tr.—M. Dokey — (2-1-0-0—.500) — 1973 5 1 1 1 $5,472 2:00³ Det¹ — 1972 20 8 2 1 $22,839 2:02² Det¹
CREEDER LINBO Br c 1969, by Widower Creed—Ellyn Sampson—Sampson Hanover — Owner: J. Sacco and A. Rosenberg, Oak Park, Southfield, Mich. — Lifetime $25,089 3, 2:02² (1)
6-29 7Spk⅝ ft 76° w100007273 1 :30² 1:00⁴ 1:30¹ 2:00 3 3 3³ 32½ 33 53¼ 2:00³ 7-2 (M.Dokey) UncleKenny, ShadHanover, Overhaul (went evenly)
6-23 Nor ft w10000 1 :30¹ 1:02² 1:33 2:03⁴ 6 1 1 1 1¹ 2¾ 2:04 8-5 (M.Dokey) DaveButler, CreederLinbo, ErlanasVally (———)
6-16 Det¹ ft pref8500 1 :30² 1:00⁴ 1:30¹ 1:59 1 2 1 1 1¹ 78 2:00³ *9-5 (M.Dokey) KeystonePonder, SkipperGneMrx, BrmbleHll (———)
6- 9 Det¹ ft pref8500 1 :30 1:00 1:30² 2:00 7 8 8 8 6⁵ 3½ 2:00 9-5 (M.Dokey) BretOverAgain, Economist, CreederLinbo (———)
6- 2 Det¹ ft w10000 1 :30³ 1:00³ 1:31 2:00³ 2 3 5 4° 31½ 13 2:00³ 7-2 (M.Dokey) CreederLinbo, ShellsGold, CampbellN (———)
9-14 H.P⅝ ft 3yrstk29700 1 :30² 1:01³ 1:32² 2:02 3 4 5 32 33 2:02³ 8-1 (M.Dokey) SilentMajority, FastClip, CreederLinbo (———)

BLACK 5 9-2 =

Driver—JIM CURRAN, Gray-Gold Tr.—R. Farrington (10-2-0-3—.267)

YANKEE BARON

B g 1967, by Baron Hanover—Princess J.,—Yankee Hanover
Owners: Farrington Stables, Inc. and J. Ludy; Richwood, Tipp City, Ohio

1973	16	2	2	4	$16,630	2:02^{2} Spk⅝
1972	34	9	3	5	$32,903	2:02^{3} Haw^{1}
			Lifetime		$57,110	4, 2:02^{1} (1)

6-30	^{4}Spk⅝ ft 78°	w10000=1	:30	1:01^{4}	1:30^{3}	2:00^{1}	1	3	4^{2½}	5^{2½}°	4^{½}	3^{3}	2:00^{4}	6-1 (W.Paisley)	AdiosArt, DoctorTom, YankeeBaron	(outpaced str)
6-23	^{7}Spk⅝ gd 66°	w10000^{7273}=1	:31^{2}	1:06	1:36^{1}	2:06^{2}	6	6	6^{5½}	6^{4½}	5^{4½}	4^{1½}	2:06^{4}	11-1 (J.Dolbee)	CafineKid, TeddyRip, WorthyBret	(raced well)
6-16	^{6}Spk⅝ sy 68°	w10000^{7273}=1	:28^{4}	1:00^{2}	1:32	2:05^{4}	5	7	7^{15}	7^{8¼}	4^{1¼}	1^{nk}	2:05^{4}	6-1 (W.Paisley)	YankeeBaron, AdiosArt, Chaw	(last ½ good)
5-23	^{8}Haw^{1} ft 61°	nw2100^{8} 1	:30^{2}	1:01^{2}	1:32^{3}	2:01^{3}	4	5	5	6^{3½}	5^{5}	3^{4½}	2:02^{3}	5-1 (W.Paisley)	Overhaul, StarboardButler, YankeeBaron	(went evenly)
5-12	^{2}Haw^{1} ft 52°	w10000 1	:31^{1}	1:00^{1}	1:31^{3}	2:01^{1}	6	8	8	7^{6½}°	5^{5}	5^{5½}	2:02^{2}	12-1 (J.Dolbee)	G.T.Skipper, TheFooler, NobleSkipper	(too much speed)
5-5	^{9}Haw^{1} ft 50°	w10000 1	:29^{3}	:59^{1}	1:30	1:59^{4}	3	7	ix9	7^{12}	8^{19}	8^{23}	2:04^{2}	21-1 (R.Farringtn)	ShadyCounsel, HeyChris, GameGuy	(road trouble)

YELLOW 6 8-1 =

Driver—JIM DENNIS, Green-White Tr.—J. Dennis (113-26-23-8—.367)

NICKS PAINTER

B g 1968, by Painter—Brenda Kay—True Chief
Owners: Victor Zeinfeld and Morris M. Zeinfeld; Maywood, Lincolnwood, Ill.

1973	14	3	1	2	$10,870	2:01^{1} L.A⅝
1972	34	7	7	7	$48,805	1:58^{4} Hol^{1}
			Lifetime		$76,576	4, 1:58^{4} (1)

6-30	^{9}Spk⅝ ft 74°	w10000=1	:29^{3}	1:02^{1}	1:31^{4}	2:01^{3}	1	4	4^{3¾}	4^{2¼}	5^{2¾}	8^{3½}	2:02^{2}	5-1 (J.Dennis)	GameGuy, Doc'sJerry, RobbRanger	(raced well)
6-23	^{7}Spk⅝ gd 66°	w10000^{7273}=1	:31^{2}	1:06	1:36^{1}	2:06^{2}	7	7	5^{4½}°	5^{3¾}°	6^{5½}	7^{7}	2:07^{4}	6-1 (J.Dennis)	CafineKid, TeddyRip, WorthyBret	(hung out)
6-16	^{8}Spk⅝ sy 68°	w10000^{7273}=1	:30^{3}	1:04^{4}	1:35^{2}	2:07	1	3	3^{2½}	3^{2}	2^{½}	3^{½}	2:07^{1}	*3-1 (J.MarshJr)	Cleostar, ShadyMile, NicksPainter	(bid in str)
6-9	^{4}Spk⅝ ft 78°	nw2500^{6}=1	:30^{2}	1:01^{1}	1:32^{4}	2:01^{2}	3	6	8^{4¼}°	1^{½}°	1^{1½}	1^{4¼}	2:01^{2}	5-1 (J.Dennis)	NicksPaintr BayStarBoy, MajesticBelleG	(powerful race)
6-2	^{5}Spk⅝ ft 73°	nw2500$^{4-10}$—1	:30^{3}	1:02^{2}	1:32^{3}	2:01^{2}	1	3	3^{2¼}	5^{3}	5^{4}	4^{6¼}	2:02^{3}	13-1 (J.Dennis)	GaySkipper, ByeByeBill, Folger	(rail no help)
5-19	^{8}Haw^{1} ft 55°	w10000 1	:30^{2}	1:02	1:31^{3}	2:01	5	7	4°	4^{5}	4^{3½}	7^{9}	2:02^{4}	10-1 (B.Nickells)	G.T.Skipper, PerleyHanover, TomsChoice	(no threat)

GREEN & WHITE 7 10-1 =

Driver—AUBREY PETTY, Maroon-Black Tr.—A. Petty (40-4-8-7—.269)

TEE CEE

Blk h 1968, by Shadow Wave—Bessie Fay—Faber Hanover Owner: Innes, Shaw, Hovsepian, Mendelsohn, Goodman, Brmnghm,Mch, PlmBch,Fla, HntngtnWds.Mch, FrmngtnHlls,Mch, Brmnghm,Mch.

1973	5	0	1	0	$2,811	
1972	28	7	6	5	$33,375	1:59^{2} Hol^{1}
			Lifetime		$45,415	4, 1:59^{2} (1)

6-30	^{9}Spk⅝ ft 74°	w10000=1	:29^{3}	1:02^{1}	1:31^{4}	2:01^{3}	4	3	3^{2½}	3^{1¼}°	3^{1½}	4^{2½}	2:02^{1}	7-1 (A.Petty)	GameGuy, Doc'sJerry, RobbRanger	(good effort)
6-23	^{8}Spk⅝ gd 66°	w10000^{7273}—1	:30	1:04	1:34^{2}	2:04^{1}	3	4	4^{4}	2^{hd}°	2^{½}	4^{4}	2:05	11-1 (A.Petty)	ShadyMile, YankeeCreed, ShadHanover	(strong until str)
6-16	Det^{1} ft	pref7500 1	:28^{4}	:59^{4}	1:31	1:59^{1}	5	3°	2°	3°	3^{1¼}	7^{17½}	2:02^{3}	*5-1 (H.Fisher)	BannerRanger, AdcoTux, FinalDecision	(———)
6-9	Det^{1} ft	pref8500 1	:30	1:01	1:30^{2}	2:00	5	6	6	6	7^{5¼}	7^{3½}	2:00^{3}	8-1 (H.Fisher)	BretOverAgain, Economist, CreederLinbo	(———)
6-2	Det^{1} ft	pref7500 1	:30^{1}	1:01^{2}	1:32	2:01^{1}	7	7	8	7°	5^{2}	2^{nk}	2:01^{1}	7-1 (T.Wilburn)	TrickyDale, TeeCee, GarconRoux	(———)
12-9	Hol^{1} ft	3yrcond17500 1⅛	:28^{1}	:59	1:29	2:15	1	4	4	6	4^{7½}	2^{2¼}	2:15^{2}	11-1 (T.Wilburn)	BigTime, TeeCee, AbbeChance	(———)

BLACK & YELLOW 8 8-1 =

Driver—GERALD WENTZ, Gold-Green Tr.—G. Wentz (9-0-1-1—.099)

‡FOLGER

Ch h 1965, by Top Deck—Lusty Kave—Lusty Volo Jr.
Owner: Virgil Wentz, Rock Springs, Wisc.

1973	14	0	3	2	$9,148	
1972	29	4	5	3	$18,473	2:03^{2} Was^{1}
			Lifetime		$46,943	5, 2:03 (1)

6-30	^{6}Spk⅝ ft 74°	‡nw2000^{8}=1	:29^{2}	1:00^{3}	1:31^{1}	2:01^{2}	7	7	7^{9½}	7^{6}	5^{3}	2^{2¼}	2:01^{4}	10-1 (G.Wentz)	FantasticDream, Folger, C.V.Yates	(closed well)
6-23	^{6}Spk⅝ gd 66°	‡nw2500^{73}=1	:31^{2}	1:04^{2}	1:35^{2}	2:06^{1}	3	4	5^{4}	7^{4}	8^{4¼}	6^{4}	2:07	7-1 (G.Wentz)	AdiosArt, M.R.Byrd, PocoPilot	(evenly)
6-9	^{5}Spk⅝ ft 78°	‡nw1750^{8}—1	:29^{3}	1:01	1:31^{1}	2:00^{4}	7	6	8^{7¼}	6^{8½}	5^{7}	5^{4}	2:01^{3}	7-2 (G.Wentz)	StarboardButlr, DonRockt, BonneFrost	(too much speed)
6-2	^{5}Spk⅝ ft 73°	‡nw2500$^{4-10}$+1	:30^{3}	1:02^{2}	1:32^{3}	2:01^{2}	4	5	5^{4¼}	4^{2}°	3^{2}	3^{5}	2:02^{2}	14-1 (G.Wentz)	GaySkipper, ByeByeBill, Folger	(rank leaving)
5-23	^{8}Haw^{1} ft 61°	‡nw2100^{8} 1	:30^{2}	1:01^{2}	1:32^{3}	2:01^{3}	6	1	1	1^{½}	4^{4½}	5^{7¾}	2:03^{1}	4-1 (G.Wentz)	Overhaul, StarboardButler, YankeeBaron	(tired badly)
5-19	^{9}Haw^{1} ft 55°	‡clm30000 1	:29^{3}	1:00	1:32	2:01^{2}	7	1	1	1^{1½}	1^{1}	2^{3}	2:02	9-1 (G.Wentz)	TheGrumbler, Folger, Mr.Rebel	(outpaced stretch)

GRAY & BLACK 9 8-1 =

Driver—TOM RATCHFORD, Gold-White Tr.—T. Ratchford (36-6-3-6—.269)

OVERHAUL

B. c 1969, by Overtrick—Little River Jane—Knight Dream
Owner: William M. Camp, Blue Island, Ill.

1973	21	5	0	5	$16.484	2:01^{3} Haw^{1}
1972	26	2	2	2	$8,734	2:02^{4} Spk⅝
			Lifetime		$14,181	2, 2:01^{4} (1) T.T.

6-29	^{7}Spk⅝ ft 76°	w10000^{7273}=1	:30^{2}	1:00^{4}	1:30^{1}	2:00	8	2°	1^{1½}	1^{1½}	1^{1}	3^{2½}	2:00^{3}	16-1 (T.Ratchford)	UncleKenny, ShadHanover, Overhaul	(good effort)
6-23	^{7}Spk⅝ gd 66°	w10000^{7273}=1	:31^{2}	1:06	1:36^{1}	2:06^{2}	9	3	x9^{13}	9^{5¾}	9^{8¾}	8^{7¼}	2:07^{4}	27-1 (T.Ratchford)	CafineKid, TeddyRip, WorthyBret	(good move, broke)
6-15	^{7}Spk⅝ ft 79°	nw25000^{7273}—1	:29^{2}	:59^{2}	1:29^{1}	1:58^{4}	5	6	6^{10}	7^{6}°	6^{5}	6^{4½}	1:59^{4}	24-1 (T.Ratchford)	SimonesSkipper, NativeExpress, WrthyBrt	(went evenly)
6-9	^{8}Spk⅝ ft 78°	inv7000=1	:29^{4}	1:01^{4}	1:31^{1}	2:00^{1}	2	ix8	8^{18}	7^{16}	7^{16}	7^{14}	2:03	21-1 (T.Ratchford)	TheGrumbler, QuakerByrd, ShadyCounsel	(botherd early)
6-1	^{7}Spk⅝ ft 73°	4yrinv7500=1	:29^{3}	1:01^{1}	1:31^{1}	1:59^{4}	6	6	6^{7½}	7^{5¼}	6^{8}	6^{5¾}	2:01	13-1 (T.Ratchford)	EllLang, DoctorTom, BigDaddysShadow	(too much spd)
5-23	^{8}Haw^{1} ft 61°	nw2100^{8} 1	:30^{2}	1:01^{2}	1:32^{3}	2:01^{3}	1	2	2	2^{½}	1^{2}	1^{1¼}	2:01^{3}	3-1 (B.Nickells)	Overhaul, StarboardButler, YankeeBaron	(ratd perfectly)

1. ARCADIA JAKE—This five year old gelding's last race was conditioned for "non-winners of $2,500 in the last six starts." On a class basis, he'll be competing against the same kinds of horses tonight. That still puts Arcadia Jake in a good position. He's coming off a good race in which he took command at the half mile mark. Although he didn't go on to win, he still was a strong factor throughout the entire contest. Evaluation—contender.

2. RIGHT GOOD—Here's another horse that finds himself well placed. He's going up against the same kinds of horses again and he's also coming off a good effort. Right Good was void of speed for the first three quarters of the mile. Then he put together a determined stretch drive which is a sign that he's starting to come around. It's the only race on his past performances where he closed any ground in the final quarter. Evaluation—contender.

3. DAN ADIOS—We can make a rather easy elimination for this horse. Since Dan Adios broke stride last time out on an off track, we'll handicap his next to last race. That effort was up against $10,000 winners and he was soundly beaten by 14 big ones. Evaluation—non-contender.

4. CREEDER LINBO—This four year old colt made a good Sportsman's Park debut in his last race. He stayed close to the pace throughout and was beaten by three and a quarter lengths at the wire. You could describe Creeder Linbo's race as an even effort. However, there are two ways a horse can go evenly. He can take it easy in the back of the pack and get beat by a large margin. Or he can stay close to the leaders and get beat by a small margin. Creeder Linbo conforms to the latter and

that's why he fits well in here. He's running for the same conditions as he competed for in his last race. Evaluation—contender.

5. YANKEE BARON—Here's another horse that's turned in a good effort within the same class level. Yankee Baron was content to sit back 2 1/2 lengths for the first three quarters of the race. He made his bid in the final quarter and got within 1/2 length of the leader in the stretch. He wasn't able to sustain his rally but he didn't finish far behind either. There's also some underlying improvement in Yankee Baron's race. It's his best finish on a fast track that's found in his past performances. That's something that can be easily overlooked with his two good off track efforts. Evaluation—contender.

6. NICKS PAINTER—His last race is the kind that can be easily underrated. Nicks Painter stayed close to the pace the entire mile but ended up finishing eighth. But his eighth-place finish should not be used as an indication of how well he performed. It's far more important to be concerned with how far back the horse finished in terms of lengths. And since Nicks Painter was beaten by only 3 1/2 lengths within the same class level, he'll have to be considered a factor in tonight's race. Evaluation—contender.

7. TEE CEE—This is the fourth straight horse who has shown the ability to stay close to the leaders, but even more importantly, to finish close to the winner. Tee Cee is also benefiting by staying within the same class level. You'll also notice that Tee Cee crossed the wire only one length in front of Nicks Painter, yet he finished four places ahead of him in the standings. Evaluation—contender.

8. FOLGER—There are three reasons why Folger cannot be overlooked in this race. He's off an extremely good effort in which he made up a ton of ground in the last half. The race also shows improvement in form over his previous efforts. The class factor is also in his favor. He's coming off a conditioned race which attracted the same kind of company he'll be facing tonight. Evaluation—contender.

9. OVERHAUL—Good speed was displayed by this four year old colt in his last race. He was sent out for the lead from the start of the race but was forced to go on the outside for the first quarter. Once he got on top, his frontrunning style almost carried him to victory. He gave way late in the final quarter but he still turned in a good race. There's no problem as far as class is concerned since he's competing against $10,000 winners again. Evaluation—contender.

Out of the nine-horse field, eight horses have raced well enough to qualify for contending roles. It's not very often that you come across a race that has this many contenders, but it will happen from time to time during the course of the season. And it's always best to be prepared for it before the occasion arises.

Since the fastest final time is shared by two of the contenders, we'll have to use numerical speed ratings. But in this particular race, we do not have to give each contender an adjusted final rating. There's such a wide variation of speed between the contenders that we're able to make some eliminations strictly off the horse's base rating.

Arcadia Jake—Final Time	2:02 4/5 =	14
Last Half	1:00 =	-
Base Rating		14
Right Good—Final Time	2:02 1/5 =	11
Last Half	58 3/5 =	-7
Base Rating		4
Creeder Linbo—Final Time	2:00 3/5 =	3
Last Half	59 1/5 =	-4
Base Rating		-1
Yankee Baron—Final Time	2:00 4/5 =	4
Last Half	58 2/5 =	-8
Base Rating		-4
Nicks Painter—Final Time	2:02 2/5 =	12
Last Half	59 3/5 =	-3
Base Rating		9
Tee Cee—Final Time	2:02 1/5 =	11
Last Half	59 2/5 =	-3
Base Rating		8
Folger—Final Time	2:01 4/5 =	9
Last Half	59 1/5 =	-4
Base Rating		5
Overhaul—Final Time	2:00 3/5 =	3
Last Half	59 4/5 =	-1
Base Rating		2

As I previously said, the maximum adjustments are capable of changing the difference between two or more horses' base rating by as much as 16 points. When you break it down, it reads like this: 4 points for class (one horse goes up; the other down), 8 points for post position (one horse goes from the one post to the nine; the other goes vice versa), 4 points for park outs (one horse was parked out for three turns; the other for one turn or none).

The contenders we're dealing with will not be changed by as much as 16 points with adjustments. All of them are running within the same class level as their last race and not one of them was parked out for two or more turns. That leaves us only with adjustments needed in the post position column which has a maximum change of 8 points. Therefore, any contender who has a base rating that's 9 or more points above the lowest base rating would be automatically eliminated. He can't possibly become the final choice even if he did receive the maximum change in post position.

The contender who has the lowest base rating is Yankee Baron with a minus four. On that basis, we can eliminate all contenders that have a base rating of 5 or more points. They are: Arcadia Jake (14 points), Nicks Painter (9 points), Tee Cee (14 points), and Folger (5 points). That leaves us with four contenders that receive adjustments in the post position column. Here's the chart:

who has an adjusted final rating that's 1 1/2 points better than the next best rating.

SEVENTH RACE — 1 MILE
PACE. Conditioned—3 Year Olds and Upward—Winners of $10,000 or more in 1972-73 — Purse $5,700.

Time—:30[1]	1:00[4]	1:30[4]	2:00[3]						Mutuel Pool—$146,029
5. Yankee Baron	5	6	6^7	64°	$33\frac{1}{2}$	1^{nk}	2:00[3]	6-1 (J.Curran)
9. Overhaul	9	3°	1^2	1^1	1^3	2^{nk}	2:00[3]	9-1 (T.Ratchford)
3. Dan Adios	3	1°	2^2	$31\frac{1}{2}$	2^3	3^1	2:00[4]	9-1 (S.Banks)
4. Creeder Linbo	4	5	5^6	$42\frac{1}{2}^o$	4^4	$41\frac{1}{4}$	2:00[4]	7-2 (M.Dokey)
2. Right Good	2	4	4^5	$53\frac{1}{2}$	8^7	$51\frac{1}{2}$	2:01	7-2 (J.Dolbee)
7. Tee Cee	7	8	$89\frac{1}{2}$	7^5	7^6	$61\frac{3}{4}$	2:01	17-1 (A.Petty)
6. Nick's Painter	6	7	$78\frac{1}{2}$	$85\frac{1}{2}$	$65\frac{1}{2}$	7^2	2:01	15-1 (J.Dennis)
1. Arcadia Jake	1	2	$33\frac{1}{2}$	21°	5^5	$83\frac{1}{4}$	2:01[1]	*5-2 (J.Ackerman)
8. Folger	8	9	9^{11}	$97\frac{1}{2}$	9^9	$94\frac{1}{2}$	2:01[3]	16-1 (G.Wentz)

Mutuels—(5) 14.20 6.80 3.80—(9) 11.00 5.60—(3) 4.80

The race turned out to be exactly what you would expect by reading the past performances. The pace was provided by Overhaul and the fastest last half was turned in by Yankee Baron. With so many contenders in the race, it's not too surprising that the last place finisher was less than 5 lengths off the winner. Overhaul did turn in a good speedy effort once he got on top, but he wasn't able to hold Yankee Baron safe in the final yards. He paid $14.20 for the win.

In the five races that were handicapped, every pertinent factor was dealt with. A horse was chosen as a contender only if his past performances revealed he fit the conditions of the race. But a contender doesn't mean anything until he's been properly analyzed. After that, the only contender who is really important, is the one who becomes the final choice.

Horse	Final Time	Last Half	Base Rating	Class		P.P.		Park	Adj. Final Rating
Right Good	11	-7	4	-	4	-½	3½	-	3½	3½
Creeder Linbo	3	-4	-1	-	-1	+½	-½	-	-½	-½
Yankee Baron	4	-8	-4	-	-4	+2	-2	-	-2	-2
Overhaul	3	-1	2	-	2	+½	2½	-	2½	2½

As you can see by the chart, none of the four remaining contenders received a drastic enough change in post position to make a difference in the final choice. It still comes out to be Yankee Baron

In the next chapter, we'll look at three situations where a horse becomes an automatic play. These are races you'll come across occasionally where you can use an angle in lieu of the two rating systems.

CHAPTER 8

Three Winning Angles

It's always been my firm belief that most playable races are won by horses that deserve to win. I won't deny the fact that you'll come across a good share of races that are won by horses strictly on pure racing luck. And there's always going to be some nag flying down the stretch with a big lead who hasn't turned in a good race in months. But for the most part, each playable race has a horse that's telling you in his own way that he's going to win.

How does a horse tell you he's going to win, you ask? Well one thing's for sure. He doesn't lean his head over during the post parade and whisper the inside info to your kid brother. Those things only happen in the movies. The only way he tells you is by the information contained in his past performance record. When the history of a horse is incorrectly translated, the racegoer is totally lost, and hence, usually walks out of the racetrack not only broke, but thoroughly disgusted as well. That's why it's so important to understand the five basic ingredients of handicapping. Without the knowledge of those five factors, a horse's past performance line turns into nothing but a bunch of mixed-up numbers and symbols.

In the last five chapters, we have thoroughly defined each one of the factors and gave each one of them a task. Class and current form had the responsibility of choosing the contenders in the race. Those two factors were combined with pace, post position, and the driver to produce the two rating systems, which, in turn, decided the final choice. But the ballgame is still far from over. The two rating systems will be applicable to most races

but not to all races. There are certain situations that are served better by a particular angle.

All angles rely on the same principle—history repeating itself. I have yet to see a regular racegoer that doesn't use at least one angle along with his handicapping. An angle can be your best friend or your worst enemy. That usually depends on what the angle is based on. If it doesn't deal with any of the five factors, I doubt very much that the angle will turn a profit in the long run. But even if it does deal with one of the five factors, I still advise caution. No matter how good the angle appears to look, it should always be given a dry run on paper first. The angles presented in this chapter are no exception to that rule.

The situations we'll look at, three in all, will probably not surface more than a half dozen times a week. The first two angles are based on the same factor—pace. One deals with it indirectly, the other one directly. The third angle deals with the post position factor.

Qualifying Races

Every time you go to the racetrack, there's bound to be at least one horse on the night's card that's coming off a qualifying race. Most of the time when a horse comes off a qualifier, he can be safely eliminated. But there are times when his race can turn into a very important handicapping tool. And if we're going to use the qualifier as the basis of an angle, it's a good idea to know why the race is run in the first place.

The most common use of the qualifying race is a mandatory one. At most tracks, when a horse breaks stride in two consecutive races, it's an automatic requirement that he compete in a qualifying race. To get back into regular competition, the horse's race must be void of breaks. If the horse goes off stride during the race, it's back to another qualifier. If the horse is successful and doesn't break stride, his trainer may enter him in a second qualifying race if he feels it's necessary.

Racetrack managements have always done their best to keep as many breakers off the raceway as possible. Nobody likes to put money on a horse and then watch him start galloping around the track. This is why a two-time breaker is not allowed to compete until he proves he has the proper racing manners. Racetrack managements always look out for the protection of the betting public despite a myth to the contrary.

A trainer may decide to enter a qualifying race if his horse has been on the sidelines for a lengthy period of time. If the horse is coming off a serious injury and has been laid up for a particularly long period of time, sometimes up to a year or more, the trainer may enter his horse in not just a second qualifying race but occasionally a third one just to be certain he's physically sound.

Trainers will also send their horses into a qualifier if it's their first attempt at racing free-legged or they're putting hopples on the animal for the first time. When a horse is shipped in from another track, it's very common to put him in the race just to let him know how many turns he'll have to negotiate on the new oval. If a horse turns in a couple of bad efforts, he may be put in the race to give him some additional activity. Time standards may also be set on the race to help determine what class level the horse should be entered in.

As you can see by now, the qualifying race is used for a variety of reasons. It's very possible that each horse entered in the race is in there for a different purpose. But they still all have something in common. Not one horse in the field is going to earn a penny for his owner. There's no purse value ever put on a qualifying race.

Horse racing is a very expensive business. Every cent the horse brings into the stable is usually needed to cover an expense. Qualifying races offer no such monetary assistance. As a result, the pace in the qualifier is much slower than in a regular race because there's no reason to ask the horse for his maximum speed capability. There's absolutely nothing to be gained by winning. This is why most horses that have just come off a qualifying race have a much slower final time as compared to the rest of the field. But this is actually a blessing in disguise. It enables the player to use the horse's race only when it's to his advantage.

If the horse is coming off a qualifying race and his final time is slower than the rest of the field, he hasn't proved anything. This type of animal can be safely eliminated like any other non-contender. But if the horse's final time equals the fastest final time, or he himself has the fastest final time, he would become a very strong possibility. But unfortunately, strong possibilities do not always reap rewards. This angle goes one step further and requires the horse to meet two extra rules.

1. The horse must be competing within 10 days of his qualifying race and;
2. His final time must be the fastest race on his past performance record.

A horse that meets these two rules would become an automatic play. If a horse doesn't conform to both of the rules, then consider him as an unratable contender.

This angle is very demanding but not without good reason. Every horse that comes off a qualifying race is assumed to be capable of running faster than his race really indicates. However, there is a small margin of error because there's no accurate way to measure just how much faster that actually is. That's why this angle plays it safe and only considers horses that have a final time which at least equals the fastest final time in the race.

Most horses that have competed in a qualifier are back on the track within a week of their race. This angle allows the trainer an extra three days to make sure he finds the right spot for his horse. We're also taking advantage of the pace factor indirectly by requiring the horse to have improved his final time over every one of his previous races that are listed. As far as the class factor is concerned, I'm leaving that to your discretion. This angle has always been one of my favorites and I've found it to be very productive at all class levels.

ONE MILE PACE

FIRST RACE

FIRST HALF OF DAILY DOUBLE

Purse $3,200

CLAIMING. Claiming price $7,000. Smooth Speed in for $8,400, all others $7,000.

PLEASE ASK FOR HORSE BY PROGRAM NUMBER

RED 1 3-1

Driver—JOE MARSH, JR., Gray-Blue-Red Tr.—J. Marsh, Jr. (180-46-30-30—.400)

FAITHFUL BOY B g 1966, by Victory Boy—Silver Faith—Silver King
Owner: Tommy Ryan, Morton Grove, Ill.

1973 8 1 0 2 $2,624 2:04 May
1972 31 4 4 2 $10,751 2:08 Aur
Lifetime $19,394 5, 2:03 (⅝)

Date	Trk Cond Temp	Class	Dist	Leader's Time ¼	½	¾	Winner's Time	PP	Order of Finish ¼	½	¾	Str	Fin	Ind.Time	Odds	Driver	First	Second	Third	Comment
8-31	^{1}May ft 81°	§clm6000	1	:31^{4}	1:03	1:33^{4}	2:04	5	5	1^{2}	1^{2}	1^{4}	1^{7¼}	2:04	2-1	(J.MarshJr)	FaithfulBoy	CollegeMan	YoungBlue	(much the best)
8-24	^{4}May ft 72°	§clm7000	1	:30^{2}	1:00^{4}	1:32^{3}	2:04	8	8	6^{10}°	4^{3}°	3^{2}x	7^{11}	2:06^{1}	6-1	(J.MarshJr)	SapphireGlow	BourbonChimes	Cheslind	(break costly)
8-16	^{7}May ft 74°	§clm8000	1	:31^{2}	1:03^{2}	1:34	2:05^{2}	7	5°	4^{1¾}°	3^{1½}°	3^{2}	3^{1¼}	2:05^{3}	8-1	(J.MarshJr)	CamdenFrisco	RustyMerrie	FaithfulBy	(3-wide briefly)
8- 9	^{6}May ft 80°	§clm9000	1	:30^{1}	1:02^{2}	1:33^{2}	2:04	3	6	5^{4}	5^{2½}	5^{2½}	3^{2½dh}	2:04^{3}	11-1	(J.MarshJr)	DtchKnght	SilvrDillr	FaithfBy-HrkWay^{dh}	(closed some)
7-24	^{7}May ft 81°	clm6000	1	:30^{1}	1:03^{1}	1:34^{3}	2:06^{3}	8	7°	4^{2½}°	4^{2}	3^{2}	4^{3¼}	2:07^{1}	13-1	(J.MarshJr)	SonnyFarvel	AdmiralJack	IrishDuane	(parked 2 turns)
7-13	^{1}Spk⅝ ft 88°	clm7000—1		:30^{2}	1:03^{4}	1:34^{1}	2:05	5	8	8^{9½}	8^{7¼}	9^{12}	8^{7½}	2:06^{3}	13-1	(J.MarshJr)	Pompidou	DutchKnight	DazzlingDeana	(rough on turn)

WHITE 2 5-1

Driver—WALTER PAISLEY, Green-White Tr.—C. Willis (198-3$0-36-36—.313)

SMOOTH SPEED Br m 1965, by Mighty Storm—Candys Comet—Pat Chief
Owner: Connel Ade Willis, Willow Springs, Ill.

1973 5 1 0 2 $2,700 2:04^{2} May
1972 14 2 4 0 $10,520 2:08^{4} Spk⅝
Lifetime $51,777 4, 2:03^{4} (⅝)

Date	Trk Cond Temp	Class	Dist	Leader's Time ¼	½	¾	Winner's Time	PP	Order of Finish ¼	½	¾	Str	Fin	Ind.Time	Odds	Driver	First	Second	Third	Comment
9- 1	^{7}May ft 80°	§clm8400	1	:30^{3}	1:02	1:33^{1}	2:03^{3}	3	4	5^{4}	3^{1½}°	2^{1½}	3^{3¼}	2:04^{1}	*9-5	(C.Willis)	RustyMerrie	ChiefsLittleStar	SmoothSpeed	(raced well)
8-25	^{1}May ft 78°	§clm7200	1	:30^{1}	1:01^{4}	1:33^{3}	2:04^{2}	3	6	6^{4¼}°	1^{1}°	1^{4}	1^{2¼}	2:04^{2}	5-2	(C.Willis)	SmoothSpeed	SeattlCindy	DazzlingStar	(3-wide briefly)
8-18	^{1}May ft 77°	§clm7200	1	:29^{3}	1:00^{3}	1:32^{1}	2:04	5	6	7^{5½}	7^{5}	7^{6}	4^{3}	2:04^{3}	7-2	(C.Willis)	SteppingHal	QuickBay	GrawlinHanover	(raced well)
8-11	^{1}May ft 77°	clm7200	1	:30^{2}	1:01^{3}	1:33	2:04^{3}	1	3	3^{4}	4^{2¼}	4^{1¾}	4^{1}	2:04^{4}	3-1	(M.Lynch)	GeneralAdios	DoctorC	CamaroHanover	(good try)
7-30	^{4}May ft 77°	clm7200	1	:31^{3}	1:03^{4}	1:35^{1}	2:06^{3}	1	3	3^{2¼}	4^{2½}°	4^{2½}	3^{¾dh}	2:06^{4}	5-1	(C.Willis)	FairyJo	CoffeeGeorge	SmoothSpd-Zhivago^{dh}	(73 debut)
9-26^{72}	Was^{1} ft	clm10800	1	:30^{4}	1:02	1:33^{3}	2:03^{3}	4	4	7	8	7^{5½}	2^{1½}	2:04	7-1	(C.Willis)	GamblingBoy	SmoothSpeed	DameFontane	(————)

BLUE 3 6-1

Driver—WAYNE MOORE, Red-Gold Tr.—W. Moore (28-2-4-2—.175)

SENATOR GLIB Ro g 1962, by Adios Senator—Mighty Deb—Mighty H.
Owner: Four Jacks Racing Stable, Harvey, Ill.

1973 25 2 3 2 $8,672 2:05^{1} Haw^{1}
1972 37 7 8 5 $25,691 2:01^{1} Hol^{1}
Lifetime $118,364 10, 2:01^{1} (1)

Date	Trk Cond Temp	Class	Dist	Leader's Time ¼	½	¾	Winner's Time	PP	Order of Finish ¼	½	¾	Str	Fin	Ind.Time	Odds	Driver	First	Second	Third	Comment
8-18	^{2}May ft 77°	§clm7000	1	:29^{3}	1:00	1:31	2:03^{2}	3	3	3^{2}	2^{nk}°	1^{1}	2^{1¼}	2:03^{3}	9-1	(W.Moore)	TommyLobell	SenatorGlib	AirBlazer	(raced well)
8-10	^{1}May ft 75°	§clm7000	1	:30^{3}	1:01^{4}	1:32^{4}	2:04^{1}	6	3°	5^{2¾}ix	8^{dis}	8^{dis}	8^{dis}		7-1	(W.Moore)	FrostyFreight	LittlePuff	AirBlazer	(road trouble)
7-31	^{6}May ft 71°	clm7000	1	:29^{1}	1:00^{4}	1:31^{4}	2:04^{1}	6	7°	3^{2}°	4^{1½}°	5^{2½}	6^{2¼}	2:04^{3}	10-1	(W.Moore)	ChiefsLittleStar	StealHome	NellieWay	(hung mile)
7-27	May ft 76°	Qua	1	:32^{1}	1:03^{3}	1:34^{2}	2:05^{1}	3	1	1^{2}	1^{2}	1^{2}	2^{1}	2:05^{2}	NB	(W.Moore)	StarGo	SenatorGlib	SteadyDown	(————)
7-18	^{6}Spk⅝ ft 82°	clm8000—1		:31^{4}	1:02	1:32^{1}	2:03^{1}	8	8	8^{14}	8^{8½}	7^{5}x	6^{5¾}	2:04^{2}	24-1	(W.Moore)	BrilliantSpeed	SiouxTime	LittleBuzz	(no threat)
7- 7	^{1}Spk⅝ ft 90°	clm9000=1		:29^{4}	1:01^{2}	1:32^{2}	2:04	5	1°	1^{1½}	1^{nk}	2^{3}	x8^{16}	2:07^{1}	11-1	(W.Moore)	BagofGold	SummertimeDirect	Tanner	(3-wide leaving)

GREEN 4 10-1

Driver—RONALD BICE, Gold-Brown-White Tr.—R. Bice (10-0-0-1—.033)

FAIR ROW BYRD B g 1968, by Poplar Byrd—Lady Free Way—Ankaway
Owner: Forest View Stable, Harwood Heights, Ill.

1973 7 1 2 0 $3,462 2:04 May
1972 18 3 3 3 $7,574 2:04^{4} Spk⅝
Lifetime $9,499 4, 2:04^{4} (⅝)

Date	Trk Cond Temp	Class	Dist	Leader's Time ¼	½	¾	Winner's Time	PP	Order of Finish ¼	½	¾	Str	Fin	Ind.Time	Odds	Driver	First	Second	Third	Comment
8-31	^{4}May ft 81°	clm7000	1	:29^{1}	1:00^{1}	1:31^{2}	2:00^{3}	8	2	2^{2}	7^{12}	8^{19}	8^{dis}		34-1	(R.Bice)	CrystalE	QuickBay	BourbonChimes	(used early)
8-24	^{7}May ft 72°	clm7000	1	:31^{4}	1:04^{1}	1:35^{2}	2:06^{1}	4	1	1^{1}	2^{nk}	1^{hd}	4^{3¾}	2:07	9-1	(R.Bice)	BaronBill	MisterAdios	MightyLoyal	(tired some)
8-17	^{4}May ft 76°	clm6000 C	1	:30^{1}	1:01^{4}	1:32^{2}	2:04	1	1	1^{1½}	1^{ns}	1^{hd}	1^{1¼}	2:04	*6-5	(N.Willis)	FairRowByrd	FireBomb	LoGoAdios	(tough mile)
8- 8	^{2}May ft 82°	clm5000	1	:29^{1}	1:01^{1}	1:32	2:03^{1}	4	2	2^{2½}	2^{4}	2^{4½}	2^{6¾}	2:04^{3}	9-2	(N.Willis)	BourbonChimes	FairRowByrd	Chickadee	(2nd best)
7-24	^{4}May ft 81°	clm6000	1	:30	1:00^{3}	1:33^{1}	2:05^{2}	7	3°	1^{1}°	1^{hd}	2^{1½}	6^{8¼}	2:07	5-1	(C.Willis)	RksCrkKthy	GenrlAdios	RushStrtBoss	(parked too long)
7-17	^{5}Spk⅝ ft 80°	clm6000+1		:30	1:01^{3}	1:33	2:03^{3}	3	3	3^{2½}	1^{½}	2^{2}	4^{3½}	2:04^{2}	8-1	(N.Willis)	PortSam	BedfordBrush	AaronMeridale	(¾ bid, hung)

BLACK 5 8-1

Driver—HENRY LUNSFORD, Red-Blue Tr.—E. Cogan (0-0-0-0—.000)

CIRCLE SAMBO Gr g 1968, by Majestic Hanover—Kathleen Grattan—Task Force
Owner: Karen Ann Quinlan, Alsip, Ill.

1973 12 6 3 0 $5,435 2:05^{2} Nfld
1972 0 0 0 0 (——)
Lifetime $1,741 3, 2:09^{1}

Date	Trk Cond Temp	Class	Dist	Leader's Time ¼	½	¾	Winner's Time	PP	Order of Finish ¼	½	¾	Str	Fin	Ind.Time	Odds	Driver	First	Second	Third	Comment
9- 4	May ft 75°	Qua§	1	:30	1:00	1:30	2:01^{3}	7	4	4^{12}	3^{10}	3^{7½}	3^{5}	2:02^{3}	NB	(H.Lunsford)	TomsChoice	LusciousLady	CircleSambo	(————)
8-30	^{7}May ft 78°	clm6000	1	:29^{3}	1:00^{2}	1:33	2:04^{2}	6	2	1^{2}	3^{nk}	4^{5½}	5^{14}	2:07^{1}	8-1	(E.Waszak)	DriftFisher	Eyreton	SpringWave	(set blistering pace)
8-18	Nfld ft	clm5000 C	1	:30^{1}	1:03	1:33^{4}	2:05^{2}	7	4°	4°	3°	5^{4½}	6^{7}	2:06^{4}	*9-5	(M.Turcotte)	LetaHall	DoubleD	CaptainCarlith	(————)
8-11	Nfld gd	clm5000	1	:30^{2}	1:03^{2}	1:35^{2}	2:07^{2}	2	1	1	1	1^{1¾}	1^{2}	2:07^{2}	*6-5	(M.Turcotte)	CircleSambo	BaronAdios	LetaHall	(————)
8 4	Nfld ft	clm4000	1	:30^{2}	1:02^{3}	1:34^{1}	2:05^{2}	3	1	1	1	1^{2}	1^{3}	2:05^{2}	*1-1	(M.Turcotte)	CircleSambo	BaronAdios	RugbyPick	(————)
8-27	Nfld ft	clm4000	1	:29^{2}	1:01^{1}	1:33^{1}	2:04^{2}	1	1	1	2	2^{5}	2^{10}	2:06^{2}	2-1	(M.Turcotte)	JudgeErv	CircleSambo	BaronAdios	(————)

YELLOW 6 7-2

Driver—JIM DOLBEE, Green-White-Red Tr.—R. Asaph (68-15-11-8—.350)

EYRETON B g 1961, by Adorian—Trusty Lady—U Scott
Owner: Thomas R. Heston, Des Plaines, Ill.

1973 22 4 6 1 $15,859 2:07^{2} Spk⅝
1972 39 1 5 5 $11,526 None at Mile
Lifetime $100,262 7, 2:03

Date	Trk Cond Temp	Class	Dist	Leader's Time ¼	½	¾	Winner's Time	PP	Order of Finish ¼	½	¾	Str	Fin	Ind.Time	Odds	Driver	First	Second	Third	Comment
8-30	^{7}May ft 78°	§clm6000 C	1	:29^{3}	1:00^{2}	1:33	2:04^{2}	3	6	6^{8½}	5^{2½}°	3^{4½}	2^{8½}	2:06^{1}	5-1	(S.Banks)	DriftFisher	Eyreton	SpringWave	(soundly beaten)
8-23	^{7}May sy 65°	§clm6000	1	:32^{2}	1:05^{3}	1:39	2:12	3	7	8^{6½}	6^{2½}°	3^{1½}	1^{1¼}	2:12	7-2	(S.Banks)	Eyreton	DriftFisher	YoungBlue	(good last ½)
8-14	^{7}May ft 70°	§clm7000	1	:30^{4}	1:02^{1}	1:33^{4}	2:05^{3}	5	6	6^{5}°	5^{4}°	4^{2}	4^{1¼}	2:05^{4}	4-1	(S.Banks)	SilentTona	CrystalE	BaronsStorm	(3-wide briefly)
8- 3	^{7}May ft 72°	clm7000	1	:30^{4}	1:02	1:33^{3}	2:06^{2}	8	8	7^{7}°	7^{3}	7^{3¼}	6^{1¾}	2:06^{4}	18-1	(S.Banks)	AljeansDon	EddieForbes	MickeySupreme	(closed well)
7-27	^{4}May sy 79°	clm7000	1	:32^{4}	1:06^{1}	1:37^{1}	2:09^{1}	7	7	7^{10}°	5^{9½}	5^{11}	4^{6¼}	2:10^{2}	10-1	(S.Banks)	BuddyTime	GoranHanover	CrystalE	(closed some)
7-17	^{10}Spk⅝ ft 80°	clm7000—1		:31	1:02^{2}	1:33^{2}	2:03^{3}	3	6	6^{4½}	6^{4}	7^{5}	7^{5}	2:04^{3}	4-1	(S.Banks)	SantosTwiggy	SnoVan	MoeWestern	(evenly)

	Driver—JOHNNY BLEVINS, White-Blue-Black		Tr.—J. Blevins	(46-5-4-4—.164)	1973	11	1	0	1	$1,796	2:05 Sem¾

BROWN 7   **6-1**

SPARKY DARES   8 h 1967, by Meadow Gene—Volynn—Volstadt

Owner: Jimmy John Stable, Peotone, Ill.   1972   21   2   3   3 $8,131   2:06 R.R   Lifetime $31,314   3, 2:02³

8-30	³May gd 78°	Šc¦m7000	1	:31⁴ 1:04¹ 1:36¹ 2:08	1	3	3¹	2¹	31½ 52½ 2:08³	9 5	(J.Blevins)	EdwinYates, Cheslind, NobleOne	(weakened)
8-22	⁶May ft 69°	Šc¦m7000	1	:31¹ 1:02³ 1:35	7	7	74¾	62°	41¼ 54¾ 2:07³	*2-1	(J.Blevins)	ReidsShadow, RksCrkKathy, S'ouxTme	(3-w'de backs'de)
8-15	⁴May ft 75°	Šc¦m7000	1	:31 1:02⁴ 1:33⁴ 2:04⁴	4	6	64¾	63°	52½ 42¾ 2:05²	7-1	(J.Blevins)	SapphireGlow, PeppersAce, WesTee	(needed room)
8- 2	⁷May ft 71°	clm7000	1	:31 1:03² 1:35¹ 2:06¹	4	6	77	54¾°	43½ 52½ 2:06⁴	6-1	(J.Blevins)	EmbassyVolo, MoeWestern, CircleEddie	(4-wide briefly)
7-20	¹⁰Spk⅝ sy 68°	clm8000+1	:32	1:04⁴ 1:36³ 2:09¹	2	7	78½	55	55 56½ 2:10³	8-1	(J.Blevins)	CadetComdr., FirstLook, ShiawayPercy	(evenly)
7-10	¹⁰Spk⅝ ft 76°	clm7000 C-1	:32	1:04⁴ 1:35³ 2:05³	9	9	76½°	42½°	54½ 55¾ 2:06⁴	8-1	(D.ShetlerJr)	StewartCraig, JoesDonJuan, Mose	(uneven course str)

	Driver—MIKE CAPONETTO, Red-Gold		Tr.—M. Caponetto	(10-0-0-0—.000)	1973	30	2	2	4	$5,938	2:08⁴ Aur

RED & YELLOW 8   **10-1**

ROSEDALE PRINCE   B g 1967, by Noble Adios—Rosedale Rita—Knox Hanover

Owner: Rosedale Stable, Oak Park, Ill.   1972   29   1   3   0 $3,674   2:12¹ Aur   Lifetime $11,246   4, 2:06³ (1)

8-30	³May gd 78°	c¦m7000	1	:31⁴ 1:04¹ 1:36¹ 2:08	4	2°	2ʰᵈ°	31°	79 79¼ 2:09⁴	31-1	(M.Capontto)	EdwinYates, Cheslind, NobleOne	(overland route)
8-22	⁶May ft 69°	c¦m7000	1	:31¹ 1:02³ 1:35	3	4	5³	73	74¼ 65½ 2:07⁴	23-1	(M.Capontto)	ReidsShadow, RooksCreekKthy, S'ouxTme	(foes too tuff)
8-14	⁷May ft 70°	clm7000	1	:30⁴ 1:02¹ 1:33⁴ 2:05³	2	4	4³	43	31½ 52 2:06	19-1	(M.Capontto)	SilentTona, Crysta'E, BaronsStorm	(raced well)
8- 2	⁷May f¦ 71°	clm7000	1	:31 1:03² 1:35¹ 2:06¹	7	4°	44½°	44½°	710 714 2:09	54-1	(M.Capontto)	EmbassyVolo, MoeWestern, CircleEddie	(never saw rail)
7-24	⁶May ft 81°	clm7000	1	:30² 1:02¹ 1:33¹ 2:04¹	7	6	68½	67	79 66¼ 2:05²	66-1	(M.Capontto)	SpoiledBrat, MoeWestern, LittlePuff	(foes too tough)
7-17	¹⁰Spk⅝ ft 80°	c¦m7000-1	:31	1:02² 1:33² 2:03³	8	2°	21°	32°	98 99¼ 2:05²	39 1	(M.Capontto)	SantosTwiggy, SnoVan, MoeWestern	(parked mile)

We'll look at two example races to get a better understanding of how this angle works in practice. The first one is a $7,000 claiming race that took place at Maywood Park on September 7. A check of the program reveals that the only horse in the race coming off a qualifier is Circle Sambo. Three days earlier, the five year old gelding was timed for the mile in 2:02 3/5. It's the best time on his past performance record and it's also the fastest final time turned in by any of the competitors in the eight-horse field. Circle Sambo meets all requirements and becomes an automatic play.

Even though Circle Sambo was listed at 8-1 in the morning line, he still received a lot of backing. His qualifying race doesn't fool too many people and he was sent off as the second choice at 2-1.

Circle Sambo was sent out for the lead from the start. He set extremely fast fractions for this class level and coasted home to an easy victory. The winning time for the mile was 2:01 1/5, an

FIRST RACE — 1 MILE

PACE. Claiming $7,000. Purse $3,200.

Time—:29² 1:00¹ 1:30⁴ 2:01²   Mutuel Pool—$37,796

Hd.No.	Horse	PP	¼	½	¾	Str	Fin	Ind.Time	Odds	Driver
5.	Circle Sambo	5	1	1³	1³	1²	12¼	2:01²	2-1	(H.Lunsford)
1.	Faithful Boy	1	3	2³	2³	22	22¼	2:01⁴	*6-5	(J.MarshJr)
2.	Smooth Speed	2	4	56½	39	35	35	2:02²	5-1	(W.Paisley)
6.	Eyreton	6	6	68½	513°	411	414	2:04¹	14-1	(J.Dolbee)
7.	Sparky Dares	7	7	714	716°	613	517	2:04⁴	28-1	(J.Blevins)
8.	Rosedale Prince	8	8	816	817	715	619	2:05¹	65-1	(M.Capontto)
3.	Senator Glib	3	5	46°	412	512	723	2:06	6-1	(S.Banks)
4.	Fair Row Byrd	4	2	35	614	815	8ᵈⁱˡ		30-1	(R.Bice)

Mutuels—(5) 6.60 3.20 3.00—(1) 3.00 2.20—(2) 2.60

improvement of 1 1/5 seconds over his qualifying race. He returned $6.60 to win.

The next race we'll look at is a $3,500 claiming event. This one took place at Sportsman's Park on July 2. There are two horses in the race that are coming off qualifiers—Flaming Parker and Idlewhiles Bruce. But Flaming Parker would not be considered for play. There are three horses in the race that have turned in a faster final time than he has. That automatically eliminates him as a non-contender.

ONE MILE PACE

FIRST RACE
FIRST HALF OF DAILY DOUBLE

Purse $2,500

CLAIMING. Claiming price $3,500 — 3 Year Olds and Upward — Illinios Bred. Dusty G. Hayes, Miss Roscoe, Flaming Eyre, Select Ways and Poplar John in for $4,200, all others $3,500.

PLEASE ASK FOR HORSE BY PROGRAM NUMBER

	Date	Trk Cond Temp	Class	Dist	Leader's Time ¼ ½ ¾	Winner's Time	PP	¼	½	¾	Str	Fin	Ind.Time Odds	Driver	First	Second	Third	Comment

RED 1   **4-1**

	Driver—ED CONLEY, Red-Green-White			Tr.—F. Hicks	(9-1-4-2—.432)	1973	12	1	1	2	$1,926	2:13¹ Aur

CRYSTAL BARON   Br g 1968, by Crystal Byrd—Irene Heberling—Tony The Great

Owner: Glen Dunham, Waupun, Wis.   1972   11   2   4   2 $507   2:11 Rchln   Lifetime $507   4, 2:11

6-19	²Spk⅝ ft 78°	clm4000+1	:28³	:59¹ 1:32¹ 2:05²	2	5	519°	46½	2¹	21¼ 2:05³	25-1	(E.Conley)	FannyMorgen, CrystalBaron, WorthyByrd	(raced well)
6- 5	¹Spk⅝ sy 70°	clm3500—1	:32³ 1:07³ 1:39	2:09	6	4°	11¼	21½	35½ 36¾ 2:10²	41-1	(E.Conley)	RooksCreekKathy, KingSelka, CrystalBaron	(used early)
5-15	²Haw¦ ft 61°	clm5000	1	:32¹ 1:04¹ 1:36¹ 2:06	9	9	9	88½	77½ 77¼ 2:07²	57-1	(E.Conley)	AprilArt, DunksBoy, CadetCommander	(no threat)
5- 2	²Haw¦ gd 44°	clm5000	1	:32³ 1:03² 1:36	2:07²	6	9	9	913	811 811 2:09³	55-1	(E.Conley)	HastiDoc. GoJohnnyGo. Bock	(dull effort)
3-17	³Spk⅝ ft 36°	345yrstk5000=1	:30⁴ 1:02⁴ 1:32⁴ 2:03³	2	8	86	910	817 823 2:08¹	79-1	(F.Hicks)	TheGreatByrd, SeaEmerald, Littlefuse	(lagged at start)
3-10	³Spk⅝ gd 58°	3-5yrnw3R=1	:31¹ 1:03² 1:35² 2:08	2	6	9⁸¼	916	920 9ᵈⁱˡ	66-1	(F.Hicks)	PatrickByrd, SkipalongStew, ShiawaySandy	(lagged)

BLUE **2** 10-1 —

Driver—JESSIE WILLIS, Maroon-Gray-White Tr.—C. Jacobs (28-0-4-2—.103)

DUSTY G. HAYES B m 1965, by Gene Hayes—Direct Dust—Dusty Hanover
Owner: Clarence and Randall Jacobs, Harvard, Ill.

1973 20 2 2 5 $4,957 2:091 Haw1
1972 19 2 4 3 $6,148 2:073 Was1
Lifetime $11,023 7, 2:073 (1)

6-14 1Spk⅝ ft 74° clm4800=1 :313 1:04 1:36 2:064 3 5 65 85½ 96½ 73¾ 2:073 25-1 (J.Willis) GeeGeeKnox, KirksFlight, CarelessLew (couldn't close)
6- 4 2Spk⅝ gd 67° clm4800=1 :332 1:082 1:403 2:113 6 6 43½° 43½° 65½ 86½ 2:13 16-1 (J.Willis) GeeGeeKnox, WorthyByrd, AdmiralJack (tough trip)
5- 9 1Haw1 ft 71° clm4800 1 :31 1:022 1:341 2:061 7 8 9 96 86 73½ 2:07 8-1 (J.Willis) MightyNalim. LukesChip, HazeyCreede (no threat)
4-17 3Haw1 ft 66° clm4800 1 :304 1:034 1:374 2:091 5 6 5 53 2½ 1½ 2:091 21 1 (J.Willis) DustyGHayes, SusiesPride, Douglass (just up)
4-10 2Spk⅝ ft 33° clm4800=1 :31 1:05 1:361 2:081 4 6 69½ 55½° 54 56 2:092 7-1 (J.Willis) ProudTime, GeneseeTime, VoloPurdue (went evenly)
4- 3 1Spk⅝ ft 37° clm4800=1 :304 1:033 1:362 2:074 2 4 54½ 42¼° 43 34½ 2:084 6-1 (H.Burright) Talaria, GeeGeeKnox, DustyG.Hayes (lacked suff close)

WHITE **3** 10-1 —

Driver—CONNEL WILLIS, Red-White-Green Tr.—C. Willis (16-1-2-2—.174)

MISS ROSCOE B f 1969, by Daddio—Denises Plutocrat—Plutocrat
Owner: Connel Ade Willis, Willow Springs, Ill.

1973 3 0 0 0 $368
1972 6 1 0 1 $1,424 2:09 Spk⅝
Lifetime $1,602 3, 2:09 (⅝)

6-14 1Spk⅝ ft 74° clm4800—1 :313 1:04 1:36 2:064 5 6 55° 21° 22 96 2:08 11-1 (H.Burright) GeeGeeKnox, KirksFlight, CarelessLew (parked 2 turns)
6- 1 1Spk⅝ ft 79° clm6000—1 :292 1:01 1:312 2:031 1 2 21½ 25 611 8dis 8-1 (H.Burright) RmsPrincss, AgnsMeridle, RomnDancr (too much speed)
5-23 3Haw1 ft 61° fmnw2R 1 :301 1:034 1:341 2:043 3 2 2 21½ 38 411 2:064 12-1 (H.Burright) MayByrdKing, Deceit, StarlaGo (tired badly)
8-14 Spr1 gd 3yr-ec4880 1 :311 1:023 1:34 2:051 1 6 6° 6° 116¾ 119 2:07 NB (C.Willis) JaneJester. HeatherAlma, VelmaCreed (————)
7-28 Camb ft 3yr ec1160 Dash in 2:09, Fin. 3 Dash in 2:082, Fin. 4 NB (C.Willis)
7-23 Hnry ft 3yr-ec1160 Dash in 2:103, Fin. 6 Dash in 2:11, Fin. 5 NB (C.Willis)

GREEN **4** 6-1 —

Driver—HAM ADAMS, Maroon-Gray Tr.—H. Adams (8-0-0-2—.083)

FLAMING EYRE Ch g 1969, by Plutocrat—Rosa The Rusher—Rush Hour
Owner: A. H. Adams, Mandarin, Fla

1973 4 0 1 1 $234
1972 20 3 1 2 $1,973 2:11 Mtvrn
Lifetime $1,991 3, 2:11

6-18 3Spk⅝ ft 77° clm7200=1 :293 1:012 1:323 2:041 9 9 912 811 713 717 2:073 27-1 (J.Dolbee) JollyGeneGiant, AndysJake, GenerlAdios (foes too tough)
6- 13 Spk⅝ ft 74° Qua 1 :32 1:04 1:36 2:063 5 1 35½ 22 23 26¾ 2:08 NB (H.Adams) ArcadiaJake, FlamingEyre, MissPeggyFrisc (————)
4-19 4Haw1 ft 67° nw2R 1 :33 1:054 1:381 2:081 1 3 4 67 914 920 2:121 8-1 (H.Adams) ReallyBombed, SirPrinceAdios. KappysDancer (tired)
4- 5 LouD ft nw300 1 :312 1:041 1:364 2:083 2 1 1 1 12½ 2¾ 2:084 *3-5 (R.Guhy) WhizKidWillie, FlamingEyre, LndaLouEnsgn (————)
3-31 LouD ft nw1000 1 :313 1:042 1:362 2:09 5 2° 1 1 12 3¼ 2:09 8-1 (R.Guhy) NancyBeeOakwood, TVPart, FlamingEyre (————)
10-26 Aud ft 2 5yrcond500 1 :322 1:063 1:39 2:122 2 2 2 2 21 21 2:123 31-1 (R.Guhy) AdiosLorene, FlamingEyre. DeemsTime (————)

BLACK **5** 5-1 —

Driver—JIM DENNIS, Green-White Tr.—J. Dennis (91-23-17-7—.388)

FLAMING PARKER Ch g 1965, by Parker Byrd—Flaming Beauty—Try Wyn
Owner: Victor and Morris Zeinfeld, Maywood, Lincolnwood, Ill.

1973 3 0 0 0 $290
1972 33 5 6 2 $14,946 2:031 Hol1
Lifetime $63,792 7, 2:031 (1)

6-27 Spk⅝ ft 72° Qua 1 :303 1:043 1:35 2:051 5 3 32½ 22° 23 44½ 2:06 NB (J.Dennis) MajorBill, MisterAdios, ByeByeWinter (————)
6-21 Spk⅝ ft 76° Qua 1 :294 1:02 1:314 2:041 5 3 38 412 411 416 2:072 NB (J.Dennis) BranchRockyGuy, MissPggyFrsco, DzzlngStr (————)
4- 3 L.A⅝ ft clm5000 1 :322 1:033 1:344 2:053 5 6 6 3 41¼ 64 2:062 5-1 (J.Dennis) SecondRaid, MissAmyAdios. IrishCam (————)
3-24 L.A⅝ ft clm6000 1 :303 1:031 1:334 2:044 7 1 2 2 21½ 52¾ 2:052 7-1 (J.Dennis) SilverRoyal, Shany, Berkey (————)
3-17 L.A⅝ ft clm6000 1 :32 1:033 1:342 2:05 2 3 3 4 75 55¼ 2:06 7-1 (J.Dennis) BonnieLaddieN, MyDough, MajesticBrewer (————)
12- 2 Hol1 ft clm6000 1 :302 1:013 1:331 2:031 5 9 9 6 67½ 85¾ 2:042 7-2 (J.Dennis) NeveleBlaze, DiamontePace, BillBlaine (————)

YELLOW **6** 3-1 =

Driver—STANLEY BANKS, White-Purple Tr.—K. Vander Schaaf (107-13-18-11—.244)

SELECT WAYS Blk m 1965, by Chief Strong—Colossal Ways—Colossal
Owner: Gary A. Fatland, Sandwich, Ill.

1973 18 1 3 5 $5,617 2:052 Spk⅝
1972 31 6 6 7 $12,846 2:062 Haw1
Lifetime $24,133 6, 2:061 (1)

6-13 1Spk⅝ ft 73° clm4200=1 :311 1:043 1:35 2:051 3 2 21 43 32½ 33¼ 2:054 *2-1 (S.Banks) HighPaintr, MountainCaptain, SelctWys (no closing kick)
5-31 1Spk⅝ ft 74° clm4200=1 :301 1:032 1:334 2:052 4 3 32¼ 31½ 12½ 11½ 2:052 8-1 (S.Banks) SelectWays, FrostyAbbe, RocketW.Ring (powerful winnr)
5-15 1Haw1 ft 61° clm4200 1$\frac{1}{16}$:291 :593 1:233 5 1 2 21 1½ 23 1:241 *5-2 (S.Banks) TorpidsGold, SelectWays, BoutTurn (early speed)
4-27 1Haw1 ft 45° clm4200 1$\frac{1}{16}$:292 1:012 1:233 8 8 8 710 54 21 1:234 7-1 (S.Banks) SatinGrattan, SelectWays. RexG. (closed strong)
4-16 1Spk⅝A ft 45° clm4200=1 :302 1:043 1:35 2:093 5 1 41¼ 89¼° 65½ 42½ 2:101 6-1 (S.Banks) RareEvent, KingSelka, TonkaChief (rallied)
4- 2 2Spk⅝ ft 44° clm4200—1 :303 1:033 1:36 2:084 2 3 42½ 42¾ 32 32 2:091 10-1 (S.Banks) LandesFortune, RexG., SelectWays (went evenly)

GREEN & WHITE **7** 10-1 =

Driver—CLAUDE LORANCE, SR., Gold-Blue Tr.—C. Lorance, Sr. (13-0-0-0—.000)

IDLEWHILES BRUCE B g 1967, by Callahan Hanover—Spot Hal—Hal Dale
Owner: Claude R. Lorance, Laura, Ill.

1973 4 0 0 0 (——)
1972 3 0 0 0 (——)
Lifetime $5,551 4, 2:072

6-27 Spk⅝ ft 72° Qua 1 :301 1:02 1:34 2:051 4 2° 12 11½ 2½ 21 2:052 NB (C.LoranceSr) DrFarr, IdlewhilesBruce, RosgoKid (————)
6-21 Spk⅝ ft 76° Qua 1 :30 1:044 1:36 2:072 4 3 33½ 43 34½ 33 2:08 NB (C.LoranceSr) FlyingRed, RosgoKid, IdlewhilesBruce (————)
6- 7 1Spk⅝ ft 81° clm3500—1 :294 1:014 1:333 2:054 3 x9 9dis 9dis 9dis 9dis 32-1 (CLoranceSr) TonkaChief, SmokePuff, SolsCreed (no threat)
5-29 4Spk⅝ gd 49° clm5000—1 :32 1:062 1:381 2:094 6 8 8dis x8dis 8dis 8dis 31 1 (C.LoranceJr) DunksBoy, Papa, BomberG. (out of it)
5-11 2Haw1 ft 55° clm7000 1 :34 1:061 1:374 2:09 8 8 8 89 911 811 2:111 41-1 (C.LoranceJr) HighJimmy, Aggregate, HeyBoyRanger (no chance)
5 1 3Haw1 gd 66° nw2R 1 :314 1:03 1:354 2:061 3 1 1 11 65 912 2:083 49-1 (C.LoranceJr) DykeM, BattleshoeFlame. LyricEyre (early foot)

BLACK & YELLOW **8** 10-1 —

Driver—NELSON WILLIS, Maroon-Gray-White Tr.—J. Wolfe (68-5-9-10—.196)

POPLAR JOHN Br g 1969, by Poplar Byrd—June Tide—Tide Water
Owners: Francis J. Barrett, Warren W. Ecklund, Oak Lawn, Tinley Pk., Ill.

1973 14 0 0 0 $1,177 2:084 Spk⅝ Qua
1972 21 1 1 2 $1,533 2:141 BmlP
Lifetime $1,561 3, 2:141

6-19 2Spk⅝ ft 78° clm4800+1 :283 :591 1:321 2:052 7 8 924 913 75½ 56¼ 2:063 31-1 (N.Willis) FannyMorgn, CrystlBaron, WorthyByrd (too much speed)
6- 5 1Spk⅝ sy 70° clm4200—1 :323 1:073 1:39 2:09 5 x9 911 98½ 513 x616 2:121 29-1 (J.Wolfe) RooksCreekKathy, KingSelka, CrystlBron (made breaks)
5 17 2Haw1 ft 53° clm4800 1⅛ :304 1:023 2:06 2:214 7 1 2 42½ 88 88¼ 2:232 30-1 (J.Wolfe) MountainCapt., MelodyLucky, RocketWRing (away well)
5- 1 1Haw1 gd 66° clm4200 1 :323 1:05 1:371 2:083 6 2° 1 11½ 31½ 85¼ 2:093 5-1 (J.MarshJr) GayTona, RosgoKid, MelodyLucky (early foot)
4-16 1Spk⅝ ft 43° clm4200=1 :314 1:06 1:363 2:08 2 5 76½ 710 79 54¾ 2:09 6-1 (P.Milburn) LuckyEddieAdios, TennsseeDoll, SquawMan (lost ground)
4- 4 1Spk⅝ gd 36° clm4200=1 :313 1:05 1:364 2:092 6 8 74¼ 33¼° 32¼ 43¾ 2:101 15-1 (J.Curran) LusciousLady, KingSelka, LincolnsGayWench (good try)

GRAY & BLACK **9** 10-1 =

Driver—GENE VALLANDINGHAM, Red-White-Blue Tr.—G. Vallandingham (60-5-9-3—.183)

BYEMAR B g 1967, by Poplar Byrd—Cadmar—Killarney Hal
Owner: Neil Kelly, Elgin, Ill.

1973 21 5 4 0 $6,979 2:061 Spk⅝
1972 17 3 4 1 $5,300 2:121 BmlP
Lifetime $12,451 4, 2:062 (1)

6-13 1Spk⅝ ft 73° clm3500=1 :311 1:043 1:35 2:051 2 3 42½ 64½ 55 56¼ 2:062 14-1 (GVllndnghm) HighPaintr, MountainCaptain, SelctWys (no closing kick)
6- 7 Spk⅝ ft 75° Qua 1 :312 1:043 1:342 2:051 9 4 45½ 44½ 44 46¼ 2:062 NB (GVllndnghm) SunsetJeanne, PaulinesBoy, MissGift (————)
5-24 1Haw1 ft 60° clm3500 1$\frac{1}{16}$:30 1:02 1:241 6 3° 2° 2½° 45½ 79½ 1:261 15-1 (GVllndnghm) HastyAdios, RooksCreekKthy, CoalmntFrtz (tired badly)
5- 2 1Haw1 gd 44° clm4000 1⅛ :321 1:062 2:102 2:264 9 1 2 21½ 65½ 913 2:292 31-1 (GVllndnghm) AprilArt, DoctorMarches, CarelessLew (tired badly)
4-17 1Haw1 ft 56° clm4000 1 :31 1:041 1:361 2:062 9 1° 1 12 55 913 2:09 17-1 (GVllndnghm) GayFamous, EmpireGold, TorpidsGold (tired)
4-10 5Spk⅝ ft 33° clm4000=1 :304 1:042 1:354 2:073 7 8 811 ex920 9dis 9dis 20-1 (GVllndnghm) KayCarmichael, Muley, RosgoKid (not a factor)

One of the horses that has a faster final time than Flaming Parker is Idlewhiles Bruce. He turned in a 2:05 2/5 in a qualifying race five days earlier. That time is faster than any of the races on his past performance record. It's also a faster final time than any of his competitors have turned in. That qualifies Idlewhiles Bruce on all counts and turns him into an automatic play.

FIRST RACE — 1 MILE
PACE. Claiming price $3,500 — 3 Year Olds and Upward — Illinois Bred — Purse $2,500.

Time—:31 $1{:}03^{2}$ $1{:}33^{3}$ $2{:}04^{2}$ Mutuel Pool—$38,653

Hd.No. Horse	PP	¼	½	¾	Str	Fin	Ind.Time	Odds	Driver
7. Idlewhiles Bruce	7	1°	1^{1}	1^{nk}	2^{nk}	$1^{1¾}$	$2{:}04^{2}$	8-1	(C.LoranceSr)
5. Flaming Parker	5	3	3^{2}	$2^{nk\circ}$	1^{nk}	$2^{1¾}$	$2{:}04^{4}$	3-1	(J.Dennis)
2. Dusty G. Hayes	2	5	$5^{4¼}$	$5^{4¼}$	$4^{3¾}$	$3^{3¼}$	2:05	15-1	(J.Willis)
6. Select Ways	6	2	2^{1}	$3^{1¼}$	$3^{1¾}$	4^{4}	$2{:}05^{1}$	*2-1	(S.Banks)
3. Miss Roscoe	3	7	$7^{7¼}$	$7^{5½}$	$6^{4¾}$	5^{4}	$2{:}05^{1}$	20-1	(C.Willis)
1. Crystal Baron	1	6	$6^{6¼}$	$6^{5¼\circ}$	$7^{6¾}$	$6^{7¼}$	$2{:}05^{4}$	4-1	(E.Conley)
4. Flaming Eyre	4	4	4^{3}	$4^{2¾}$	$5^{3¾}$	7^{10}	$2{:}06^{2}$	5-1	(H.Adams)
8. Poplar John	8	8	$8^{8¾}$	8^{8}	$8^{8¾}$	8^{11}	$2{:}06^{3}$	43-1	(N.Willis)
9. Byemar	9	9	9^{11}	9^{14}	9^{19}	9^{23}	2:09	28-1	(GVilndnghm)

Idlewhiles Bruce claimed for $3,500 by R. M. and R. A. Haddad, trainer—E. Lutes.
Mutuels—(7) 18.80 9.00 6.00—(5) 5.20 3.20—(2) 10.00

Idlewhiles Bruce left the gate well and took over the lead at the first quarter. The only challenger he encountered along the way was Flaming Parker. He was briefly headed by that one in the stretch but came on again to win the race going away. The mile was timed in 2:04 2/5, an improvement of one full second over his qualifying race. This time there was no short price. Idlewhiles Bruce returned a good $18.80 to win.

Both Circle Sambo and Idlewhiles Bruce had something in common—they both were sent out for the lead. You'll find that most of the horses that qualify as an automatic play will attempt to go wire to wire. Speed is the main asset behind this angle and naturally the best place for a speed horse is on the front end.

This angle should only be used for horses coming off qualifying races. Races for qualifying drivers do not reflect the capability of the horse. They are run strictly to give young drivers experience in the sulky. When you come across a horse that's off a qualifying driver race, simply throw it out and handicap his next to last effort.

Fast Time—Fast Quarter

This angle is almost self-explanatory. It's used only when a horse has both the fastest final time and the fastest final quarter. The first impression you might get is that this is the kind of angle that pops up about four or five times a night. But actually that's pretty far from the case. I'd be mighty surprised if you were able to use the fast time-fast quarter angle more than four or five times a week.

The reason you won't be able to get a lot of action out of this angle is because there are several safeguards attached to it for protection. Not every horse that has the fastest final time and the fastest final quarter will become an automatic play. If you were to put your money down on that kind of horse every night, you would probably go broke in less than a month.

This is a speed angle which deals directly with the pace factor. Like any other angle of this type, you cannot select just any horse that comes along. When we were working with the qualifying race angle, we confined play only to horses that figured to improve on an already fast final time. This angle is similar in that respect. This one confines play only to horses that have the fastest final time and figure in the race.

If we're going to be dealing with horses that have the fastest final time in the race, we'll have to locate the ones that have seriously made an attempt to win. Speed is something that can often be deceiving because horses are capable of running faster when losing a race than when actually winning. For a prime example of this, I refer you to page 00 in Chapter 1. The event was the prestigious "Governor's Cup" and it produced the fastest race in the history of harness racing. There were five horses entered in the field that night but we'll concentrate on only one—Ed Byrd. A check of his past performances reveal the following two items:

1. The fastest final time that's listed anywhere on the program was on June 2 when he was timed for the mile in 2:00 4/5.
2. The best winning time he has ever turned in was a 2:01 3/5 at the age of six.

I want you to keep those two items in mind and take a look at the result chart. Ed Byrd, in a losing effort, covered the mile in a speedy 1:57 3/5. Now

Chief Sammy, number three, is the winner of this photo finish. (Photo by Kuprion.)

I'll ask you a question. Is Ed Byrd really a sub-two-minute pacer?

The answer is a definite no. True, Ed Byrd stopped the teletimer in 1:57 3/5, but only because he was carried in the race. His fast final time is the direct result of competing against a horse that's able to cut out extremely fast fractions. Most drivers describe a fast race like Ed Byrds as "being sucked along for the ride." If you want to get a more realistic final time for him, you'll have to go to the finish line where he was handed a 15-length defeat. Add those lengths on to his final time and you come out with 2:00 3/5. That's a lot closer to how fast Ed Byrd is really capable of turning in a winning effort.

The dividing line we'll need to seriously consider the fastest final time in the race is a long way off from 15 lengths. The requirement used for this angle is set at 3 lengths. If a horse lost his race by more than that amount, he cannot become an automatic play. That's a very small margin to work with but it's a margin that definitely assures us of not getting hung up on a horse that was carried in a race.

Another redeeming factor that's added on to this angle is that the horse must have closed faster in his final quarter than any of his competitors. That will include non-contenders as well as contenders. That also means we'll have to work strictly with fast track races. If a horse's last race was on an off track or he parked out for two or more turns, it does not give a true indication of his speed.

The only problem you'll confront is when you have to reach back more than 30 days to get a fast track race. If that situation occurs and the horse turns out to be a non-contender, then it's safe to eliminate him from the race. But if the horse is a contender, then consider him to be an unratable contender—and of course two unratable contenders in a race make it unplayable. Here's how the angle looks when it's put in rule form:

1.   Eliminate the following:

A.   All non-contenders that do not have a ratable race (fast track) within the last 30 days.

B.   All horses that have broken stride in their last ratable race.

C. All horses that have competed in a qualifying race their last time out.

2. An automatic play must have:

A. The fastest final time in the race.

B. Lost his race by no more than 3 lengths. Winners are acceptable.

C. The fastest final quarter in the race.

It might appear that rule 1-C is contrary to the qualifying race angle. But it's actually impossible for these two angles ever to come up an automatic play in the same race. Let's say a horse comes off a qualifier and his final time is equal or better than the fastest final time in the race. If that ever happens, this angle will not produce an automatic play. Even if the qualifying horse doesn't meet the requirements of his own angle, it's still impossible for this angle to come up with a horse. The two angles will never contradict each other.

Horses that have broken stride on a fast track in their last ratable race are eliminated in this angle as in any other handicapping situation. The only breaks that are ever thrown out are ones that are due to interference, equipment, or an off track.

We'll test out the fast time-fast quarter angle on two example races. The first one is a $7,000 claimer that took place at Maywood Park on September 8. It's a good race to work on because it has more than its share of the difficult situations you're bound to come across eventually. An explanation is given for each horse whose last race wasn't used for handicapping.

ONE MILE PACE — **FOURTH RACE** — **Purse $3,200**

CLAIMING. Claiming price $7,000. Robin's Choice in for $8,400, all others $7,000.

PLEASE ASK FOR HORSE BY PROGRAM NUMBER

RED 1 — 5-1

Driver—NELSON WILLIS, Maroon-Gray-White Tr.—C. Carroll (97-9-10-12—.190)
CHIEF OSCEOLA B g 1964, by Chief Lenawee—Date Time—Good Time
Owner: Charles Carroll, Marseilles, Ill.
1973 28 7 6 5 $17,016 2:03 Spk⅝
1972 28 5 5 5 $11,198 2:05^4 Spk⅝
Lifetime $44,528 6, 2:04^2 (1)

Date	Trk Cond Temp	Class	Dist	Leader's Time ¼	½	¾	Winner's Time	PP	¼	½	¾	Str	Fin	Ind.Time	Odds	Driver	Order of Finish: First, Second, Third	Comment
9-4	May ft 75°	Qua§	1	:31^1	1:02^1	1:33^4	2:04^3	2	2	2^{2½}	2^{1½}	2^{1½}	2^{1¾}	2:05	NB	(N.Willis)	FrostyKing, ChiefOsceola, Integrated	(————)
8-8	^{8}May ft 82°	clm7000	1	:32	1:04^3	1:35^1	2:06	8	7	5$^{3°}$	6$^{3¼°}$	6^{5½}	7^{5½}	2:07^1	15-1	(N.Willis)	BethExpress, MisterAdios, NobleOne	(parked 2 turns)
7-27	^{4}May sy 79°	clm7000	1	:32^4	1:06^1	1:37^1	2:09^1	1	2	2^{1½}	2^2	3^{4½}	x8^{dis}		*2-1	(N.Willis)	BuddyTime, GoranHanover, CrystalE	(break costly)
7-14	^{2}Spk⅝ ft 75°	clm9000+	1	:29^3	1:00^4	1:31^2	2:02	7	9	9^{9¾}	8$^{7¾°}$	9^{11}	9^{14}	2:04^4	11-1	(N.Willis)	AprilArt, LookawaySun, Amigo'sGirl	(followed)
7-4	^{10}Spk⅝ ft 82°	clm8000−	1	:31	1:03^2	1:34	2:04^3	3	2	2^{1½}	4^{2¼}	3^{2½}	4^3	2:05^1	9-2	(N.Willis)	SengaMarie, PortSam, LittlePuff	(evenly)
6-23	^{1}Spk⅝ gd 74°	clm9000=	1	:30^3	1:04^2	1:35^4	2:05^1	7	1	2^1	2^{1¼}	2^{3½}	3^8	2:06^4	9-2	(N.Willis)	ReMark, SharpStar, ChiefOsceola	(3-wide for lead)

WHITE 2 — 4-1

Driver—CONNEL WILLIS, Red-White-Green Tr.—A. Dorman (76-9-9-8—.219)
LADYS KING Br g 1960, by Potomac Lad—Lady Iosola Miller—Athlone Iosola Guy
Owner: Adolph E. Dorman, Albert Lea, Minn.
1973 8 2 2 0 $4,610 2:04 May
1972 16 3 1 3 $5,942 2:05 Was^1
Lifetime $65,924 7, 2:02 (⅝)

Date	Trk Cond Temp	Class	Dist	Leader's Time ¼	½	¾	Winner's Time	PP	¼	½	¾	Str	Fin	Ind.Time	Odds	Driver	Order of Finish: First, Second, Third	Comment
9-1	^{4}May ft 85°	clm6000	1	:29^4	1:02	1:32^4	2:04	5	2	1$^{½°}$	1^{2¼}	1^2	1^{1¼}	2:04	10-1	(N.Willis)	LadysKing, SteppingSal, JollyGeneGiant	(well placed)
8-25	^{2}May ft 78°	clm5000	1	:29^4	:59^4	1:32^1	2:04^2	2	1	2^{½}	1^{½}	2^3	2^5	2:05^2	9-2	(C.Willis)	WillieGranda, LadysKing, Cindilla	(tired)
8-9	^{4}May ft 80°	clm5000	1	:31^2	1:03^3	1:34^4	2:05^3	4	5	5^3	3$^{nk°}$	1^2	1^{1¼}	2:05^3	*2-1	(J.Dennis)	LadysKing, MissTrojan, FrankDazzleway	(perfectly drivn)
7-24	^{2}May ft 81°	clm5000	1	:30^3	1:02	1:33^3	2:05^3	2	3	1^{1½}	2^{ns}	2^1	2^{nk}	2:05^3	15-1	(C.Willis)	Pellaire, LadysKing, SirWarwick	(just missed)
7-4	^{3}Spk⅝ ft 82°	clm5000=	1	:29^4	1:03^3	1:34^3	2:05^4	4	2	2^{1¼}	3^{1½}	ix9^{16}	9^{13}	2:08^2	7-2	(N.Willis)	Chickadee, RomanDancer, SissySassy	(break costly)
6-20	^{4}Spk⅝ ft 76°	clm5000−	1	:30^3	1:05^2	1:36^3	2:07^4	8	8	8$^{11°}$	8^{5¾}	7^{4¾}	5^{4¼}	2:08^3	9-1	(N.Willis)	DionnaDiller, FairyJo, GladstoneBabe	(slow leaving)

BLUE 3 — 6-1

Driver—WALTER PAISLEY, Green-White Tr.—W. Paisley (198-30-35-36—.313)
ROBINS CHOICE Br c 1969, by Choice H—Clara Parker—Parker Byrd
Owner: Walter Paisley, Wilmington, Ill.
1973 9 1 0 2 $3,144 2:04^4 May Qua
1972 3 1 0 0 $1,300 2:06^2 Haw^1
Lifetime $1,300 3, 2:06^2 (1)

Date	Trk Cond Temp	Class	Dist	Leader's Time ¼	½	¾	Winner's Time	PP	¼	½	¾	Str	Fin	Ind.Time	Odds	Driver	Order of Finish: First, Second, Third	Comment
8-30	^{6}May gd 78°	clm8400	1	:31^3	1:03^3	1:34	2:05^2	1	2	3^2	4^{1¾}	5^3	3^5	2:06^2	*6-5	(W.Paisley)	MisterAdios, LovinLuLu, RobinsChoice	(no close)
8-22	^{7}May ft 69°	clm10800	1	:29^1	1:00^2	1:31^3	2:02	3	4	4^{4½}	4$^{1½°}$	2^6	x5^{9¾}	2:04	*8-5	(W.Paisley)	NobleChoice, EyreFire, IdlewhilesEarl	(dull mile)
8-15	^{10}May ft 75°	clm12000	1	:30^1	1:01^3	1:32^3	2:02^2	2	3	3$^{3½°}$	3$^{2°}$	7^{7½}	8^{14}	2:05^1	9-2	(W.Paisley)	ColMoffitt, JHazenAdios, Knoxella	(tired badly)
8-8	^{10}May ft 82°	clm9600	1	:29^2	:59^4	1:31^4	2:03^1	4	5	5^4	7^{5½}	5^5	3^{1¼}	2:03^2	2-1	(W.Paisley)	LunarHill, Goodare, RobinsChoice	(shuffled back)
7-31	^{8}May ft 71°	clm8400	1	:30^3	1:01^4	1:33^4	2:05	3	5	4$^{2½°}$	1^2	1^4	1^{3¾}	2:05	*2-1	(W.Paisley)	RobinsChoice, SonnyFarvl, TmmyLobell	(3-wide for lead)
7-27	May ft 76°	Qua	1	:30^4	1:02^3	1:33^2	2:04^4	2	4	3^3	1$^{1°}$	1^3	1^{5¼}	2:04^4	NB	(W.Paisley)	RobinsChoice, WalterJPick, EdgewoodDevan	(————)

GREEN 4 — 8-1

Driver—JAMES MORRISSEY, Green-White-Yellow Tr.—J. Morrissey (30-4-2-6—.219)
DAZZLING STAR B g 1965, by Dazzleway—Leola V. Grattan—White Mountain Boy
Owner: J. Morrissey and J. Schilling, Chicago, Ill., St. John, Ind.
1973 21 2 1 4 $6,951 2:06^3 May
1972 41 3 5 2 $11,850 2:04^1 Was^1
Lifetime $22,906 7, 2:04^1 (1)

Date	Trk Cond Temp	Class	Dist	Leader's Time ¼	½	¾	Winner's Time	PP	¼	½	¾	Str	Fin	Ind.Time	Odds	Driver	Order of Finish: First, Second, Third	Comment
9-1	^{7}May ft 80°	§clm7000	1	:30^3	1:02	1:33^1	2:03^3	5	3°	2$^{½°}$	5$^{3°}$	6^7	5^{8½}	2:05^2	10-1	(J.Morrissey)	RustyMerrie, ChiefsLittleStar, SmoothSpd	(parked mile)
8-28	May ft 84°	Qua§	1	:31^3	1:03^1	1:34	2:04^4	2	2	3^{2½}	3^2	3^3	3^2	2:05^1	NB	(J.Morrissey)	SherwoodDancer, JavelonJeantte. DzzlngStr	(————)
8-25	^{1}May ft 78°	clm6000	1	:30^1	1:01^4	1:33^3	2:04^2	1	3	4^{2½}	5$^{2½°}$	4^6	3^{2¾}	2:05	8-1	(J.Morrissey)	SmoothSpeed, SeattleCindy, DazzlingStar	(raced well)
8-17	^{1}May ft 76°	clm7000	1	:31	1:03^1	1:34^1	2:05^1	8	8	8^{5½}	7$^{3½°}$	7^{3¼}	8^{3¼}	2:05^4	27-1	(J.Morrissey)	MisterAdios, RamsPrincess, MightyLoyal	(no excuse)
8-8	^{6}May ft 82°	clm6000	1	:30^3	1:01^4	1:33^4	2:05	2	4	4$^{1¾°}$	7^{4½}	7^5	4^{3½}	2:05^4	6-1	(J.Morrissey)	BitOCreed, FireBomb, Zhivago	(raced well)
7-26	^{2}May ft 73°	clm5000	1	:31^2	1:02^2	1:34^2	2:06^3	5	2°	2^{¾}	1^{nk}	1^{nk}	1^{1¼}	2:06^3	6-1	(J.Morrissey)	DazzlingStar, FoxyTime, Torpion	(parked early)

BLACK **5** 3-1

Driver—KEN VANDER SCHAAF, Gold-Black Tr.—K. Vander Schaaf (10-0-0-1—.033)

AQUARIUS B h 1965, by Advocator—Eric's Winnie—Eric Hanover
Owner: Ken Vander Schaaf, Sandwich, Ill.

1973 20 7 1 3 $12,004 2:04 May
1972 20 4 3 1 $3,744 2:03^1 V.D⅝
Lifetime $16,832 7, 2:03^1 (⅝)

9-3 ^{10}May gd 74°	§clm6000 C	1	:31^3	1:03^3	1:35	2:06^1	2	5	1^{1½}	1^2	1^{2½}	1^{3¼}	2:06^1	*4-5 (J.Dolbee)	Aquarius, RoyDares, MightyNaHm	(much the best)
8-27 ^{4}May ft 82°	§clm5000	1	:31^4	1:03	1:33^2	2:04	5	1	1^1	1^{1¼}	1^{2½}	1^{2¼}	2:04	7-2 (J.Dolbee)	Aquarius, KristyLynn, NevadasSonA	(easy win)
8-14 ^{2}May ft 70°	§clm6000	1	:30^2	1:02^1	1:32^3	2:03^2	6	7	6^{6½}°	x8^{24}	8^{dis}	8^{dis}		7-2 (H.Adams)	HastiDoc, SnoVan, FairyJo	(on move, broke)
8-3 ^{4}May ft 72°	clm6000	1	:31^1	1:04^2	1:35^4	2:06	1	4	3^{1½}°	2^{nk}°	2^{1½}	2^{1¾}	2:06^2	3-1 (J.Dolbee)	TrueOne, Aquarius, RushStreetBoss	(2nd best)
7-23 ^{3}Spk⅝ ft 81°	clm5000=	1	:31^2	1:04	1:34	2:04^3	1	3	1^1	1^2	1^{3½}	1^{1½}	2:04^3	*8-5 (J.Dolbee)	Aquarius, NevadasSonA, J.C.Stormy	(easy win)
7-19 ^{4}Spk⅝ ft 84°	clm5000=	1	:31^2	1:04	1:34	2:05^3	7	7	7^7°	6^7°	3^{2½}	3^{¾}	2:05^4	11-1 (J.Dolbee)	HastiDoc, KristyLynn, Aquarius	(closed some)

YELLOW **6** 10-1

Driver—DWIGHT BANKS, White-Purple-Gold Tr.—D. Banks (13-0-2-1—.111)

REGGIE COMMANDER B g 1967, by Bay Prince—HelenCmmandr—Lieut. Cmmandr
Owner: Larry Williams, Lessee, East Moline, Ill.

1973 27 1 3 4 $4,253 2:06^2 E.M.D ⅝
1972 25 2 1 3 $4,219 2:05^4 Was^1
Lifetime $12,113 5, 2:05^4 (1)

9-4 ^{7}May gd 73°	clm7000	1	:31^2	1:03^2	1:35	2:08^2	6	7	7^6	8^{7½}	7^7	7^{8¼}	2:10	56-1 (D.Banks)	WindaleGuyTraux, AljeansDon, TrudyBurns	(evenly)
8-28 ^{10}May ft 85°	clm7000	1	:30^2	1:00^4	1:33	2:04^2	5	7	8^{8½}	5^3°	5^{3¼}	4^{4¼}	2:05^1	10-1 (D.Banks)	HastiDoc, FlatPass, CamaroHanover	(3-wide briefly)
8-20 ^{7}May ft 69°	clm7000	1	:30	1:00^4	1:32^4	2:04^4	4	4	4^5	4^2°	3^1	2^{1¼}	2:05	13-1 (D.Banks)	TrudyBurns, ReggieCmmndr, GoranHanover	(raced well)
8-13 ^{7}May ft 77°	clm7000	1	:30^3	1:01^3	1:32^1	2:03^2	1	5	6^{7¼}	5^5	4^6	3^{3¾}	2:04^1	10-1 (D.Banks)	BedfordBrush, FlatPass, ReggieCommander	(raced well)
8-2 ^{7}May ft 71°	clm7000	1	:31	1:03^2	1:35^1	2:06^1	6	8	8^{7¼}°	8^{7¼}	6^6	4^{2½}	2:06^4	17-1 (D.Banks)	EmbassyVolo, MoeWestern, CircleEddie	(3-wide briefly)
7-24 ^{1}May ft 81°	clm7000	1	:29^3	1:01^1	1:33^3	2:04	4	5	6^{5½}	6^{8½}	3^{5½}	2^{7¾}	2:05^3	18-1 (D.Banks)	LunarHill, ReggieCommander, SnoVan	(soundly beaten)

BROWN **7** 6-1

Driver—EDDIE LUTES, Red-White Tr.—E. Lutes (31-4-5-2—.240)

LO GO ADIOS B g 1968, by Ellens Adios—Siss Dream—Sallys Dream
Owner: Thomas and Peter Russian, Burbank, Ill.

1973 27 3 2 6 $5,252 2:05 May
1972 26 4 4 2 $3,430 2:04^4 Cka⅝
Lifetime $3,778 4, 2:04^4 (⅝)

8-31 ^{4}May ft 81°	clm7000	1	:29^1	1:00^1	1:31^2	2:00^3	7	8	8^{13}	5^{9½}	5^{9½}	4^{19dh}	2:04^2	18-1 (E Lutes)	CrystalE., QuickBay, BourbonChimes	(too much speed)
8-25 ^{4}May ft 78°	clm6000 C	1	:30^4	1:02^4	1:33^3	2:05	6	4	4^{5½}	4^5	3^{3½}	1^{½}	2:05	9-2 (W.Paisley)	LoGoAdios, ProudDelight, AaronMeridale	(strong on rail)
8-17 ^{4}May ft 76°	clm6000 C	1	:30^1	1:01^4	1:32^2	2:04	2	3	2^{1½}°	2^{ns}°	2^{hd}x	3^{2¾}	2:04^3	7-1 (E.Lutes)	FairRowByrd, FireBomb, LoGoAdios	(tough trip)
8-10 ^{1}May ft 75°	clm7000	1	:30^3	1:01^4	1:32^4	2:04^1	5	7	8^9	7^{25}	7^{25}	7^{17}	2:07^3	17-1 (E.Lutes)	FrostyFreight, LittlePuff, AirBlazer	(out of it)
8-1 ^{7}May ft 67°	clm8000	1	:30	1:02	1:32^4	2:04	5	7	5^3°	5^3°	6^{6½}	6^{7¾}	2:05^3	16-1 (E.Lutes)	WillFly, FlyingFool, SpoiledBrat	(parked 2 turns)
7-24 ^{3}May ft 81°	nw4000^{73}	1	:29^1	:59^1	1:30^2	2:01^1	1x	8	8^{dis}	8^{dis}	8^{dis}	8^{dis}		10-1 (E.Lutes)	KeystneJournal, NobleLand, MargretSue	(elimnated self)

RED & YELLOW **8** 8-1

Driver—DARYL BUSSE, Gray-Red Tr.—Da. Busse (107-9-11-13—.182)

CHIEF'S LITTLE STAR B g 1968, by Dazzle Lee—Chief Star's Time—No Time
Owner: K. M. Rutherford, Manistee, Mich.

1973 22 3 4 2 $13,558 2:04^1 May
1972 33 9 7 7 $10,132 2:04^1 Was^1
Lifetime $13,858 4, 2:04^1 (1)

9-1 ^{7}May ft 80°	§clm7000	1	:30^3	1:02	1:33^1	2:03^3	2	2	3^{1½}	4^2	4^3	2^{1¼}	2:03^4	6-1 (Da.Busse)	RustyMerrie, ChiefsLittleStar, SmoothSpeed	(raced well)
8-25 ^{7}May ft 78°	§clm7000	1	:30^3	1:02^3	1:33	2:03^1	7	1	2^{1¼}	4^{2¾}	5^{5¼}	7^{6¾}	2:04^3	8-1 (Da.Busse)	LittlePuff, QuickBay, AirBlazer	(used early)
8-18 ^{2}May ft 77°	§clm7000	1	:29^3	1:00	1:31	2:03^2	4	2	2^1	3^{1¼}	4^{2¼}	4^{2½}	2:04	*2-1 (Da.Busse)	TommyLobell, SenatorGlib, AirBlazer	(evenly)
8-10 ^{4}May ft 75°	clm8000	1	:30^1	1:01^1	1:33	2:03^2	1	3	4^{2½}	6^3	5^{3½}	5^{3¾}	2:04^1	9-2 (Da.Busse)	BuddyTime, RustyMerrie, FlyingFool	(evenly)
7-31 ^{6}May ft 71°	clm7000	1	:29^1	1:00^4	1:31^4	2:04^1	4	2	2^{1½}	2^{hd}°	1^{½}	1^1	2:04^1	12-1 (Da.Busse)	ChiefsLitteStar, StealHome, NeHieWay	(good mile)
7-24 ^{1}May ft 81°	clm7000	1	:29^3	1:01^1	1:33^3	2:04	7	1°	1^{1½}	2^5	6^{7½}	5^{16}	2:07^1	6-1 (D.Bird)	LunarHill, ReggieCommander, SnoVan	(early speed)

1. CHIEF OSCEOLA—Eliminated. Last time out, he competed in a qualifier but his final time does not equal the fastest final time in the race.
2. LADYS KING—31^1 2:04.
3. ROBINS CHOICE—Eliminated. His last race is thrown out because of an off track. His next to last race eliminates him for breaking stride on a fast track.
4. DAZZLING STAR—30^4 2:05. His last race is thrown out because he was parked out. A qualifying race is significant only if it's the horse's last effort. The August 25 race is used for handicapping,
5. AQUARIUS—30^3 2:04. His last race is thrown out because of an off track. The August 27 race is used for handicapping.
6. REGGIE COMMANDER—31^3 2:05^1. His last race is thrown out because of an off track. The August 28 race is used for handicapping.
7. LO GO ADIOS—Scratched.
8. CHIEF'S LITTLE STAR—30^1 2:03^4.

The fastest final time and the fastest final quarter belong to Chief's Little Star. He closed in 30^1 which is 2/5 of a second faster than the final quarter turned in by Aquarius. He covered the mile in 2:03 4/5 which is one tick faster than the final times turned in by both Aquarius and Ladys King. The margin of defeat in Chief's Little Star's race was a length and a quarter. That qualifies him on all three counts and turns him into an automatic play.

FOURTH RACE — 1 MILE
PACE. Claiming $7,000. Purse $3,200.
Time—:30^3 1:03^3 1:33^1 2:04 Mutuel Pool—$45,405

8. Chief's Little Star	7	2	2^{hd}°	1^1	1^{2¼}	1^{½}	2:04	9-2	(Da.Busse)
1. Chief Osceola	1	4	4^{3½}	4^{2½}	4^3	2^{½}	2:04^1	3-1	(N Willis)
2. Lady's King	2	3	3^2	3^{1½}°	3^{2½}	3^3	2:04^3	5-1	(C.Willis)
4. Dazzling Star	4	6	6^{7½}	6^6	5^4	4^{3¾}	2:04^4	16 1	(J.Morrissey)
6. Reggie Commander	6	7	7^{11}	7^9	6^{5½}	5^{4¼}	2:04^4	40-1	(D.Banks)
5. Aquarius	5	1°	1^{hd}	2^1	2^{2¼}	6^5	2:05	*2-1	(K.VndrSchf)
3. Robin's Choice	3	5	5^{5½}	5^{5½}°	7^{6½}	7^8	2:05^3	3-1	(W.Paisley)

Aquarius claimed for $7,000 by Amadio Bruni and J. Dolbee, trainer—J. Dolbee.
Mutuels—(8) 11.40 5.60 4.60—(1) 4.60 4.00—(2) 3.40 Scratched—Lo Go Adios

Chief's Little Star left the gate well from the outside post position. He was content to sit behind the leader for the first half of the race. After that point, he took command, opened up a good lead and still had enough left to win clear at the wire. He returned $11.40 in the win slot.

6 RACE

ONE MILE PACE — Claiming Price $8,000. — Purse $4,600

PLEASE ASK FOR HORSE BY PROGRAM NUMBER

PROGRAM NUMBER

Red **1** $8,000 9-2

MOSE

B g 66 by Adios Bomber—Lady B. Sampson—Sampson Hanover
Owner: Ken Vander Schaaf, Sandwich, Ill.
1973 15 1 4 1 $8,128 2:08^4 gd Y.R.
1972 24 8 0 2 $15,587 2:02^2 Spk$\frac{5}{8}$
Lifetime thru 1972 $43,986

Driver—STANLEY BANKS, White-Purple **Trainer—K. Vander Schaaf**

Date	Trk	Cd	Tem	Class	Dis	Leader's Time ¼	½	¾	Winner's Time	PP	¼	½	¾	Str	Fin	Ind Time	Odds	Driver	First	Second	Third
4-27	^{10}Haw^1	ft	45°	clm8000	1	:30^4	1:02^3	1:34^1	2:05	3	3	4	5^3	4^2	2$^{2\frac{1}{4}}$	2:05^2	3-1	(SBanks)	ReMark	Mose	SengaMarie
4-18	^{10}Haw^1	sy	61°	clm9000	1	:30^2	1:03^3	1:37^2	2:09	8	1	1	1$^{1\frac{1}{2}}$	9^8	9^{16}	2:12^1	*8-5	(SBanks)	IdlewhilesEarl	RosedalePrince	MissLekram
4-11	^{6}Spk$\frac{5}{8}$	sy	35°	clm9000	1	:33^1	1:06^3	1:38	2:10^3	2	1	2	2	2^3	2$^{5\frac{3}{4}}$	2:11^4	2-1	(SBanks)	BoldGene	Mose	Crawdad
3-31	^{2}Spk$\frac{5}{8}$A	sy	44°	clm9000	1	:30^3	1:03^3	1:37^2	2:08^4	2	3	3	6°	3^1	2$^{1\frac{1}{2}}$	2:09^1	7-2	(SBanks)	NearChief	Mose	DutchKnight
3-21	^{7}Spk$\frac{5}{8}$	ft	35°	clm9000	1	:30^3	1:04^1	1:34^4	2:06^2	6	1	1	1	1^2	7^{3}p6	2:07	9-2	(SBanks)	NobleScot	SengaMarie	SilverDiller
3-14	^{8}Spk$\frac{5}{8}$	ft	58°	clm10000	1	:29^3	1:01^4	1:32^3	2:05	1	3	1	1	1$^{\frac{1}{2}}$	9$^{7\frac{1}{4}}$	2:06^2	*9-2	(SBanks)	HopeImperial	NobleChoice	Cheslind

White **2** $8,000 8-1

TUCKABUCK

Blk g 68 by Addio Byrd—Silvers Jewel—Harlan
Owner: Daryl D. Busse, Merlyn H. Welch, Kingston, Ill., Sharon, Wis.
1973 5 0 1 0 $1,900 2:09 Spk$\frac{5}{8}$ Qua
1972 0 0 0 0 (——)
Lifetime thru 1972 $15,896

Driver—DARYL BUSSE, Gray-Red **Trainer—Da. Busse**

Date	Trk	Cd	Tem	Class	Dis	Leader's Time ¼	½	¾	Winner's Time	PP	¼	½	¾	Str	Fin	Ind Time	Odds	Driver	First	Second	Third
4-28	^{1}Haw^1	ft	43°	clm8500	1	:31^1	1:02^2	1:33^4	2:04^1	9	7°	3°	3$^{1\frac{1}{2}}$°	2$^{1\frac{1}{2}}$	5$^{3\frac{1}{2}}$	2:05	12-1	(DaBusse)	WesternsJody	TerryJeansByrd	Goodare
4-20	^{3}Haw^1	gd	71°	clm8000	1	:32^1	1:03^2	1:35	2:06^4	6	2	2	3$^{1\frac{1}{4}}$	2nd	4$^{4\frac{1}{2}}$	2:07^4	9-1	(DaBusse)	WesternsJody	SampsonCreed	HaveAChance
4-13	^{2}Spk$\frac{5}{8}$	ft	39°	clm6000	1	:31^2	1:03^1	1:34^2	2:05^1	4	2	3	1	1^1	2^{nk}	2:05^1	24-1	(DaBusse)	RioDean	Tuckabuck	HedgeAppleJohn
4- 4	^{3}Spk$\frac{5}{8}$	gd	36°	clm5000	1	:31^3	1:03^4	1:35^1	2:07^4	5	1°	1	2	3^3	4$^{6\frac{3}{4}}$	2:09^1	8-1	(DaBusse)	SissySassy	FlubAdubAdoo	FairyJo
3-28	Spk$\frac{5}{8}$	ft		Qua	1	:31	1:03^3	1:35^3	2:06	5	3°	1	2^2	2^4	2$^{4\frac{1}{2}}$	2:07	NB	(DaBusse)	LincolnsBid	Tuckabuck	Braidwood
3-21	^{6}Spk$\frac{5}{8}$	ft	35°	clm6000	1	:31	1:04^4	1:34^4	2.05^4	2	x9	x9	9	9^{24}	9^{21}	2:10	5-2	(DaBusse)	FlashHarry	L.A.Parker	RacerWave

Blue **3** $8,000 12-1

SAMPSON CREED

Blk h 67 by Sampson Direct—Creeds Queen—Widower Creed. Owners: Eugene Waszak & Jim Talarek, Chicago, Markham, Ill.
1973 9 0 1 1 $1,800
1972 7 2 2 0 $437 2:11^2 Vnwrt
Lifetime thru 1972 $12,244

Driver—EUGENE WASZAK, White-Gold-Blue **Trainer—E. Waszak**

Date	Trk	Cd	Tem	Class	Dis	Leader's Time ¼	½	¾	Winner's Time	PP	¼	½	¾	Str	Fin	Ind Time	Odds	Driver	First	Second	Third
4-28	^{1}Haw^1	ft	43°	clm8500	1	:31^1	1:02^2	1:33^4	2:04^1	6	3°	2	2$^{1\frac{1}{2}}$	3^2	7$^{7\frac{1}{2}}$	2:05^4	10-1	(EWaszak)	WesternsJody	TerryJeansByrd	Goodare
4-20	^{3}Haw^1	gd	71°	clm8000	1	:32^1	1:03^2	1:35	2:06^4	9	8	7	7^7	6$^{3\frac{1}{2}}$	2$^{\frac{3}{4}}$	2:07	50-1	(EWaszak)	WesternsJody	SampsonCreed	HaveAChance
4-14	^{2}Spk$\frac{5}{8}$A	ft	56°	clm8000	1	:30^1	1:04	1:34^2	2:05^1	3	4	4	x6	9^{16}	9^{11}	2:07^2	37-1	(EWaszak)	TinyForbes	CarlenDirtyBird	HaveAChance
4- 7	^{5}Spk$\frac{5}{8}$	ft	45°	clm9000	1	:31	1:02^4	1:34^2	2:06^1	1	3	3	3°	3$^{1\frac{1}{2}}$	6$^{6\frac{1}{4}}$	2:07^2	14-1	(EWaszak)	HandsomeDate	SeattleCindy	JewelThief
3-29	^{7}Spk$\frac{5}{8}$	gd	40°	Cclm7500	1	:31^2	1:05^4	1:36^4	2:08^3	8	8	7	8°	7$^{3\frac{1}{4}}$	5^{nk}	2:08^3	23-1	(CAlessi)	Danella	TeeniTime	TinyForbes
3-22	^{10}Spk$\frac{5}{8}$	ft	36°	clm7500	1	:30^2	1:02^2	1:34	2:05^3	4	5	4	7	6^8	6$^{6\frac{1}{4}}$	2:06^4	6-1	(WPaisley)	Danella	DaveWestern	BartByrd

Green **4** $8,000 6-1

MISTER ADIOS

B g 64 by Adios Mite—Rushmor—Rush Hour
Owners: William Luttrell & Wilbur Boren, Marseilles, Ill.
1973 7 2 1 0 $5,168 2:06^2 Spk$\frac{5}{8}$
1972 0 0 0 0 (——)
Lifetime thru 1972 $41,431

Driver—PHILIP MILBURN, Blue-Gold **Trainer—D. Henert**

Date	Trk	Cd	Tem	Class	Dis	Leader's Time ¼	½	¾	Winner's Time	PP	¼	½	¾	Str	Fin	Ind Time	Odds	Driver	First	Second	Third
4-27	^{10}Haw^1	ft	45°	Cclm8000	1	:30^4	1:02^3	1:34^1	2:05	8	9	2°	2^1°	3$^{1\frac{1}{2}}$	4$^{4\frac{3}{4}}$	2:06	7-1	(JGrevengoed)	ReMark	Mose	SengaMarie
4-17	^{6}Haw^1	ft	56°	clm7000	1	:32	1:05^4	1:37^2	2:07^3	2	4	4	2^{nk}	1$^{\frac{3}{4}}$	1$^{\frac{3}{4}}$	2:07^3	*3-1	(JGrevengoed)	MisterAdios	GrandClara	MelodyWarrior
4-10	^{10}Spk$\frac{5}{8}$	ft	33°	clm6000	1	:31^3	1:04	1:35^3	2:06^2	1	2	2	2	2$^{\frac{1}{2}}$	1^{nk}	2:06^2	6-1	(JGrevengoed)	MisterAdios	GrandClara	DionnaDiller
4- 2	^{10}Spk$\frac{5}{8}$	ft	42°	Cclm6000	1	:30^2	1:03^3	1:34^1	2:07	4	1°	2	2°	4$^{3\frac{1}{2}}$	8$^{6\frac{1}{4}}$	2:08^1	6-1	(GIsom)	WindlAnaTrux	EdgwdWllce	HdgeAppleJhn
3-26	^{4}Spk$\frac{5}{8}$	ft	44°	clm6000	1	:30^2	1:02	1:34^2	2:06	3	6	5	6°	6^5	6$^{3\frac{1}{2}}$	2:06^4	*2-1	(GIsom)	CarlenDrtyBrd	JubileeTme	HedgeAppleJhn
3-19	^{10}Spk$\frac{5}{8}$	ft	33°	clm6000	1	:30^1	1:01^2	1:32^4	2:04^4	5	5	5	2	2$^{1\frac{1}{2}}$	2$^{2\frac{1}{2}}$	2:05^2	8-1	(GIsom)	LoisAmigo	MisterAdios	CarlenDirtyBird

Black

5

$8,000
8-1

BARONS STORM

B g 67 by Baron Hanover—The Gray Storm—Storm Cloud
Owner: Forest View Stable, Harwood Heights, Ill.

1973	13	1	2	0	$4.350	2:111	BmlP
1972	31	4	7	3	$5,313	2:034	Lat1
Lifetime thru 1972					$11,757		

Driver—JERALD GREVENGOED, Gold-Black **Trainer—R. Bice**

4-26 10Haw1	ft 51°	clm9000	1	:31	1:024	1:351	2:054	7	7	8	96	79½	65¾	2:07	6-1	(JGrevengoed)	DillerVolo, HalKnox, BillCarlith
4-14 1Spk⅝A	ft 56°	clm7500	1	:292	1:002	1:31	2:033	2	2	2	2	2½	2½	2:034	13-1	(JGrevengoed)	MajorBlack, BaronsStorm, HarkWay
4- 6 3Spk⅝	ft 64°	clm8000	1	:303	1:031	1:333	2:041	6	7	7	7	67	610	2:061	33-1	(JGrevengoed)	BillCarlith. SilentTona, HaveAChance
3-31 3Spk⅝	sy 45°	clm7000	1	:322	1:064	1:381	2:092	6	6	6	5°	56½	23¼	2:10	20-1	(JGrevengoed)	CarlnDrtyBrd,BaronsStorm,MeldyWarrior
3-23 2Spk⅝	ft 45°	clm7000	1	:311	1:03	1:351	2:064	3	4	4	3°	11	43	2:072	16-1	(JGrevengoed)	MortiesPride, SengaMarie, LuckyPeak
3-16 2Spk⅝	sy 34°	clm7000	1	:321	1:06	1:384	2:103	4	9	8°	6°	65	x611	2:124	10-1	(JGrevengoed)	SilverDiller, ReidsShadow, SengaMarie

Yellow

6

$8,000
7-2

GOODARE

B g 66 by Times Square—Little Goody—Good Time
Owner: Four Jacks Racing Stable, Harvey, Ill.

1973	4	0	1	1	$2.149		
1972	37	7	7	3	$27.614	2:012	Brd⅝
Lifetime thru 1972					$52,998		

Driver—WAYNE MOORE, Red-Gold **Trainer—D. Paulik**

4-28 1Haw1	ft 43°	clm8500	1	:311	1:022	1:334	2:041	7	9	7	74¾°	74½	32¾	2:044	7-2	(WMoore)	WesternsJody, TerryJeansByrd. Goodare
4- 7 6Spk⅝	ft 45°	clm10000	1	:313	1:043	1:36	2:062	3	4	5	4	44	65¾	2:073	*2-1	(WMoore)	G.T.Winter, ForbesTime, SilverDiller
3-27 10Spk⅝	ft 38	clm10000	1	:303	1:04	1:341	2:043	6	7	7	6°	42¾	22¾	2:051	5-1	(WMoore)	SenatorBerry, Goodare, SnoVan
3-17 1Spk⅝A	ft35°	Cclm10000	1	:303	1:031	1:333	2:052	7	8	8	8	65	42½	2:06	*3-1	(JCurran)	Edstime, Knoxella, AljeansDon
12- 2 6Was1	ft 36°	clm12000	1	:31	1:04	1:364	2:053	6	7	6°	5°	43	1nk	2:053	3-1	(WPaisley)	Goodare, VictorysHorn, McNavi
11-24 8Was1	ft 38°	clm12000	1	:303	1:004	1:331	2:042	4	6	6	8	44	12	2:042	9-2	(JCurran)	Goodare, BengalSong, McNavi

Brown

7

$9,600
5-1

SENGA MARIE

B m 66 by Adios Pick—Greta Han—Ogden Hanover
Owner: Norma G. Jensen, Edmonton, Alberta

1973	18	3	1	4	$6.907	2:044	Spk⅝
1972	42	4	9	5	$7.234	2:10	Reg
Lifetime thru 1972					$27,224		

Driver—JOHN SEARLE, Green-Gold **Trainer—O. Jaffke**

4-27 10Haw1	ft 45°	clm9600	1	:304	1:023	1:341	2:05	4	6	9	85½°	64	33½	2:054	5-1	(JSearle)	ReMark, Mose, SengaMarie
4-14 2Spk⅝A	ft 56°	clm9600	1	:301	1:04	1:342	2:051	5	6	7	9	811	57½	2:064	5-1	(JSearle)	TinyForbes,CarlenDirtyBird,HaveAChance
4- 5 5Spk⅝	ft 53°	clm8400	1	:304	1:031	1:34	2:044	3	5	4	5	32½	11	2:044	40-1	(JSearle)	SengaMarie, GrandAce, DameFontane
3-30 10Spk⅝	ft 40°	clm8400	1	:32	1:033	1:35	2:051	6	9	9	8°	812	79	2:07	9-1	(FKeener)	Ferdinand. MohicanGold. DaveWestern
3-23 2Spk⅝	ft 45°	clm8400	1	:311	1:03	1:351	2:064	4	5	5	6	53x	21¼	2:07	10-1	(JSearle)	MortiesPride, SengaMarie, LuckyPeak
3-16 2Spk⅝	sy 34°	clm8400	1	:321	1:06	1:384	2:103	5	3	5	5	54½	36¼	2:114	19-1	(JSearle)	SilverDiller, ReidsShadow, SengaMarie

Red & Yellow

8

$9,600
12-1

ALJEAN'S DON

B c 69 by Jet Hanover—Tahoe—Bristol Hanover
Owner: J. Schilling & J. Morrissey, St. John, Ind., Chicago, Ill.

1973	10	0	0	2	$1.404		
1972	19	2	5	3	$9.038	2:034	W.R.⅝
Lifetime thru 1972					$10.856		

Driver—JAMES MORRISSEY, Green-White-Yellow **Trainer—J. Morrissey**

4-27 10Haw1	ft 45°	clm9600	1	:304	1:023	1:341	2 05	7	8	5°	42½°	97½	99¼	2:064	19-1	(JMorrissey)	ReMark, Mose, SengaMarie
4-18 10Haw1	sy 61°	clm10800	1	:302	1:033	1:372	2:09	1	5	5	64	86	79½	2:104	19-1	(JMorrissey)	IdlewhilesEarl,RosedalePrince,MissLekram
4-11 6Spk⅝	sy 35°	clm10800	1	:331	1:063	1:38	2:103	6	9	8	8	716	612	2:13	29-1	(JMorrissey)	BoldGene, Mose, Crawdad
4- 3 7Spk⅝	ft 37°	clm10800	1	:311	1:04	1:34	2:051	5	6	6	6	76½	67	2:063	12-1	(JMorrissey)	RuthsChoice. Brindanette. LovinLuLu
3-28 8Spk⅝	sy 50°	clm12000	1	:322	1:062	1:374	2:101	3	5°	3°	5°	78¼	810	2:121	9-2	(JMorrissey)	FrostyWil, FirstLook, Dr.Conway
3-23 4Spk⅝	ft 45°	nw3000	1	:303	1:023	1:333	2:042	8	9	9	9	811	811	2:063	18-1	(JMorrissey)	ChrisButler, Concourse, MaidOfKnight

Orange

9

$8,000
6-1

GINNY'S GENE

Br g 64 by Gene Abbe—Ginny Widow—The Widower
Owner: George G. Hardie, Santa Monica, Calif.

1973	13	4	1	0	$6,105	2:043	Haw1
1972	29	2	5	2	$10,628	2:044	L.A.⅝
Lifetime thru 1972					$59,466		

Driver—GENE VALLANDINGHAM, Red-White-Red **Trainer—G. Vallandingham**

4-27 2Haw1	ft 45°	clm5000	1	:31	1:014	1:342	2:043	1	3	4	43	11½	12½	2:043	5-2	(GVallndnghm)	GinnysGene, BethExpress, ChiefOsceloa
4-14 L.A.⅝	ft	clm4500	1	:30	1:021	1:324	2:034	4	7	7	7	66	57½	2:051	5-1	(GHardie)	GladstneBbe,FreemnsDream.FlyngDtchmn
4- 3 L.A.⅝	ft	clm5000	1	:322	1:033	1:344	2:053	6	3	4	5	62¾	54	2:062	3-1	(GHardie)	SecondRaid, MissAmyAdios, IrishCam
3-24 L.A⅝	ft	clm6000	1	:30	1:021	1:333	2:042	5	6	6	6	44	42½	2:044	13-1	(GHardie)	WorthyPacingTme,PepprDrive,SundwnLass
3-17 L.A.⅝	ft	clm5000	1	:314	1:041	1:344	2:051	7	8	8	8	823	824½	2:10	19-1	(GHardie)	SilverRoyal, C.F.Sincous. ScottysColt
3- 3 B.M.1	sy	clm5500	1	:33	1:061	1:394	2:11	7	5	4	5	610½	612½	1:132	8-1	(GHardie)	C.F.Sincous, MyDough, Newstead

TRACKMAN'S SELECTION — 6-1-7 LONGSHOT HOPE — No. 2 PHIL'S PICKS —2-1-3 SIXTH RACE

The next race we'll look at is an $8,000 claiming event. This one took place at Hawthorne Race Course on May 8. It's a fairly simple race to handicap compared to the last one. If you go through each horse, you'll come out with the following results:

1. MOSE—30^3 $2:05^2$.
2. TUCKABUCK—30^4 $2:05^1$.
3. SAMPSON CREED—31^3 $2:05^4$.
4. MISTER ADIOS—30^1 $2:07^3$.
5. BARONS STORM—30^3 $2:07$.
6. GOODARE—30 $2:04^4$.
7. SENGA MARIE—30^2 $2:05^4$.
8. ALJEANS DON—Eliminated.
9. GINNYS GENE—29^3 $2:04^3$.

Again we come up with a horse from the outside. Ginnys Gene closed in 29^3 and finished the mile in $2:04^3$. Since the veteran pacer is coming off a winning effort, he's fully qualified to become an automatic play.

SIXTH RACE—ONE MILE PACE—PURSE $4,600
Claiming Price $9,600-$8,000.
GOODARE claimed for $8,000 by Rursch, Kadel & Williams,
Tr.—Da. Busse
Time—:31^1 1:01^3 1:31^4 2:04   Mutuel Pool $103,288

9 Ginnys Gene	9	5	5	5^6	2^4	$11\frac{1}{2}$	2:04	7-1	(GVallndnghm)
4 Mister Adios	4	6	6	6^9	3^5	$21\frac{1}{2}$	$2:04^1$	5-1	(PMilburn)
5 Barons Storm	5	7	7	$7^9\frac{1}{2}$	6^{10}	$35\frac{1}{2}$	$2:05^1$	11-1	(JGrevengoed)
1 Mose	1	1	1	1^3	1^4	$45\frac{3}{4}$	$2:05^1$	5-2	(SBanks)
8 Aljeans Don	8	2	2	2^3	4^7	$58\frac{3}{4}$	$2:05^4$	51-1	(JMorrissey)
7 Senga Marie	7	9	9	9^{15}	7^{15}	$69\frac{1}{2}$	2:06	10-1	(JSearle)
3 Sampson Creed	3	4	4	4^5	5^8	7^{11}	$2:06^1$	19-1	(EWaszak)
6 Goodare	6	8	8	8^{15}	8^{15}	8^{13}	$2:06^3$	*5-2	(WMoore)
2 Tuckabuck	2	3	3	3^4	$x9^{dis}$	9^{18}	$2:07^3$	6-1	(DaBusse)

MUTUELS—(9) $16.00 $6.60 $5.80—(4) $6.60 $5.20—(5) $7.00

Ginnys Gene also secured good position from the start. He dropped into the fifth spot and remained there until the field hit the three quarter mark. Ginnys Gene then put together a good stretch drive and eventually won the race going away. He rewarded his backers with a $16.00 payoff.

The question that now remains is, would you have wagered on Ginnys Gene? He's going up $3,000 in class and that's something that can't be overlooked. On the other hand, he's coming off a winning effort within the claiming ranks which makes him fully qualified for a contending role. I think you'll find it to your advantage if you play

this angle by the previous rules set down. If a horse is going up in class in a claimer and hasn't won his last race—no play.

CRISS CROSS

This angle is very similar to the numerical speed rating system. It's based directly on the post position factor but it also takes into consideration three other factors—class, form, and pace. On the other hand, it *doesn't* consider class, form, and pace. I'm sure that sounds a bit confusing but I'll clear that up in a minute.

Handicapping a horse race is something that's been defined by turf writers in a hundred different ways. My personal definition of handicapping is: evaluating the chance each horse has at winning and then comparing the animals to one another. That's not exactly a unique definition because, after all, there aren't too many other ways you can handicap a horse race.

Let's say you come across two horses that appear to have similar past performance lines. They are both in relatively good form, have handled the same kind of pace, and are leaving from the same post positions they received in their last race. Then you look at their class levels. One horse competed against $18,000 claimers and the other one was up against horseflesh worth $15,000. That immediately terminates their equality. The nod naturally goes to the horse that raced at the highest class level.

That is an oversimplified example at evaluation and comparison. Not every race is going to be gift wrapped like that one. But there are still a good number of races each week where you can separate two or more horses on the basis of one factor. It doesn't have to be class either. It can be pace, which we've already seen, or current form, a mandatory factor that every contender should meet.

You can also separate two or more horses on the basis of post position. However, post position is not the strongest factor you can work with. If you're going to use it to separate a potential winner from an also ran, it's always best that the other factors are as close as can possibly be. Preferably, it is used with horses that are running within the same class level and have had to handle a similar pace.

The criss cross angle is able to make a choice between two or more horses solely on the basis of post position. That's because it deals with horses that only need to be handicapped in that one area. These are horses that have raced in exactly the same class level and have had to handle the exact same pace. In other words, these are horses that have competed against each other their last time out.

The criss cross angle, like the previous two, will not provide a lot of action. You'll come across very few races where the same field happens to be competing twice in a row. But this angle doesn't require the same competitors to be running against each other, although it would be preferable. A working situation would occur if at least one half of the field is facing itself for a second time. For example, a seven- or eight-horse field has to have a minimum of four horses competing against each other a second time.

There's still another requirement that must be fulfilled before the criss cross angle can be put into operation. The other horses that are entered in the field, the ones that were not involved in the last race, must be safely eliminated as non-contenders. If one or more of them are in a contending role, then this angle should not even be considered.

The only handicapping we'll have to do for those horses is to make adjustments for their post position. Class and pace are no longer of any concern because each horse has competed in the same class level and has had to handle the same pace. Even current form isn't important because that will be reflected once the horse receives the adjustment for his post position.

The criss cross angle and the numerical speed rating system use the same adjustment for post position. That involves the time element which is approximately equal to 1/2 length per post position. Here's how to use the adjustments:

1. All horses receiving a better post position than they had in their last race get 1/2 length subtracted from their final time for every post they move in.

2. All horses receiving a less desirable post position than they had in their last race get 1/2 length added on to their final time for every post they move out.

3. The horse that has the best adjusted final time, as long as it's one full length faster (1/5 of a second) than the next closest horse, becomes an automatic play.

We'll look at two example races involving the criss cross angle. The first one is an $11,000 claimer that took place at Hawthorne Race Course on May 22. The race is made up of nine horses, six of which are facing each other for the second time in a row. The other three horses in the field have already been safely eliminated as non-contenders. That leaves us only with adjustments needed for post position.

8 RACE

ONE MILE PACE — Claiming Price $11,000. — Purse $6,400.

Date	Trk Cd Tem	Class	Dis	1/4	1/2	3/4	Winner's Time	PP	1/4	1/2	3/4	Str	Fin	Ind Time	Odds	Driver	First	Second	Third

WESTERN'S JODY — Red 1 — $13,200 — 8-1
Ro m 64 by Everett Chief—Abbes Only—Poplar Abbe
Owners: Lyle Lenz & Richard Wilczek, Schiller Park, Chicago, Ill.
1973 9 3 2 0 $9,250 2:04¹ Haw¹
1972 20 1 2 3 $4,912 2:07 Was¹
Lifetime thru 1972 $51,976

Driver—JAMES WONDERGEM, Orange-Black   Trainer—J. Wondergem

5-15	⁹Haw¹ ft 56°	clm13200	1	:294	1:00¹	1:32	2:04	9	9	9	8¹¹°	7⁶	5²	2:04²	5-1	(JWondergem)	NobleChoice, ForbesTime, SeattleCindy
5- 7	¹⁰Haw¹ sy 60°	clm12000	1	:304	1:03³	1:36	2:06	8	8	8	6⁵	4⁶	2²½	2:06²	*2-1	(JWondergem)	ValiantSampson, WesternsJody, NobleScot
4-28	¹Haw¹ ft 43°	clm10200	1	:311	1:02²	1:33⁴	2:04¹	1	2	4	4²½	4³	1¹½	2:04¹	*1-1	(JWondergem)	WesternsJody, TerryJeansByrd, Goodare
4-20	³Haw¹ gd 71°	clm9600	1	:321	1:03²	1:35	2:06⁴	8	7	6	6⁵½	5²½	1¾	2:06⁴	7-2	(JWondergem)	WesternsJody,SampsonCreed,HaveAChance
4-13	¹⁰Spk⅝ ft 39°	clm9000	1	:304	1:02²	1:33³	2:04⁴	8	9	9	4°	3¹	2ns	2:04⁴	14-1	(JWondergem)	C.R.Purdue, WesternsJody, GrandAce
4- 6	¹Spk⅝ ft 64°	clm6000	1	:303	1:04	1:35²	2:06	4	5	5	5°	4²	1¹¼	2:06	22-1	(JWondergem)	WesternsJody,JustlyIrishHonor,ScotMiser

Blue

3

$11,000
6-1

NOBLE CHOICE

Br g 67, by Race Time—Entreat Me Not—Royal Blackstone
Owner: Edward Walston, Chicago, Ill.

1973	16	1	2	3	$7.833	2:04	Haw^1
1972	31	5	2	3	$18,480	$2{:}01^4$	Spk$\frac{5}{8}$
Lifetime thru 1972					$39,683		

Driver—AUBREY PETTY, Maroon-Black **Trainer—A. Petty**

5-15	^{9}Haw^1 ft 56°	clm11000	1	$:29^4$	$1{:}00^1$	1:32	2:04	4	5	5	$5^{6\frac{1}{2}}$	$3^{2\frac{1}{2}}$	1^{nk}	2:04	11-1	(APetty)	NobleChoice, ForbesTime, SeattleCindy
5- 7	^{8}Haw^1 sy 60°	clm13000	1	$:32^3$	$1{:}04^2$	$1{:}36^1$	$2{:}05^4$	1	2	3	$3^{1\frac{1}{4}}$	$3^{1\frac{1}{2}}$	6^3	$2{:}06^2$	11-1	(APetty)	C.F.Guy, DeltaDirect, GoranHanover
4-30	^{7}Haw^1 sy 50°	clm13000	1	$:30^4$	1:02	1:33	$2{:}03^2$	4	1	3	5^5	6^5	$6^{7\frac{3}{4}}$	2:05	14-1	(JDolbee)	SenatorBerry, GoranHanover, C.F.Guy
4-20	^{6}Haw^1 sy 64°	clm12000	1	$:34^2$	$1{:}05^1$	$1{:}37^2$	$2{:}06^4$	4	4	4	$4^{4\frac{1}{2}}$	4^3	$3^{4\frac{1}{2}}$	$2{:}07^4$	6-1	(APetty)	SenatorBerry, LittlePuff, NobleChoice
4-13	^{4}Spk$\frac{5}{8}$ ft 39°	Cclm12000	1	$:30^1$	$1{:}02^3$	$1{:}33^2$	$2{:}04^3$	3	3	3	3	4^5	$7^{5\frac{3}{4}}$	$2{:}05^4$	7-2	(CWillis)	StewartCraig, EyreFire, TecklaAdiosB.
4- 9	^{8}Spk$\frac{5}{8}$ gd 33°	clm13000	1	$:30^4$	$1{:}04^2$	1:36	$2{:}08^1$	1	4	5	6°	$4^{4\frac{1}{2}}$	$3^{3\frac{1}{2}}$	2:09	8-1	(CWillis)	KnoxAbout,SummertimeDirct,NobleChoice

Green

4

$13,200
8-1

SOONER RACE

Br g 69 by Addio Byrd—Princess Meridale—Tempered Volo
Owner: Corman and Armstrong, Mt. Sterling, Ill.

1973	14	3	2	2	$5.986	$2{:}04^3$	F.P.^{1}
1972	23	2	2	2	$3,296	$2{:}10^2$	MtStr
Lifetime thru 1972					$3,296		

Driver—J. DOUGLAS HOLFORD, Burgundy-White **Trainer—J. D. Holford**

5-15	^{9}Haw^1 ft 56°	clm13200	1	$:29^4$	$1{:}00^1$	1:32	2:04	7	8	8	9^{11}	$6^{5\frac{1}{2}}$	$4^{1\frac{1}{4}}$	$2{:}04^1$	10-1	(JDHolford)	NobleChoice, ForbesTime, SeattleCindy
5- 7	^{7}Haw^1 sy 60°	nw8000^{7273}	1	$:30^4$	1:02	$1{:}33^2$	$2{:}03^3$	5	6	7	7^3	$8^{3\frac{1}{2}}$	$5^{3\frac{1}{2}}$	$2{:}04^2$	24-1	(JDHolford)	Paladin, NeverSayDieA., AnchorBoy
4-26	^{5}Haw^1 ft 51°	nw7000^{7273}	1	$:30^4$	$1{:}02^2$	$1{:}34^4$	$2{:}04^2$	8	8	8	8^5	7^6	$7^{5\frac{1}{2}}$	$2{:}05^3$	31-1	(JDHolford)	SherwoodDancer, H.W.Express, BretsTune
4-16	^{7}Spk$\frac{5}{8}$ ft 45°	nw8000^{7273}	1	$:30^3$	$1{:}04^2$	$1{:}33^4$	$2{:}05^3$	1	5	5	5	6^6	$3^{2\frac{1}{4}}$	2:06	7-2	(JDHolford)	H.W.Express, SpyderWright, SoonerRace
4- 9	^{7}Spk$\frac{5}{8}$ gd 33°	nw7000^{7273}	1	$:31^2$	$1{:}05^4$	$1{:}36^1$	$2{:}08^3$	6	7	6	6	$5^{6\frac{1}{2}}$	$2^{2\frac{1}{4}}$	2:09	8-1	(JDHolford)	ShiawaySandy, SoonerRace, Winter
4- 3	^{10}Spk$\frac{5}{8}$ ft 37°	nw8000^{7273}	1	$:31^3$	$1{:}04^4$	$1{:}35^3$	2:06	9	4	4	5	$5^{4\frac{1}{4}}$	$4^{3\frac{1}{4}}$	$2{:}06^3$	16-1	(JDHolford)	Tarabay, NeverSayDieA, DearBaroness

Yellow

6

$11,000
6-1

SEATTLE CINDY

B spayed 68 by Scottish Pence—Seattle Call—Diplomat Hanover
Owner: Wall Bros., Cicero, Ill.

1973	19	4	4	2	$11.895	$2{:}04^1$	Spk$\frac{5}{8}$
1972	21	3	6	2	$5.450	$2{:}04^3$	Was^1
Lifetime thru 1972					$5,647		

Driver—JIM DOLBEE, Green-White-Red **Trainer—W. Wall**

5-15	^{9}Haw^1 ft 56°	clm11000	1	$:29^4$	$1{:}00^1$	1:32	2:04	6	7	6	6^8	$4^{3\frac{1}{2}}$	3^{nk}	2:04	6-1	(JDolbee)	NobleChoice, ForbesTime, SeattleCindy
5- 7	^{10}Haw^1 sy 60°	clm10000	1	$:30^4$	$1{:}03^3$	1:36	2.06	7	7	7	$9^{7\frac{1}{2}}$	8^{10}	$4^{5\frac{1}{4}}$	2:07	4-1	(BShuter)	ValiantSampson, WesternsJody, NobleScot
4-30	^{10}Haw^1 sy 50°	clm10000	1	$:32^3$	$1{:}04^2$	1:36	2:07	4	7	7°	6^5	$2^{\frac{1}{2}}$	$2^{\frac{3}{4}}$	$2{:}07^1$	9-1	(BShuter)	DeltaDirect, SeattleCindy, VarsitySignal
4-19	^{7}Haw^1 ft 67°	clm11000	1	$:31^1$	$1{:}01^4$	1:34	$2{:}04^1$	8	8	8	8^7	x8^{13}	8^{dis}		7-1	(RKnox)	Rozella, G.T.Winter, HandsomeDate
4-14	Spk$\frac{5}{8}$ ft	clm9000	1	$:30^1$	$1{:}02^2$	$1{:}34^2$	$2{:}05^4$	9	9	9	7	$6^{2\frac{3}{4}}$	$3^{1\frac{1}{4}}$	2:06	14-1	(RKnox)	TeeniTime, EyreNavarch, SeattleCindy
4- 7	^{5}Spk$\frac{5}{8}$ ft 45°	clm9000	1	:31	$1{:}02^4$	$1{:}34^2$	$2{:}06^1$	7	5	5	4	4^2	$2^{\frac{1}{2}}$	$2{:}06^2$	8-1	(RKnox)	HandsomeDate, SeattleCindy, JewelThief

Brown

7

$13,200
8-1

LOOKAWAY SUN

B g 69 by Mighty Sun—Janie Dorwood—Tactful Guy
Owners: Busse and Welch, Kingston, Ill.; Sharon, Wis.

1973	12	0	3	0	$2,725		
1972	38	10	7	5	$22,888	$2{:}01^2$	DuQ^1
Lifetime thru 1972					$22,888		

Driver—DARYL BUSSE, Gray-Red **Trainer—Da. Busse**

5-15	^{9}Haw^1 ft 56°	clm13200	1	$:29^4$	$1{:}00^1$	1:32	2:04	5	1	1	$1^{1\frac{1}{2}}$	$2^{\frac{1}{2}}$	$7^{2\frac{1}{2}}$	$2{:}04^3$	5-1	(DaBusse)	NobleChoice, ForbesTime, SeattleCindy
5- 4	^{10}Haw^1 ft 45°	clm15000	1	$:29^4$	1:01	$1{:}32^4$	$2{:}03^1$	8	1°	1	$1^{1\frac{1}{2}}$	$1^{\frac{1}{2}}$	$6^{5\frac{3}{4}}$	$2{:}04^2$	9-1	(DaBusse)	SequoiaHanover, MerryRuler-^{dh}-FrostyWil
4-26	^{6}Haw^1 ft 51°	clm18000	1	$:31^2$	$1{:}02^4$	$1{:}34^2$	$2{:}03^2$	8	1	1	1^{hd}	8^6	9^{11}	$2{:}05^3$	14-1	(DaBusse)	DutchKnight, TinaKnox, PeterBrown
4-14	^{4}Spk$\frac{5}{8}$A ft56°	nw9000^{7273}	1	$:30^1$	1:03	1:34	$2{:}03^1$	2	1°	2	4	8^{14}	8^{15}	$2{:}06^1$	8-1	(DaBusse)	PrimsKnight, StarPop, AwayAmigo
4- 5	^{10}Spk$\frac{5}{8}$ ft 53°	nw1R^8	1	$:29^1$	$1{:}00^4$	$1{:}31^4$	2:03	4	1	2	1	$2^{\frac{1}{2}}$	$5^{6\frac{1}{2}}$	$2{:}04^2$	9-1	(DaBusse)	TomsChoice, DocsJerry, PatrickTime
3-31	^{8}Spk$\frac{5}{8}$Asy44°	nw16500^{7273}	1	:31	$1{:}03^1$	$1{:}34^2$	$2{:}05^4$	8	3°	4°	9	9^{19}	9^{20}	$2{:}09^4$	40-1	(SBanks)	Integrated, PromsEasy, C.V.Thor

Red & Yellow

8

$11,000
7-2

FORBES TIME

B g 67 by Freight Forwarder—M. A. G.—Grattan Forbes
Owner: Nicholas J. Wall, Cicero, Ill.

1973	18	0	4	4	$8,175		
1972	36	4	7	3	$16,569	2:05	Spk$\frac{5}{8}$
Lifetime thru 1972					$42,561		

Driver—JOE MARSH, JR., Gray-Blue-Red **Trainer—J. Marsh, Jr.**

5-15	^{9}Haw^1 ft 56°	clm11000	1	$:29^4$	$1{:}00^1$	1:32	2:04	2	2	2	$2^{1\frac{1}{2}}$	$1^{\frac{1}{2}}$	2^{nk}	2:04	7-2	(JMarshJr)	NobleChoice, ForbesTime, SeattleCindy
5- 7	^{8}Haw^1 sy 60°	clm13000	1	$:32^3$	$1{:}04^2$	$1{:}36^1$	$2{:}05^4$	4	6	4°	$4^{1\frac{1}{2}}$	$2^{1\frac{1}{2}}$	$5^{2\frac{1}{2}}$	$2{:}06^2$	16-1	(JMarshJr)	C.F.Guy, DeltaDirect, GoranHanover
4-30	^{7}Haw^1 sy 50°	clm13000	1	$:30^4$	1:02	1:33	$2{:}03^2$	3	5	9	8^9	8^8	8^{12}	$2{:}05^4$	10-1	(JMarshJr)	SenatorBerry, GoranHanover, C.F.Guy
4-18	^{8}Haw^1 sy 61°	clm13000	1	$:31^4$	1:02	1:35	$2{:}05^4$	5	7	7	5^6	4^5	$4^{6\frac{1}{2}}$	$2{:}07^1$	23-1	(RKnox)	TinaKnox, Edstime, DutchKnight
4-12	^{6}Spk$\frac{5}{8}$ ft 36°	Cclm11000	1	$:31^2$	$1{:}02^4$	$1{:}34^2$	2:05	1	4	4	6	5^4	6^4	$2{:}05^4$	*7-2	(RKnox)	DutchKnight, ByrdMark, G.T.Winter
4- 7	^{6}Spk$\frac{5}{8}$ ft 45°	Cclm10000	1	$:31^3$	$1{:}04^3$	1:36	$2{:}06^2$	6	6	6°	6°	3^3	$2^{\frac{3}{4}}$	$2{:}06^3$	5-2	(JMarshJr)	G.T.Winter, ForbesTime, SilverDiller

1. WESTERNS JODY   Final Time - 2:04²
   P.P. Adj. -4   (9-1)   Adj. Final Time - 2:03³
3. NOBLE CHOICE   Final Time - 2:04
   P.P. Adj. -½   (4-3)   Adj. Final Time - 2:03⁴½
4. SOONER RACE   Final Time - 2:04¹
   P.P. Adj. -1½   (7-4)   Adj. Final Time - 2:03⁴½
6. SEATTLE CINDY   Final Time - 2:04
   P.P. Adj. -   (6-6)   Adj. Final Time - 2:04
7. LOOKAWAY SUN   Final Time - 2:04³
   P.P. Adj. +1   (5-7)   Adj. Final Time - 2:04⁴
8. FORBES TIME   Final Time - 2:04
   P.P. Adj. +3   (2-8)   Adj. Final Time - 2:04³

After the adjustments have been completed, the best final time is Westerns Jody with a 2:03³. Her final time is 1 1/2 lengths faster than the next closest horse. That makes Westerns Jody an automatic play.

EIGHTH RACE—ONE MILE PACE—PURSE $6,400
Claiming Price $13,200-$11,000.

Time—:31¹   1:02⁴   1:34²   2:04   Mutuel Pool $92,095

		¼	½	¾	Str	Fin		Odds	Driver
1 Westerns Jody	1	3	3	3³	2¹	12½	2:04	*5-2	(JWondergem)
3 Noble Choice	3	4	4	4⁴½	4³½	22½	2:04²	7-1	(APetty)
5 Delta Direct	5	6	6	6⁷½	5⁴	3²½	2:04²	7-2	(NTrimble)
8 Forbes Time	8	8	8	7⁹½	3²½	4³½	2:04⁴	7-1	(JMarshJr)
2 Birthday Delight	2	2	2	2¹½	1¹	5⁴	2:04⁴	6-1	(SLeRoy)
4 Sooner Race	4	5	5	5⁵½	6⁷½	6⁶¾	2:05²	9-1	(JDHolford)
9 First Look	9	9	9	9¹¹	7⁸	7⁸	2:05³	15-1	(JGrevengoed)
6 Seattle Cindy	6	7	7	8¹⁰	8¹¹	8¹²	2:06²	6-1	(JDolbee)
7 Lookaway Sun	7	1	1	1¹½	9¹³	9¹⁴	2:06⁴	14-1	(DaBusse)

MUTUELS—(1) $7.80 $4.80 $3.00—(3) $6.20 $3.80—(5) $3.00

The race turned out to be decided by one factor—post position. Westerns Jody got the biggest break in post out of the six horses and took advantage of it. She was able to secure a closer position to the leaders this time and had less ground to make up in the stretch. She finally drew out late in the race and proved to be a convincing winner. The pacing mare returned $7.80 to win.

ONE MILE PACE   SEVENTH RACE   Purse $6,000

CLAIMING. Claiming price $20,000-$25,000 — 3 Year Olds and Upward. Perfect Weapon in for $25,200, Mr. Rebel $25,000, Right Lane $24,000, Can Tar Rebel and Patrick Time $22,000 and Mi Grande Amigo $20,000.

PLEASE ASK FOR HORSE BY PROGRAM NUMBER

Date	Trk Cond Temp	Class	Dist	¼	½	¾	Winner's Time	PP	¼	½	¾	Str	Fin	Ind.Time	Odds	Driver	ORDER OF FINISH First Second Third	Comment

RED 1   5-2 =

Driver—WALTER PAISLEY, Green-White   Tr.—R. Farrington   (39-8-7-4—.334)
MI GRANDE AMIGO   B g 1968, by Newport Amigo—Rio Purdue—Arden Hanover
Own: Farrington Sta. Inc.-Arnold Cattle Co. Inc.; Richw'd, O., Ch'go, Ill.

1973 14 2 1 2 $11,090   2:04⁴ Spk⅝
1972 44 7 7 7 $44,434   1:59⁴ Haw¹
Lifetime $79,394   3, 1:59³ (1)

5-26	4Spk⅝ ft 60°	clm22000=1	:30³ 1:01¹ 1:30³ 2:00²	6	6	6⁵		4¹¾°	42¼	42¼	2:00⁴	7-1	(J.MarshJr)	YankeeCreed, RightLane, PerfectWeapon	(too much spd)
5-18	9Haw¹ ft 66°	clm24000	1 :31¹ 1:01⁴ 1:31³ 2:01³	9	4°	1		1½	6⁵	6⁷	2:03	7-1	(J.Dolbee)	BgDaddysShadw, PerfectWeapn, RomnLeadr	(tird badly)
5-12	7Haw¹ ft 52°	3yrup7700	1 :31¹ 1:04¹ 1:34¹ 2:03³	3	4	3°		2¹°	9⁸	9⁷¾	2:05¹	*2-1	(J.MarshJr)	BrindaAnnsWinner, C.V.Thor, Chaw	(hung out)
5- 7	5Haw¹ sy 60°	w70007273	1 :30 1:00 1:30² 2:01	6	6	1		1²	12½	34½	2:01⁴	6-1	(J.MarshJr)	SimonesSkppr, TmsChce, MiGrndeAmgo	(faltered in str)
4-28	8Haw¹ ft 43°	3yrup7500	1 :32² 1:03³ 1:33¹ 2:02³	9	9	9		acc dnf				12-1	(J.Curran)	LincolnsBid, BrindaAnnsWinner, CVThor	(unseated drivr)
4-20	9Haw¹ gd 64°	stk11000	1 :30² 1:01⁴ 1:34¹ 2:03⁴	7	10	8		9⁵½	42½	6³¾	2:04³	4-1	(J.Curran)	C.V.Thor, Chaw, HarkWon	(game effort)

BLUE 2   7-2 =

Driver—JIM DENNIS, Green-White   Tr.—J. Dennis   (15-2-2-2—.252)
PERFECT WEAPON   B c 1969, by Adios Bomber—Elvida Hanover—Tar Heel
Owner: Rudolph R. Gurrola, Elgin, Ill.

1973 16 2 3 1 $12,256   2:03³ LA⅝
1972 13 3 1 2 $21,505   2:05¹ Was¹
Lifetime $48,511   2, 2:01 (1)

5-26	4Spk⅝ ft 60°	clm25200=1	:30³ 1:01¹ 1:30³ 2:00²	1	2	2½		3¹½	3²	3²	2:00⁴	*2-1	(J.Dennis)	YankeeCreed, RightLane, PerfectWeapon	(in close qtrs)
5-18	9Haw¹ ft 66°	clm25200	1 :31¹ 1:01⁴ 1:31³ 2:01³	3	5	4°		4¹¼	1¹	2½	2:01⁴	7-2	(B.Nickells)	BgDaddysShadw, PrfectWeapn, RomnLeadr	(just missed)
5-12	4Haw¹ ft 52°	clm25200	1 :31¹ 1:02⁴ 1:32⁴ 2:02³	1	3	6		6⁴	5²½	12	2:02³	7-1	(J.Dennis)	PerfectWeapon, Propeller, DonRocket	(well handled)
5- 5	8Haw¹ ft 50°	3yrup7500	1 :31¹ 1:03¹ 1:33³ 2:02	6	1	1		2¹	6⁵	8⁵½	2:03¹	36-1	(T.Ratchford)	GuyDaniel, BrindaAnnsWinner, C.V.Thor	(used early)
4-28	8Haw¹ ft 43°	3yrup7500	1 :32² 1:03³ 1:33¹ 2:02³	1	2	2°		2ⁿᵏ°	65½	7⁸	2:04¹	21-1	(T.Ratchford)	LincolnsBid, BrindaAnnsWinner, CVThor	(bid, hung)
4-20	9Haw¹ gd 64°	stk11000	1 :30² 1:01⁴ 1:34¹ 2:03⁴	6	6°	3°		3ⁿᵏ°	9⁹	10¹⁰	2:05⁴	17-1	(T.Ratchford)	C.V.Thor, Chaw, HarkWon	(never saw rail)

GREEN 4   6-1 =

Driver—NELSON WILLIS, Maroon-Gray-White   Tr.—C. Willis   (12-1-2-2—.231)
PATRICK TIME   B g 1968, by Winter Time—Cindy P. Hal—Purdue Hal
Owner: Connel Willis, Willow Springs, Ill.

1973 13 1 0 1 $4,779   2:01² Haw¹
1972 28 3 5 8 $17,185   2:03² Spk⅝
Lifetime $19,727   4, 2:03² (⅝)

5-26	4Spk⅝ ft 60°	clm22000—1	:30³ 1:01¹ 1:30³ 2:00²	7	7	7⁷		5³¼	5³¾	5⁴½	2:01²	10-1	(H.Burright)	YankeeCreed, RightLane, PerfectWeapon	(too much spd)
5-18	8Haw¹ ft 66°	stk10900	1 :29⁴ 1:00² 1:31³ 2:00⁴	8	8	7°		5²½	5⁴½	8⁴¼	2:01³	7-1	(J.MarshJr)	Chaw, BrindaAnnsWinner, C.V.Thor	(no chance)
5-11	7Haw¹ ft 55°	3-5yrnw2R	1 :33 1:05¹ 1:36¹ 2:05²	5	6	6		4²	4³	5⁵¼	2:06²	6-1	(J.MarshJr)	ShadHanover, StarPop, SteveMilam	(went evenly)
5- 4	9Haw¹ ft 45°	clm20000	1 :29⁴ 1:00¹ 1:31³ 2:01²	5	7	6		6⁵½	22	12¼	2:01²	12-1	(J.MarshJr)	PatrickTime, CanTarRebel, PatPlutocrat	(strong rush)
4-26	8Haw¹ ft 51°	nw20006	1 :32¹ 1:02⁴ 1:34⁴ 2:04²	8	9	9		9⁵	8⁷	8⁹	2:06¹	21-1	(J.Dolbee)	PocoPilot, AdiosArt, Cleostar	(no threat)
4-20	5Haw¹ gd 64°	nw20006	1 :31¹ 1:01² 1:33³ 2:04⁴	5	7	7		7⁶½	6⁸½	7¹¹	2:07	8-1	(C.Willis)	RightGood, WithoutWarning, GameGene	(no threat)

The next race that fits the criss cross angle is a claimer with prices ranging from $20,000 to $25,000. This one took place at Sportsman's Park on June 5. The race attracted a very small field. Only six horses were scheduled to go to the starting gate. Out of the six horses, three had faced each other their last time out. The other three horses in the race have already been eliminated as non-contenders. One of those non-contenders, Right Lane, was originally in that same last race, but he performed in the interim and turned in an effort which lost him a contending status. The three horses facing each other again received the following adjustments for post position:

1. MI GRANDE AMIGO   Final Time - 2:00^4
    P.P. Adj. -2½   (6-1)   Adj. Final Time - 2:00^{1½}
2. PERFECT WEAPON   Final Time - 2:00^4
    P.P. Adj. +½   (1-2)   Adj. Final Time - 2:00^{4½}
4. PATRICK TIME   Final Time - 2:01^2
    P.P. Adj. -1½   (7-4)   Adj. Final Time - 2:01^{½}

An automatic play is found to be in Mi Grande Amigo. His final time has been reduced to 2:00^{1½}, which is 3 full lengths faster than Perfect Weapon's final time.

Mi Grande Amigo was given a perfect trip by driver Walter Paisley. The five year old gelding was in good position at the half mile mark and slowly edged closer to the leaders. He finally put away Perfect Weapon in midstretch and held a safe margin over Patrick Time at the wire. He paid a respectable $10.40 to win.

The three angles we've looked at all have something in common—they all involve horses that appear to have a marked edge over their competitors. You might want to make the rules more lenient to provide more action or even tighten them up to suit your personal taste. Either way, I still suggest you give the angles a dry run on paper first. If there's any one thing you can be sure about when it comes to horse racing, it's that there's always going to be a next race.

SEVENTH RACE — 1 MILE
PACE. Claiming price $20,000-$25,000 — 3 Year Olds and Upward — Purse $6,000.

Time—:30^2 1:03^2 1:33^4 2:03^3								Mutuel Pool—$93,403	
1. Mi Grande Amigo	1	4	4^{3½}	4^2	3½	1¾	2:03^3	4-1	(W.Paisley)
4. Patrick Time	4	5	5^5	5^{3½}	4^{1½}	2¾	2:03^4	15-1	(N.Willis)
3. Can Tar Rebel	3	2	2^1	3^{1½}	5^2	3¾	2:03^4	*2-1	(J.Graham)
5. Right Lane	5	6	6^{6½}	6^5	6^3	4^1	2:03^4	5-2	(GVllndnghm)
2. Perfect Weapon	2	3	3^2	2$^{ns\ o}$	1½	5^{2½}	2:04^1	7-2	(J.Dennis)
6. Mr. Rebel	6	1	1^1	1^{ns}	2½	6^{2¾}	2:04^1	5-1	(J.MarshJr)

Can Tar Rebel claimed for $22,000 by R. Langer and J. Albert, trainer—S. Stucker.
Mutuels—(1) 10.40 5.80 3.40—(4) 9.80 4.60—(3) 2.80

In the next chapter, we'll take on an even different aspect of the sport by looking at some handicapping situations where a horse can easily go underrated.

CHAPTER 9

Expecting the Unexpected

How many times have you wagered on a horse you really didn't like? No, I'm not just talking about before you made the bet. I'm talking about something that every horseplayer does at least once during the racing season. That's when you walk away from the sellers window and ask yourself this question, "Why in the world did I just make that bet?"

If that question rings a bell, then you're definitely a full fledged horseplayer. Bad bets are, unfortunately, part of the game. It's the price you have to pay to gain experience. Everybody makes a bad bet once in a while and the interesting thing about it is you can usually figure it out before the race even takes place. Just picture this situation:

You place your money on a horse, one you don't particularly care for, but you just want to have a little something going in the race. Then, as you walk away from the window, you decide to take a second look at the program. You come across a horse that you didn't take a good look at before. All of a sudden you spot something about him you missed earlier and you wish that green stuff was back in your pocket. Why? Because now you realize that your money would have been better off had it been on this other horse. There's nothing you can do about it because it's almost post time. The horses are nearing the starting gate and with every passing moment, he looks more and more like a standout. Needless to say, he wins, you lose, and you want to kick yourself.

Probably the easiest thing to do at the racetrack is to underrate a horse. All you have to do is to forget to take a close look at each horse's class level in the race. If you take it for granted that so-and-so horse is running against the same kind of company again, you might find out the hard way that the animal is really taking a big class drop. And when you make the mistake of underrating one horse, you end up overrating the rest of the field.

In this chapter, we'll look at four different situations where a horse has an important factor going for him that very often gets overlooked. Each horse is the type that frequently goes underrated. Some of the animals still end up returning a short price, but occasionally you can get away with a nice box car payoff. They're the kind of horses that might not stand out at first glance, but each one has that something extra going for him that the rest of the field lacks.

Rested and Ready

The tenth race at Sportsman's Park on June 27 brought together a field of ordinary $8,000 claimers. Well, at first they may look ordinary, but actually there's one horse in the race that has a little bit more going for him than first meets the eye. That's the five year old pacer Bag of Gold. Take a close look at his past performance record and then compare his chances to the only other contender in the race, Little Puff, and then to the eventual favorite, Idlewhiles Earl.

The first thing you'll notice is that Bag of Gold and Little Puff are coming off the same race. Both

RED 1   **10-1** =

Driver—TOM RATCHFORD, Gold-White	Tr.—T. Ratchford	(29-4-3-4—.241)	1973 14 0 0 0 $1,551

BAG OF GOLD — Br h 1968, by Race Time—Blossom Hal—Hal Dale — Owner: J. McGregor, and R. Viehover, San Jacinto, Pasadena, Calif.
1972 32 1 2 7 $10,389 2:04² L.A⅝   Lifetime $21,778 3, 2:02³ (1)

6-15	¹Spk⅝ ft 79°	clm8000+1	:31¹ 1:03 1:35² 2:05¹	6	8	8⁶½°	6³°	54	5³	2:05⁴	34-1 (T.Ratchford)	RikiNoc, MightyLoyal, ChiefsLittleStar	(went evenly
5-10	L.A⅝ ft	clm6500	1 :31⁴ 1:02² 1:13² 2:04²	4	4°	2°	5	79¾	710	2:06²	9-1 (J.McGregor)	ScottishDon, JohnDee, FreemansDream	(———
5- 5	L.A⅝ ft	clm7500	1 :30 1:01¹ 1:32³ 2:03³	6	8	8	8	72½	6²	2:04	17-1 (F.ToddJr)	GreenbergO'Brien, PepperDrive, LumberBrt	(———
5- 1	L.A⅝ ft	clm7500	1 :30² 1:01² 1:33² 2:04³	3	2	3	3	3¹	51½	2:04⁴	8-1 (J.McGregor)	ComoHanover, MissMelrose, AndrasBoy	(———
4-25	L.A⅝ ft	clm8000	1 :30¹ 1:01⁴ 1:33¹ 2:03⁴	1	4	6	6	44	41¾	2:04¹	7-1 (R.Williams)	PepperDrive, PagesRebel. AndysDud	(———
4-18	L.A⅝ ft	clm7000	1 :31² 1:04⁴ 1:35¹ 2:05²	5	5	6	7	86¾	76	2:06³	5-1 (R.Williams)	PepperDrive, GeneralGray, HurryingHenry	(———

WHITE 3   **7-2** =

Driver—JERRY GRAHAM, Green-Orange	Tr.—J. Graham	(43-12-5-6—.390)	1973 10 3 1 1 $7,864 2:04¹ L.A⅝

LITTLE PUFF — B h 1968, by Poplar Byrd—Charlotte—Southern Tryax — Owner: Misty Farm & Walter Myers, Salem, Ill.
1972 18 2 3 4 $6,991 2:02⁴ Haw¹   Lifetime $13,719 4, 2:02⁴ (1)

6-15	¹Spk⅝ ft 79°	clm8000—1	:31¹ 1:03 1:35² 2:05¹	9	2°	21°	2½°	3¹	42¾	2:05⁴	12-1 (J.Graham)	RikiNoc, MightyLoyal, ChiefsLittleStar	(tough mile
6- 5	¹⁰Spk⅝ sy 65°	clm8000—1	:32 1:06² 1:37³ 2:08¹	3	3	11½	1ⁿᵏ	2ʰᵈ	1ⁿᵏ	2:08¹	*5-2 (J.Graham)	LittlePuff, SengaMarie, IdlewhilesEarl	(held on well
5-31	Spk⅝ ft 69°	Qua	1 :30¹ 1:04 1:34³ 2:06⁴	3	2	3²	2²	2¹	12½	2:06⁴	NB (J.Graham)	LittlePuff, SunsetJeanne, PotsPlayBoy	(———
5-17	⁸Haw¹ ft 53°	clm11000	1 :31¹ 1:02 1:34¹ 2:04²	4	2°x8	8ᵈⁱˢ	8ⁱⁱˢ	8ᵈⁱˢ			5-1 (J.Graham)	PlutoHal, Dod:eDee, TerryJeansRocket	(out of it
5- 8	⁹Haw¹ ft 60°	clm11000	1 :31² 1:03² 1:34² 2:05²	3	4	6x	916	815	818	2:09	5-2 (J.Graham)	G.T.Winter, FirstLook, LyricEyre	(no chance
4-30	⁷Haw¹ sy 50°	clm13000	1 :30⁴ 1:02 1:33 2:03²	8	2°	2	3²	4³	57¾	2:05	19-1 (J.Graham)	SenatorBerry, GoranHanover, C.F.Guy	(tired

GREEN 4   **6-1** +

Driver—JAMES WONDERGEM, Orange-Black	Tr.—J. Wondergem	(11-2-2-3—.374)	1973 22 5 5 2 $11,337 2:04⁴ Haw¹

IDLEWHILE'S EARL — B g 1969, by Mighty Sun—Miss Guy Counsel—Chief Counsel — Owner: Lyle Lenz & Richard Wilczek, Schiller Park, Chicago, Ill.
1972 0 0 0 0 (——)   Lifetime (——)

6-18	¹⁰Spk⅝ ft 77°	clm8400 C—1	:30³ 1:02¹ 1:33² 2:03²	1	5	54	75½°	53½°	46¼	2:04³	*5-2 (G.Conley)	SpdyChestnt, KngryExprss, ReidsShdw	(road trouble ¾
6- 5	¹⁰Spk⅝ sy 65°	clm9600—1	:32 1:06² 1:37³ 2:08¹	1	4	43½	51¾°	41¾	3ⁿᵏ	2:08¹	9-2 (G.Conley)	LittlePuff, SengaMarie, IdlewhilesEarl	(good last ⅛
5-28	¹⁰Spk⅝ sy 52°	clm9600—1	:30⁴ 1:04² 1:36³ 2:06⁴	8	8	73¾°	73°	38	49¼	2:08³	6-1 (G.Conley)	Mr.Thunderbyrd, ElBarb, Eyreton	(hung out
5-16	⁶Haw¹ ft 43°	clm10800	1 :31 1:03⁴ 1:34³ 2:04⁴	4	5	7	64½	711	78¾	2:06³	9-2 (G.Conley)	GinnysGene, LangCreed, TerryJeansByrd	(no chance
5- 9	⁷Haw¹ ft 66°	c!m10800	1 :30⁴ 1:02 1:34¹ 2:04⁴	9	9	9	74½	31½	11¼	2:04⁴	20-1 (G.Conley)	IdlewhilesEarl, DodieDee. TerryJeansByrd	(strong rally
4-30	¹⁰Haw¹ sy 50°	clm12000	1 :32³ 1:04² 1:36 2:07	7	9	9	97½	88½	68¾	2:08⁴	12-1 (G.Conley)	DeltaDirect, SeattleCindy, VarsitySignal	(no factor

horses have turned in good efforts and they figure to do well since they are staying within the same class level. Bag of Gold found himself parked out for two turns of the track and Little Puff was on the outside for three turns. They are both getting a big break in post position for tonight's race and they finished only one quarter of a length apart from each other in their last effort. So when you get down to the real nitty gritty, it's pretty hard to make a decision between the two horses.

Idlewhiles Earl would not receive the same consideration as Bag of Gold or Little Puff. If you take a closer look at his class level, you'll see that he was entered for a claiming price of $8,400. He's only a four year old so that translates his last race into a $7,000 claimer. Since Idlewhiles Earl is going up in class in a claiming race off a losing effort, he's automatically eliminated as a non-contender.

If you wanted to use numerical speed ratings to separate the two horses, you would come out with 31 1/2 for Bag of Gold and 36 for Little Puff. On that basis alone, Bag of Gold would be considered the final choice. However, the speed rating in this situation does not give a true indication of his ability. Actually, it underrates his potential because Bag of Gold has an important factor in his favor that is not found on the past performance record of Little Puff: He was away from the racing wars for almost five weeks prior to his last effort.

On the other hand, Little Puff has been a steady competitor of late and shows no layoffs within the last two months. That gives a definite edge to Bag of Gold because he figures to show more improvement over his last race than Little Puff.

It's always a good idea to take special notice of horses that have been away from competition for a month or more. Not for betting purposes, but for future reference. Usually when a horse sits on the sidelines for that period of time or longer, he's going to be in need of a race in order to get back into shape. Some trainers prefer to use a qualifying race, while others send their horse directly into competition. The horses you should keep your eye out for are ones that have raced well after a layoff, especially if they are placed in approximately the same class level.

TENTH RACE — 1 MILE
PACE. Claiming price $8,000 — 3 Year Olds and Upward — Purse $3,600.

Time—:30² 1:03² 1:34³ 2:06   Mutuel Pool—$34,318

1. Bag Of Gold	1	6	52½°	1½	1³	11¼	2:06	7-1 (T.Ratchford)
3. Little Puff	3	5	64	41¾°	2³	21¼	2:06¹	7-2 (J.Graham)
4. Idlewhiles Earl	4	8	75½°	73¾°	56¼	33½	2:06⁴	*7-2 (J.Wondergm)
9. Byrd Mark	9	9	98¾	95¼	66¼	44	2:06⁴	22-1 (R.Knox)
5. El Barb	5	4	42½	62¾	36	54¼	2:06⁴	4-1 (GV!lndnghm)
2. Wes Tee	2	7	85¾	84¼	98¾	67¼	2:07²	16-1 (J.Ackerman)
8. Dazzling Star	8	3°	21°	52¾°	88¼	78	2:07³	8-1 (J.Morrissey)
7. First Look	7	1	3¹	31½	77¼	88¼	2:07³	9-1 (S.Banks)
6. Chief's Little Star	6	2	1¹	2½	46	911	2:08¹	4-1 (Da.Busse)

First Look claimed for $8,000 by Arnold Cattle Co. and Farrington Stables, Inc., trainer—R. Farrington.

Mutuels—(1) 16.00 11.60 3 60—(3) 5.20 2.80—(4) 3.40
$3 Trifecta—(1-3-4)—Paid $490.20   Trifecta Pool—$106.250

Bag of Gold returned a healthy $16.00 to win. That's quite an overlay considering he looked good enough to win just off his last race alone. Since the tenth race is the last event on the card, there's also trifecta wagering. The trio of horses finished one, two, three and provided a payoff of $490 plus enough change for a cup of coffee. However, I can truthfully say that I would not have spent a single penny on the trifecta in this race. It's hard enough selecting winners, let alone picking three horses to finish in order. And it's not going to do you any good to watch a $16.00 payoff go down the drain if you put all your money on a gimmick bet. When the price is there, take it.

FIRST RACE — 1 MILE
PACE. Claiming price $9,000 — 3 Year Olds and Upward — Purse $3,800.

Time—:29^4 1:01^2 1:32^2 2:04   Mutuel Pool—$54,005

Hd.No. Horse	PP	¼	½	¾	Str	Fin	Ind.Time	Odds	Driver
7. Bag Of Gold	7	9	$74\frac{1}{2}°$	$64\frac{3}{4}°$	4^8	1^{nk}	2:04	13-1	(T.Ratchford)
1. Summertime Direct	1	3	4^3	$54\frac{1}{2}$	$36\frac{1}{2}$	2^{nk}	2:04	*3-1	(J.MarshJr)
2. Tanner	2	5	$53\frac{1}{4}°$	$2^{nk}°$	1^3	$3\frac{1}{2}$	2:04^1	13-1	(G.Vllndnghm)
6. Col. Moffitt	6	8	9^8	$97\frac{1}{4}$	6^9	$41\frac{3}{4}$	2:04^2	8-1	(J.Blevins)
4. Carol Chief	4	6	$64\frac{1}{2}$	$85\frac{1}{4}$	5^9	$51\frac{3}{4}$	2:04^2	5-1	(C.Alessi)
3. Daddio Mac	3	$2°$	$21\frac{1}{2}$	$33\frac{1}{4}$	7^{10}	6^6	2:05^1	5-1	(A.G.Shaw)
8. Worthy Reward	8	$4°$	$31\frac{1}{2}°$	$43\frac{1}{2}°$	8^{14}	7^{14}	2:06^4	15-1	(H.Burright)
5. Senator Glib	5	$1°$	$11\frac{1}{2}$	1^{nk}	2^3	$x8^{16}$	2:07^1	11-1	(W.Moore)
9. Sports Arena	9	7	8^6	$74\frac{3}{4}°$	$x9^{24}$	9^{17}	2:07^2	9-1	(J.Graham)

Carol Chief claimed for $10,800 by Indigan Stable, trainer—D. Pletcher.
Mutuels—(7) 28.00 13.80 6.40—(1) 4.20 3.00—(2) 3.60

Speaking of price, I have also reproduced the result chart of Bag of Gold's next race. He returned to the race track after a ten-day rest and was sent up against $9,000 claimers, a mere $1,000 class hike. He closed very strong on the outside of the track and just got up for the win. He paid $28.00, which almost doubles the payoff he returned for his first winning effort.

Horses reflecting the history of Bag of Gold win many a race during the season. If you follow horses that have raced well after being rested, make sure the animal is not entered in a race where he's overclassed. For claiming races, the horse should be within $1,000 of his last claiming price. In conditioned races, the conditions should be almost the same. If the horse comes through with a winning effort, you might find it profitable to follow him in his next race.

WHEN CLASS MAKES THE DIFFERENCE

The class factor is something that is often talked about but rarely ever explained. It's not that turf analysts are trying to avoid the subject, it's just that it's very difficult to explain something that borders on the obvious, and yet is theoretical at the same time.

Another reason that makes the class factor not only too difficult to explain, but also difficult to understand, is that it's the only factor that must be first evaluated and then compared to other horses to make any sense. Form, pace, post position, and the driver can all be immediately evaluated, but even they must be put in their proper perspective. Or to put it another way, you cannot take those four factors separately and use them to compare a horse to his rivals solely on their own merits. But you can evaluate the class status of a horse and compare him to his competitors, thereby using class as an important handicapping tool.

Form, whether it's current or overall, is dealt with without comparison because a horse is categorized as being either in good or bad form. If a horse is found to be in bad form, he would be immediately eliminated from the race as a non-contender without the need of going into any further investigation. If a horse is in good form, you still wouldn't compare him to his competition until you have first taken into consideration his class standing. The same is also true for pace. You can evaluate exactly how successful or unsuccessful an animal handled the pace in his last race, but it won't do you any good to compare his chances to the rest of the field until you have first settled the issue with his class and current form.

Post position is evaluated and compared, but not with other horses in the race. The only way post position is compared is by referring to the animal's last effort. You can also evaluate the man in the sulky but not until you have fully handicapped the horse by using the other four factors. And if you want to start comparing drivers, you're really going to run into trouble. Always keep in mind that the best horse in the race doesn't need the best driver in the race to turn in a winning effort.

That brings us back to class. It also brings us up to the ninth race at Maywood Park on September 6. It's a conditioned event for "non-winners of $7,500 in 1973." Two horses in the race, Desoto

Duke and Noble Land, appear to have the best chance at winning. But the class differences between the two horses almost makes it look as if a Cadillac were going up against a ten-speed bicycle. Look at their past performances.

encountered a fast pace was the August 16 race when he broke stride.

Noble Land has a lot more going for him than just his ability to handle a fast pace. The class factor is also overwhelmingly in his favor. Take

WHITE 2 3-1

Driver—WILLIAM BECKLEY, Blue-Gold   Tr.—W. Beckley   (48-5-6-9—.236)   1973 7 5 1 0 $6,311 2:03² May

DESOTO DUKE   B g 1970, by Henry T. Adios—Miss Rip—Rip Hanover   1972 0 0 0 0   (——)

Owner: Herman F. Beckley, Albany, Ind.   Lifetime   (——)

8-31 ²May ft 81°	nw4R	1 :31² 1:03 1:34 2:03³	2	4	1²	1⁵	1²	11¼	2:03³	*3-5 (W.Beckley)	DesotoDuke, FrostyKing, MayByrdKing	(easy win)
8-16 ⁸May ft 74°	§nw500073	1 :29⁴ 1:00¹ 1:31⁴ 2:02¹	8	2°x8ᵈⁱˢ	8ᵈⁱˢ	8ᵈⁱˢ	8ᵈⁱˢ		*6-5 (W.Beckley)	EdgewdDvn, JoansGne, OakLndRdr	(rank broke dueling)
8- 7 ⁷May ft 81°	§nw3R	1 :31⁴ 1:02³ 1:33⁴ 2:03²	6	8	7⁴	1¹⁰	1²	15¼	2:03²	*2-5 (W.Beckley)	DesotoDuke, MiracleDeal, JustlyGnius	(big 3-wide move)
7-29 Munc.e ft	3yrstk1030	Dash in 2:07, Fin. 2				Dash in 2:05³, Fin. 1				NB (W.Beckley)	DesotoDuke, MightyPeggy, GoldenDanDean	(——)
7-11 ⁶Spk⅝ ft 71°	3-5yrnw2R+1	1 :31¹ 1:03³ 1:36² 2:05²	6	1	11¼	1²	12½	13¼	2:05²	9-5 (W.Beckley)	DesotoDuke, JointEndvr, TranquillityBay	(much the best)
7- 4 ²Spk⅝ ft 82°	3-4yrnw1R+1	1 :30² 1:02⁴ 1:33² 2:05¹	6	8°	5²¾°	11½	13	12¾	2:05¹	*4-5 (W.Beckley)	DesotoDuke, MerryDragon, DrHayes	(big 3-wide move)

GRAY 7 9-2

Driver—CONNEL WILLIS, Red-White-Green   Tr.—C. Willis   (69-7-8-8—.205)   1973 11 2 2 2 $6,787 2:02² Spk⅝

NOBLE LAND   B g 1966, by Lehigh Hanover—Entreat Me Not—Royal Blackstone   1972 28 2 5 3 $13,447 2:05¹ Was¹

Owner: Connel Willis, lessee, Willow Springs, Ill.   Lifetime $73,942 5, 1:59³ (1)

9- 3 ⁹May gd 74°	§nw600073	1 :30⁴ 1:03³ 1:34¹ 2:04²	5	2	3²½	42½°	3²½	3¹½	2:04⁴	8-1 (C.Willis)	Ironworks, MightyButler, NobleLand	(raced well)
8-28 May ft 84°	Qua§	1 :30⁴ 1:02 1:32⁴ 2:02	2	3	3⁸	3¹³	2¹⁵	2¹⁸	2:05³	NB (C.Willis)	Ironworks, NobleLand, ChpmansCandy	(——)
8-24 ⁶May ft 72°	nw800073	1 :31 1:02³ 1:32² 2:01⁴	8	8	6⁵½	6⁴½	6⁶	6⁹	2:03³	9-1 (C.Willis)	KeystoneStormy, TarrsChief, Concourse	(no chance)
8-14 ⁵May ft 70°	nw550073	1 :30³ 1:02 1:31³ 2:02	3	2	3¹½	3¹	2¹	21¼	2:02¹	3-1 (C.Willis)	Ironworks, NobleLand, RamblingShorty	(good try)
8- 4 ³May ft 77°	nw600073	1 :31 1:00⁴ 1:31³ 2:03²	4	2°	2ʰᵈ	1ⁿᵏ	1¾	1¹	2:03²	*3-5 (C.Willis)	NobleLand, Concourse, GusMinbar	(dueled the mile)
7-24 ³May ft 81°	nw400073	1 :29¹ :59¹ 1:30² 2:01¹	3	3	3³½	3¹	2½	2ⁿᵏ	2:01¹	5-2 (C.Willis)	KeystoneJournal, NobleLand, MargaretSue	(was gaining)

The three year old Desoto Duke has had a successful campaign thus far. He has started seven times for the year and has made it to the winner's circle on five separate occasions. The only time the gelding finished out of the money was on August 16 when he broke stride.

Noble Land also boasts a consistent record for the year. The seven year old gelding has finished in the money six times for his eleven efforts.

A pace analysis of the two horses brings out some interesting information. Desoto Duke came home in 1:00 3/5 for his last win after going the first half mile in 1:03. Noble Land also turned in a last half in 1:00 3/5, but the pace was a little bit slower in his race. However, the only reason the pace was slowed down was because the race was contested on a good track. A conservative estimate of the track conditions would have an effect of about two seconds. That's an indication that Noble Land is capable of overcoming a fast pace much more easily than Desoto Duke.

As you can already tell, it wouldn't be any problem for me to make a strong case for Noble Land solely on the basis of pace. If you take a look at some of his previous efforts, you'll see that he's able to handle a fast pace quite well. That's something you won't find on the past performance record of Desoto Duke. The only time he

another look at the past performances of the two horses and you'll see what I mean. Desoto Duke has been winning races but the extent of his efforts have come in lifetime non-winner events. The only time Desoto Duke competed in open company was once again that race in which he broke stride. That appears to be a speed break which is a possible clue that the class of horses he faced might have been a little too much for him. An important handicapping hint to remember is that class can usually handle pace but pace never has a chance against class.

As far as the class status of Noble Land is concerned, he's considered to be running in approximately the same class level. His last effort was against horses for "non-winners of $6,000 in 1973." That still puts him within $2,000 of the monetary conditions of tonight's race.

Another thing that is working for Noble Land is age. Desoto Duke is only a three year old while Noble Land is a seasoned veteran. When three year olds go up against older horses and all other things are equal, a slight edge is always given to the older horse. Things are far from equal between these two horses but the age factor is still on the side of Noble Land.

An evaluation of the two horses would look like this: Noble Land fits the race well classwise, appears to be capable of handling a fast pace if needed and has shown good consistency so far this season. Desoto Duke is taking a big class hike, has handled a medium pace with good success, and has also been a consistent sort.

When you compare the two horses, it puts a completely different light on things. Noble Land is given a big edge on class, has the credentials that reveal a definite pace advantage, and also will benefit from the fact that Desoto Duke is only a three year old. The latter two advantages are plus factors for Noble Land, but they are not nearly as important as that big edge on class.

Desoto Duke eventually went postward as the even odds favorite. Because the youngster was so immensely overrated, it left Noble Land as a very attractive overlay. He was sent off at odds of 9-1 and scored an easy victory. He paid $20.00 to win. Desoto Duke probably would have finished second but he was bothered by another horse at the half mile mark. The judges placed him in the number two spot through a disqualification.

Anyone who is familiar with Chicago racing will immediately recognize the vast difference in class between Desoto Duke and Noble Land. Horses coming off non-winner races are difficult to handicap in regular conditioned events because their class status is obscure against other horses. That's why it's very important to know the class of horses that generally compete in conditioned events at your local racetrack. You'll have a definite advantage in those races because non-winner types that look good on paper very frequently are overrated in the betting.

Horses coming off non-winner races also go the claiming route. But the class status of non-winner

NINTH RACE — 1 MILE
PACE. Conditioned. N-W $7,500 in 1973. A-E Fillies and Mares that have started 3 or more times at this meet and are N-W $1,000 at this meet. Purse $3,800.

Time—:30⁴ 1:02² 1:33² 2:02³   Mutuel Pool—$74,889

7. Noble Land	7	1	1¹¼	1²	1⁴	1⁴½	2:02³	9-1 (C.Willis)
8. Jicarill Byrd	8	2°	2¹¼	2²	2⁴	2⁴½p3	2:03³	16-1 (J.Ferguson)
2. DeSoto Duke	2	3	3²'m	3³°	3⁵½	36¼p2	2:03⁴	*1-1 (W Beckley)
6. First Cash	6	7	6⁵½	55	4⁶½	4⁶¼	2:03⁴	41-1 (S Banks)
3. Amigo's Girl	3	4	4³½	44	6⁸½	5⁹¾	2:04³	10-1 (A.Petty)
4. Jane Jester	4	5	5⁴½	67	5⁸½	6¹⁰	2:04³	30-1 (J.Curran)
1. Royal Prince	1	6	x7⁷½	715	7¹⁶	7¹⁷	2:06	10-1 (K.Heeney)
5. Sherwood Dancer	5	x8	8¹³	8¹⁷	8¹⁸	8¹⁸	2:06¹	2-1 (C.Alessi)

Jicarill Byrd disqualified and placed 3rd for impeding the progress of Desoto Duke.
Mutuels—(7) 20.00 6.00 4.60—(2) 3.20 3.00—(8) 6.20

Horse and driver give it all they have with just a few yards to go. (Photo by Kuprion.)

horses is much more easily defined in claiming races than in conditioned events. That's because claiming prices are a good measuring stick when trying to evaluate the animal's true class.

Serious minded players are advised to keep records of how non-winner horses fare when they are dropped into claiming races. It's a little extra work but it will be extremely useful in the long run. The only horses you'll have to keep track of are ones that win their first attempt in a claiming race. Keep a record of the claiming price the horse won for and also the type of non-winner race he last competed in. Then, average out the claiming price to the nearest $1,000. This way you'll have a good idea if the non-winner horses are going up or down in class in claiming races.

Players that were energetic enough to keep records on the 1973 season in Chicago would have come out with the following results:

Non-Winners of One Race	- $4,000
Non-Winners of Two Races	- $7,000
Non-Winners of Three Races	- $10,000
Non-Winners of Four Races	- $13,000

As you can see, the claiming prices are quite consistent with the class level of the race. But when you think about it, that's not really too surprising. What is surprising is the kind of prices you can get when non-winner horses drop into claiming races that are priced lower than the amounts listed. For instance, a $7,000 claimer race which took place on June 21 at Sportsman's Park.

The four year old gelding, Pompidou, was in a conditioned event his last time out for "non-winners of three races." His stiffest competition, Majestic Layne and Beth Express, are both coming off the same race which was a $6,000 claimer. All three horses were clocked in almost the same final time and the speed in each one's last half is just as close. Pompidou and Beth Express both closed in 1:00 4/5. Majestic Layne was timed in 1:01 2/5 while taking the overland route.

The three horses aren't really as closely matched as they appear to be on paper. The astute handicapper would immediately recognize that Pompidou is taking a big class drop. Horses that compete on the Chicago circuit win claiming affairs in approximately $10,000 company when coming off races for non-winners of three. That doesn't necessarily mean that Pompidou is taking a $3,000 class drop in claiming terms. It could be more or it could be less. But anyone who bothered to set aside about five minutes a week to maintain records on non-winner races would have known that Pompidou still has a big edge on class.

SIXTH RACE — 1 MILE

PACE. Claiming price $7,000—3 Year Olds and Upward —Purse $3,700.

Time—:30 1:03 1:34 2:05^{3} Mutuel Pool—$94,893

5. Pompidou	5	7	7^{8}°	3^{1¼}	2^{hd}	1^{3}	2:05^{3}	6-1 (J.Wondergm)
3. Majestic Layne	3	6	5^{6½}°	1^{nk}°	1^{hd}	2^{3}	2:06^{1}	*2-1 (N.Willis)
8. Beth Express	8	8	8^{9½}	5^{3¾}	3^{4}	3^{4¼}	2:06^{2}	9-2 (A.G.Shaw)
6. Robins Choice	6	1	1^{1½}	2^{nk}x	4^{5}	4^{5½}	2:06^{4}	16-1 (W.Paisley)
1. Clem K	1	4	4^{5½}	7^{8¼}	6^{7¼}	5^{12}	2:08	8-1 (Da.Busse)
2. Julie Way	2	3	3^{3½}	6^{6¼}	5^{7}	6^{13}	2:08^{1}	11-1 (R.Kline)
7. Crawdad	7	2	2^{1½}	ix4^{2¼}	8^{15}	7^{13}	2:08^{1}	5-2 (S.Banks)
4. Fire Bomb	4	5	6^{7}	8^{9¼}	7^{11}	8^{14}	2:08^{2}	23-1 (E.Magee)
9. Spring Wave	9	9	9^{13}	9^{10}	9^{16}	9^{17}	2:09	46-1 (J.Blevins)

Mutuels—(5) 15.80 6.60 3.40—(3) 3.80 2.80—(8) 3.00

WHITE **3** 6-1 +

Driver—NELSON WILLIS, Maroon-Gray-White Tr.—J. Turner (39-3-5-6—.199)

MAJESTIC LAYNE Blk h 1968, by Majestic Hanover—Ensign Ann—Ensign Hanover
Owner: John Turner, Downers Grove, Ill.

1973 6 0 1 2 $2,655
1972 26 4 4 7 $13,093 2:05^{2} Spk⅝
Lifetime $19,020 4, 2:05^{2} (⅝)

6-13 ^{5}Spk⅝ ft 73°	clm6000=1	:29^{4}	1:02^{1}	1:33^{3}	2:04^{1}	9	9	6^{3¾}°	6^{4}°	5^{3¾}	4^{1}	2:04^{2}	21-1 (N.Willis)	HighJimmy-BethExpress^{dh}, LakewoodQuick	(big race)
6- 5 ^{4}Spk⅝ sy 70°	clm6000=1	:31^{1}	1:03^{2}	1:35^{3}	2:06^{2}	7	9	9^{9}	7^{5½}	4^{3}	3^{1¼}	2:06^{3}	11-1 (N.Willis)	TimelySpeed, ChipmansCandy, MajstcLyne	(last ½ gd)
5-25 ^{1}Haw^{1} ft 58°	clm6000 1	:30^{4}	1:01	1:32	2:05	5	5	5	5^{3½}	5^{5}	5^{5}	2:06	*7 2 (N.Willis)	GayFamous, KingeryExpress, SonnyFarvel	(went evenly)
5-14 ^{2}Haw^{1} ft 47°	clm6000 1	:31	1:02^{2}	1:33^{4}	2:05	6	8	8	7^{6}	4^{5½}	2^{1¼}	2:05^{1}	5-1 (N.Willis)	SonnyFarvel, MajesticLayne, R.MagicPride	(good try)
5- 1 ^{6}Haw^{1} sy 66°	clm6000 1	:32^{3}	1:03:	1:35	2:08^{1}	2	3	4	4^{3½}	4^{4}	3^{4½}	2:09^{1}	8-1 (N.Willis)	MrTinkerByrd, BitOCreed, MajesticLayne	(even effort)
2-12 ^{9}BmlP ft 26°	clm7000+1	:33^{1}	1:04	1:34^{4}	2:07^{1}	1	5	6^{12}	7^{14}	7^{13}	5^{11}	2:09^{2}	7-1 (N.Willis)	SilverCreekTilly, HaveAChance, LangCrd	(lagged behind)

BLACK **5** 6-1 −

Driver—JAMES WONDERGEM, Orange-Black Tr.—J. Wondergem (9-1-2-2—.309)

POMPIDOU B g 1969, by Owen Hal—Mrs. Reif—Dominion Grattan
Owner: Lyle Lawson, Elburn, Ill.

1973 17 1 3 2 $1,994 2:19^{3} sy Aur
1972 19 4 0 2 $3,020 2:14^{4} Sndwh
Lifetime $3,291 3, 2:14^{4}

6- 8 ^{4}Spk⅝ ft 85°	nw3R=1	:29^{3}	1:02^{2}	1:32^{3}	2:03^{2}	8	9	8^{6¼}°	5^{9}	6^{5}	6^{4¾}	2:04^{2}	21-1 (J.MarshJr)	SpeedyAlmahurst, JoansGene, TwinkleBlue	(went evenly)
5-28 E.M.D⅝ ft	nw2000^{73} 1	:31^{3}	1:02^{1}	1:34^{2}	2:07	1	6	6	6°	4^{3½}	3^{3}	2:07^{3}	5-1 (W.Carney)	TimelyLassie, EddiePluto, Pompidou	(————)
5-19 E.M.D⅝ ft	w2500^{73} 1	:31	1:03^{4}	1:34^{4}	2:05^{2}	7	7	7	6°	6 ½x	6^{14}	2:08^{1}	13-1 (J.Dagenais)	TubbyZam, Stratamaid, Camptown	(————)
5- 9 E.M.D⅝ ft	nw2000^{73} 1	:31^{1}	1:03^{2}	1:33^{3}	2:05^{2}	2	4	5	4	4^{3½}	3^{2½}	2:06	5-1 (J.Dagenais)	LoGoAdios, VelvetsHarry, Pompidou	(————)
5- 5 E.M.D⅝ ft	nw2000^{73} 1	:30^{2}	1:04^{2}	1:35^{4}	2:07^{1}	1	4	4	6	4^{1½}	2^{3½}	2:07^{4}	9-1 (W Carney)	MissHatton, Pompidou, BethalsLizzie	(————)
4-28 LouD ft	nw2000^{7273} 1	:30^{4}	1:03^{4}	1:35^{4}	2:07^{3}	4	5	5	4°	3^{1}	2^{hd}	2:07^{3}	43-1 (J.Dagenais)	CandyKeys, Pompidou, LikeAGirl	(————)

BLACK & YELLOW **8** 9-2 +

Driver—A. GEORGE SHAW, Blue-White Tr.—A. G. Shaw (16-1-3-3—.229)

BETH EXPRESS B m 1963, by Adios Express—Nibbles Beth—Nibble Hanover
Owner: Joseph Caruso, Chicago, Ill.

1973 12 4 2 2 $9,827 2:04^{1} Spk⅝
1972 19 1 4 0 $4,331 2:11 gd LaPorte
Lifetime $52,356 8, 2:03

6-13 ^{5}Spk⅝ ft 73°	clm7200=1	:29^{4}	1:02^{1}	1:33^{3}	2:04^{1}	8	7	9^{6¼}	9^{8}	7^{4¾}	1^{¾dh}	2:04^{1}	18-1 (A.G.Shaw)	HighJimmy-BethExprss^{dh}, LakwdQuick	(powerful last ¼)
6- 4 ^{5}Spk⅝ gd 67°	clm7200 C=1	:30^{2}	1:02^{2}	1:33^{4}	2:06	7	2	2^{1½}°	2^{nk}	7^{10}	7^{14}	2:08^{4}	*9-5 (J.MarshJr)	WorthyAdvice, ProudDelight, PatsysGal	(tired badly)
5-24 ^{4}Haw^{1} ft 60°	clm7200 1	:31^{2}	1:03^{3}	1:34^{4}	2:04^{3}	4	3	3	2^{½}	1^{2}	3^{2½}	2:05^{1}	*2-1 (W.Paisley)	ChiefOsceola, BitOCreed, BethExpress	(tired sme)
5-10 ^{6}Haw^{1} ft 62°	clm7200 1	:31	1:03^{1}	1:34^{3}	2:06^{1}	3	6	6	2^{1}°	1^{2}	1^{nk}	2:06^{1}	*2-1 (W.Paisley)	BethExpress, AndysJake, BitOCreed	(under the whip)
4-27 ^{2}Haw^{1} ft 45°	clm6000 C 1	:31	1:01^{4}	1:34^{2}	2:04^{3}	7	2	2	2^{1¼}	2^{1½}	2^{2½}	2:05^{1}	*2-1 (A.G.Shaw)	GinnysGene, BethExpress, ChiefOsceola	(2nd best)
4-18 ^{6}Haw^{1} gd 61°	clm7200 1	:31	1:03^{1}	1:36^{3}	2:07^{2}	7	7	7	5^{5}	4^{6¼}	4^{9¾}	2:09^{2}	7-2 (A.G.Shaw)	HedgeAppleJohn, BitOCreed, MrTinkerByrd	(even)

Pompidou was able to sneak off at odds of 6-1. He proved he was worth more than $7,000. The four year old gelding won going away by three open lengths. He returned a generous $15.80 to win.

Non-winner events for lifetime wins are run at virtually all racetracks. If you want to keep ahead of this game, it's important to know the approximate class status of the horses entered in those races. As far as wagering on non-winner events is concerned, it's a whole different ballgame. We'll get into that in the next chapter.

Switch in Racing Strategy

When you're looking through the racing program for your selection, there will be times when you come across a horse whose last race was run in a completely different style than any of his previous efforts. This is when the driver changes the racing strategy for the horse. These kinds of horses are usually worth following because it's a tactic that's often employed for a very good reason.

The switch in racing strategy is about as old as the game itself. It can be used for both stretch runners and frontrunning types. The idea behind the change is to give a horse needed stamina in an area in which it's been lacking. When a horse does his best running in the stretch, he'll occasionally go into a losing streak because he leaves the starting gate too slow. The result of this would cause the horse to have too much ground to make up in the stretch. This is especially true if the horse lacks a good strong close. The animal might be able to get within striking distance at the three quarter mark, but he still falls short at the finish line by a couple of lengths.

Many drivers will try to remedy this kind of predicament by asking the horse for gate speed. This way, when the horse is sent out for his next race, his chances are much improved that he'll leave the starting gate fast. This, in turn, will allow the horse to stay close to the leaders and put him in a good position for the stretch drive.

Frontrunners that have been tiring out just before reaching the finish line also benefit from a switch in racing strategy. In this situation, the driver again reverses the animal's usual kind of race. Instead of sending the horse directly out for the lead, he'll keep him off the pace and ask him for as much speed as possible in the final quarter. By doing this, the animal will gain enough stamina for his next race to carry him to the wire without quitting.

The first thing to look for when you spot a switch in racing strategy is success. If the horse hasn't responded well to the switch, then there's no reason whatsoever to expect an improved effort from him his next time out. But, if the horse does come around and throw in a good race, one where he makes definite improvement on his loss margin over his previous race, then there's more than enough reason to follow him in his next race.

The most important thing these horses have going for them is versatility. Even though a frontrunner may be successful in his first try at coming off the pace, it doesn't necessarily mean that the driver will revert to another wire to wire attempt. Nor does it mean that a stretch runner who turned in a good speed race will once again return to a come-from-behind type of strategy. What it does mean is that these kinds of horses are capable of going either way. If a horse turned in a good effort, the driver may decide to repeat the same kind of race. He can also go back to the racing strategy of the animal's previous races because now the horse has the needed stamina that was once lacking.

The switch in racing strategy is not something that's used to predict how a driver and horse are going to run their race in tonight's contest. The importance of it is to uncover the change that took place in the horse's last race. That may sound simple enough, but these kinds of horses still are generally underrated in the betting. We're dealing with horses that have a good race behind them so you'll rarely get big longshots. However, most people overlook the switch, so you can still get away with a decent price on most horses.

Take a look at the past performance record of Col. Moffitt and you'll see an example of a switch in racing strategy. The six year old gelding was entered in a $7,000 claiming race on June 11 at Sportsman's Park. Col. Moffitt was strictly a speed horse up until his last effort. After going in two qualifying races, he showed some of that good speed by winning a photo on April 25. But in his next two races, he wasn't quite able to put it all together. On May 7, the gelding stayed close to the leaders but eventually he faltered when it came time for the stretch drive. On his next to last effort, he led for more than three quarters of the mile but again he gave way late in the race.

RED
1
5-1
—

Driver—JESSIE WILLIS, Maroon-Gray-White **Tr.—J. Willis** **(10-0-1-1—.089)**

CRAWDAD B g 1967, by Addio Byrd—Princess Meridale—Tempered Volo
Owner: William McEnery, Evergreen Park, Ill.

1973	21 5 1 3	$11,589	2:06^1 Spk⅝
1972	34 4 4 1	$12,819	2:05^1 Haw^1
	Lifetime	$18,131	4, 2:04^3 (1)

5-31 ^{7}Spk⅝ ft 74°	clm9000—	1	:30	1:03	1:33^1	2:03^3	6	7	7^{11}	7^{7½}°	7^{5½}	6^{5¾}	2:04^4	25-1 (W.Rosebm)	TinyForbes, LangCreed, LookawaySun	(went evenly
5-19 ^{10}Haw^1 ft 55°	clm10000	1	:30^4	1:02^4	1:34	2:04^3	9	9	6	6^8	6^{8½}	6^{14}	2:07^2	12-1 (J.Willis)	TeeniTime, NoCredit, SpeedyChestnut	(post hurt
5-10 ^{7}Haw^1 ft 62°	clm10000	1	:30^3	1:00^4	1:31^2	2:04	7	8	8	6^{6¼}°	6^6	6^{4¼}	2:04^4	7-1 (J.Willis)	GoldBerry, TeeniTime, ChiefsLittleStar	(even trip
5- 2 ^{8}Haw^1 gd 44°	clm9000	1	:30^4	1:01	1:31^4	2:04^3	7	5	6	6^4	4^4	2^{½dh}	2:04^4	17-1 (J.Willis)	SilverDiller, BillyTime-Crawdad^{dh}	(closed good
4-25 ^{8}Haw^1 ft 46°	clm11000	1	:31	1:00^4	1:32	2:03^4	7	8	9	8^{15}	8^{12}	8^{14}	2:06^2	10-1 (J.Willis)	BengalSong, JewelThief, PlutoHal	(no threat
4-16 ^{6}Spk⅝A ft 45°	clm10000+	1	:30^4	1:04^1	1:34^3	2:06^1	1	2	3^3	3^2	2^1	1^{1½}	2:06^1	6-1 (J.Willis)	Crawdad, LoisAmigo, LovinLuLu	(perfect trip

BLACK & YELLOW
8
7-2
=

Driver—JOHNNY BLEVINS, White-Blue-Black **Tr.—J. Blevins** **(15-0-3-1—.133)**

COL. MOFFITT B g 1967, by Don Adios—Orphan Nellie—Lieut. Commander
Owner: John Limparis, Palos Park, Ill.

1973	5 1 1 0	$2.775	2:07^4 Haw^1
1972	33 8 4 3	$16,559	2:02^4 Spk⅝
	Lifetime	$20,432	5, 2:02^4 (⅝)

5-30 ^{10}Spk⅝ ft 59°	clm7000=	1	:30^4	1:03^3	1:33^3	2:05	1	4	4^5	5^4	4^{2½}	2^{hd}	2:05	8 1 (J.Blevins)	PortSam, Col.Moffitt, BigDavid	(just missed
5-17 ^{5}Haw^1 ft 53°	clm7000 C	1	:31	1:02^3	1:33^4	2:04^4	3	1	1	1^{1½}	1^1	6^{3½}	2:05^3	7-2 (H.Burright)	BobbyBaron, BigDavid, JerryDuke	(weakened
5- 7 ^{2}Haw^1 sy 60°	clm7000	1	:31^2	1:03	1:35^4	2:06^3	2	3	4	3^1	7^{4½}	8^{5½}	2:07^4	4-1 (C.McDermtt)	KayCarmichael, BillCarlith. Zhivago	(faded
4-25 ^{5}Haw^1 ft 50°	clm6000	1	:32^4	1:05	1:37^3	2:07^4	5	5	1	1^2	1^1	1^{ns}	2:07^4	3-1 (C.McDermtt)	Col.Moffitt, SeafieldGlobe, CleverRod	(well handled
4-20 Haw^1 ft 68°	Qua	1	:31^4	1:04	1:35^4	2:08	5	2	1	1^3	1^7	1^{11}	2:08	NB (CMcDermtt)	Col.Moffitt, AppolloMascot, YatesBoy	(———
4-11 Spk⅝ ft	Qua	1	:32	1:05^2	1:36	2:08^1	5	5	1	2^5	3^{4½}	5^{8½}	2:10	NB (CMcDermtt)	TheIdler, GayFamous, JointEndeavor	(———

In Col. Moffitt's last race, the switch in racing strategy is clearly defined. Since he was leaving from the rail, there's little doubt what his driver had in mind. Instead of trying to make a speed contest out of the race, he was kept slightly off the pace and closed well in the final quarter.

SEVENTH RACE — 1 MILE
PACE. Claiming $7,000. 3 Years and Up. Purse $3,700.

Time—:30^2 1:02^3 1:33^2 2:04^3 Mutuel Pool—$95,451

8. Col. Moffitt	8	8	9^{9½}	8^{7¼}	6^{2¾}	1^{nk}	2:04^3	7-2 (J.Blevins)
1. Crawdad	1	4	3^3	3^{1¾}	1^1	2^{nk}	2:04^3	*2-1 (J.Willis)
5. Dear Baroness	5	6	6^{5½}	5^{4½}	2^1	3^{2¼}	2:05	7-1 (H.Burright)
4. Rusty Merrie	4	7	7^7	6^{5½}	5^{2¼}	4^{2¼}	2:05	9-1 (A.G.Shaw)
7. Senator Haven	7	2	2^{1½}	2^{1¼}	4^{1¼}	5^{3½}	2:05^2	7-1 (E.Waszak)
2. Hal Knox	2	5	4^{4¼}	4^3	3^1	6^{3½}	2:05^2	7-1 (J.Searle)
9. Penrod Prior	9	9	8^{7½}°	7^{5¾}°	8^{4¾}	7^{4¾}	2:05^3	5-1 (N.Willis)
6. Ballard's Rodney	6	1	1^{1½}	1^{1¼}	7^{4¼}	8^7	2:06	12-1 (H.Ballard)
3. Slick Sail	3	3°	5^{4½}°	9^{10}	9^{17}	9^{19}	2:08^2	46-1 (J.Harry)

Mutuels—(8) 9.80 4.80 4.80—(1) 3.60 3.00—(5) 4.00

Col. Moffitt was asked to repeat the same kind of performance in his June 11 race. This time he was kept far off the pace but he made an even stronger close in the final quarter. Although Col. Moffitt was listed as the morning line favorite, Crawdad, whose past performance record has also been reproduced, went off as the people's choice. Col. Moffitt returned a respectable $9.80 to win.

Jetway Sue also reflects a switch in racing strategy. The pacing mare was entered in a $5,000 claiming race on August 22 at Maywood Park. Look at her past performance record.

As you can see, it's the complete opposite type of switch that took place with Col. Moffitt. Jetway Sue is a stretch runner that was sent out for a wire to wire attempt. A successful one at that. But look at her two previous efforts that were contested on the local circuit. In each race, she was a bit slow leaving the starting gate. She had an inside post position in both efforts but she was unable to take advantage of it in either race.

Jetway Sue is a stretch runner but she lacks a good strong close. It appears from her previous efforts that the only way she can win in that fashion is if she's less than five lengths off the pace after three quarters of the mile. However, her driver has another option open. Since he was able to get good gate speed out of her last time, he can try to go wire to wire again.

FOURTH RACE — 1 MILE
PACE. Claiming price $5,000 — Illinois Bred — Purse $3,000.

Time—:30^4 1:03^4 1:34^4 2:06^4 Mutuel Pool—$31,016

7. Jetway Sue	7	2	4^2	5^{2½}	5^{2½}	1^{½}	2:06^4	7-2 (E.Lutes)
5. Friskey May	5	7	5^3°	4^{1½}°	2^{nk}	2^{½}	2:07	21-1 (R.Knox)
3. Brooks Colt	3	3	6^{3½}	8^{4¼}	6^{4½}	3^{¾}	2:07	30-1 (J.Searle)
6. Chickadee	6	8	3^{1½}°	2^1°	3^{½}	4^{1¼}	2:07	3-1 (Da.Busse)
2. Gladstone Babe	2	5	1^{½}°	1^1	1^{nk}	5^{2¼}	2:07^1	*7-5 (S.Banks)
8. Rusty Robin	8	1°	2^{½}	3^{1¼}	4^2	6^{8¼}	2:08^2	7-1 (W.Paisley)
4. Donz Sparkler	4	6	7^{4½}°	6^{2¾}°	7^5	7^{12}	2:09^1	8-1 (C.Willis)
1. Hi Land Knight	1	4	8^{5½}	7^{3¾}°	8^7	8^{13}	2:09^2	11-1 (C.Daly)

Mutuels—(7) 11.80 6.40 6.00—(5) 15.80 5.40—(3) 12.80

BROWN
7
9-2

Driver—EDDIE LUTES, Red-White **Tr.—B. Shuter** **(20-2-4-1—.228)**

JETWAY SUE B m 1967, by Torpedo Hanover—Jet Princess—Amscot
Owners: Bo Anthers, Grammer, Ind.

1973	3 1 0 1	$1,624	2:05^1 May
1972	26 1 0 2	$996	2:08^4 LouD
	Lifetime	$1,341	5, 2:08^4

8- 9 ^{1}May ft 80°	clm4800	1	:31	1:03^1	1:34^1	2:05^1	8	1	1^{1½}	1^{nk}	1^{1½}	1^{½}	2:05^1	29-1 (E.Lutes)	JetwaySue, CleverRod, Lang'sFilly	(big mil
7-19 ^{4}Spk⅝ ft 84°	clm6000+	1	:31^2	1:04	1:34	2:05^3	3	4	6^{6½}	7^5	7^{6½}	7^{4¼}	2:06^2	19-1 (B.Shuter)	HastiDcc, KristyLynn, Aquarius	(no excus
7- 9 ^{2}Spk⅝ ft 92°	clm4800=	1	:30^3	1:03^3	1:34^1	2:05	2	6	6^7	5^5	5^{5½}	3^{3¼}	2:05^3	21-1 (B.Shuter)	AdmiralJack, FannyMorgen, JetwaySue	(raced wel
7- 5 Spk⅝ ft 75°	Qua	1	:30	1:01^4	1:33^2	2:05^3	8	7°	6^{19}	6^{8½}	6^5	6^{2½}	2:06^1	NB (Bo.Shuter)	FirePilot, LittleDaddy, TennesseeSid	(———
6-21 Spk⅝ ft 76°	Qua	1	:31	1:04	1:35	2:06^3	4	x6	6^{dis}	6^{dis}	6^{dis}	6^{dis}		NB (B.Shuter)	LunarHill, WonderByrd, DeMarYoung	(———
9-25 LouD sy	clm4800	1	:32	1:05^1	1:37^2	2:09^4	6	4°	2°	2°	4^2	7^{8¼}	2:11^2	31-1 (B.Anthers)	MyMySmith, KemoSabay, VikingPick	(———

Jetway Sue wasn't sent out for another frontrunning attempt, but she was successful in securing good position. At the quarter, she dropped into the number two spot despite the fact that she left from the seven post. In doing so, she was much closer to the leaders than usual at the three quarter mark and, as a result, she had less ground to make up in the stretch. The result chart has her at 7-2 but she actually went off at 9-2 and returned $11.80 to win.

The switch in racing strategy is something that is often overlooked. But if you come across a horse similar to Col. Moffitt or Jetway Sue, remember that it's only important if the animal raced well in his last effort. A successful switch is an added edge that most horses don't have. If the horse didn't respond to the change, don't follow him.

Quality Class Drops

Earlier in the chapter, we looked at some situations where class was used as a deciding factor when considering horses that were coming off non-winner races. In those particular races, we were able to use class as a very strong handicapping factor. Class, of course, is *always* a very strong handicapping factor—when it's used correctly, that is.

The class status of a horse is partially dependent on his current form. In other words, there is a class-form relationship. So if you really wanted to use class incorrectly, it wouldn't be too difficult. All you would have to do is totally ignore current form, and in the long run that would have a drastic effect on your bankroll. Even though class is the most independent of all handicapping factors, there is still a certain amount of attention that must be paid to current form.

The exact role that current form plays on class is proportional to the class function itself. For instance, if a horse is taking a class hike he should automatically be in good form just for you to consider him a contender in the race. When a horse is taking a big class hike, then you should not only be very selective in your choice but also demand that the animal be in peak form. Horses that are staying within the same class should be in good form to the point where they show you they can compete successfully within that level. If a horse is dropping down in class, then you should give a certain amount of leeway on his current form since the animal is going up against lesser competition than he faced in his last start.

The best advantage a horse can derive from the three class functions is the class drop. This is especially true if the animal also happens to be in good form. However, there are very few situations where you can have both factors working for you at the same time. In claiming races if a horse is in good form, he simply doesn't go down in class—he goes up. The only time you'll see a horse in good form taking a class drop in a claimer is if he's coming off a conditioned race.

Horses that compete strictly in conditioned races occasionally are able to drop down in class while in good form. A trainer has much more flexibility with class in conditioned races because there's never any risk of losing a horse on a claim. If a horse wins a conditioned race for "non-winners of $15,000" this week, he still may be eligible to compete for "non-winners of $10,000" next week.

Another kind of horse that drops down in class while in good form is the high class competitor. A horse that races well against free-for-allers, stakes horses, or invitational types is occasionally dropped into a conditioned race. Wagering on a quality horse in a conditioned race usually doesn't offer a great monetary reward, but betting against the animal will get you even less.

RED **1** 2-1	Driver—DARYL BUSSE, Gray-Red		Tr.—Da. Busse		(59-7-5-8—.211)			1973	22	4	4	4	$24,095	2:01³ Spk⅝
	BIG DADDY'S SHADOW		B c 1969, by Shadow Wave—Big Spree—Good Time					1972	29	7	4	1	$18,723	2:01² Hol¹
			G. Williams, Kadel & Rursch, Dvnprt, Io., Joy, Tylr Rdg, Ill.					Lifetime					$20,282	3, 2:01² (1)

8-17	⁹May ft 76°	§w1000073	1 :284 :584 1:29¹ 1:59¹	3	5	55½	43½	34	21¼ 1:59²	5-1 (Da.Busse)	AdiosArt, BigDaddysShadow, YankeeBaron	(nice try)
8-11	¹⁰May ft 77°	w1000073	1 :282 :584 1:28 1:57²	8	8	81¹⁰	815	719	51² 1:59⁴	19-1 (S.Banks)	Starboard Butler, Jefferson, C.V.Thor	(broke 2 minutes)
8- 6	⁵May ft 81°	nw1000073	1 :30¹ 1:01 1:30² 2:00⁴	7	7	65°	54½	54½	4¾ 2:01	9-2 (Da.Busse)	NicksPainter, YankeeBaron, DoctorAndy	(parked 2 turns)
7-28	¹⁰May ft 64°	inv7500	1 :30 1:01¹ 1:30⁴ 2:00⁴	4	5	55½	53½	43½	64¼ 2:01³	15-1 (Da.Busse)	UncleKenny, GaySkipper, EliLang	(evenly)
7-21	⁷Spk⅝ ft 75°	nw17506	1 :29³ 1:01¹ 1:31⁴ 2:01³	3	7	53½	31¼°	21	12¼ 2:01³	5-2 (Da.Busse)	BigDaddysShadow, Overhaul, FlamingosPride	(easy win)
7-14	⁶Spk⅝ ft 75°	clm30000	1 :29² 1:02 1:31⁴ 2:01²	8	9	75°	63½°	73¼	31½ 2:01⁴	9-2 (Da.Busse)	Airfare, LincolnsBid, BigDaddysShadow	(hung out)

WHITE **2** 7-2

Driver—WALTER PAISLEY, Green-White Tr.—A. Petty (122-20-23-23—.332)

ELI LANG
B c 1969, by Lang Hanover—Jerry's Joy—Jerry. H.
Owner: Edward Walston, Chicago, Ill.

1973	23	3	7	5	$31,776	1:59^4 Spk⅝					
1972	33	4	4	7	$24,779	2:02^1 Haw^1					
Lifetime					$31,216	3, 2:02^1 (1)					

8-18 ^{9}May ft 77°	§inv10000	1	:29^3	1:01^2	1:32^2	2:00^2	5	1°	1^{1¼}	2^1	2^3	2^{5¾}	2:01^3	7-1 (W.Paisley)	StarboardButler, EliLang, GameGuy	(dueled 1st ¼
8-10 ^{5}May ft 75°	inv10000	1	:29^1	:59	1:29^1	1:58^4	6	3	3^{4½}	6^{2½}	6^{3¾}	6^{4¾}	1:59^4	22-1 (A.Petty)	ShadHanover, HastyEd, UncleKenny	(broke 2 minutes
8- 4^{10}May ft 73°	inv7500	1	:29^4	1:01^1	1:30^3	2:00	7	7	7^{6¼}	6^{3¼}°	7^5	7^{5½}	2:01^1	12-1 (A.Petty)	GameGuy, ShadHanover, UncleKenny	(no close
7-28^{10}May ft 64°	inv7500	1	:30	1:01^1	1:30^4	2:00^4	3	4	4^4	4^{2½}	5^4	3^{3½}	2:01^3	5-1 (A.Petty)	UncleKenny, GaySkipper, EliLang	(evenly
7-20 ^{5}Spk⅝ sy 73°	inv7000−1		:31	1:03^3	1:35^4	2:06	6	1	2^{1½}	2^{1¼}	2^2	3^{2½}	2:06^3	3-1 (A.Petty)	AdiosArt, YankeeBaron, EliLang	(raced well
7- 7 ^{9}Spk⅝ ft 90°	stk50000+1		:27^4	:58^1	1:26^3	1:56	8	9	9^{6½}	8^{8¾}	8^{14}	8^{14}	1:58^{4}e	13-1 (J.Dolbee)	SirDalrae, ElPatron, Breadwinner	(too much speed

GREEN **4** 7-2

Driver—JIM CURRAN, Gray-Gold Tr.—R. Farrington (111-15-23-12—.286)

YANKEE BARON
B g 1967, by Baron Hanover—Princess J.,—Yankee Hanover
Owners: Farrington Stables, Inc. and J. Ludy; Richwood, Tipp City, Ohio

1973	23	3	5	5	$24,330	2:00^3 Spk⅝
1972	34	9	3	5	$32,903	2:02^3 Haw^1
Lifetime					$57,110	4, 2:02^1 (1)

8-17 ^{9}May ft 76°	§w1000073	1	:28^4	:58^4	1:29^1	1:59^1	5	6	8^7	7^5	4^6	3^{2¼}	1:59^3	4-1 (J.Curran)	AdiosArt, BgDaddysShadow, YankeeBaron	(closed some
8- 6 ^{5}May ft 81°	nw1000073	1	:30^1	1:01	1:30^2	2:00^4	2	4	5^4	4^{2½}°	3^{2¾}	2½	2:01	*5-2 (J.Curran)	NicksPainter, YankeeBaron, DoctorAndy	(good effort
8- 1 ^{5}May ft 67°	nw1000073	1	:30^3	1:03^1	1:33^1	2:03	2	3	4^3	4^{2½}	2^{2½}	2^{ns}	2:03	2-1 (J.Curran)	NativeExpress, YankeeBaron, Samtree	(just missed
7-28 ^{9}May ft 64°	w1000073	1	:30^3	1:02^3	1:33	2:02^3	8	8	7^5°	6^4°	7^5	7^{5½}	2:03^4	18-1 (J.Curran)	GameGuy, StarboardButler, DoctorAndy	(hung out
7-20 ^{5}Spk⅝ sy 73°	inv7000+1		:31	1:03^3	1:35^4	2:06	4	4	4^6	6^5	4^{4½}	2^{2¼}	2:06^2	7-1 (J.Curran)	AdiosArt, YankeeBaron, EliLang	(good finish
7-14 ^{9}Spk⅝ ft 75°	w10000^{7273}=1		:30	1:00^4	1:31	2:00^4	9	4°	2^{1¼}°	4^{1¾}°	8^{6½}	8^{11}	2:03	9-1 (J.Curran)	NicksPainter, RightGood, Overhaul	(parked mile

Take a look at the past performance record of Eli Lang and you'll see a good example of a quality class drop. The four year old colt was entered in a conditioned event for "winners of $10,000 in 1973." The race took place on August 22 at Maywood Park. The only competition that Eli Lang appears to have is from Big Daddy's Shadow and Yankee Baron. However, the class of horses on their past performances nowhere matches the class of horses that Eli Lang has faced. Even though they both performed well against $10,000 winners, a big class edge is still given to Eli Lang. He turned in a good effort in his last race in a $10,000 invitational.

FIFTH RACE — 1 MILE
PACE. Conditioned — Winners of over $10,000 in 1973 that are Non-winners of a race this meet—Purse $5,000

Time—:30^2 1:01^3 1:32^1 2:00^3 Mutuel Pool—$85,926

2. Eli Lang	2	2	1^{1¼}	1^1	1^{2½}	1^3	2:00^3	*3-2	(W.Paisley)
4. Yankee Baron	4	5	5^3°	2^1°	2^{2½}	2^3	2:01^1	2-1	(J.Curran)
6. Doc's Jerry	6	1	2^{1¼}	4^{2¼}	3^{6½}	3^{10}	2:02^3	44-1	(S.Banks)
1. Big Daddy's Shadow	1	3	4^{2½}	6^{3¾}°	6^{10}	4^{11}	2:02^4	2-1	(Da.Busse)
3. Bret's Tune	3	4	6^5	5^{3¼}°	4^{9½}	5^{14}	2:03^2	10-1	(J.MarshJr)
7. M. R. Byrd	7	7	3^{1½}°	3^2°	5^{9½}	6^{14}	2:03^2	55-1	(C.Willis)
5. Meg's Rhythm	5	6	7^9	7^{4¾}	7^{11}	7^{14}	2:03^2	18-1	(H.Fabert)

Mutuels—(2) 5.00 3.00 3.00—(4) 3.60 2.80—(6) 5.60

Eli Lang didn't exactly light up the board. He returned an even $5.00 to win. But when all things are considered, this wasn't a bad price. He could have just as easily gone off at odds on. You'll also notice the advantage that class has over pace. Eli Lang closed in 28^2 which forced every other horse in the field to lose ground in the final quarter.

The past performance record of Stormy Filter also exemplifies a quality class drop. The three year old colt was entered in a conditioned event for "non-winners of $10,000 in 1972 and 1973" on May 4 at Hawthorne Race Course. Stormy Filter is coming into the race with excellent credentials. He's fresh off a win against stakes caliber horses which saw him parked the entire mile. The only other horse in the race with a chance of winning is Star Pop. He's coming off an impressive win himself. But the class of horses he recently faced is a long way off from the kind of company that Stormy Filter has been keeping.

Red **1** 7-2

STORMY FILTER
B c 70 by Filter—Sally D. Purdue—Purdue Hal
Owner: Abraham Schultz, Bal Harbour, Fla.

1973	7	1	0	1	$16,518	2:04^3 Haw^1
1972	14	9	3	0	$25,160	2:02^4 DuQ^1
Lifetime thru 1972					$25,160	

Driver—JERRY GRAHAM, Green-Orange Trainer—J. Graham

4-25 ^{7}Haw^1 ft 46°	3yrstk21305	1	:29^3	1:02	1:34^3	2:04^3	8	7°	6°	2½°	1^2	1^{1¼}	2:04^3	*6-5	(JGraham)	StormyFilter, PellaireByrd, P.B.Mar
4-11 ^{7}Spk⅝ sy 35°	3yrstk42300	1	:31	1:04^2	1:36^2	2:07^3	4	6°	4°	1	2^{nk}	3^{12½}	2:10^1	5-2	(JGraham)	RobbRanger, SlippinBy, StormyFilter
4- 6 L.A.⅝ ft	nw20000	1	:30^2	1:02^1	1:31^4	2:02^1	8	8	8	7	8^4	5^{2¾}	2:02^4	11-1	(JGraham)	Mr.Jazz, HobbyHorseLupe, VivaLobell
3-31 L.A.⅝ ft	nw20000^{7273}	1	:32	1:03	1:32^3	2:02^1	2	ix7	7	7	7^{5¼}	6^{6¼}	2:03^2	7-1	(JGraham)	R.DsBeauty, HyMinbar, LuckyPiece
3-23 L.A.⅝ ft	3-4yr6000	1	:30^2	1:02^2	1:32^3	2:01^2	1	3	3	5^{2¼}ix	6^{dis}	6^{dis}		8-1	(JGraham)	DoctorTom, AdiosRick, HappyHeart
3-16 L.A.⅝ ft	3-4yr6000	1	:30	1:01	1:30^3	2:00^2	6	6	7	7	6^{4½}	5^{5¾}	2:01^3	20-1	(JGraham)	VeriSpecial, NicksPainter, St.ClairCarl

Red & Yellow **8** 5-1

STAR POP

B g 70 by Poplar Byrd—Star Gem Wick—Gene Abbe
Owner: Estelle Walston, Chicago, Ill.

1973	7	4	2	1	$8,647	2:04^{2} Spk⅝
1972	10	0	5	0	$2,210	
Lifetime thru 1972					$2 210	

Driver—AUBREY PETTY, Maroon-Black **Trainer—A. Petty**

4-25	^{4}Haw^{1} ft 50°	nw5000^{7273}	1	:31^{4}	1:04^{2}	1:35^{3}	2:05^{1}	2	3	1	1^{2}	1^{4}	1$^{7\frac{1}{2}}$	2:05^{1}	*2-5	(WPaisley)	StarPop, SpeedTicket, FlyingBaron
4-14	^{4}Spk⅝A ft56°	nw9000^{7273}	1	:30^{1}	1:03	1:34	2:03^{1}	3	5	5	3	3$^{5\frac{1}{2}}$	2$^{3\frac{1}{2}}$	2:04	5-2	(APetty)	PrimsKnight, StarPop. AwayAmigo
4- 6	^{5}Spk⅝ ft 64°	nw3R	1	:30^{2}	1:03^{3}	1:33^{4}	2:04^{2}	7	7	7	3°	3$^{\frac{3}{4}}$	1$^{2\frac{1}{4}}$	2:04^{2}	5-1	(APetty)	StarPop, DodgeAcresElla, JaneJester
3-31	^{4}Spk⅝ sy 45°	3-5yrnw2R	1	:32^{4}	1:05^{2}	1:37^{4}	2:10	1	1	1	1	1$^{1\frac{1}{2}}$	1$^{1\frac{1}{4}}$	2:10	*3-5	(APetty)	StarPop, KeystoneDandy, TarportPalmer
3-23	^{3}Spk⅝ ft 45°	3-5yrnw2R	1	:31	1:03^{4}	1:34^{4}	2:05^{3}	8	9	8°	3°	2^{4}	3^{3}	2:06^{1}	*2-1	(APetty)	DodgeAcresElla, GalaNite. StarPop
3-14	^{5}Spk⅝ ft 63°	3-4yrnw1R	1	:31^{2}	1:04	1:35^{1}	2:07^{3}	6	9	6°	1	1$^{1\frac{1}{2}}$	1$^{\frac{3}{4}}$	2:07^{3}	*6-5	(APetty)	StarPop, TheIdler, GoodLittleArab

FIFTH RACE—ONE MILE PACE—PURSE $4,800

Non-Winners of $10,000 in 1972-73. 3-Year-Olds $1,000 Allowance.

Time—:31^{4} 1:03^{2} 1:34^{1} 2:03^{4} Mutuel Pool $136,779

1 Stormy Filter	1	3	3	3$^{1\frac{1}{2}}$	1^{1}	1$^{1\frac{1}{4}}$	2:03^{4}	*2-1	(JGraham)
8 Star Pop	8	8	8°	7$^{5\frac{1}{2}}$	3^{5}	2$^{1\frac{1}{4}}$	2:04	6-1	(APetty)
6 Steady Blaze	6	6	6	8$^{7\frac{1}{2}}$	6$^{7\frac{1}{2}}$	3$^{1\frac{1}{4}}$	2:04	18-1	(DShetlerJr)
4 Shadow Luck	4	4	4	4$^{3\frac{1}{2}}$	4^{6}	4$^{1\frac{3}{4}}$	2:04^{1}	5-2	(DwPletcher)
2 Break Water	2	1	2	1$^{\frac{1}{2}}$	2^{1}	5^{2}	2:04^{1}	10-1	(BShuter)
5 WinterSymphony	5	5	5	6^{5}	5$^{6\frac{1}{2}}$	6$^{2\frac{1}{4}}$	2:04^{1}	6-1	(JAckerman)
7 Steve Milam	7	7	7°	5$^{4\frac{1}{2}}$	7$^{8\frac{1}{2}}$	7$^{4\frac{3}{4}}$	2:04^{4}	10-1	(BNickells)
9 KeystoneStormy	9	9	9	9^{8}	8^{12}	8^{7}	2:05^{1}	38-1	(JFerguson)
3 Cherry Coke	3	2°	1	2$^{\frac{1}{2}}$	9^{15}	9^{13}	2:06^{2}	10-1	(JWillis)

MUTUELS—(1) $6.60 $3.60 $3.00—(8) $5.60 $3.20—(6) $5.60

The price on Stormy Filter was also far from a box car payoff. He returned a modest $6.60 to win. But Stormy Filter and Eli Lang were so well placed that their payoffs were only secondary. There are horses that go off at 4-5 every week that find themselves facing stiffer competition. So I would have to say that both horses were pretty much underrated despite their small return.

If you're going to look for quality class drops, it's a good idea to become familiar with the better horses at your local racetrack. It's also a good idea to know some of the classier types across the country that may visit there from time to time. The United States Trotting Association sponsors the HARNESS RACING HOTLINE at (312) 782-5100. A call to that number brings you the latest harness racing news and also the results of major stakes and feature races at all North American harness tracks on a 24-hour basis.

In the next chapter, we'll take a second look at off tracks, try to pick a winner in one of those tough non-winner races, and also see what effect the single shaft sulky has on handicapping a race.

CHAPTER 10

Unfinished Business

In this chapter, we'll look at three different situations that were briefly mentioned earlier in the book. We've pretty thoroughly discussed what to do if a horse competed on an off track in his last race, but we're still left with another kind of off track performer, the kind of horse that won his last race on an off track and is well situated for a repeat performance on a fast track.

We've already handled the problem of horses coming off non-winner races, but we haven't actually handicapped a non-winner race itself. It's a fairly high risk situation, so it demands an extremely well placed horse. We'll see exactly what that horse looks like a little later in this chapter.

The single shaft sulky is the most revolutionary piece of equipment that's been introduced to the sport of harness racing since the mobile starting gate. Some drivers swear by it; others swear at it. We'll see what effect it has on handicapping a race. But first, we'll settle the off track issue.

OFF TRACK REPEATERS

One of the most confusing things about handicapping a race is how to deal with a horse that won on an off track in his last effort. Many people come to the conclusion that if a horse turns in a good race when the track is off, that he's only capable of repeating his good performance under similar conditions. This might be true for some horses to a certain extent, but for the great majority, it is not.

First of all, if a horse is not in form, it's very doubtful that he'll turn in a good race regardless of the fact that he has a preference for a wet racing surface. Second, and more important, is that a horse may just be coming into his own and he wins on a night that it happens to rain. However, there's still going to be that occasional mudrunner that wakes up when the track turns into a total mess. So the important thing to do is to separate those horses that won only because the track was wet from those that were more than capable of winning despite the fact that the conditions were off.

The first thing to look for when trying to make the separation is to consider only horses that won their last race by a large margin. In most situations, a win by a large margin would be considered anything that is three lengths or more. But to eliminate any possible error, the win margin should be doubled to six lengths or more.

Locating a horse that won his race by an impressive margin is a step in the right direction, but there's still an outside possibility of latching onto a mudrunner rather than a horse rounding into good form. The difference between the two can usually be told in the animal's previous races. If his past performance record indicates that he was previously beaten on an off track in one or more efforts, then there's a very good chance that his last race is a reflection of his good form. Even if he broke stride in one of his races on an off track, it would still indicate that he doesn't exactly cherish a wet racing surface.

A second type of horse that's worth locating is one that has a fast final time. An off track will usually slow down a race by at least two seconds. So any off track winner that has the fastest final time in a race would appear to be in a very good position for another victory.

9 RACE

ONE MILE PACE — Claiming Price $14,000. — Purse $6,000

PLEASE ASK FOR HORSE BY PROGRAM NUMBER

Date	Trk Cd Tem	Class	Dis	Leader's Time 1/4	1/2	3/4	Winner's Time	PP	1/4	1/2	3/4	Str	Fin	Ind Time	Odds	Driver	Order of Finish: First, Second, Third

Red 1 — DR. CONWAY — $14,000 — 6-1

B h 67 by Don Adios—Volo Dillard—John Dillard
Owner: Terry Brown, Viola, Ill.
1973 6 2 0 1 $6,580 2:05 Spk⅝
1972 33 2 5 4 $14,630 2:014 Was1
Lifetime thru 1972 $47,211

Driver—JOHNNY BLEVINS, White-Blue-Black — **Trainer—J. Blevins**

Date	Trk Cd Tem	Class	Dis	1/4	1/2	3/4	Winner's Time	PP	1/4	1/2	3/4	Str	Fin	Ind Time	Odds	Driver	Order of Finish
4-28	2Haw1 ft 43°	Cclm13000	1	:313	1:03	1:351	2:04	4	1	3	52½	53½	76½	2:052	9-2	(WPaisley)	StrongByrd, Rozella, LincolnsLogic
4-19	8Haw1 ft 67°	clm15000	1	:304	1:031	1:331	2:032	3	1	1	31½	46	512	2:054	*9-5	(WPaisley)	Airfare, McNavi, BigDaddysShadow
4-13	9Spk⅝ ft 39°	clm14000	1	:31	1:033	1:341	2:051	3	2	2	3	2½	12½	2:051	7-2	(WPaisley)	Dr.Conway, SummertimeDirect, McNavi
4- 5	8Spk⅝ ft 53°	Cclm11000	1	:294	1:022	1:332	2:05	2	4	4	5°	21¼	11½	2:05	*3-2	(SBanks)	Dr.Conway, StewartCraig, FirstLook
3-28	8Spk⅝ sy 50°	Cclm10000	1	:322	1:062	1:374	2:101	7	8	6°	2°	21½	3¾	2:102	10-1	(DaBusse)	FrostyWil, FirstLook, Dr.Conway
3-23	5Spk⅝ ft 45°	clm11000	1	:304	1:022	1:333	2:034	7	8	8°	8°	96	78½	2:053	14-1	(DaBusse)	Knoxella, ByrdMark, MataGay

White 2 — WINTER — $16,800 — 6-1

B g 69 by Winter Time—Pride's Leonard—Roxburgh Leonard
Own-r: Philip H. Benefiel, Calisle, Ind.
1973 14 2 2 3 $6 039 2:061 Spk⅝
1972 13 2 2 2 $2 921 2:053 Was1
Lifetime thru 1972 $2 921

Driver—CONNEL WILLIS, Red-White-Green — **Trainer—C. Willis**

Date	Trk Cd Tem	Class	Dis	1/4	1/2	3/4	Winner's Time	PP	1/4	1/2	3/4	Str	Fin	Ind Time	Odds	Driver	Order of Finish
5- 2	9Haw1 gd 42°	clm16800	1	:321	1:032	1:333	2:05	6	7	7	76½	45½	31½	2:052	14-1	(CWillis)	StewartCraig, EdgewoodKeene, Winter
4-24	9Haw1 ft 41°	stk8000	1	:304	1:021	1:333	2:024	8	8	8	75½	713	717	2:061	42-1	(CWillis)	PromsEasy, NobleSon, GaySkipper
4- 9	7Spk⅝ gd 33°	nw70007273	1	:312	1:054	1:361	2:083	4	6	5°	5°	46	33½	2:092	12-1	(CWillis)	ShiawaySandy, SoonerRace, Winter
3-31	7Spk⅝Asy44°	3-5yrstk5000	1	:314	1:063	1:371	2:074	8	8	8	8	811	812	2:101	17-1	(CWillis)	PrimsKnight, PacingBoy, L.E.Abbe
3-24	7Spk⅝ ft 48°	3-5yrstk5000	1	:311	1:034	1:361	2:061	2	2	2	3	61½	54¼	2:07	3-1	(CWillis)	RocketMan, LloydsTime, ArrivaByrd
3-17	10Spk⅝A ft35°	3-5ys:k5000	1	:312	1:033	1:331	2:052	4	5	5	6	54	2¾	2:053	6-1	(CWillis)	BreakWater, Winter, PacingBoy

Blue 3 — ‡SENATOR BERRY — $14,000 — 3-1

Ro g 67 by Hodgen—Miss Berry—Paul MacPherson
Owner: Ira Berger, Chicago, Ill.
1973 10 4 1 0 $12.163 2:032 sy Haw1
1972 26 4 4 4 $9.173 2:033 ScD⅝
Lifetime thru 1972 $13,775

Driver—BRENT CARTER, Blue-White — **Trainer—B. Carter**

Date	Trk Cd Tem	Class	Dis	1/4	1/2	3/4	Winner's Time	PP	1/4	1/2	3/4	Str	Fin	Ind Time	Odds	Driver	Order of Finish
4-30	7Haw1 sy 50°	‡clm13000	1	:304	1:02	1:33	2:032	6	8	6°	43	11¼	15½	2:032	5-2	(WPaisley)	SenatorBerry, GoranHanover, C.F.Guy
4-24	Haw1 ft 45°	‡Qua	1	:31	1:031	1:334	2:04	6	1°	1°	1½°	2½	21½	2:042	NB	(BCarter)	JeffersonSpeed,SenatorBerry,RangrRichrd
4-20	6Haw1 sy 64°	‡clm12000	1	:342	1:051	1:372	2:064	3	1	2	21½	11½	13¼	2:064	4-1	(WPaisley)	SenatorBerry, LittlePuff, NobleChoice
4-13	4Spk⅝ ft 39°	‡clm12000	1	:301	1:023	1:332	2:043	2	5	5	5	65½	44¼	2:052	13-1	(HGuerra)	StewartCraig, EyreFire, TecklaAdiosB.
4-11	8Spk⅝ sy 35°	‡clm12000	1	:311	1:042	1:371	2:091	7	8	8	7	87¼	911	2:112	20-1	(HGuerra)	TinaKnox, FrostyWil, FirstLook
4- 2	7Spk⅝ ft 42°	‡Cclm11000	1	:303	1:04	1:334	2:054	2	5	5	4°	21	45¾	2:07	*4-5	(JCurran)	TecklaAdiosB.,NbleChoice,SummrtmeDirct

Green 4 — CAROL CHIEF — $16,800 — 8-1

B m 66 by Mister Chief—Kay Song—Victory Song
Owner: Wrapack, Inc., Chicago, Ill.
1973 15 1 2 3 $9.675 2:062 BmlP
1972 32 8 6 4 $16.902 2:04 H.P.⅝
Lifetime thru 1972 $38.045

Driver—CARMEN ALESSI, Gold-White-Blue — **Trainer—C. Alessi**

Date	Trk Cd Tem	Class	Dis	1/4	1/2	3/4	Winner's Time	PP	1/4	1/2	3/4	Str	Fin	Ind Time	Odds	Driver	Order of Finish
4-30	9Haw1 sy 50°	clm19200	1	:304	1:01	1:323	2:032	3	5	5°	32½	88½	912	2:054	15-1	(CAlessi)	VictorysHorn, DyamiteWomen, RightLane
4-23	7Haw1 ft 51°	clm19200	1	:312	1:014	1:333	2:032	1	6	6	64	62½	42¾	2:04	7-1	(CAlessi)	BarkerBlack, TopallAdios, BirthdayDelight
4- 2	9Spk⅝ ft 42°	clm19200	1	:30	1:034	1:344	2:054	7	1	1	1	1¾	95½	2:07	7-1	(CAlessi)	MunciesAdios, PrincessJudith, Avanti
3-27	8Spk⅝ ft 38°	clm18000	1	:301	1:043	1:344	2:051	1	4	4	2°	2nk	32¼	2:053	*9-5	(CAlessi)	WardenIllmo, Avanti, CarolChief
3-20	8Spk⅝ ft 35°	clm18000	1	:312	1:041	1:341	2:053	7	2°	1	2	11	31¾	2:06	*2-1	(CAlessi)	SpringMeadow, Avanti, CarolChief
3-15	8Spk⅝ ft 46°	clm18000	1	:313	1:044	1:34	2:042	3	3	3	3	33¾	2nk	2:042	*2-1	(CAlessi)	BarkerBlack, CarolChief, Boyduplicate

Black 5 — MATA GAY — $14,000 — 6-1

Br g 65 by Matastar—Trudy Gay—The Intruder
Owners: Ralph &Paul I. Spadafore, Pontiac, Mich.
1973 8 0 1 3 $2 827
1972 16 6 3 2 $12.751 2:031 H.P.⅝
Lifetime thru 1972 $12,751

Driver—JOE MARSH, JR., Gray-Blue-Red — **Trainer—J. Marsh, Jr.**

Date	Trk Cd Tem	Class	Dis	1/4	1/2	3/4	Winner's Time	PP	1/4	1/2	3/4	Str	Fin	Ind Time	Odds	Driver	Order of Finish
3-23	5Spk⅝ ft 45°	clm11000	1	:304	1:022	1:333	2:034	8	9	9	9	53½	32	2:041	6-1	(JMarshJr)	Knoxella, ByrdMark, MataGay
3- 3	4Spk⅝ ft 50°	clm9000	1	:29	1:004	1:34	2:054	3	5	6	9	53¼	2nkdb	2:054	3-1	(JMarshJr)	G.T.Winter, MataGay, Mr.Thunderbyrd
2-24	5Spk⅝ ft 35°	clm9000	1	:314	1:043	1:361	2:063	5	6	6	7°	76	63¾	2:072	3-1	(JMarshJr)	EyreNavarch, Mose, BluCreed
2- 9	Y.R. ft	clm10000	1	:303	1:021	1:34	2:061	1	5	6	7°	52¾	32	2:063	*3-2	(WGilmour)	RoyalGenePick, CarolinaCotton, MataGay
2- 2	Y.R. sy	clm10000	1	:323	1:061	1:384	2:111	6	5	5	5°	53½	3¾	2:112	3-1	(WGilmour)	JimmyHayes, CarolinaCotton, MataGay
1-19	Y.R. sy	clm10000	1	:324	1:052	1:39	2:112	7	7	7	7	74¼	52	2:114	17-1	(WGilmour)	Cornell, McOClu, GetGoingA

Yellow 6 — C. R. PURDUE — $14,000 — 5-1

B g 67 by Purdue Hal—Lady Chuck—Parker Byrd
Owner: Ken Vander Schaaf, Sandwich, Ill.
1973 17 7 1 1 $14.359 2:033 sy Haw1
1972 41 3 7 4 $10.600 2:08 Spk⅝
Lifetime thru 1972 $16,824

Driver—STANLEY BANKS, White-Purple — **Trainer—K. Vander Schaaf**

Date	Trk Cd Tem	Class	Dis	1/4	1/2	3/4	Winner's Time	PP	1/4	1/2	3/4	Str	Fin	Ind Time	Odds	Driver	Order of Finish
5- 1	9Haw1 sy 62°	clm11000	1	:323	1:051	1:363	2:081	4	4	5	64	66½	1nk	2:081	*9-5	(SBanks)	C.R.Purdue, EyreFire, Knoxella
4-21	5Haw1 sy 58°	clm8000	1	:313	1:02	1:332	2:033	9	2	2	21½	11	15¾	2:033	7-2	(SBanks)	C.R.Purdue, QuickBay, DaveWestern
4-13	10Spk⅝ ft 39°	clm7500	1	:304	1:022	1:333	2:044	4	6	6	7°	42	1ns	2:044	5-1	(SBanks)	C.R.Purdue, WesternsJody, GrandAce
4- 4	5Spk⅝ gd 36°	clm6000	1	:31	1:04	1:352	2:072	2	5	5	7	52	11½	2:072	5-1	(SBanks)	C.R.Purdue, GrandClara, PlutoHal
3-27	6Spk⅝ ft 38°	Cclm5000	1	:322	1:052	1:363	2:072	5	6	6	5	37	34½	2:082	9-1	(DSheely)	FlubAdubAdoo. Papa. C.R.Purdue
3-19	10Spk⅝ ft 33°	clm6000	1	:301	1:012	1:324	2:044	3	8	8	8°	68½	68¼	2:062	8-1	(DSheely)	LoisAmigo, MisterAdios, CarlenDirtyBird

Brown 7 — EMPY — $16,800 — 8-1

B m 68 by Coffee Break—Banker Girl—Hector Prim
Owners: Richard J. & Merrie Gurrola, LaPorte, Ind.
1973 6 1 1 1 $3 483 2:062 L.A.⅝
1972 30 2 5 6 $14.038 2:043 Haw1
Lifetime thru 1972 $26.369

Driver—TOM RATCHFORD, Gold-White — **Trainer—T. Ratchford**

Date	Trk Cd Tem	Class	Dis	1/4	1/2	3/4	Winner's Time	PP	1/4	1/2	3/4	Str	Fin	Ind Time	Odds	Driver	Order of Finish
4-30	7Haw1 sy 50°	clm15600	1	:304	1:02	1:33	2:032	2	3	5	68	55	79½	2:052	5-1	(TRatchford)	SenatorBerry, GoranHanover, C.F.Guy
4-23	10Haw1 ft 51°	clm16800	1	:321	1:044	1:354	2:054	7	8	8°	64½	41¼	41½	2:061	7-1	(TRatchford)	EdgewoodKeene.BillsDaughtr,StwartCraig
4-10	L.A. ft	clm18000	1	:301	1:012	1:323	2:014	1	4	4	2	21	31¾	2:021	8-1	(JDennis)	RickyCounsel, Propeller, Empy
3-31	L.A.⅝ ft	Cclm12000	1	:30	1:022	1:324	2:032	1	5	5	5	65¼	51¾	2:034	4-1	(RVallesKey)	Mt.AiryBill, GoodTimeLad, ChiefRed
3-24	L.A.⅝ ft	Cclm9600	1	:314	1:052	1:354	2:062	2	3	2	1	12	1nk	2:062	*1-1	(JDennis)	Empy, MarluGus, SaintClairChief
3-17	L.A.⅝ ft	clm9000	1	:304	1:014	1:322	2:033	8	7	7	6	42½	2nk	2:033	8-1	(JDennis)	GreenbergOBrien, Empy, NeveleBlaze

Red & Yellow 8 — FRANADIO — $14,000 — 10-1

B g 66 by Adios Bomber—Franselka—Selka's King
Owner: Mayo Priebe, Jr. (Lessee), Rochester, Minn.
1973 1 0 0 0 (——)
1972 10 0 2 0 $1.820
Lifetime thru 1972 $27,333

Driver—GLEN KIDWELL, Blue-Gold — **Trainer—M. Priebe, Jr.**

Date	Trk Cd Tem	Class	Dis	1/4	1/2	3/4	Winner's Time	PP	1/4	1/2	3/4	Str	Fin	Ind Time	Odds	Driver	Order of Finish
4-25	5Haw1 ft 51°	nw70007273	1	:304	1:022	1:344	2:042	2	1	3	42¼	913	917	2:08	75-1	(GKidwell)	SherwoodDancer, H.W.Express, BretsTune
11-22	3Was1 gd 34°	nw300072	1	:302	1:032	1:36	2:071	3	3	5	7	918	9dis		9-1	(DShetlerJr)	VarsityKing, FlyingBaron, BugerBear
11- 9	6Was1 ft 43°	nw200072	1	:313	1:012	1:334	2:054	6	2°	1°	2°	64	611	2:08	6-1	(DShetlerJr)	ReggieCommandr,DearBaroness,BraveTme
10- 2	7Was1 ft 65°	nw300072	1	:30	1:00	1:323	2:033	3	5	5	54¼	912	824	2:082	7-2	(DShetlerJr)	NeverSayDieA., ArcolaKid, YathongLad
9-20	7Was1 ft 70°	nw400072	1	:304	1:003	1:331	2:034	2	1	3	42½	32½	58¼	2:052	2-1	(DShetlerJr)	FourOaks. Plunder, Katfish
9-15	5Was1 ft 69°	nw400072	1	:293	1:004	1:331	2:041	8	3°	3	32	41½	2hd	2:041	11-1	(DShetlerJr)	KimTamTime, Franadio, FireBomb

Orange 9 — AVANTI — $14,000 — 12-1

B g 67 by Diller Hanover—Tonette Hanover—Spencer Scott.
Owners: H. E. Wagley & J. Schilling, Chicago, Ill., St. John, Ind.
1973 17 2 6 4 $12 357 2:071 BmlP
1972 25 4 3 2 $6.628 2:032 ScD⅝
Lifetime thru 1972 $8,692

Driver—JAMES MORRISSEY, Green-White-Yellow — **Trainer—J. Morrissey**

Date	Trk Cd Tem	Class	Dis	1/4	1/2	3/4	Winner's Time	PP	1/4	1/2	3/4	Str	Fin	Ind Time	Odds	Driver	Order of Finish
5- 2	9Haw1 gd 42°	clm14000	1	:321	1:032	1:333	2:05	8	8	9	98	916	97¾	2:063	8-1	(JMorrissey)	StewartCraig, EdgewoodKeene, Winter
4-25	9Haw1 ft 46°	clm14000	1	:311	1:021	1:341	2:043	6	8	8	86½°	43	22¼dh	2:05	8-1	(JMorrissey)	RuthsChoice, Edstime-dh-Avanti
4-17	8Haw1 ft 56°	clm17500	1	:303	1:01	1:321	2:032	7	7	7	77½	77	78	2:05	13-1	(JMorrissey)	PatPlutocrat, SkiSlope, MountainScout
4- 2	9Spk⅝ ft 42°	clm16000	1	:30	1:034	1:344	2:054	6	2	2	2	2¾	31½	2:061	10-1	(JMorrissey)	MunciesAdios, PrincessJudith, Avanti
3-27	8Spk⅝ ft 38°	clm15000	1	:301	1:043	1:344	2:051	3	5	5	7	62¼	22	2:053	10-1	(JMorrissey)	WardenIllmo, Avanti, CarolChief
3-20	8Spk⅝ ft 35°	clm15000	1	:312	1:041	1:341	2:053	2	6	6	4	32	2¾	2:054	7-1	(JMorrissey)	SpringMeadow, Avanti, CarolChief

TRACKMAN'S SELECTIONS — 3-6-2

PHIL'S PICKS — 2-3-9

The ninth race at Hawthorne Race Course on May 9 produced such a horse. It was a $14,000 claiming race and it brought together a field of nine. The fastest final time in the race belongs to Senator Berry. The six year old gelding won his last effort in 2:03 2/5 over a sloppy track. The next closest final time that took place on a fast track is Carol Chief with a 2:04. Another final time that shouldn't be overlooked is C. R. Purdue's 2:03 3/5. His race was contested on a sloppy track, but his final time is still one tick slower than Senator Berry's final time. You'll also note the decisive class edge that Senator Berry holds over C. R. Purdue.

NINTH RACE—ONE MILE PACE—PURSE $6,000
Claiming Price $16,800-$14,000.
Time—:31 1:02^{3} 1:33^{1} 2:03^{2} Mutuel Pool $95,027
AVANTI disqualified and Placed Eighth for impeding EMPY in stretch

3 Senator Berry	3	5	5	5^{3½}	1^{nk}	1^{1½}	2:03^{2}	*9-5	(BCarter)
4 Carol Chief	4	6	6	6^{5}	4^{2½}	2^{1½}	2:03^{4}	7-1	(CAlessi)
2 Winter	2	4	4	4^{2}	3^{1}	3^{1½}	2:03^{4}	6-1	(CWillis)
9 Avanti	9	2°	2	3^{1}	5^{3½}	4^{3¾}p8	2:04^{1}	23-1	(JMorrissey)
6 C. R. Purdue	6	8	8	7^{6}	7^{5}	5^{5}p4	2:04^{2}	7-2	(SBanks)
1 Dr. Conway	1	3	3	1^{¾}	2^{nk}	6^{5¼}p5	2:04^{2}	14-1	(JBlevins)
5 Mata Gay	5	7	7	8^{6½}	8^{6½}	7^{5¾}p6	2:04^{3}	4-1	(JMarshJr)
7 Empy	7	9	9	9^{7½}	im6^{4}	8^{6}p7	2:04^{3}	13-1	(TRatchford)
8 Franadio	8	1	1°	2^{¾}	9^{15}	9^{20}	2:07^{2}	65-1	(GKidwell)

MUTUELS—(3) $5.60 $3.60 $2.80—(4) $6.60 $3.80—(2) $3.60

The race turned out to be a fairly easy win for Senator Berry. It's not very surprising that he was sent off as the 9-5 favorite and returned only $5.60 to win. But it's not a bad price for so little an effort in handicapping.

Horses that are as well placed as Senator Berry do not exactly run every week. An off track will usually slow down a horse to the point where it's impossible to compare his final time to the rest of the field. So the best thing to do is to rely on off track winners that won their race by six lengths or more as long as they show at least one losing effort on a wet surface.

Park on June 15. Wenevir Bert won his last race going away by 8 1/4 lengths over a good track. The question of whether he's just another animal that wakes up when the conditions are off as opposed to a horse coming into his own is an easy one. Take a look at his two previous efforts that were contested on an off track. On May 1, he turned in a pretty good race but there were still five horses that crossed the finish line in front of him. The race that's really a dead giveaway is the one just prior to that. He was clobbered by Senator Berry by 11 lengths.

If we were to handicap Wenevir Bert off his last race on a fast track, we would be giving him an unfair analysis of his current form. That, in turn, creates another problem. When a horse makes a major improvement in his current form, he's also increasing his class capability. So a $2,000 class hike for Wenevir Bert would not appear to be out of line. An 8-length plus triumph in $10,000 company indicates that he would fit in well against $12,000 claimers.

TENTH RACE — 1 MILE
PACE. Claming $12,000. 3 Years & Up. Purse $5.000.
Time—:30^{2} 1:03^{2} 1:33 2:03^{2} Mutuel Pool—$56.360

1. Wenevir Bert	1	2	4^{3}	4^{2}°	1^{1}	1^{2½}	2:03^{2}	3-1	(J.MarshJr)
2. Pleasem	2	5	8^{6}	6^{4}	5^{3}	2^{2½}	2:04	12-1	(S.Banks)
3. Tommy Lobell	3	3°	1^{1½}	2^{ns}	2^{1}	3^{2¾}	2:04	4-1	(J.Dolbee)
4. Ruth's Choice	4	6	3^{2½}°	1^{ns}	3^{2}	4^{3¾}	2:04^{1}	*5-2	(W Moore)
9. Pluto Hal	9	1	2^{1½}	3^{1}	4^{2½}	5^{4¼}	2:04^{1}	18-1	(W.Beckley)
8. Dr. Conway	8	9	9^{7}	9^{7½}	7^{6}	6^{4¼}	2:04^{1}	20-1	(Da.Busse)
7. Hardy Bob	7	8	7^{5½}°	8^{5½}	8^{7}	7^{5½}	2:04^{3}	11-1	(A.Petty)
6. Tina Knox	6	7	5^{4}°	7^{4½}°	9^{7½}	8^{5½}	2:04^{3}	4-1	(W.Pasley)
5. Brilliant Speed	5	4	6^{4½}	5^{2½}	6^{4}x	9^{13}	2:06	12-1	(C.McDermtt)

Mutuels—(1) 8.60 7.00 6.80—(2) 9.80 9.20—(3) 6.00

Wenevir Bert not only went out and won the race, but he also lowered his lifetime mark in the process. His time for the mile was 2:03 2/5, the fastest winning time ever for Wenevir Bert. His price wasn't that bad either. He returned a respectable $8.60 to win.

RED
1
9-2
+

Driver—JOE MARSH, JR., Gray-Blue-Red Tr.—J. Marsh, Jr. (83-13-7-11—.245)
1973 8 1 0 1 $4,291 2:07 gd Spk⅝
1972 25 4 3 3 $12,686 2:05^{2} gd Was^{1}
Lifetime $16,344 4, 2:05^{2} (1) gd

WENEVIR BERT Ch g 1968, by Newport—Mighty Sis—Mighty H
Owner: Nicholas J. Wall, Cicero, Ill.

6- 4^{10}Spk⅝ gd 67°	clm10000=	1	:31^{1}	1:05^{4}	1:37^{2}	2:07	3	5	6^{5½}°	3^{1½}°	1^{3}	1^{8¼}	2:07	*3-1	(J.MarshJr)	WenevirBert, TerryJeansRocket, C.F.Guy	(big win)
5-25 ^{2}Haw^{1} ft 58°	clm10000	1	:32	1:03^{3}	1:33^{3}	2:05	5	7	3°	2^{hd}	1^{1½}	3^{hd}	2:05	*2-1	(J.MarshJr)	DaddioMac, BillyTime, WenevirBert	(just failed)
5-18 ^{6}Haw^{1} ft 66°	clm12500	1	:31^{4}	1:03^{3}	1:35	2:04^{1}	2	3	5	5^{2½}	6^{3½}	5^{2¼}	2:04^{3}	3-1	(J.MarshJr)	LocalLie, Boyduplicate, MunciesAdios	(went evenly)
5-10^{10}Haw^{1} ft 62°	clm10000 C	1	:32^{1}	1:02^{4}	1:34^{1}	2:05^{4}	5	6	8	8^{7}°	2^{½}	4^{½}	2:06	9-1	(G.Wentz)	ChiefRagtime, NoCredit, ShiawayPercy	(good effort)
5- 1 ^{9}Haw^{1} sy 66°	clm11000	1	:32^{3}	1:05^{1}	1:36^{3}	2:08^{1}	9	9	9	9^{9½}	8^{9}	6^{2}	2:08^{3}	37-1	(G.Wentz)	C.R.Purdue, EyreFire, Knoxella	(late brush)
4-20 ^{6}Haw^{1} gd 64°	clm12000	1	:34^{2}	1:05^{1}	1:37^{2}	2:06^{4}	8	8	8	6^{7}	5^{4}	7^{11}	2:09	15-1	(G.Wentz)	SenatorBerry, LittlePuff, NobleChoice	(tired)

The past performance record of Wenevir Bert is a good case in point. The five year old gelding was entered in a $12,000 claiming race at Sportsman's

The past performance record of Near Chief reflects another off track winner coming into good form. The five year old gelding was entered in a

$9,000 claiming race on June 9 at Sportsman's Park. Near Chief, like Wenevir Bert, was an impressive winner in his last race. He romped home by more than 9 lengths on a track labeled sloppy. Although Near Chief turned in a good effort on an off track on April 20, there's no reason to believe that he's strictly an off track performer. On May 7, he tested a sloppy racing surface and it turned out to be a poor effort. He had the lead at the quarter, was second at the half mile mark, dropped back to fourth position after three quarters of the mile, and eventually broke stride in the stretch. Not exactly the kind of race you would expect from a good mudrunner.

board again. This time he beat $12,000 claimers and returned $17.00 to win.

Horses that do their best running on an off track will usually flop when the conditions are labeled fast. That's why you must know how to separate a mudrunner from a horse that would have won regardless of the conditions. Picking winners is important, but eliminating losers is part of the game too.

NON-WINNER CHOICES

When it comes to those tough non-winner events, you'll find the maiden race on the bottom of the totem pole. It's the one type of race that can

WHITE **3** 6-1 +	Driver—DARYL BUSSE, Gray-Red				Tr.—R. Searle		(22-3-2-3—.232)			1973	13	3	2	0	$7,565	2:07³ sy Spk⅝	
	NEAR CHIEF	B g 1968, by Newport—Blackhawks Queen—Knight Pilot								1972	9	1	1	0	$2,532	2:08⁴ sy Haw¹	
	Owner: Ed & Estell Caudell & T. Bretsnyder, N. Aurora, Wheaton, Ill.											Lifetime			$2,569	4, 2:08⁴ sy (1)	

5-28	⁶Spk⅝ sy 52°	clm7000—1	:31¹ 1:04⁴ 1:35⁴ 2:07³	6	2	2½	1³	1⁵	1⁹¼	2:07³	5-1	(Da.Busse)	NearChief, ShadyByrd, EllyMarie	(tons best)
5-15	⁸Haw¹ ft 56°	clm8000	1 :32¹ 1:04² 1:36² 2:06	7	7	8	7⁹	7³	7⁴½	2:07	10-1	(E.Lutes)	T.D.Blaze, HopeImperial, RealBlast	(raced well)
5- 7	¹⁰Haw¹ sy 60°	clm10000	1 :30⁴ 1:03³ 1:36 2:06	6	1	2	4³	x9¹¹	89½	2:08	8-1	(E.Lutes)	ValiantSampson, WesternsJody, NbleScot	(costly break)
4-28	¹⁰Haw¹ ft 43°	clm10000 1¹⁄₁₆	:29 :59²		1:22³	8	7	7°	5⁶½°	3²½	5³	1:23¹ 14-1 (E.Lutes)	HarkWay, LovinLuLu, SenatorGlib	(3-wide turn)
4-20	¹⁰Haw¹ gd 64°	clm10000 1¹⁄₁₆	:32 1:05¹² 09¹ 2:17²	6	2	3	3³	1²	2¹	2:17³	5-1	(E.Lutes)	SilentTona, NearChief, SandBandit	(good move)
4-13	⁵Spk⅝ ft 39°	nw4R—1	:31¹ 1:03² 1:34¹ 2:04	6	7	7⁷½	8⁵¼	8⁷	89¾	2:06	54-1	(E.Lutes)	ApoloMeridale, NoFear, DodgeAcresElla	(soundly beaten)

If we were to throw out Near Chief's last race, we would encounter the same kind of problem that occurred with Wenevir Bert. Near Chief's next to last race does not represent his true class or current form. But with the information from his previous races, we would know there's no need to use his next to last race. His runaway victory for $7,000 is more than enough to compensate a $2,000 class hike.

SIXTH RACE — 1 MILE
PACE Claiming $9,000. 3 Years & Up. Purse $4,200.
Time—:29⁴ 1:02³ 1:32³ 2:02³   Mutuel Pool—$11,591

dd.No.	horse	PP	¼	½	¾	Str	Fin	Ind.Time	Odds	(Driver)
3.	Near Chief	3	1	2¹½	2¹¼	3½	1ⁿˢ	2:02³	10-1	(Da.Busse)
5.	C. R. Purdue	5	7	6⁷½°	7⁶°	5²	2ⁿˢ	2:02³	7-2	(S.Banks)
1.	Re Mark	1	5	5⁶½	5⁵°	6⁴	3¹¾	2:03	7-2	(W.Paisley)
8.	Senator Glib	8	2°	1¹½	1¹¼	1ʰᵈ	4²	2:03	14-1	(W.Moore)
4.	Chief Ragtime	4	6	7⁸	6⁶	7⁶	5⁵¼	2:03³	10-1	(J.Dolbee)
2.	Mr. Thunderbyrd	2	3	3³	4³	4¹ix	6⁶	2:03⁴	*2-1	(J.MarshJr)
9.	Aljean's Don	9	8	8¹¹	8⁸	8⁸	7⁶¼	2:03⁴	20-1	(J.Morrissey)
7.	El Barb	7	4	4⁴½	3²¼°	2ʰᵈx	8⁸¼	2:04¹	6-1	(GVllndnghm)
6.	Eldora's Boy	6	x9	x9²³	9²³	9²³	9¹⁸	2:06¹	33-1	(N.Willis)

Mr. Thunderbyrd claimed for $9,000 by Steven Vollaro and Stephen Levenson, trainer —S. Vollaro.
Mutuels—(3) 23.80 8.00 6.80—(5) 4.40 3.60—(1) 5.20

Near Chief also took a new lifetime mark with his winning effort. He paced the mile in 2:02 3/5, something you might not expect him to do by reading his past performance record. He paid $23.80 to win for one of the better overlays of the year. Just nine days later, Near Chief lit up the

either make or break the handicapper. If you want to try to recoup some of your earlier losses, then look no further than a race confined to maidens only. Big payoffs are as common in maiden races as tomato juice is in bloody marys. But if you want to keep your money, or better yet, keep your sanity, then forget maiden races entirely.

The reason why big payoffs are so common in maiden races is because there's no such thing as a horse that figures. The animals have yet to establish their true racing abilities, so the unexpected is very likely to happen. A horse can take it on the chin by 20 lengths in his last race and then turn in a big effort his next time out. That kind of thing can happen in any contest, but let's face it, it happens much more frequently in maiden races.

The best alternative you have to wagering on maiden races is a simple one: Never play the race no matter how good a horse looks on paper. Why risk any money on a race where current form is something that changes from week to week and where the class factor is totally nonexistent.

Events that are conditioned for "non-winners of two races in lifetime" are not much more appealing than maiden affairs. You still must be a bit suspicious of current form. The only class edge a competitor can have is if he's facing a maiden. Of course, there will be times when you come across a horse that looks like an absolute standout. But I doubt very much that a horse like this will be overlooked. There's a very good chance that he'll go off at odds on. There's also a very good chance that he'll turn in a losing effort. Dependability is still something that is rare, so it's best that races for non-winners of two are never played.

Bordering on the line which divides the playable race from the unplayable are events conditioned for "non-winners of three or four races in lifetime." The majority of these races are somewhat on the risky side, but occasionally you can pinpoint a horse that is worth following. The idea behind handicapping a race is to locate a horse that is well placed. But these events demand a little bit more than just a well-placed horse, so we'll have to take it one step further.

In Chapter 6, we used advantage ratings to handicap a race. The contender with the fastest final time became the prime horse. To become a final choice, it was mandatory that the prime horse comply with at least three of the remaining seven advantages. A similar approach is used for locating the final choice in races for non-winners of two or three. Again the prime horse must have the fastest final time out of all the contenders. But in this situation, two more advantages have been added. Now a prime horse must meet at least five advantages to become a final choice.

1. FASTEST FINAL TIME: The contender with the fastest final time becomes the prime horse. Final times are only compared to conten-

ders, not non-contenders. When a prime horse is found, proceed to advantages two through ten to see which ones apply to him.

2. FASTEST LAST HALF: The prime horse's last half must be at least 1/5 of a second faster than all other contenders.

3. FASTEST FINAL QUARTER: The prime horse's final quarter must also be at least 1/5 of a second faster than all other contenders.

4. EDGE ON CLASS: This advantage applies to the prime horse only if the class level in his contending race is higher than that at which all other contenders raced in their contending race.

5. BREAK IN POST POSITION: The prime horse must be moving in at least two posts over the post position he received in his contending race.

6. PARKED OUT RACE: The prime horse receives this advantage if he was parked out for two or more turns in his contending race.

7. GOOD MOVE IN STRETCH: This advantage applies to the prime horse if he made up three lengths or more in the final quarter.

8. OFF A WINNING EFFORT: The prime horse must be coming off a win. If he won his contending race and was disqualified, he's still considered to be coming off a winning effort.

9. BETTER THAN AVERAGE DRIVER: Experience tells the handicapper which drivers are better than average. If you prefer, use this advantage if the driver has been averaging one win for every six drives or if he has a driver percentage of .275 or better.

10. SHORT LAYOFF: This advantage applies to the prime horse if he's returning to the race track within ten days of his last start.

GREEN **4** 6-1 +

Driver—WALTER PAISLEY, Green-White Tr.—D. Frederick (235-46-40-36—.343)

TIME MAKER B c 1970. by Mahone Time—Sis King—Royal King
Owner: Robert H. Venable, Champaign, Ill.

1973 7 2 2 1 $4,279 2:02^3 Spk⅝
1972 19 10 2 2 $5,903 2:08 Char
Lifetime $5,903 2, 2:08

7- 7	^{3}Spk⅝ ft 90°	nw3R=1	:30^1	1:01	1:31^2	2:02	6	[illegible]	[illegible]	$5^{3\frac{3}{4}}$°	2^3	2^{ns}	2:02	3-1 (J.MarshJr)	BarbaraAlmahurst, TimeMaker, JoansGene (late close)
6-28	^{7}Spk⅝ ft 64°	nw3R+1	:31^1	1:03	1:32^3	2:03^3	7	7	$7^{6\frac{3}{4}}$	$6^{5\frac{1}{4}}$°	5^3	$3^{1\frac{1}{2}}$	2:04	9-2 (W.Paisley)	LoyalTime, JoansGene, TimeMaker (good last ½)
6-20	^{6}Spk⅝ ft 76°	3-4yrnw2R+1	:30^1	1:02^2	1:33^4	2:04^3	6	5	$5^{4\frac{1}{4}}$	$2^{\frac{3}{4}}$°	2^{hd}	5^2	2:05	*6-5 (DwPletcher)	MayzieWellmnr, BrbraAlmhrst, CmdrBrks (str bid, hung)
6-11	^{2}Spk⅝ ft 89°	nw1R−1	:30^2	1:03	1:33	2:02^3	1	3	2^2	$3^{1\frac{3}{4}}$	$1^{\frac{1}{2}}$	$1^{1\frac{1}{2}}$	2:02^3	*1-2 (W.Paisley)	TimeMaker, MarshallRanger, StaceyTime (fast time)
5-31	^{9}Spk⅝ ft 74°	3yrstk5700=1	:29	1:00^3	1:32^2	2:02^4	2	2	3^1	3^1	$1^{\frac{1}{2}}$	$2^{\frac{3}{4}}$	2:03	15-1 (G.Montgmry)	P.B.Mar, TimeMaker, GoldenTimmy (hung tough)
5-26	^{3}Spk⅝ ft 60°	3yrstk9630+1	:29^4	1:00^1	1:31^2	2:01	1	4	$5^{5\frac{1}{2}}$	5^3	$4^{6\frac{1}{2}}$	6^{10}	2:03	20-1 (G.Montgmry)	RobbRanger, SlippinBy, CarryOnChief (not gd enough)

BLACK **5** 5-1 +

Driver—STANLEY BANKS, White-Purple Tr.—D. Perrin (144-17-23-14—.239)

HEATHER RUSS B g 1970, by Meadow Russ—Breezemor—Eddy Scot
Owner: Carson L. Perrin, Beloit, Wisc.

1973 17 2 2 2 $8,432 2:03^3 Spk⅝
1972 11 3 1 2 $2,891 2:10 Aldo
Lifetime $2,891 2, 2:10

7- 6	^{4}Spk⅝ ft 83°	nw3R−1	:29^3	1:02^1	1:32^4	2:03^3	1	3	$3^{2\frac{1}{4}}$	$5^{3\frac{1}{4}}$	$5^{2\frac{1}{2}}$	1^{nk}	2:03^3	*5-2 (S.Banks)	HeatherRuss, GoldenTimmy, MannartDuer (just up)
6-22	^{4}Spk⅝ ft 76°	nw14000^{7273}=1	:29^4	1:02^4	1:32^2	2:02	2	4	$4^{4\frac{1}{2}}$	4^3	6^5	3^3	2:02^3	16-1 (S.Banks)	BrennaScot, BretsTune, HeatherRuss (closed some)
6-12	^{7}Spk⅝ ft 65°	nw12500^{7273}=1	:30	1:01^2	1:31	2:01^3	2	4	$4^{3\frac{1}{2}}$	1^1	2^3	$2^{7\frac{1}{4}}$	2:03	14-1 (S.Banks)	BrennaSct. HeathrRuss, WntrSymphny (bid, weakened)
6- 5	^{9}Spk⅝ sy65°	nw12000^{7273}+1	:33	1:06	1:37	2:06^3	5	6	7^7	$8^{4\frac{1}{2}}$	$6^{5\frac{1}{2}}$	$4^{2\frac{1}{2}}$	2:07^1	23-1 (S.Banks)	SlippinBy, BrennaScot, L.R.Adios (last ½ good)
5-25	^{3}Haw^1 ft 58°	nw3R 1	:31	1:01	1:31^1	2:01	1	3	5	5^5	3^8	5^{11}	2:03^1	6-1 (S.Banks)	BigBub, BarbaraAlmahurst, GrandClara (no chance)
5-16	^{5}Haw^1 ft 43°	nw3R 1	:31^3	1:02^4	1:33^2	2:04^1	1	3	7	$7^{7\frac{1}{2}}$	3^5	3^{nk}	2:04^1	13-1 (S.Banks)	LollipopWave, ReallyBombed, HeatherRuss (strong rally)

Any prime horse that complies with at least five advantages would have enough factors going for him to outweigh the protests of even the most conservative spot player. Those of you who wait for a horse to be in the right spot would not ordinarily have to demand this much out of your selection. But in tough non-winner races, it's best to get as much out of the horse as possible.

A good example of this type of horse is Time Maker. The three year old colt was entered in a conditioned event for "non-winners of four races in lifetime." The race took place at Sportsman's Park on July 12. Three horses, Golden Timmy, Loyal Time, and Heather Russ, appeared to be the stiffest competition for Time Maker. Or at least at a glance they appear to be. Time Maker's final time of 2:02 is the fastest out of the contenders, which makes him the prime horse. The advantages that make him the final choice are as follows:

2. FASTEST LAST HALF:
   Time Maker 59 3/5
   Loyal Time 1:00
   Golden Timmy 1:00 2/5
   Heather Russ 1:01
3. FASTEST FINAL QUARTER:
   Time Maker 29 4/5
   Loyal Time 30 1/5
   Golden Timmy 30 1/5
   Heather Russ 30 3/5

5. BREAK IN POST POSITION: Time Maker moves in two slots from the six to the four over his last race.

7. GOOD MOVE IN STRETCH: The three year old colt made up 3 3/4 lengths in the final quarter.

9. BETTER THAN AVERAGE DRIVER: In the sulky is the very capable Walter Paisley with a driver's percentage of .343.

10. SHORT LAYOFF: Time Maker returns to the race track after a five day rest.

EIGHTH RACE — 1 MILE

PACE. Conditioned — 3 Year Olds and Upward — Non-winners of 4 races or $8,000 in Lifetime. (Races for $750 or less not considered as wins.) Purse $3,300.

Time—:30^3 1:03^3 1:32^3 2:02^4 Mutuel Pool—$99.779

4. Time Maker	4	1	2^1°	$1^{\frac{1}{2}}$	1^2	1^1	2:02^4	*2-1 (W.Paisley)
8. Jan Byrd	8	2°	1^1	$3^{1\frac{1}{2}}$	2^2	2^1	2:03	14-1 (C.LoranceSr)
3. Loyal Time	3	5	5^4	7^5	$7^{6\frac{1}{2}}$	$3^{4\frac{1}{4}}$	2:03^3	5-1 (J.Curran)
5. Heather Russ	5	6	$8^{6\frac{1}{2}}$	6^4°	5^5	$4^{5\frac{1}{2}}$	2:04	6-1 (S.Banks)
6. Native Gem	6	7	6^5°	4^3°	$4^{4\frac{1}{2}}$	$5^{5\frac{1}{2}}$	2:04	6-1 (J.Dennis)
1. Golden Timmy	1	4	4^3°	2^1°	3^4	$6^{7\frac{1}{4}}$	2:04^1	7-2 (Da.Busse)
7. Little Will	7	9	7^6	$8^{5\frac{1}{2}}$°	8^7	$7^{8\frac{1}{2}}$	2:04^3	12-1 (B.Nickells)
2. Embassy Volo	2	3	$3^{2\frac{1}{2}}$	$5^{3\frac{1}{2}}$	6^6	8^{10}	2:04^4	19-1 (L.Rapone)
9. Star Check	9	8°	$9^{8\frac{1}{2}}$	9^{14}	9^{17}	9^{14}	2:05^3	23-1 (J.Vollaro)

Mutuels—(4) 6.40 4.40 3.40—(8) 12.00 5.60—(3) 4.20

Time Maker had a fairly easy time of it, winning the race with a mile in 2:02 4/5. He returned $6.40 to win even though he was listed at 6-1 in the morning line. It's interesting to note that Time Maker faced Loyal Time on June 28 with the latter getting the win. But the improvement that Time Maker made in his last race is more than enough to compensate for that losing effort. The fans certainly noticed it because it was Loyal Time that was the morning line favorite.

Events that are conditioned for "non-winners of three or four races in lifetime" are difficult to handicap. Relying on horses such as Time Maker may not be the whole answer. A horse that reflects his past performance record in a similar situation would probably not go off at better than 3-1 odds. But it's better to play it safe than to play it broke.

The Single Shaft Sulky

On June 20, 1970 at Garden City Raceway in St.

Catherines, Ontario, a pacer by the name of Meadowview Ben took a new lifetime mark. I doubt very much that this piece of news was ever picked up by the wire services. After all, how many people would have been interested in knowing that a five year old gelding just paced the mile in 2:04 2/5, even if it was the fastest winning mile in Meadowview Ben's racing career.

Although the story of Meadowview Ben will remain in total obscurity forever, it was actually the beginning of the most revolutionary change in sulky design since 1892. The five year old gelding was the first horse ever to pull a single shaft sulky in an actual race.

The inventor of the single shaft sulky is Joe King, an aeronautical engineer from Ormond Beach, Florida. Unlike the conventional sulky, which has one wooden pole on either side of the horse, the single shaft sulky is exactly what its name implies. It has one large steel shaft that arches over the horse's back and attaches to a single point behind his neck. On the conventional buggy, the driver sits with his legs wide apart; on the SSS, the driver keeps his legs together with his feet passing through two stirrups that are placed on a small steel crossbar.

A pacer with the single shaft sulky enters the winners circle. (Photo by Kuprion.)

The single shaft sulky has been known to improve some horses' time by as much as five full seconds. It's been especially beneficial to older horses that have suffered lameness in their front legs. Because the shaft comes over the horse's back, rather than on his sides, the animal gets a lift up front which takes valuable weight off his legs. The SSS has also done wonders for horses that have had problems negotiating turns. The bike trails directly behind the horse, which allows him freer movement and reduces air friction at the same time.

The first indication that the single shaft sulky would not only be a great aid to horsemen, but also to handicappers, were the events that took place at Monticello Raceway during its 1972 meeting. This was the first racetrack that allowed the bike to be used for an entire meeting. Here's what happened:

- Out of the 470 races which had at least one SSS in it, 255 (or 54%) were won by horses pulling a single shaft.
- Of the 180 horses that used the single for the first time, 115 (or 69%) came home winners.
- Over 90% of the horses that won with the sulky, either took a new season or lifetime mark.
- Regardless of current form, post position, or odds, an average of 25% of the 974 horses that started with the single shaft sulky eventually won during the meeting.

The 1973 Maywood Park meeting produced evidence that the results at Monticello were no fluke. The single shaft sulky was used in 345 races and 225 horses were on the winning end. That's an average of almost two winners for every three races. Of the 1,124 horses that started with the SSS, 565 finished in the money for a 50% clip.

BLUE **3** 10-1

Driver—ROBERT KNOX, Gold-Brown — **Tr.—R. Knox (97-8-17-14—.228)**

CRYSTAL E. Blk g 1967, by Crystal Byrd—Crystal Worthy—Worthy Boy
Owner: Priscilla Knox and Robert Rosenbury, Homewood, Ill, Rochester, Ind.

1973 16 3 1 2 $7,460 2:00^{3} May
1972 17 1 5 1 $6,598 2:05^{1} May
Lifetime $6,598 5, 2:05^{1}

8-31	^{4}May ft 81°	§clm7000	1	:29^{1}	1:00^{1}	1:31^{2}	2:00^{3}	5	1	1^{2}	1^{1}	1^{2}	1^{6¾}	2:00^{3}	7-2 (R.Knox)	CrystalE., QuickBay, BourbonChimes	(blistering speed)
8-28	May ft 84°	Qua§	1	:30^{3}	1:00^{4}	1:33	2:05^{4}	7	1	1^{7}	1^{3}	1^{3}	1^{nk}	2:05^{4}	NB (R.Knox)	CrystalE, VolcPurdue, TrueGift	(————)
8-24	^{7}May ft 72°	clm7000	1	:31^{4}	1:04^{1}	1:35^{2}	2:06^{1}	8	8	5^{4}°	7^{6}°	8^{8½}	8^{13}	2:08^{4}	20-1 (R.Knox)	BaronBill, MisterAdios, MightyLoyal	(no chance)
8-14	^{7}May ft 70°	clm7000	1	:30^{4}	1:02^{1}	1:33^{4}	2:05^{3}	3	5	5^{4}°	3^{2½}°	2½	2½	2:05^{4}	*2-1 (R.Knox)	SilentTona, CrystalE, BaronsStorm	(3-wide briefly)
8- 4	^{1}May ft 77°	clm7000	1	:30^{3}	1:01^{1}	1:32^{4}	2:03^{2}	4	1°	2½	1½	1^{1½}	3^{4¼}	2:04^{1}	5-1 (R.Knox)	LakewoodQuick, ReidsShadow, CrystalE	(tired)
7-27	^{4}May sy 79°	clm7000	1	:32^{4}	1:06^{1}	1:37^{1}	2:09^{1}	4	5	3^{6½}°	3^{2½}°	2^{4}°	3^{3¾}	2:10	3-1 (R.Knox)	BuddyTime, GoranHanover, CrystalE	(tough trip)

GREEN **4** 6-1

Driver—JOE MARSH, JR., Gray-Blue-Red — **Tr.—J. Marsh, Jr.**

STARBOARD BUTLER B g 1968, by Adios Butler—Portside—Ensign Hanover
Owner: Wm. Lewis and Ross Siverling; Mansfield, Ashland, Ohio

1973 21 3 2 3 $16,646 2:00^{4} Spk⅝
1972 33 2 6 3 $18,794 2:02^{3} Was^{1}
Lifetime $35.596 4, 2:02^{3} (1)

7-20	^{8}Spk⅝ sy 68°	w10000^{7273}=1		:30^{3}	1:03^{1}	1:34^{4}	2:05^{3}	1	1	1^{1}	1^{1}	1^{4}	1^{4¼}	2:05^{3}	5-1 (J.MarshJr)	StarboardButlr, NbleKnghtTme, DnasRybil	(wire to wire)
7-13	^{8}Spk⅝ ft 77°	w10000^{7273}=1		:29^{3}	1:01	1:30^{1}	1:59^{3}	9	9	9^{7½}	8^{5}	9^{4}	7^{4¼}	2:00^{2}	19-1 (J.MarshJr)	CreederLinbo, C.V.Thor, TheGrumbler	(raced well)
7- 4	^{8}Spk⅝ ft 82°	w10000^{7273}=1		:29^{3}	1:00^{3}	1:30^{1}	1:59^{4}	2	3	4^{3¾}	4^{2}°	2^{1}	5^{3¼}	2:00^{2}	15-1 (R.Knox)	ShadHanover, NativeExpress, TeddyRip	(str move, hung)
6-30	^{4}Spk⅝ ft 78°	w10000=1		:30	1:01^{4}	1:30^{3}	2:00^{1}	3	4	6^{4½}	6^{3}	6^{4¼}	4^{3}	2:00^{4}	6-1 (J.MarshJr)	AdiosArt, DoctorTom, YankeeBaron	(evenly)
6-23	^{8}Spk⅝ gd 66°	w10000^{7273}=1		:30	1:04	1:34^{2}	2:04^{1}	7	1	1^{1½}	1^{hd}	7^{7}	7^{11}	2:06^{2}	8-1 (J.MarshJr)	ShadyMile, YankeeCreed, ShadHanover	(away very fast)
6-16	^{6}Spk⅝ sy 68°	w10000^{7273}=1		:28^{4}	1:00^{2}	1:32	2:05^{4}	8	1°	2^{2½}	2^{1½}	1^{hd}	4^{3¼}	2:06^{2}	5-1 (J.MarshJr)	YankeeBaron, AdiosArt, Chaw	(brushed twice)

BLACK **5** 3-1

Driver—JOE MARSH, JR., Gray-Blue-Red — **Tr.—J. Marsh, Jr. (180-46-30-30—.400)**

STARBOARD BUTLER B g 1968, by Adios Butler—Portside—Ensign Hanover
Owner: Wm. Lewis and Ross Siverling; Mansfield, Ashland, Ohio

1973 25 5 3 3 $27,096 1:57^{2} May
1972 33 2 6 3 $18,794 2:02^{3} Was^{1}
Lifetime $35.596 4, 2:02^{3} (1)

8-31	^{5}May ft 81°	§ffa15000	1	:28^{4}	:58^{2}	1:28^{1}	1:57^{3}	3	1°	2^{1}	3^{2}	3^{1½}	4^{2}	1:58	*3-2 (J.MarshJr)	StringsHank, GdByColumbus, Jeffersn	(needed room str)
8-18	^{9}May ft 77°	§nv10000	1	:29^{3}	1:01^{2}	1:32^{2}	2:00^{2}	1	2	2^{1¼}	1^{1}	1^{3}	1^{5¾}	2:00^{2}	*4-5 (J.MarshJr)	StarboardButler, EliLang, GameGuy	(:28 last ¼)
8-11	^{10}May ft 77°	§w1000073	1	:28^{2}	:58^{4}	1:28	1:57^{2}	1	2	2^{1¼}	2^{1¼}	2^{1}	1^{nk}	1:57^{2}	9-2 (J.MarshJr)	StarboardButler, Jefferson, C.V.Thor	(new track record)
7-28	^{9}May ft 64°	§w1000073	1	:30^{3}	1:02^{3}	1:33	2:02^{3}	4	2	2^{1½}	3^{1¼}	3^{1½}	2^{1¼}	2:02^{4}	*2-1 (J.MarshJr)	GameGuy, StarboardButler, DoctorAndy	(boxed in)
7-20	^{8}Spk⅝ sy 68°	w10000^{7273}=1		:30^{3}	1:03^{1}	1:34^{4}	2:05^{3}	1	1	1^{1}	1^{1}	1^{4}	1^{4¼}	2:05^{3}	5-1 (J.MarshJr)	StarboardButlr, NbleKnghtTme, DnasRybil	(wire to wire)
7-13	^{8}Spk⅝ ft 77°	w10000^{7273}=1		:29^{3}	1:01	1:30^{1}	1:59^{3}	9	9	9^{7½}	8^{5}	9^{4}	7^{4¼}	2:00^{2}	19-1 (J.MarshJr)	CreederLinbo, C.V.Thor, TheGrumbler	(raced well)

YELLOW **6** 5-2

Driver—JIM DOLBEE, Green-White-Red — **Tr.—D. Ranachowski (52-11-8-4—.336)**

MIGHTY BUTLER B c 1970, by Adios Butler—Dream Lady—Knight Dream
Owner: Ivanhoe Stables, Inc., Chicago, Ill.

1973 12 2 1 1 $5,210 1:59^{4} May
1972 11 2 1 1 $3,268 2:05^{2} V.D¾
Lifetime $3,268 2, 2:05^{2} (¾)

8-27	^{6}May ft 82°	§nw400073	1	:30^{1}	:59^{3}	1:29^{3}	1:59^{4}	2	1	1^{2}	1^{7}	1^{14}	1^{15}	1:59^{4}	*2-5 (GVlIndnghm)	MightyButler, DSTime, AnnsAmigo	(blistering mile)
8-17	^{2}May ft 76°	§nw3500	1	:30^{1}	1:00^{3}	1:30^{2}	2:01^{1}	4	1	1^{2½}	1^{8}	1^{5}	1^{5}	2:01^{1}	3-1 (GVlIndnghm)	MightyButler, WhtneyFarr, BarbaraAlmahurst	(tons best)
7-26	^{6}May ft 73°	nw500073	1	:29^{4}	1:02^{2}	1:33^{4}	2:03^{4}	3	4	4^{3½}	4^{5}	6^{10}	6^{14}	2:06^{3}	3-1 (J.MarshJr)	EasyDude, HundredPipers, JicarillByrd	(out of it)
7-13	^{5}Spk⅝ ft 88°	nw12000^{7273}+1		:31^{3}	1:03^{1}	1:32^{4}	2:02^{4}	2	3	4^{4½}	4^{4¼}	3^{3}	3^{5¼}	2:03^{4}	6-1 (J.MarshJr)	WinterSymphony, SpeedTickt, MghtyBtler	(mild bid str)
6-20	^{8}Spk⅝ ft 76°	nw8000^{7273}−1		:29^{3}	1:01^{4}	1:31^{4}	2:04	8	6	6^{4¼}	6^{3}	x7^{12}	7^{14}	2:06^{4}	6-1 (C.Alessi)	RareButterfly, KeystoneDandy, EmbssyVlo	(break costly)
6- 9	^{6}Spk⅝ ft 78°	3yrstk31000+1		:29^{4}	:58^{4}	1:28^{3}	1:58^{3}	13	12	11^{21}	11^{11}	9^{9}	8^{8½}	2:00^{2}	e26-1 (C.Alessi)	GaySkipper, RacingKnight, RicciReenieTime	(raced well)

A stable hand displays a conventional sulky. (Photo by Kuprion.)

Many of the horses at Maywood Park that won with the single shaft sulky lowered their lifetime marks to incredibly fast times. Crystal E.* stopped the teletimer in 2:00 3/5. The fact that the six year old gelding was only a $7,000 claimer makes his winning time even more amazing.

Mighty Butler, a three year old colt, put the single shaft sulky on for the first time and quickly sped to a 2:01 1/5 victory, not exactly the kind of speed that was indicated by his previous effort. Just ten days later, the son of Adios Butler covered the mile in 1:59 4/5.

The most remarkable winning effort of the meet was turned in by another Adios Butler offspring—Starboard Butler. This five year old gelding hovered near the two-minute mark during the last few weeks of the Sportsman's Park meeting. When he was shipped over to the Maywood oval and got hold of the single shaft, he became a brand new horse. On August 11, he won by a neck in 1:57 2/5, the world's record for aged geldings on a half mile track. Had Starboard Butler not lacked racing room on August 31, he might even have lowered the record again.

Let us not forget that the single shaft sulky also has an effect on the handicapper. One might jump to the conclusion that the SSS would only confuse the racegoer to the point where he starts wagering on sulkies rather than horses. But a detailed study put together by Greg Magreta, research analyst for Harness Tracks of America, proves that the single shaft sulky is a legitimate aid in handicapping.

nomical 55% during the Laurel meeting to 39% during the final three weeks of the Windsor summer meeting when use of the bike was permitted. The winning favorite is generally selected by the public about 33% of the time, so it seems that racegoers benefit from the invention almost as much as horsemen.

The single shaft sulky is only in the infancy stage. There are many racetracks in North America that have not allowed its usage in regular competition. Some observers of the sport believe it will be a decade or more before it gains full acceptance. If the single shaft is presently being used at your local track, there are four things that are advised to improve your handicapping. (Even if the SSS has not been permitted in your home town, it's still a good idea to keep these four items in mind for future reference):

1. Watch out for older horses that were once clumsy. The SSS may relieve some of the aches and pains the horse has accumulated through a lengthy career. One or two races over the track and he may return to the form he achieved as a youngster.

2. Don't knock a couple of seconds off every horse's final time just because he's using the single shaft sulky for the first time. Many horses are not affected by the bike.

3. Speed horses pulling the SSS have a slight edge over stretch runners. If the animal has been stopping in the stretch, the switch to the single may be the answer.

4. Why not keep a record of horses that make

TRACK	NUMBER OF SINGLE SHAFT RACES	NUMBER OF RACES WITH SSS FAVORITES	NUMBER OF SSS WINNING FAVORITES	PERCENTAGE OF SSS WINNING FAVORITES
Vernon Downs	295	103	51	50%
Laurel Raceway	113	42	23	55%
Windsor Raceway	158	127	50	39%
Maywood Park	345	230	100	43%
TOTALS	911	502	224	45%

In the 911 races that were studied at the four racetracks in 1973, the wagering public correctly named the favorite 45% of the time. The percentage of winning favorites ranged from an astro-

an enormous reversal of form in their first attempt with the SSS? A horse may be shipped out of town where the buggy is not allowed. When he returns, you'll be one step ahead of the game.

*Denoting the single shaft sulky is a linked-S symbol which precedes the class of the race.

CHAPTER 11

Final Notes

The principles that have been laid out in this book derive from research and analysis of over 5,000 races that took place from 1970 through 1972. The data I collected from those races are responsible for the handicapping procedures that were set forth in the preceding pages. For the sake of consistency, and to put theory into practice, all example races that were used in combination with handicapping procedures were selected from the 1,270 races that were contested in 1973 at Hawthorne, Sportsman's (Chicago Downs Association Meeting), and Maywood Park.

Although there was a large number of races used for research and analysis, it still doesn't mean that handicapping a horse can be reduced to a perfect science. Far from it, in fact. What happened yesterday doesn't necessarily have to repeat itself tomorrow even if you come across almost the exact same race. We work only with probabilities, not absolutes. When a horse wins a race and reflects a certain pattern, we take note. If another horse wins a race and reflects a similar record, the pattern then falls into an experimental group. Then it must pass the test of time. If the percentages are in our favor over the long run, we then look for that pattern to reoccur. After that, all we can do is hope for the best.

One thing that might have disturbed some of the more serious players about this book is that I used only example races that produced a winning horse. I will not deny that any dummy can handicap a race in retrospect, especially when he can make a good case for the winner. But there's nothing to be

served by illustrating a handicapping procedure and then backing it up with a losing result. We're working in a game where the best handicappers in the world select more losers than winners. If I were writing a book on how to play baseball, I certainly wouldn't have a picture of a man striking out in my "How to Get Base Hits" chapter. Case dismissed.

The best advice I would ever give you on handicapping is—do not beat yourself. Most of that will depend largely on how much patience you have. If you decide to wager on every single race that comes along, then I wish you all the luck in the world. You're going to need it because I can't think of a better way to throw away your money.

The handicapper who decides to play this game for fun and profit will not run to the window on every given occasion. He waits for races that offer him a fighting chance. I hesitate on calling this person a spot player because I have yet to meet a real one. A serious spot player, that is. Otherwise known as the kind of guy that limits his action to one or two races a night. If two plays happen to be the second and ninth races, he's in for a lot of sitting around and doing nothing. Personally, I wouldn't stand for that (or should I say sit for it). We all like to enjoy a profit on a night's visit, but there's no reason to turn into a two-hour statue in the process.

Limiting action to races that offer a fighting chance need not be anything less than five races on a full night's card. Rarely will there ever be an occasion when there's less playable races on the night than that. When you want to determine if the race is playable, just look for the opposite—the

117

unplayable race. A race that is not suitable for play would be (a) any one of the eight high risk races listed in Chapter 2, and (b) any race that has two or more unratable contenders in it. All races that do not fall into these two categories would be considered playable.

I am confident that the handicapping principles in this book will satisfy you once they are put into practice on a playable race. The one area in which I advise caution, and this is especially directed to the beginner, is the numerical speed rating system. The only problem with it is that it specifically assigns a number to a horse. Numbers are extremely helpful when handicapping a race, but they still do not replace knowledge. Numbers can't think. People think. A number can't tell the difference between two or three wide. A number can't see that a horse was boxed in his last race. A number will never understand the difference between a big and small class drop. Therefore, I strongly advise you to use your own knowledge over the numerical speed rating system whenever possible. Its principles are sound, but so is the mind.

Purposely left out of this book were a number of less important handicapping factors. If I wanted to fill space, I could have discussed something like, "Why It's Important to Look for Horses That Were Gelded Over the Winter." That kind of thing *might* latch onto a winner every other year, but I won't even take your time up with a small discussion of it. Far more worthy of attention are these eight handicapping and wagering briefs that could make the difference between a winning or losing night at the races.

1. Don't get hung up on watching prerace warm-ups. When you want to make sure the horse is sound, just make a spot check of his past performance record. If the animal has been racing at regular intervals, there's a very good chance that he's not hurting. It's a lot better than counting bandages.

2. An exotic wager such as a perfecta, quiniela, or a big triple will very often return a high payoff. But what about the horse you have selected to win the race? If your perfecta doesn't come in, you

may have picked a winner for nothing. Never make an exotic wager unless you can safely narrow the field down to two or three legitimate contenders. Even in this case, always have something on the horse you think will win.

3. There's no such thing as betting against yourself when the price is right. Don't waste your time with two short-priced horses, but if two or three long ones figure to be right there—take 'em.

4. Don't throw the program away when you're ready to leave the racetrack. Take it home and make sure there's a check beside each horse that won. In your spare time, go over all the races that you lost. There's a possibility that you might have overlooked something. It's too late for what happened last night, but not for what may happen next week.

5. Forget tips and all other so-called "inside information." A trainer can tell an owner that his horse had a good workout earlier in the day. The owner tells his brother, who tells his friend, who tells his cousin, and so on and so forth. By the time you receive the word it's that the race is practically fixed. Sorry, but things just don't work that way. The most successful handicappers are people who can make an objective analysis of the information contained in a horse's past performance record.

6. Never let the odds influence you. Whether the horse is 2-1 or 20-1, if you think he's going to win, then play him. For some reason, a large number of racegoers will lay off a horse that is 9-5 or less. But even a 4-5 payoff will return an 80% profit. That's something you won't get at your local bank.

7. If you're new at the game, keep wagers to a minimum for at least three months. It's also a good idea to stay away from chalk horses during this period. Experience will eventually tell you if the horse is a good chalk or a false favorite.

8. Always watch races closely for horses that may encounter trouble along the way. Binoculars won't hurt either. A horse can get impeded, boxed in, or be forced to go three wide, all of which may not show up in the program. It's little things like this that can help you beat the harness racing game.

Good luck and good racing!

RACETRACK ABBREVIATIONS AND
COMPARATIVE SPEED RATINGS
Based on a one mile norm of 2:05

Assinboia Downs...ASD(13/16) 2:05 1/5
Atlantic City...AC(5/8) 2:03 2/5
Audubon Raceway.......................................Aud.........................2/05 2/5
Aurora Downs..Aur........................... 2:07
Balmoral Park ....BmLP 2:06
Batavia Downs...Btva 2:05 1/5
Bay Meadows..B.M.(1) 2:04
Blue Bonnets ....B.B.(5/8) 2:03 1/5
Brandywine Raceway ....Brd(5/8) 2:02 3/5
Buffalo Raceway...B.R. 2:05 1/5
Cahokia Downs..Cka(3/4)................. 2:04 1/5
Connaught Park ....Conn....................... 2:06 1/5
Delaware..Dela 2:04 3/5
Detroit (Wolverine) ....Det(1) 2:03 2/5
Dover Downs...D.D.(5/8) 2:04 2/5
Duquoin ....DuQ(1) 2:01 3/5
East Moline Downs..E.M.D.(5/8) 2:04
Fairmont Park..F.P.(1) 2:03 3/5
Foxboro (Bay State) ....Fox(5/8) 2:03
Freehold Raceway ....Fhld....................... 2:04 3/5
Frontenac Downs, Ont ..................................F.D.(5/8) 2:04 1/5
Garden City, Can...GdnC(5/8)............. 2:04 3/5
Gator Downs..G.D. 2:05 2/5
Georgetown Raceway.....................................Grgtn 2:05 2/5
Goshen (Historic Track) ....Gosh 2:05
Green Mountain ....G.M.(5/8) 2:05 2/5
Green Mountain Park....................................G.M.P.(13/16).......... 2:04 3/5
Greenwood Raceway, Ont ....GrR(5/8)................. 2:04
Hamilton Raceway ....H.R. 2:06 2/5
Harrington Raceway......................................Harr 2:05 2/5
Hawthorne Race Course................................Haw(1) 2:03 4/5
Hazel Park..H.P.(5/8) 2:04
Hinsdale Raceway ....Hin.......................... 2:06 1/5
Hollywood Park...Hol(1) 2:01 4/5
Indianapolis...Ind(1) 2:01 4/5
Jackson Raceway ....Jack 2:07
Kawartha Downs, Ont...................................K.D.(5/8) 2:04
Kentucky Raceway ....K.R.(5/8) 2:04 2/5
Latonia Raceway ....Lat(1)...................... 2:03 1/5
Laurel Raceway ....Lau(5/8) 2:03 1/5
Lebanon Raceway ....Leb 2:06 2/5
Lexington (The Red Mile)..............................Lex(1) 2:01 2/5

Liberty Bell .... L.B.(5/8) 2:02 3/5
Lincoln Downs .... L.D.(13/16) 2:03 3/5
Los Alamitos .... L.A.(5/8) 2:03 4/5
Louisville Downs .... LouD 2:05 2/5
Maywood Park .... May 2:04
Meadows, The .... Mea(5/8) 2:03 1/5
Mohawk, Can. .... Moh(5/8) 2:04 1/5
Monticello Raceway .... M.R. 2:05 1/5
Northfield Park .... Nfld 2:04 3/5
Northville Downs .... Nor 2:05
Ocean Downs .... O.D. 2:04 3/5
Pocono Downs .... PcD(5/8) 2:03 1/5
Pompano Park .... PPk(5/8) 2:03 2/5
Raceway Park .... RPk(5/8) 2:03 3/5
Richelieu Park .... Rich 2:04 4/5
Rideau Carlton Raceway .... RidC(5/8) 2:04 1/5
Rockingham Park .... Rock 2:05 4/5
Roosevelt Raceway .... R.R. 2:04 1/5
Rosecroft Raceway .... RcR 2:04 1/5
Sacramento, Calif .... Sac(1) 2:03 2/5
Saratoga Harness Racing .... Stga. 2:03 2/5
Scioto Downs .... ScD(5/8) 2:02 3/5
Sportsman's Park .... Spk(5/8) 2:02 4/5
Springfield .... Spr(1) 2:01 3/5
Suffolk Downs .... S.D. 2:06 2/5
Vernon Downs .... V.D.(3/4) 2:01 4/5
Washington Park .... Was(1) 2:03 1/5
Wheeling Downs .... W.D. 2:05 3/5
Windsor Raceway .... W.R.(5/8) 2:03 1/5
Woodbine .... Wdn(3/4) 2:05 4/5
Yonkers Raceway .... Y.R. 2:04

GLOSSARY OF HARNESS RACING TERMS

ACROSS THE BOARD—three separate bets represented by a "combination ticket." A $6 ticket is $2 across the board (win, place, show). A $15 ticket is $5 across the board.

AGE—all horses have a universal birthdate of January 1st. If a horse is foaled during the year, he automatically becomes one year old on the next January 1st regardless of his real birthdate.

AGED HORSE—any horse that is four years old or older.

ALL OUT—when a horse, in a race or during a workout, is being driven at its maximum speed.

ALLOWANCE—a 20% increase in claiming price which is given to three and four year olds and mares. If a three year old is entered in a $6,000 claiming race, his claiming price is $7,200.

ALSO RAN—said of a horse when his finish position is not in the money.

BABY—a yearling or a two year old.

BABY RACE—an event for two year olds.

BACKSTRETCH—the stretch on the far side of the track.

BEST TIME—the fastest time a horse has ever raced.

BIG TRIPLE—see TRIFECTA

BOLT—when a horse fails to go a straight course during a race.

BOXED IN—when a horse, during a race, is surrounded by other horses and is unable to get free.

BREAK STRIDE—when a trotter or pacer goes off his gait and breaks into a gallop.

BROODMARE—a mare used strictly for breeding purposes.

BRUSHING—racing a horse at his fastest speed.

BUGGY—see SULKY

CALL—the announcer's description of a race given over the track's public address system.

CARD—(1) all races on a particular day; (2) a racing program.

CATCH DRIVER—one who picks up a drive although not the horse's regular driver.

CHALK—the favorite.

CHALKEATER—a player who bets on favorites most of the time.

CIRCUIT—all racetracks within a certain geographical area. The local circuit.

CLAIM—to purchase a horse from a claiming race. The U.S.T.A. rule is "no person shall be permitted to claim any horse unless he is an owner who has declared a horse programmed to start."

CLAIMING PRICE—the horse's best monetary value which is determined by the owner or trainer.

CLAIMING RACE—a race where horses are entered for a specific claiming price.

COLT—a male horse aged four years or under.

COMMISSION—see TAKE

CONDITIONED RACE—a race where horses are grouped together according to a certain number of conditions. Gait, age, sex, winnings, etc.

COUPLED—two horses going as a single betting unit.

COURSE—a racetrack.

DAILY DOUBLE—traditionally the first and second race. Bettors select one horse to win each race. Both horses must win in order to collect.

DAM—mother of a horse.

DASH—a race decided in a single trial.

DEAD HEAT—when two or more horses cross the wire at exactly the same moment.

DEBUT—a horse's first race.

DISQUALIFY—(1) when a horse is placed in a lower position in a race than it actually finished because of a rule violation; (2) when a driver is suspended from racing; (3) when an official is suspended from his duties.

DISTANCED—a horse that lost his race by more than 25 lengths.

DIVISION—an event which is divided into two or more races.

DOG—a slang term used to describe a worthless horse.

DRAW—to withdraw a horse from a race.

DRIVER—the person who drives a trotter or pacer. A driver must be at least sixteen years old to drive at a county fair, eighteen at a pari-mutuel race track.

EARLY CLOSING EVENT—a race in which horses are entered at least six weeks prior to the race.

ENTRY—two or more horses going as a single betting unit that are owned or trained by the same stable.

EVENLY—when a horse, during a race, secures position and doesn't gain or lose any significant ground.

EXACTA—a race where the bettor must select the first two finishers. To collect, the horses must be in exact order.

EXOTIC WAGER—betting a race other than win, place, and show. Exacta, quiniela, trifecta, etc.

EXTENDED PARI-MUTUEL MEETING—a meeting, or meetings at which time no agricultural fair is in progress, and having a duration of ten days or more with pari-mutuel wagering.

FAST TRACK—a dry and hard racing surface.

FAVORITE—the horse with the highest amount of money wagered on him in the win pool.

FEATURE—the race with the highest purse value on the program.

FIELD—(1) the horses competing in a race; (2) two or more horses grouped together as a single betting unit.

FILLY—a female horse aged four years or under.

FINAL TIME—the actual amount of time it took a horse to complete his race.

FINISH LINE—see WIRE

FOAL—(1) a new born horse; (2) a mare giving birth.

FORM—the ability of a horse as indicated in his past performance record.

FORM PLAYER—a player who chooses his horses on the basis of current form.

FREE-LEGGED—a trotter or pacer who competes without hobbles. Almost all pacers wear hobbles since the pace is an acquired gait. Most trotters are free-legged although there are some that wear trotting hobbles.

GAIT—the manner in which the horse moves his legs. The most common gaits are: trot, pace, gallop, rack, walk and running walk.

GATE—(1) the total attendance at the race track; (2) the mobile starting gate.

GELDING—any desexed male horse.

GIMMICK BET—see EXOTIC WAGER

GOING AWAY—when a horse wins his race while increasing his margin.

GRAND CIRCUIT—harness racing's most prestigious tour which has member tracks all over the United States and Canada. The Grand Circuit is a non-profit organization.

GREEN HORSE—(1) a trotter or pacer that has never competed in a race; (2) a term generally applied to a horse that does not have a lot of experience on the racetrack.

HAND—a unit of measurement used to determine the height of a horse from the ground to the highest part of his back. A hand equals four inches.

HANDICAP—a race which takes into consideration performance, sex, or distance. The Racing Secretary may assign post positions.

HANDICAPPER—a person who attempts to select winners by handicapping a race.

HANDICAPPING—evaluating the chance each horse has at winning and then comparing the horses to one another.

HANDLE—the total amount of money wagered on a race or during an entire meeting.

HOBBLES—straps of nylon, leather, or plastic with loops on both ends which circle the legs on the same side of the pacer to keep him on stride. Trotting hobbles run diagonally under the horse's belly. Also spelled hopples.

HOMESTRETCH—the stretch part of the track from the last turn to the finish line.

HORSE—a male horse aged five years or older.

HUNG OUT—a horse on the outside of the field, unable to get to the rail.

IMPEDED—when the progress of a horse is obstructed momentarily during a race.

IN HAND—when a horse wins a race with speed to spare.

IN HARNESS—when the race is said to be "in harness," the performance shall be in the sulky.

INQUIRY—a sign that flashes on the tote board to indicate a possible rule violation during the running of a race.

IN THE MONEY—said of a horse that finishes first, second, or third in a race.

INVITATIONAL—a race in which horses are selected personally by the Racing Secretary, or by conditions limiting the field to the best horses on the grounds.

JUMPER—a horse that frequently breaks stride in a race.

LAPPED ON—when a horse breaks stride at the finish line and there are one or more horses next to him (within one length). The breaking horse is placed behind all lapped on horses.

LATE CLOSING EVENT—a race in which horses are entered less than six weeks but more than three days prior to the race.

LENGTH—the distance between the horse's nose and the base of his tail.

LIFETIME MARK—the fastest time ever made by a horse in a race which he won.

LONGSHOT—a horse not receiving much money wagered on him in the win pool. Horses are generally considered longshots if their odds are 6-1 or more.

MAIDEN—a horse that has never won a race with purse value at the gait in which it is entered to start.

MAIDEN RACE—a race confined to maidens only.

MARE—a female horse aged five years or older.

MATCH RACE—an arranged race with the conditions already agreed upon between the contestants.

MATINEE RACE—a race with no entrance fee and where the premiums, if any, are other than money. Trophy, ribbon, blanket, etc.

MEET—see EXTENDED PARI-MUTUEL MEETING

MOBILE STARTING GATE—a car, with a set of wings mounted on the chassis, use to bring the horses up to the starting line.

MORNING LINE—the opinion of an experienced track handicapper as to the possible payoff of each horse should it win. This appears in the program and is the first set of odds posted on the tote board before the race.

MUDRUNNER—a horse that does his best racing on an off track.

MUTUEL POOL—the total amount of money wagered on any race, any one night, or any one meeting.

MUTUELS—see PARI-MUTUELS

ODDS BOARD—the part of the tote board where the odds are listed on each horse in the race.

ODDS ON—when the odds on a horse are even money or less.

OFFICIAL—a sign that lights up on the tote board to indicate the results have been approved by the judges.

OFF THE BOARD—when the odds on a horse are more than 99-1.

OFF TRACK—when the racing strip is listed as anything other than a fast track. Good, slow, sloppy, etc.

ON THE RIM—racing on the outside of the field.

ON THE WOOD—racing along the rail.

ON TOP—the horse leading in the race.

OPEN RACES—races that are reserved for the best horses on the grounds. The Racing Secretary controls eligibility to these races.

OUT OF THE MONEY—said of a horse that doesn't finish first, second, or third in a race.

OVERLAND ROUTE—said of a horse that is racing on the outside (parked out).

OVERLAY—when the odds on a horse are high considering his past performance record.

PACEMAKER—the horse, leading the race, that is said to be making the pace.

PACER—a horse that moves both legs on the same side of his body forward at the same time.

PADDOCK—an area or enclosure where horses are prepared for a race.

PARI-MUTUELS—a wagering system which divides the money bet into three pools (win, place, show). Winning ticket holders receive a payoff according to the amount of money wagered. Before the payoff is made, the "take" is deducted as described by law.

PARKED OUT—when a horse is on the outside of the track and there's one or more horses between him and the rail.

PARLAY—when a bettor takes the winnings on one horse and places it all on another horse.

PAST PERFORMANCES—a charted record which has information on the horse's previous races. The pp's usually list the horse's last six races.

PAYOFF—the amount of money returned on each successful $2 wager.

PERFECTA—see EXACTA

PHOTO FINISH—when two or more horses are so close when they cross the finish line that a photograph is needed to decide the winner.

PLACE BET—a wager that a horse will come in first or second in a race.

PLACE MONEY—the payoff on a place bet.

PLACE POOL—the total amount of money wagered on all horses to place in a race.

POLE—the inside rail.

POOL—see MUTUEL POOL

POST PARADE—the procession of horses in a race from the paddock to the stretch in front of the grandstand.

POST POSITION—the lining up of horses at the start of the race from the inside rail out. Horses pick up speed behind the starting gate in order of their post position number.

POST TIME—the time a race is scheduled to start.

PROGRAM—(1) a publication sold at the racetrack, or on the newsstand, which contains the past performance record for all horses scheduled to compete on the card; (2) the combined races for one day.

PROVISIONAL DRIVER—a driver not possessing one year of driving experience and 25 satisfactory starts at extended pari-mutuel meetings.

PULLED—when a horse is taken from the rail to the outside of the track to pass other horses.

PULL UP—bringing a horse to a stop.

QUINIELA—a race where the bettor must select the first two finishers. A winning ticket is held regardless of the order of finish.

QUIT—when a horse tires during a race.

RACING SECRETARY—an official who writes the races and tries to bring together fields of equal ability.

RAIL—the position next to the fence surrounding the inside of the race track.

RATING—when the driver takes a firm hold on a horse to conserve his best speed for the stretch drive.

RECORD—see LIFETIME MARK

RESULT CHART—a detailed record of a race which gives the position of all horses at the quarter, half, three quarters, stretch call, and finish. Other information is provided, such as breaks, parked outs, accidents, etc.

RIDGELING—an incomplete male horse.

RINGER—a horse competing under a false name.

SCRATCH—the withdrawal of a horse from a race prior to its actual start.

SET DOWN—when a driver is suspended from racing for a specified amount of time.

SHORT PRICE—a small payoff compared to the amount of money wagered.

SHOW BET—a wager that a horse will come in first, second, or third in a race.

SHOW MONEY—the payoff on a show bet.

SHOW POOL—the total amount of money wagered on all horses to show in a race.

SIRE—father of a horse.

SPOT PLAYER—a person who doesn't wager unless a horse appears to have an excellent chance to win.

STABLE—(1) all horses owned by one individual; (2) the people hired to care and train for a group of horses; (3) a building where horses are sheltered and fed.

STAKES RACE—a race, generally with a high purse value, in which horses are entered or nominated sometime prior to the actual racing date.

STALLION—a male horse used primarily for breeding purposes.

STANDARDBRED—a registered breed of horse developed for trotting or pacing.

STRAIGHT—see WIN BET

STRETCH—(1) the straight part of the course from the last turn to the finish line; (2) any section of the track without turns.

STUDHORSE—any male horse used for breeding purposes.

SUCKLING—a horse that has yet to reach its first birthday (January 1st).

SULKY—a light, two-wheeled racing vehicle used to carry a driver.

TAKE—the amount of money, fixed by law, which is deducted from the mutuel pool before the payoff is calculated.

TELETIMER—an electronic device on the tote board that times the race.

TIP—supposedly inside information as to the winner of a race yet to be contested.

TOTE BOARD—a sophisticated information board located on the infield in front of the grandstand. It lists the top four finishers, payoffs, odds, post time, official time of day, mutuel pools, the teletimer, and the condition of the track.

TOUT—a person who makes his living by giving tips on races. Touts will either sell their tips or work on a commission basis.

TRACK CONDITION—the rating of the racing surface as set by the State Steward and Judges. Conditions are fast, good, slow, sloppy, muddy and heavy.

TRIFECTA—a race where the bettor must select the first three finishers. The horses must run exactly one, two, three in order to collect.

TROTTER—a horse that moves his right front leg and left rear leg forward at the same time, followed by the same movement of the other two legs.

UNDERLAY—when the odds on a horse are low considering his past performance record.

UNITED STATES TROTTING ASSOCIATION—the governing body of the sport which is devoted to the betterment of harness racing.

UNPLACED—a horse that fails to finish in the money. To the bettor, first through third. To the owner, first through fourth.

USED UP—when a horse tires out after showing good speed in a race.

VEER OUT—see BOLT

WEANLING—see SUCKLING

WHEEL—a system of wagering where the bettor chooses one horse and ties him in a combination with all other horses. Used in races such as daily doubles, exactas, and quinielas.

WIN BET—a wager that a horse will come in first in a race.

WIN MONEY—the payoff on a win bet.

WINNER—the first horse whose nose reaches the wire. If there's a dead heat, both horses are considered winners.

WIN POOL—the total amount of money wagered on all horses to win in a race.

WIRE, THE—the finish of a race which can be either a real or an imaginary line from the center of the judges stand to a point immediately across.

WIRE TO WIRE—a horse that takes the lead from the start of a race and never gives it up.

WITH COVER—when a horse, during a race, has one or more horses in front of him.

WITHOUT COVER—when a horse is racing parked out and there are no other horses in front of him.

WORKOUT—a training exercise to keep a horse in racing condition.

YEARLING—any horse between its first and second birthday.